THE SUBJECT OF VIOLENCE

THE SUBJECT
OF VIOLENCE
The Song of Roland *and the*
Birth of the State

Peter Haidu

Indiana University Press

Bloomington and Indianapolis

The paper used in this publication meets the minimum require-
ments of American National Standard for Information Sciences—
Permanence of Paper for Printed Library Materials, ANSI
Z39.48-1984.
∞™
Manufactured in the United States of America

Library of Congress Cataloging-in-Publication Data

Haidu, Peter, date.
    The subject of violence : the Song of Roland and the birth
of the state / Peter Haidu.
        p.   cm.
    Includes bibliographical references.
    ISBN 0-253-30548-9
    1. Chanson de Roland.   2. Semiotics and history.   3. Epic
poetry, French—History and Criticism.   4. Narrative, ideology,
subjectivity.   5. Violence in literature and society.   6. State—
formation and subjectivity.   7. Literature and society—France—
History.   I. Title.
    PQ1522.H33   1993
    841'.1—dc20   92-33892

1 2 3 4 5 97 96 95 94 93

for Rachel and Noah

in love
and the hope that theirs may be a better world

Contents

Acknowledgments

THIS BOOK HAS been a long time in the making. It has accumulated a number of debts, intellectual, professional, and financial.

Two sections of this book appeared, in part or in whole, in earlier publications. "The Semiotization of Death" was published in *Style* 20 (1986): 220–51, in its special number on medieval semiotics. "Funerary Rituals" appeared in *Continuations: Essays on Medieval French Literature and Language in Honor of John L. Grigsby*, ed. Norris J. Lacy and Gloria Torrini-Roblin, Birmingham, AL: Summa Publishers, 1989, pp. 187–202. I am grateful to the editors and publishers concerned for permission to use these sections here.

The initial occasion for the intellectual quest whose first result is the present work was the grant of a year's leave under Yale University's generous Morse Fellowship program for untenured faculty in 1970–71. The proposal for an Aristotelian genre study of medieval romance led to the encounter with the structuralist theories that demonstrated the inappropriateness of genre theory, especially for medieval texts: that is when my reading in semiotics and deconstruction began. A fellowship from the National Endowment for the Humanities in 1977–78 enabled me to seriously turn to medieval history, to review my understanding of narrative semiotics, and to establish initial formulations for historicizing that methodology. Regular and continuing support by the Research Board of the Academic Senate in recent years, as well as occasional support in the form of research assistance from the Center for Medieval and Renaissance Studies, both at UCLA, have greatly facilitated my work. Early drafts of this book were typed by the Word-Processing Center for Social Sciences and the Humanities, directed by Jane Bitar; this small office was shut down by administrative fiat during the recession of 1991.

Throughout the years of research, hesitation, and pondering, I have benefited from the knowledge, resourcefulness, and kindness of librarians at Columbia, Yale, the University of Virginia, the University of Illinois, and at the Bibliothèque Nationale in Paris. Recent experience has driven home the lesson that competence and respect for faculty research needs are not to be taken for granted.

I received a major impetus in the reformulation of the semiotic theory which subtends this book from an extraordinarily intense and fruitful seminar in the semiotic theory of C. S. Peirce which I taught for the Comparative Literature

Program at UCLA in 1988, in spite of the personal rigidities and the shortsighted institutional politics which block serious efforts of interdisciplinary research and teaching. I am indebted to the administrators concerned for an exemplary lesson in the institutional violence allowed and encouraged by the bureaucratized university. Cathy Brimhall, Elena Kristova, and Amy Morris not only participated in that seminar, but consistently and fruitfully challenged my thinking.

My reflection has benefited from the kind, generously open, and occasionally sharp discussions and exchanges of letters and manuscripts I have enjoyed over the years with friends, students, and colleagues. To list all of the valuable interlocutors would occupy too many pages. Let me only mention a few individuals whose contributions to this particular book have been marked: Guy Bennett, Robert Benson, Ted Blodgett, John Bonham, Bernard Cerquiglini, Denyse Delcourt, Belinda Egan, Saul Friedländer, Harold Garfinkel, A. J. Greimas, Hans-Robert Jauss, Henry A. Kelly, Benjamin Kilborne, Jacques Le Goff, Donald Maddox, Christiane Marchello-Nizia, Claire Nouvet, Vincent Pecora, Michèle Perret, David Raybin, Timothy Reiss, Joe Riddel, Richard Rouse, Sarolta Takacs, Eugene Vance, Rainer Warning, Hayden White, and Paul Zumthor. All will recognize that the benefits of such communication are often indirect, and sometimes dialectically oppositional: they are real nonetheless, and all have my enthusiastic thanks.

My editors at Indiana University Press have been kind, patient, and resourceful in shepherding the manuscript through publication: Bob Sloan, Terry Cagle, and Jack Ford have my sincere gratitude for their humane performance of an institutional process. A special word of thanks is due Tom Sebeok, for reasons he will appreciate.

For their detailed, sympathetic, and conscientious reading of the penultimate version of the manuscript, I owe Howard Bloch and Larry Crist a substantial professional debt. They saved me from errors and omissions, and helped shape this work for the better. Needless to say, they bear no responsibility for remaining errors, omissions, or assertions!

Three dear friends, busy with demanding lives, careers, and administrative responsibilities, took the time to read and comment on early versions of this book as it approached a difficult and often delayed completion. Their extraordinary generosity, in the gifts of both time and critical attention, helped sustain a difficult and laborious intellectual quest. To Matilda Tomaryn Bruckner, Alexandre Leupin, and Mark Rose, I can only offer an expression of the most heartfelt gratitude for the sustenance given in warmest friendship.

Finally, the only person who can have an inkling of how crucial the force of her delicate love has been over the past years is the companion who has shared that time with me: Sarah.

THE SUBJECT OF VIOLENCE

Introduction

Violence: Modern Perspectives on the Medieval and the Modern

> The joyous appropriation of culture harmonizes with a climate of military
> music and paintings of battle-scenes. What distinguishes dialectical from
> cultural criticism is itself negated, fulfilled and surmounted in one.
> Theodor Adorno, "Cultural Criticism and Society"

> . . . consciousness does not accede to the real through its own internal develop-
> ment, but by the radical discovery of what is *other than itself*.
> Louis Althusser, "The 'Piccolo Teatro' "

CELEBRATING VIOLENCE AND desperately negotiating its aporias, the *Chanson de Roland* opens the genealogy of a postclassical tradition of European textualities at the sources of both medieval culture and our own. That these textualities have been labeled "literature" since the eighteenth century is simultaneously liberation and captation, not to say castration. Removing the texts from their social and historical embeddedness, the label of "literature" has legitimated research into the cultural conditions of possibility that allowed for the particular techniques and structures of the texts, a happy empowerment which has produced major advances in textual understanding. Simultaneously, however, "literature's" radical dispossession of the texts, their excision from the social world of signification they assumed and addressed, has prompted an unparalleled proliferation of "interpretations" which testify brilliantly to their own impossibilities and to those of their authors' societies, allegories revealing the aporias of their own initiations and masking the content of the texts concerned. The hope of the present work is that the turn, not to "origins," but toward genealogical "beginnings"[1] may serve to illuminate, not only a distant, receding and determinative past, but also a present still struggling with the issues around which the European Middle Ages constructed its social formations, its polities, its complex cultural hegemonies and marginalities. The ultimate focus of this book is on the problematic to which Walter Benjamin's notion of a "constitutive violence" was a response.[2]

Whatever the prior disintegration in the Roman socius, the European Middle Ages were born of the tumult of external invasions, from the east and from the north, repeated across a span of centuries. The disintegration of centralized powers, at the level of empire, of region, of any governmental entity, until the polity turned into a small community of those who could be ruled from the focal point of a single fortress and its complement of warrior-knights, left men and women in

> a state of permanent and painful insecurity. . . . A daily threat weighed on each individual fate. It reached, in addition to goods, flesh itself. Besides, war, murder, the abuse of force, there is hardly a page of the present analysis [after more than 500 pages] against which their outline has not been profiled.[3]

The "mark of an epoch and a social system," Marc Bloch continues, violence was anchored "at the deepest level of social structure and mentality. It inhered in the economy. It inhered in law. . . . Violence, finally, inhered in the mores." In these mores, the gesture of violence is foregrounded by a framework of human law that is mere illusion, and a divine law that always allows repentance after transgression. Beyond such illusion and occasionality,

> it is the recourse to brutal gesture which appears normal, even when right is not infringed. There is no point in enumerating the excesses of warriors . . . violence appears at all social levels: aggressions which may be individual or not in the cities, the destruction of property or vengeance upon persons are constant. Bearing arms, even if only a pruning hook, is generalized. . . . But no moral judgment is required by these abuses: there is no deliberate cruelty or sadism in these murders or rapes, or hardly any; merely a propensity to not flinch at blood.[4]

It is precisely in the *chanson de geste*, the sung epics of medieval France, that violence is repeatedly displayed. The narrative kernel of these narrative poems is the social turbulence, the "irrepressible violence" (*"cette violence incoercible"*) of a political conflict.[5] A poem such as the *Song of Roland* provides the social historian extensive documentation of the theme:

> the *chansons de geste* or the crusade chronicles recount for us, to the point of satiation, their heroes' murderous exploits . . . [in a] veritable anthology of the mortal blow: any epic song is crawling with them; in five stanzas, the author of the *Roland* explains to us five different forms: the lance straight in the chest, sword-point in the side, sword-edge on the head, sword-point in the small of the back . . . , and the sword whirled about with both hands.[6]

Is the historian's reading anomalous? A perfectly respectable and traditional literary historian, untainted by contemporary theory, limns the epic and its hero as follows:

> Strike! . . . That's the key word of Roland's language. . . . This violence, inherent to the character, mental violence, verbal violence, manifests itself by a

privileged object which presses and translates its personality. The object: the sword: the personal translation: Durendal.[7]

The hero himself is a character "marked by the exclusive love of war."[8]

Violence must not be hypostasized. It is a relational concept, not a thing. Its structures are to be found in all medieval textuality, from the epic to the fabliau, from the courtly lyric to the nonsense verse of the fatrasie, from romance to all forms of drama. One might hazard the hypothesis that it is precisely the relational structure addressed by medieval civilization.[9] But our modern language constitutes an impediment to understanding its earlier forms. There is no single equivalent to "violence" in Old French, even though the term itself derives from Old French *violer*, meaning the use of force in general, as well as its particular use meaning "rape." One source lists a total of forty-five Old French equivalents for the modern French *violence*.[10] Not all of the words listed bear the moral disapproval inherent in the modern term. The rough, injurious, or unjust use of force[11] did not invariably bear coded, moral disapproval, however much individuals may have suffered from it. Our term "violence" perforce bears a seme of disapproval, of condemnation: our culture assumes peace as the desired and desirable norm, and negativizes its opposite. In other cultures, such as the nomadic and the early feudal, the use and display of force were positively coded, at least in a particular class, as sources of profit, honor, social rank, and release from various servitudes. To some degree, and from some perspectives, the use of force in forms we consider violent was a social norm in medieval society: society was unimaginable without its presence.

As a social practice, violence is ubiquitous in both the modern and the medieval periods. The superiority modernity can claim over the Middle Ages is a technical one: our means of production and delivery are immeasurably greater and more devastatingly efficient than those of the Middle Ages. In addition, the great national empires of modernity have developed the technical and political techniques of exporting their violences to other countries for surrogate warfare, so that the rhythm of resurgent violence appears—to their own subjects—somewhat more spaced in modern times than in the medieval: after all, a bit over twenty years did elapse between the two world wars that mark the first half of the twentieth century, by contrast to the daily razzias with lance, sword, and mace wielded from horseback of the Middle Ages. The Spanish "civil" war provided the clearest example of such surrogacy, but the lower-level colonial wars such as Vietnam and Afghanistan, the military enforcements of political hegemonies such as various American adventures in South America, the Soviet in Eastern Europe between the end of the Second World War and the revolutions of 1989, and the United Nations-sponsored "TV war"—a latter-day, airborne "blitzkrieg"—against Iraq of 1991 have all been carried out "elsewhere," leaving their originating populations largely untouched. These populations are thereby ideologically constituted in the illusion of the fundamental rationality and peacefulness of their world—their social, political, and economic conditions of existence. The multiple holocausts of Jews, Gypsies, and Armenians—to which list the Muslim population of the former nation-state of Yugoslavia is being added as this book goes through the publication process—deploy human resources of will, intelligence, and imagination at the service of human destruction, made possible, among other inventions of civilization, by technology and the bureaucratic organization of society. They horrify in their cruelty, their demonization of difference, their totalizing persecution of ethnic alterity in the name of fictitious purity married to greed. They unhesitatingly redefine humanity in the narrowest, most clannish sense, raising fear and resentment of the other above all other values. They have not undermined the assumption of peace, decency, and rationality.

Modernity's technological superiority is not necessarily matched by greater sophistication in the understanding or management of violence. The idea of holy war, total war without negotiated surrender, entered Europe during the eleventh and twelfth centuries, with crusades directed against both external and internal enemies. What can seem to us small-scale holocausts of Jews such as those of 1096 in Speyer, Worms, and Mainz, or that of 1099 in Jerusalem, were replicated in the extermination of Christians labeled "heretics" by the Mother Church, such as the extermination of the entire population of the town of Beziers during the Albigensian Crusade. The monk Caesarius of Heisterbach, prior of his monastery, recounts the event in his *Dialogus miraculorum*, written in the first half of the thirteenth century for the instruction of novices. All the inhabitants of the city—men, women, and children—were killed without mercy, under the watchful eye of Arnaud-Amaury, the Papal legate. Faced with the question of possible dissembling on the part of heretics claiming to be Catholics, his reported response to the knights of the *militia Christi* cut the Gordian knot, citing Scripture: "*Caedite eos. Novit enim Dominus qui sunt eius*": "Kill them all. God will recognize his own."[12] Caesarius' syntax leaves the authenticity of his own report open to doubt. Even if the story is apocryphal, however, Arnaud-Amaury's report to Pope Innocent III was authentic: "Without regard for sex and age, nearly 20,000 of these people were put to the edge of the sword."[13] Seven and a half centuries later, another Papal legate, in the city of Bratislava in Czechoslovakia, also was faced with the issue of the innocent victims of mass extermination. His response, as theological as Arnaud-Amaury's, provided a distant echo of his predecessor's *dictum*. Among the Jewish children being exterminated by the Nazi death machine, he said: "Es gibt kein unschuldiges jüdisches Kinderblut, jedes jüdische Blut ist schuldig": "There is no innocent Jewish children's blood, all Jewish blood is guilty."[14] If anything, the difference between the two legates suggests a degradation of ecclesiastical morality.

Above all, however, it is the continuity which is remarkable. The holy war of the crusades prefigures the Nazis' "holy war" against "Judeo-Bolshevism."[15] Reciprocally, the Allies of World War II viewed their own effort similarly, as is revealed by the title of Dwight D. Eisenhower's book *Crusade in Europe.*[16] The continuities between the Middle Ages and modernity have been obscured by the self-serving ideologies of successive "modernities"—from the sixteenth-century "renaissance" to the twentieth-century rediscovery of a medieval semiotic problematic—which use the Middle Ages as a negativized counterimage of modernity's desired ideals. Modern scholars continue the denigrating gesture of their renaissance predecessors who imposed the term *"medium aevum"* to designate the supposed interruption of contact with classical antiquity—an interruption we now know to be fictive. Twentieth-century scholarship and theory repeat the denial of their own paternity in the gesture of exclusion, even as the pertinence of medieval sign theory and the problematics of signification to contemporary theory are increasingly recognized.

The denial is especially marked in the domain of theory. It goes deeper than the surface incongruity—to speak crudely—between new methods and old matters: the phenomenological reference that undergirds contemporary theory, acknowledging the interdependence of subject and object, sidesteps that simpleminded binarism. There is something inherently disquieting about the thoughtful address of medieval textuality—call it signification, call it representation, call it what you will—for contemporary thought.[17] It is an unease that affects not only the old guard of medievalism, from which one would expect nothing other than the sly and arrogant self-defensiveness it has displayed, often in the violence of passive academic aggression; it can be seen among the specialists in other, more recent periods of European literature, most of whom work in willful and often boastful ignorance of anything medieval. It can be seen even among those from whom we might expect more understanding of its pertinence to contemporaneity, those who have specifically addressed the issues of theory and methodology. Some of the greatest minds of "postmodernity" have circumnavigated the Middle Ages, one would almost think intentionally, even when their topic might have dictated a particular focus upon that period. What period of human history might seem, at first sight, more exemplary of overt logocentrism than the Middle Ages? Yet, outside its appearance as an occasional example toward the beginning of the *Grammatology*, Derrida avoids the period, even when dealing with negative theology, one of whose greatest representatives was Maimonides.[18] And what of Foucault, who, retracing the classical history of the constitution of Western subjectivity after having outlined Western epistemes, skipped the Middle Ages in both cases, as if he had swallowed the ideology of Renaissance poetic polemicists hook, line, and sinker, viewing the medieval period as a mere interruption of the true genealogy of the Occident?[19]

As a group, semioticians have been more open to the fact of medieval textuality, but few have allowed themselves more than an occasional and incidental incursion into the medieval domain.[20] A major exception has constituted itself around the issue of "open" and "closed" texts, and the forced use of medieval textuality as an example of the latter.[21] This supposedly "semiotic" categorization continues a much older tradition, which sees in the entire Middle Ages a single, monocultural entity—regardless of geographical, temporal, national, class, or linguistic location—whose values are entirely determined by the Church, bearing a message drastically reduced and simplified vis-à-vis its original status as doctrine.[22] This assumption succeeds all too well in obfuscating the historical fact that, with the entry of vernacular textuality into the domain of even marginally institutionalized culture, something radically new happened in the twelfth century, something which is not adequately explained by a presumed ideological continuity of the preceding centuries.[23] In the ideologically colored domain of culture, the vernacular texts that surface in the twelfth and thirteenth centuries constitute a new cultural territorialization, best identified as that of a "minor literature": one in which a subordinate group—minor at least within the sphere of culture and ideology—constructs its own textuality, as against an official and formally institutionalized culture (that of the Church), a construction in which everything is to be read politically, as implying collective values.[24] In this context, the reading of medieval textuality as representing a closed ideological and semiotic monophony is as gross a travesty of historicism as one can find!

In fact, the texts of this territorialization, responding simultaneously to political urgencies and their hazardous venture into uncharted waters—or perhaps, to mix an impossible metaphor, into the waters of a cultural space that simply did not exist before their traversal—are as "open" as one chooses to read them. The texts of modernity, in their attempted rejection of social signification, can be read as equally "closed" and conservative in their import as the texts of medieval patronage. The medieval texts respond with profound resonance to readings attentive to the undisclosed, to the as-yet-unformulable, to the exigencies of "making it new"—indeed, of inventing newness itself: it is entirely a question of the interpreter's optic. The medievals considered themselves "moderns," in relation to and in distinction from the ancients with whom they entertained such complex relations.

The historical continuities between the Middle Ages and their future are not real only at the level of culture, textuality, and ideology. They are, if anything, more pronounced at the level of institutions. The practices of local and international banking (including even double-entry bookkeeping), the establishment of an organized military according to hierarchies recognizable to a modern eye, the capitalization and resultant captation of intellectual life in the institution of the university, the creation of the foundations of the nation-state itself, as well as various forms of representation, and along with the last named, the bases of an appropriate kind of subjectivity, are all creations of the Middle Ages which we live today. For all its weaknesses, traditional Marxist historiography was correct in realizing the historical unity of the period stretching from the earliest part of the Middle Ages to the French Revolution by its denomination of that millenium (roughly speaking) as the "feudal period." What this historiography could not anticipate was that post-revolutionary modernism would place issues fought over and only apparently resolved during the Middle Ages at the center of its own political problematic.

The (partial) identity of modern times with the medieval period is profound. Whether this should be a matter of self-gratulations or commiseration is a matter of variable individual judgment. More important than the pleasure or displeasure particular individuals may take at this identity, however, is the recognition of its facticity. And that facticity casts a strange light indeed upon the efforts to disregard it. Its denial by modernists—those students of the intervening periods who work in the dual disregard of medieval beginnings—proceeds through a parricidal symbolic murder which repeats the absurdity of the negation of renaissance theorists, without its historical rationale. Joachim du Bellay, writing his *Deffence et illustration de la langue française* in 1549, in the name of the Brigade (the military term is fascinating: the renaissance engaged in a military war against its cultural and political antecedence: a nonnegotiable crusade to the death against its origins?), also known as the Pléiade, called for creative imitation of classical authors, including within the idealized past of "classicism" the Italian poet of the Italian Renaissance, Petrarch. Apparently, neither Du Bellay nor his mates in the Brigade realized that the love sonnets to Laura (to be imitated by all the poets of the Pléiade) were the most recent form of a tradition of love poetry reaching back through Dante and the *dolce stil nuovo* to its beginnings in the love poetry of the troubadours of the twelfth and thirteenth centuries: it was the presence of their own genealogy that Renaissance poets denied, as it is their own genealogy that is denied by the majority of modernists.

This denial, however, is not the product of stupidity or ignorance. There is reason for it, in the character of the medieval texts as perceived from the vantage point of the later developments of textual history. If the modernist's denial is a rejection of genealogical identity in favor of an asserted Difference, it is a fact that the texts in question wear an appearance of alterity that is, to put it mildly, off-putting to modern readers. From the Middle Ages until the postrevolutionary invention of romanticism, textuality—at the surface—asserts identity over difference. It is a literature of convention, of re-cognizable forms, in which difference is disguised by the forms of sameness. It looks like a literature of overt submission to rule, the rule of audience, the rule of patronage, the submission to the reign of the same. The degree to which this is merely a sameness of appearances, which vehiculates deeper and profound differences, has been amply understood in the case, say, of classical drama and eighteenth-century neoclassicism. The very labels of "classical" and "neoclassical," tired and timeworn, reveal the progress made in reading the later texts.

Medieval texts present a face of alterity which does not readily yield to naturalization, and which effectively disguises meaning and significance to an untrained eye, either modernist or postmodernist, rejecting what appear to be easy conventionalisms. Repetitions, however, decried from romanticism to Flaubert, have returned to the forefront in both postmodernism and post-structuralism, largely in the wake of their deployment in movements of modern art, from Picasso and Braque to the abstract expressionists. Indeed, it is the rehabilitation of repetition by contemporary art and theory movements that presents the best hope for a retrieval of the medieval heritage. It is the re-admission of repetition to the house of theory, an entry performed first under the aegis of structuralism, and then by post-structuralism, that promises at least the possibility of approaching medieval textuality from a cognitive position that is not inherently hostile to the conditions of its existence.[25] It is only with such an approach, negotiated with due attention to the particularities of both texts and the social and cultural systems of which they are an integral part, which they bear within their linguistic and nonlinguistic structures, that medieval textuality can fulfill its promise of becoming an essential cognitive way station on the way to self-understanding of men and women facing the mutations of the twenty-first century.

The negotiation of the multiple alterities between contemporary consciousness and medieval texts must be overtly acknowledged. The particular combinations of this multiplicity remain equally determinative and unpredictable. This book will address a single text and attempt to elucidate, not all its structures or meanings, but those structures of significance which, largely disregarded by traditional scholarship, combine to produce a radically new understanding of the text's performances. The text, however, is subject to "reading" by multiple disciplines. "Textuality," today, implies a necessary methodological pluralism, in recognition of its complexity. Text is composed of at least two elements: a medium of manifestation, which in our case is language; and a principle of overall organization, which in our case is narrativity. Language and narrativity exceed each other's reach. The polysemanticity of language means always more than it seems: language is the medium of unsuspected and unspecified significations, working through the wide variety of forms at the definition of which rhetoric has been working for millenia. Language frequently works in indirect fashion, by implication, and contradictorily. The poem's language will be examined in detail, according to several parameters. These include traditional rhetoric, the new rhetoric of deconstruction, and the proto-logical relations of literary implication. All of these will be worked to reveal dimensions of meaning not recognized heretofore.

These forms of linguistic analysis are not inherently related to the text's narrativity, in spite of attempts, deriving ultimately from Roman Jakobson's historic paper on aphasia, to recast narrative as a mode of linguistic organization.[26] As a narrative text, it will be examined according to models provided by narrative semiotics, one of the forms of the post-structuralist enterprise.[27] These models are remarkably supple, of extraordinary breadth, and—contrary to misrepresentations current in the fashions of academic opinion—do not necessarily produce logocentric or fascistic results. They are tools of analysis, analytic templates analogous to the figures and tropes of traditional grammar and rhetoric. They are instruments of research, means of discovery, models for the constitution of objects of research, applied to representations of the most fundamental problematics of social value: they are not substitutes for the consideration of the latter. On the contrary, they recognize and incorporate the specific materiality of textuality: structures and forms of representation. It is their positive utility that determines their use, however: the structures of narrativity, the complex structures of exchange they identify, provide the dynamic of transformation in textuality. Even the absence of narrativity may be a marked one, so that the absence of transformation is the textual result, which, however frustrating, does provide a major dimension of meaning, as in Samuel Beckett's novels or the medieval courtly lyric.[28] More frequently, however, the function of narrative transformation can be represented, with one additional comment, in the classic formula of the fundamental narrative: $a1 \rightarrow b \rightarrow a2$, with the comment that $a1$ does not equal $a2$: not to have accomplished a goal is not the same as not having tried to accomplish it.

Given the relative newness of the discipline of narrative semiotics—its major texts have appeared in English only during the last few years—this text does not present its arguments in full-blown technical form. An adaptation has been attempted, in response to the limited readiness of a presumed audience to accept "semiotese." The present work devolves from a particular rewriting of what may be referred to as the "standard theory": its historicization, an effort far from complete.[29] This historicization of semiotics, which formalizes unacknowledged presuppositions in the practice of semiotic analysis, has as its effect the cancellation of an opposition which bedevils criticism: that of the formal and structural on the one hand, and that of the social and the historical on the other. It is as the result of a properly grounded analysis of textual structures that the text's production of socio-historical signification is to be achieved.

Language and narrative constitute each other's "remainders," those aspects of the text which the respective models do not represent.[30] Since both are integral parts of the text, language and narrative, or rather, linguistically based forms of analysis and a form of narratology, are each other's necessary complement. Rather than ignore the illumination that each brings to the text—which has been the strategy of both semiotics and deconstruction, each denying the existence of what it does not illuminate, and which another discipline does—these two major approaches of post-structuralism must be conjoined in an effort to give adequate representation to the recognized structures of textuality.[31] Both deconstruction and semiotics are simultaneously based on the analysis of linguistic texts, and aim at far more than textual analysis. Their common virtue (in the strong, Italian sense of *virtù*) lies in their address of the concrete materialities of language and text. For both, "meaning" and the structures that produce meaning are not to be "read off" the linguistic or narrative surface. For both deconstruction and semiotics, meaning is constructed from textual specifics, even when illimitably deferred. For both, *how* structure and meaning are constructed is prior to content, both temporally and logically: structure is what produces meaning.

More important is another metatheoretical consideration. The models of narrative semiotics, and those of the linguistic disciplines named, are essential analytic tools, but they cannot suffice unto themselves. They are models for the analysis and representation of structure or syntax, and the recuperation of meaning(s). But the alterity of the texts, and the unrecognizability of their encodings, make of these disciplines models as insufficient as they are essential. It is a fact that, with the best will in the world, a semiotic reading will overlook even the numerous repetitions which ought to make an "isotopy" (a kind of micro-theme) perceptible. Were the semiotician less human, less limited in his or her perceptions by the blinders of expectations, both in syntax and in semantics, there might be no need for complementary knowledge. But the semiotician is not a cognitive superhero: nor is a deconstructionist, a rhetorician old or new, or a logician. Semiotics and other post-structuralist research is as subject to the vagaries of cognitive predetermination and the effects of epistemic shift as the research of other disciplines. The deployment of formal models does not, in itself, overcome the limitations imposed by cultural and historical blinders or lenses. Hence the necessity of complementing the necessary methodological instrumentalities derived from contemporary theory with other mental frames that alert the decoder to possible encodings.

The phrasing is all-important. Historical research cannot provide ready-made meanings as substitutes for textual readings. It can only provide a repertoire, and a non-limitative repertoire at that, of possible vectors of meaning. It is always a possibility that some element of social or cultural signification will appear for the first time in the particular text one is reading, unpredicted by the preceding historical record. "History" cannot be introduced into the problematics of textual analysis as a security blanket of referential certainty, assuring an ultimate reference that anchors the text in an elsewhere of stability and self-identity. A contemporary historiography, cognizant that history itself is ineluctably caught in the processes and debits of textualization, refuses to hypostasize history and will not impose closure on textual signification.[32] On the contrary, in its elucidation, historical perspectives are additional potentials of signification, no more, no less.

Does the textual status of actually existing works of history negate their status as representations of past evenementiality or structures, implying immeasurable stretches of human experience, of joy and suffering? Hardly. It defines that representation as a constructed and a hazardous one, subject to analysis as a textual construct. Such a historiography will readily see the domain of evenementiality as always already inscribed by a kind of "writing." At both levels, the relations of the forms of textuality known as "history" to textualities of other types can be seen as intertextual ones. History brings no absolute certainty, no closure, no insurance policies of validity or correctness. It can only offer potentials of signification whose actual incorporation, utilization, and transformations are subject to the hazards of a common textuality.

For the fact is that texts are not passive reflections of prior "realities." They are not, it is true, human actors, nor can they conceivably be read as if they were. A text does not possess "intentionality," nor is an author's stated intent a reliable guide to its meanings or significance. In the medieval case, authorial statements as to intention or desired effect are invariably incorporated within the text in question, and they must therefore be seen as functions within the text rather than external determinations of its purport. In addition, the epistemological problematics of medievalism would displace such "intention[alitie]s" even if they were available. Beyond that lie larger considerations. Not only medieval texts but all texts are inhuman in both a superficial and in a more profound sense. They cannot be reduced to the issuance of a single human voice: they are far too social for that. So is the human voice itself. For text, discourse, or language to exist, a prior displacement is required, a displacement, precisely, of the individual human speaker. The text is not a representation of a single voice's issuance, it is itself a violent substitute. It is thanks to this violent substitution that texts are also transformative machines, complex entities working in largely unpredictable and indeterminate ways to reproduce meanings and values (as do all ideological artefacts) but also to deflect them, to inflect them, to transform them, to critique them, to re-elaborate the historical encodings, with which texts cannot help but start, into new structures of signification that sometimes anticipate social and political history. It is not only the conflict of later interpretations that makes of the text an ideological battleground, it is the fact that the text is constituted as a negotiation of contradictions, a negotiation which is not merely the imaginary solution of real problems, but—at least sometimes—a far more concrete gesture approaching "problem solving" in its ability to index and anticipate historical reality. It is as a result of its transformational potential that the textual machine can become, not a reflective passivity, but a performative historical agent. Its effectivities are inevitably mediated, but they may well operate at the deepest levels of culture, ideology, and society.

The codes which are constitutive of such operations are not simply created *ex nihilo.* They are continuities between the textual body and the social text, local extensions of continuities that traverse the various social areas our episteme designates as politics, economics, culture, ideology, textuality, etc. It is only insofar as it incorporates the codes of its social formation (from the immediately linguistic to the most recondite semiotic figures) that the text can exist at all: textuality cannot help but exist on the basis of the "languages" (including all forms of semiotic significance) of its own time. As it employs those languages, it cannot help but take along, with the words and figures that compose and are composed by the words, significances that are ultimately and must ultimately be social. Text exists, and can only exist, as an element within a social formation, even when its material and structures desperately seek an escape from sociability.

This intimate relation between the entities traditionally designated and differentiated in our episteme as "text" and "history" or "society" is best expressed by the neologism of "co-textuality." The older notion of "context" proceeds as a predetermined cognitive division and hierarchy which may be heuristically necessary, but which must be deployed with permanent questioning. In this conception, the terms one wishes to "contextualize"—text, discourse, psyche, culture, society, history: the list can be extended indefinitely—are always already part of the same entity, part of each other, and necessary to each other's construal, even as they are differentiated by the disciplinary compartmentalizations of our episteme. It is only because of the filtration of "reality" through these epistemic diffractions, and the reconstitution of "reality" within those disciplinary divisions, that their objects appear not only different from each other but actively hostile to each other. The literary scholar or student, asked to read extensively in the kind of writing produced by members of departments of history, economics, or sociology, feels unquestionably displaced and imposed upon. In such reading, the "literary" person is dispossessed of the controls and references which provide his or her own mode of power/knowledge. Submitting to the discomfort of this temporary disempowerment is the cost of re-knitting what the institutionalization of our episteme has sundered: the (partial) identity of text with its alterities.

This identity of text with its alterities, as this relation is categorized in our episteme, works both ways, however. If the reading considered "literary" in our epoch must be historicized, not at some supposedly ulterior stage of reading, but from the very inception of the act of reading, the reverse is equally true. Most working historians inherit a notion of textuality which, from the perspective of contemporary theoretical developments, remains remarkably naive, assuming that the text we consider "literary" functions primarily as a repository of images which "reflect," well or poorly, reliably or unreliably, the social realities that are their contemporaries. The complexities revealed by contemporary reworkings of textuality both limit the mimetic reliability of texts and focus attention on far different modes of textual functioning. These alternative conceptualizations of the text are disregarded by the historian at his or her own peril, because they multiply the historical valences of the text many times. It is true that contemporary textual theory, largely centered in the discipline of literature, has sometimes adopted an anti-historical stance, leveling differences between historical periods, their societies, their cultures, and their texts. In fact—and it is one of the not-so-hidden agendas of this book to make the point—the overlapping techniques of rhetorical analysis, deconstruction, and narrative semiotics, among others, have a historical potential which has only begun to be explored. Needless to say, their assimilation by the historian is not an easy task. It requires the very same dispossession of self, of disciplinary control and mastery described in the preceding paragraph as the necessity imposed by historicity on the student of literature. The identity of text with its alterities requires of the historian the same effort, the same acceptance of a temporary disempowerment, required of the student of literature before the problematics of history. If the literary scholar and reader must recast the image of the text as ineluctably historical from its very beginning, the historian is required to grasp the complexities that attend contemporary notions of "textuality." It is only insofar as the historian goes to school at the modern critic's table that he or she can begin to make full use of the so-called "literary" text's historical potential. If literary study today is required to historicize, history must equally well grasp the full signification of the contemporary use of the term "text" and the problematics attendant thereto.

Such an operation is neither painless nor easy. It requires—to use the term already employed—cautious negotiation, simultaneously cognizant of the differences of disciplines as well as the urgency of their ultimate co-textualization. Thus it is that the reader of the present book will find in the pages that follow not only finicky pursuits of verbal collocations and their implications or contradictory underpinnings, allied to the quest for larger, narrative structures whose presence would always make itself felt because it provides both an organizational principle of textual coherence and its major mode of transformation: the reader will also find extended discussions of historical matters. These are nourished by extensive reading of medieval history;[33] they also include interpretation of this reading, and some outright speculation. The literary reader will undoubtedly find these sections—the two longest are designated as "excursus"—excessively detailed, supererogatory, and self-indulgent; the historian reader ought to find them somewhat reductive, and at least mildly out-of-date. Such are the perils of interdisciplinarity, the tolls imposed upon knowledge by the separations of disciplines upon those who would negotiate that separation. Within the economy of the present text, these discussions of "history" can be considered as representing the "internal referent" constructed on the basis of a fairly broad historical intertextuality for the purpose of apprehending the *Roland*'s significations.

The reader who has come thus far will recognize the complex problematic of the project, which seeks to recapture elements of identity through the recognition of a necessary phase of alterity. The project does not foresee a reduction of difference but a comprehension of the necessarily dialectical relation between the terms being related and the terms by which they are being related (since axes of relations themselves become terms at a further level of analysis). The constitutions requisite of all knowledge—that of the knower and that of the object of discussion—can only proceed by the negotiations of appropriate forms of mediation. The degree to which these mediations allow for the production of representations that are not only useful and worthy of some effectivity but, in some strange way, "true" to the past they seek to represent in an active reconstitution, is what is at stake in the enterprise. Within the object of study and in the relation of that object to the study itself, the imbrication of text and its alterities is in play.

These negotiations ineluctably bring about some discomfort. They implicate readers at the deepest level of ideological interpellation: that is, where they really live as Subjects. Two issues, outside the textual, form cruces: Marxism and Christianity. Marx's writings work, in these pages, not as a doctrine, coherent and totalizing, explicating all major questions of social life, but rather as a recurrent interrogation, a permanent challenge to historical reflection, one which I am convinced is necessary to the analysis of medieval history. A contemporary consciousness of the imbrication of materialism and the ideational does not cancel or erase the necessity of the concept of class as a model for medieval social structure. It hovers just behind the surface of the medieval sociology of the three orders: those who pray, those who fight, those who labor. Class conflict erupts, bloody, spontaneous, and unpredictable, throughout the Middle Ages, even if the presence of class consciousness is arguable. The crucial roles of wealth and power, of production and privileged distribution, both as constitutive of the social formation and as inhering in its cultural life at any level beyond the most superficial, are unavoidable. Class, its signs and privileges, were constantly present in the life and practices of medieval society: culture and textuality were among these practices.[34]

Marxism is necessary, but it is also insufficient. Historiographical forms and modes of cultural analysis which were unknown to Marx have burgeoned. Far from inimical, these new forms of thought further the critical analysis of society, rendering it more supple, accounting for phenomena neglected by or unknown to Marx. The correlations between the fundamental concepts of Marx and these new forms of historical questioning are indeterminable. In this book, textual analysis is performed according to models that were, in their invention, entirely independent of Marxist notions; medieval society is represented largely in terms Marx would recognize; but medieval society is presented as an amalgam of cultures, at least one of which—the nomadic—Marx never considered, as far as I know.

That all cultural practices display an ideological side, have an ideological value, is generally accepted today. Most broadly, this implies a generalized readerly suspicion that issues of power, class, and the relation to material issues are implicit in all cultural and ideational processes and artefacts. Often experienced as transcending mundane interests of wealth and power, the objects and processes of "art" sustain and disseminate value systems of social groups in positions of privilege. They also constitute a field of contestation in which are represented the value systems of other classes. Most particularly, however—and this grows out of the specific modern version of Marxism developed by Louis Althusser—ideology, considered as the lived relations of individuals to their conditions of material existence and labor, operates in and through works of art, literature, and the intellect, as a perpetual negotiation of oppositions and contradictions and as constitutive of subjectivity.

The issue of subjectivity is at the core of this book. Subjectivity, in the Middle Ages as in our times, is split and contradictory in its very constitution. On the one hand, the *Song of Roland* operates prior to a specific and historical form of subjectivity, one which is related to modern forms of subjectivity at its most profound level. On the other hand, the poem focuses on a crucial element of the process of subjectification, one without which the subject, as understood today, cannot exist. Indeed, the poem does more than focus on it: it is the claim of this book that it is in and by the *Song of Roland* that a specific form of subjection is performed, perhaps for the first time in European history, in a manner that is constitutive of later European subjectivity and history—a "beginning" of European history, hardly the only "beginning" but, as with the name of "Marx," a necessary one!

This claim implicitly reverses much of what passes for traditional, "vulgar" Marxism: the cultural determinism in which the operations of the "superstructure" "reflect," in epiphenomenal position, the workings of an "infrastructure."[35] The domain of text, culture, and ideology, while always already connected to that of material production and power, possesses sufficient opacity as well as the coherence of internal structural complexity to produce independent significations, which in turn have their own, causative effects upon the rest of the social formation. While text, as cultural phenomenon, cannot be understood without reference to distributions of power and the class organization of society, it can be the source of unforeseen transformations that implicate the entire social formation. That is the meaning of "relative autonomy," and one reason why Marxism appears, in these pages, as a mode of interrogating the historical record, a privileged epistemological framework which is not necessarily subsumptive of the production of meaning: "Marx" is not a metonym for doctrine but the name of a necessary interlocutor.

Historically, Marxism partially devolves from Christianity, and does so in the very dialectic of its opposition to religion! This devolution is rich in ironic contradictions. Both paradoxically conjoin the *plebe* with the highest idealism; both postulate the *plebe* as bearer of humanity's highest idealism—a proposition contested in neo-Marxism but disregarded by Western religiosities. Christianity, a world religion, is nonetheless often identified with the European Middle Ages, when all ideation and culture are thought to have been dominated by the Church. Even for a Marxism which viewed the Church as providing the "opiate of the people," the Middle Ages precede capitalism as the period of communitarianism disintegrated by corrosive capitalist alienations. Classics of modern sociology which would substitute for Marxism, such as the works of Ferdinand Tönnies and Max Weber, continue that perspective. That communitarianism, in one historiography of the West, was given form by the institutions and ideology of the Church. That historical ideologeme bears large investments, a representation in which faith, charity, and love were made real in human society—the most admirable versions of modern-day Christianity, in other words. It has inspired extraordinary, self-sacrificing social activism. In some cases, this activism has allied itself with a Christianized form of Marxism.

In the world of the academy, however, such investments, frequent in the disciplines of medievalism, tend far more to a conservative nostalgia, both politically and theoretically. Insofar as such a medievalism pays attention to theory at all, it tends to ally itself to hermeneutics, imposing closure on the "text" of the Middle Ages, even as history was read in Augustinian theology, as a "text" produced by God and communicating a predefined message to man. A work of scholarship which demystifies this vision, which deconstructs its idealistic pretensions, which recombines the material and the ideational, which relocates the medieval in a field of force, violence, and brutality, and which implicates the Church in that field, will be an irritant to such investments, especially as these investments are identified with ongoing institutional interests. A certain ahistoricism is at work here. The Church of today is not the Church as it was in 1935, for instance, or as it was in 1095, the year a Pope promulgated and urged a policy of aggressive war upon the class of European knights, and French knights in particular. The institutional continuities between the medieval Church and the modern ought not to obscure the profound changes it has undergone. Those changes are most marked for an ethical and political consciousness that recognizes the challenge posed the Church by its own history, medieval and modern.

Insofar as subjective energies are invested in Christianity as a challenge, insofar as Christians understand the message of their religion as a challenge to be met in the daily ethical, social, and political moments of their lives—as a mitzvah, in other words—this study of a medieval text can only reinforce the urgency of that challenge. The Christian crux rejoins the Marxist at this crossroad. Both have attempted to articulate the thirst for an implementation in daily life of ideals of justice and sustainability which would cohere with charity. Anyone who imagines that we are living that coherence, or who accepts the present as the best humankind can do to implement it, is mad and dangerous. Both Marxism and Christianity, like Rimbaud's love, need to be reinvented continually. It is my hope that anyone who has accepted the respective challenges as an incitement to seek that conjunction will find evidence of a kindred spirit in these pages: a fellow traveler.

1 | The Semiotization of Death: Open Text or Closed?

C'est l'enjeu d'une littérature, d'une philosophie, peut-être d'une politique, de témoigner des différends en leur trouvant des idiomes.

Jean-François Lyotard, *Le différend*

THE RECEIVED OPINION, forwarded by the grand tradition of interpretation, presents the value system of the poem as unitary and cohesive, representing in a single text the cultural and ideological unity postulated of the entire period. One reader stresses the effective presence of "the feudal Christian ethos" within a "feudal Christian setting"; another stresses the subsumption of feudalism by the royal figure of Charles and the Christian monarchy he represents; and a third considers the poem a song of propaganda for the Capetian kings; all concur that the *Chanson de Roland* is a "historical metanarrative of Christian triumph and hegemony," whose semiosis is monological, whatever variations may be allowed for in the relative weight accorded feudal, monarchical, and religious values.[1] This monologism would constitute a closed text of coherent ideological values, however fragmented its narrative surface might be.

The narrative displays courageous feudal warriors whose loyal service leads to their heroic death and revenge, capped by ample signs of heavenly inspiration and approval. These warriors are vassals to their suzerain, the legendary emperor Charlemagne, in reciprocal love and loyalty. The narrative displays a human system of extraordinary strength, cemented by mutual love, loyalty, and dedication, transcendent of the limits of human life, a transcendence guaranteed by the repeated signs of an approving Divinity. The values displayed by this narrative are those of courage, loyalty, love, cohesive in the service of king and emperor, nation and religion. Little wonder that, rightly or wrongly, it can be read as "a song of propaganda" for the early, Capetian embodiment of these values. The semiosis of the text then is closed, a monologism of coherent ideological values, however fragmented its narrative surface might be by the conditions of communication that prevailed at its composition: those of orality and its somewhat varied audiences in the parameters of place and relative position in a social hierarchy whose ideological cohesion is guaranteed by the monopoly over cultural values held by the Church.

This reading is not wrong. It is the predominant reading, and for good reason. It is a kind of reading that responds to the value system of the readership attracted to medieval studies, which, like most readerships, looks for confirmation of its initiating value system. It is also a reading that is permitted by the text: it is a kind of reading which allowed, not only for the composition of the text in its originating social co-text, but its survival and its reception as a major text in the history of European literature—perhaps the first major text, since classical antiquity, along with *Beowulf*—of postclassical European literature. The greatness of the text is a combination of inherent characteristics that can only be postulated abstractly (we never know inherent characteristics directly) and made functional within the larger schemes—of the history of literature, of the history of culture—brought to the text by the anticipations of the readers' codes. The *Song of Roland* is a great text of European literature, because its inherent characteristics can be made to produce the kind of "reading" which enters readily into our assumptions of what to find in the texts of the period we call "medieval," and does so brilliantly, according to aesthetic standards which have become normative in our culture.

The argument of this book will not be that this reading is wrong but that it is profoundly incomplete. It is a reading which, while responsive to particular features of the text, disregards others, both on the level of specific verbal collocations and on the level of narrative structure. It is a reading, as well, which disregards the text's social embeddedness and the full measure of its performance within a political co-text. The critique of the received tradition of interpretation—with which any new interpretation begins—is not that of error but that of partiality: only a part of the text's significatory potential has been elicited by that grand tradition of interpretation. As usual, its critique can be performed only on top of, after, and to a large degree, thanks to the tools provided by that grand tradition.

It is the assumption of monological unity and closure that is to be tested first.

Roland performs his death semiotically: he transforms himself into a complex sign.[2] The significations of this sign are problematic. What is not problematic is the religious sanction accorded the hero's death by the text. The Christian tradition normalizes the moment of death for accession to the transcendental.[3] Not only does the Angel Gabriel come down to accept Roland's glove in his final submission to the Divinity; the text specifies the hero's assumption:

Deus tramist sun angle Cherubin
E seint Michel del Peril;
Ensembl'od els sent Gabriel i vint.
L'anme del cunte portent en pareis. (ll. 2393–96)[4]

God sent his angel Cherubin
and Saint Michael of the Peril;

along with them Saint Gabriel came there.
The soul of the count they bear to Paradise.

And the first line of the following *laisse* reiterates the semantic content:

Morz est Rollant, Deus en ad l'anme es cels. (l. 2397)
Roland is dead, God has his soul in the heavens.

This transumption of Roland's soul is textualized by the use of a metaphor which is anything but transcendental. The dying hero demonstrates his religious submission in a metaphorical gesture: he offers God his glove. Stating one's loyalty and submission by handing over a glove is the gesture of a vassal toward his feudal lord and suzerain. As will be the case in the later Old French love lyric as well, the semantic representation of inchoate emotions, such as awe before divinity and woman experienced as mystery, is regularly structured in the Old French culture by appeal to the feudal vocabulary.[5] Such metaphorization implies the priority of the metaphorical code employed: the textual ontology of politics takes priority to religion. While this specifically semiotic argument is entirely valid, Dame Theology might respond that such priority is purely cognitive and has nothing to do with ontological priority. The Deity is traditionally defined—both by Maimonides and by Christian theologians—as ineffable in nature; hence the inevitability of referring to it metaphorically. To which a semiotics focused on narrative would respond that there is, in the texts in question, no ambition to represent the Deity in it/his/herself but—at most—to represent the relationship of humans to the divine. And that relationship is inherently one of power and subordination, and hence a political one. Depending on their interpretation of earlier segments of the text—particularly those dealing with Roland's pride and *démesure*, if such it be—critics tend to emphasize his profound religiosity or God's ultimate grace, forgiving the hero his trespasses. Roland's death is recounted in a series of three *laisses similaires*, among the most moving of the text. Jean Rychner noted some thirty years ago the fundamental opposition, in the oral epic, of the narrative and the lyric.[6] What Rychner called the lyric is a particular interruption of the simplest linear narrative flow. It is an interruption of developing temporality and an opening of the text to some expansion of signification. I print the three *laisses* in parallel, indicating the reappearances of semantic contents:

174

Ço sent Rolland que la mort le tresprent
Devers la teste sur le quer li descent.
Desuz un pin i est alet curant,
Sur l'erbe verte s'i est culchet adenz,
Desuz lui met s'espee e l'olifan,
Turnat se teste vers la paiene gent:
Pur ço l'at fait que il voelt veirement
Que Carles diet e trestute sa gent,
Li gentilz cuens, qu'il fut mort cunquerant.

175

Ço sent Rollant de sun tens n'i ad plus:

Devers Espaigne est en un pui agut,

176

Li quens Rollant se jut desuz un pin
Envers Espaigne en ad turnet sun vis.

De plusurs choses a remembrer li prist,
De tantes teres cum li bers conquist,
De dulce France, des humes de sun lign,
De Carlemagne, sun seignor, kil nurrit;
Ne poet muer n'en plurt e ne suspirt.
Mais lui meïsmes ne volt mettre en ubli,

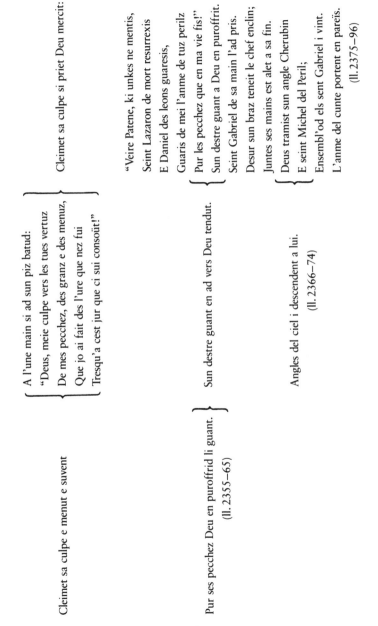

Cleimet sa culpe e menut e suvent

A l'une main si ad sun piz batud:
"Deus, meie culpe vers les tues vertuz
De mes pecchez, des granz e des menuz,
Que jo ai fait des l'ure que nez fui
Tresqu'a cest jur que ci sui consoüt!"

Cleimet sa culpe si priet Deu mercit:

Pur ses pecchez Deu en puroffrid li guant.
(ll. 2355–65)

Sun destre guant en ad vers Deu tendut.

"Veire Patene, ki unkes ne mentis,
Seint Lazaron de mort resurrexis
E Daniel des leons guaresis,
Guaris de mei l'anme de tuz perilz
Pur les pecchez que en ma vie fis!"
Sun destre guant a Deu en puroffrit.
Seint Gabriel de sa main l'ad pris.
Desur sun braz teneit le chef enclin;
Juntes ses mains est alet a sa fin.

Angles del ciel i descendent a lui.
(ll. 2366–74)

Deus tramist sun angle Cherubin
E seint Michel del Peril;
Ensembl'od els sent Gabriel i vint.
L'anme del cunte portent en pareïs.
(ll. 2375–96)

174

This Roland feels, that death seizes him
It climbs down from head to heart.
Under a pine he goes running
on the green grass, he lays down prone,
under himself, he places sword and
oliphant,
turned his head toward the pagan tribe:
He did it so, for he truly wanted
that Charles should say, and all his
tribe,
the noble count, that he died conqueringly.

175

This Roland feels, of his time none is left

He faces Spain, on a steep hill,

176

{ Count Roland lies down under a pine
{ toward Spain he turns his face.

Many things he began to recall,
the many lands the noble baron conquered
sweet France, his lineages' men,
Charlemagne, his lord, who brought him up
He cannot help but weep and sigh.
But he himself he will not forget,

He calls *mea culpa* rapidly and often

With one hand he beat his chest:
"God, *mea culpa*, before your strength and glory
for my sins, both great and small,
which I committed from the instant of birth
until this very day when I have been struck down."

He calls *mea culpa* and begs God for mercy.

"True Father, who never lied,
You resurrected Saint Lazarus from death
and protected Daniel from the lions,
protect my soul from all dangers
due to the sins I committed in my life!"

On account of his sins he presented God = his glove.

His right glove stretched to God. =

His right glove he presented to God.
Saint Gabriel took it from his hand.
Upon his arm he held his head bowed down;
hands joined he went to his end.

Angels come down from heaven to him.

God sent his angel cherubim
and Saint Michael of the Danger;
along with them Saint Gabriel came.
The soul of the count they carry to Paradise.

The common elements of all three *laisses* are the following: a topographical junction of the subject, either with a pine or with the proximity of Spain; his final confession; and the gesture in which he offers God his glove. These common, repeated elements can provide a summary narrative whose content-translation would run something like this: "Roland, under a pine close to Spain, made his confession at the moment of his death and, dying, offered God his glove." That he confesses his sins marks the subject not only as a heroic warrior but a proper Christian; in spite of the extraordinary feats of arms performed and punishments endured, he remembers his religious duty at the moment of death. This religiosity is reinforced and enriched by the third textual moment, that of offering his glove to God. As gesture, this semiotic integer is part of "the semiotics of the natural world," playing on the word "natural" in the same way linguists speak of "natural" languages.[7] The verbal signifiers "mean" the somatic gesture, and the somatic gesture of feudal ritual comportment "means" religious submission: the *verba* mean the narrative *res*, and the narrative *res* in turn mean the particular relationship between man and God. That relationship is one of /submission/, which is the semic element common to the religious and the feudal codes. This reduced narrative in fact conveys the crucial, fundamental significations that are required at this point of the narrative: the subject's successful achievement of his narrative program; his appropriate performance of a culturally required ritual which allows for his transformation from a successful narrative subject into the destinatee of the final sanction from the religious destinator; and the actual communication of the sanction. Granting as nonproblematic the required significations, these essential moments state the Subject-hero's final moments as apotheosis.

The text varies its presentation of the common narrative content with the textual expansion of amplification.[8] The major example of amplification is the notation of the Christian ritual of final confession. What is baldly stated in a single line the first time around—*cleimet sa culpe e menut e suvent*—is divided by the second *laisse* into the somatic notation of beating his breast—as sign of the narrative act of making confession—and the verbal performance of confession itself. In this *laisse*, its content is the extent of his unspecified sins, their variety, and their temporal extension from the day of his birth to the present: all are presented to God as aspects of behavior to be forgiven. In the third *laisse*, the general and more abstract statement of the first *laisse* is repeated—*cleimet sa culpe*—and amplified with a statement of a second verbal act. Not only is guilt confessed, but a subsequent mercy is implored: *si priet Deu mercit*. Where his sins were stressed in the preceding *laisse*, now it is God's power to produce miracles that is stressed, and by a well-known technique of argumentation—if the greater, then more easily the smaller—it is suggested that it could equally well be in God's power to save this sinner's soul.

These passages, even though they comport not only amplification but also the increased verbal concretization that amplification allows, nevertheless operate by reference to a transcendent realm of meaning and existence. Not only are they direct invocations of the Deity; the second amplification (in *laisse* 176) proceeds by a verbal covering which is quite specific and linguistically transcendental in character. Latinisms such as *Veire Patene, resurrexis,* and *guaresis,* particularly in combination with the references to Lazarus and the story of Daniel and the lions, have a strongly ecclesiastical character, invoking both biblical narrative and the Latin language in which that narrative normally exists. Certainly, the apotheosis and transumption of Roland, narrated in this final *laisse,* support a mode of signification that is vertical, referring to a transcendental realm, and hence a "closed" mode of signification.

If such traits of "closedness" are undoubtedly present, are they the only mode of signification at work in the three *laisses similaires* that constitute our text? At the moment of death, Roland deals with two sets of relations: those with the divinity we have just considered and those that tie him to the human society he is about to leave. In the first *laisse* quoted, the somatic notations are expanded as follows:

> Sur l'erbe verte s'i est culchet adenz.
> Desuz lui met s'espee e l'olifan,
> Turnat se teste vers la paiene gent. . . . (ll. 2358–60)

> On the green grass he lay himself face down.
> Under his body he placed his sword and horn,
> his head he turned toward the Saracen tribe. . . .

The scene is a marked one, a striking geographical location, just as the temporal moment is a marked one humanly. We are on a hillock, looking toward Spain, with four blocks of marble under two handsome trees. A stage is being set; elements of decor and properties, including even the body of the actor, are being disposed upon the stage of evenementiality for their importance, for their significance, and even, as we read, for their dramatic signification:

> Pur ço l'at fait que il voelt veirement
> Que Carles diet e trestute sa gent,
> Li gentilz cuens, qu'il fut mort conquerant. (ll. 2361–63)

> He did it so, because he truly wants
> Charles to say, and all his men as well,
> the noble knight, he died a conqueror.

These three lines are a metadiscourse, explaining the preceding action that has been narrated. But they are also part of the narrative discourse itself, whose cognitive component has been recognized by semiotics for some time.[9] As far as I know, this particular moment of textual "psychology" has not been noted by earlier criticism. At the moment of death, what Roland is thinking of is what has always preoccupied him, namely the social value that will be accorded him by his society after his death, the "honor" in which his memory will be held. What occupies Roland's mind at this moment of death is an entirely worldly, even "carnal" concern, in the sense defined by D. W. Robertson, Jr.[10] It is a question of "what will people say when I am gone," what will be the valorization attached to the name of "Roland" after the individual himself is dead. But the text does not present this in an interrogative form: it attributes willfulness and intent to the actor: *pur ço l'at fait que il voelt veirement. . . .*

The entire death scene is Roland's own stage-setting of himself and his props in such a manner that they will produce a specific pragmatic response among Charles and his troops. Roland textualizes himself and the scene in which he dies so as to make it mean and communicate a particular message to those who survive him:

> Pur ço l'at fait que il voelt veirement
> Que Carles diet e trestut sa gent,
> *Li gentilz cuens, qu'il fut mort cunquerant.* (ll. 2361–63)

"The noble count, he died a conqueror": that is the meaning Roland himself attributes to the scene as he disposes it, and that is also the meaning he attributes to his life and death as that which will survive the death among the men who constitute his companions and the society of his peers. If there is a transcendence here, it is the transcendence that can be devised by a willfully constructed semiosis, in which the destinator's own corpse is turned into an element of meaning, a complex sememe, which finds its intended effect, not in some transcendental realm located elsewhere, in another world and dimension of being, but in the society of men which continues to function beyond any individual death and whose functioning includes the memory of the dead. If transcendence is to be found in Roland's thought and intent at the moment of death, it is the purely temporal and social transcendence of human life that is achieved by the memorialization of the heroic individual among those who survive his death.[11] This "transcendence" is borne by a signification, a process of making meaning, which the communicative sender wishes to "close." The scene is set so as to be transformed into a complex signifier whose signified will be specifiable and limited: "the noble count, he died a conqueror." If there is closure in this syntagm, it is the closure willed by the representation of a strictly human speaking subject, intent on giving his life a specific value. That value, moreover, is entirely secular: it asserts power and reputation and does so in terms that would be identical did the institution of the Church not exist.

Roland proves to be a thoroughly effective semiotic operator: his message will be received in exactly the manner, and with exactly the sense, he wished attributed to the signifiers he organizes on the field of battle which is also his "deathbed" and final text. The communication elicits perfect "uptake," according to shared and purely secular codes. After Roland's death, Charles will take revenge on the fleeing Saracens, thanks to the divine intervention which interrupts the flow of time and allows him to catch up with Marsile's troops at the river crossing of the Ebre. Exhausted, Charles and his troops will rest that night and then return to Roncevaux the following day. There, they find the bodies of the 20,000 Franks, dead in battle, and look for the most precious among them. Charles explains to his companions, between accesses of tears, that he goes forward looking for Roland for a particular reason:

> "Segnurs, le pas tenez,
> Kar mei meïsme estoet avant aler
> Pur mun nevold que vuldreie truver.
> A Eis esteie, a une feste anoel,
> Si se vanterent mi vaillant chevaler
> De granz batailles, de forz esturs pleners.
> D'une raisun oï Rollant parler:
> *Ja ne murreit en estrange regnet*
> *Ne trespassast ses humes e ses pers;*
> *Vers lurs païs avreit sun chef turnet;*
> *Cunquerrantment si finereit li bers.*" (ll. 2857–67)

> "Lords, hold your pace,
> I myself must go forward now
> for my nephew, whom I would find.
> I was at Aix once, at a high holy day,
> and my brave knights, they boasted all
> of wondrous battles, and full-pressed attacks.
> Then I heard Roland say one thing:
> *Never in a foreign kingdom would he die*
> *without advancing beyond his men and peers;*
> *toward their country, he'd have turned his head;*
> *the baron, so would he end, conqueringly.*"

And so, among the flowers, scattered red with barons' blood among the grasses of the field of battle, crying with the pity of their deaths, Charlemagne, great emperor, will find the body of his nephew, closer than a son, and weep and pray and faint in pain and grief for Roland. Both the pragmatic and the cognitive are determined by the earlier discourse, itself proleptic, which Charles is now narrating. Both the temporal and discursive relations are complex. Charles remembers a discourse, Roland's at Aix, well before the present war, foretelling the eventuality which has been narrated by the present text. The memory of that foretelling allows him to find the corpse and to interpret the manner of its disposition: its meaning. The earlier discourse contains both pragmatic cues for finding Roland's body and interpretive elements for decoding its disposition. Remembered discourse contains the elements to decode both space and nonlinguistic signifiers.

A breach in the received notion of "closedness" has already been established. The text we are discussing is "closed" insofar as it refers to itself, not in referring to some transcendental realm of meaning. The individual syntagm does not exist simply thanks to its vertical function. At this point, the "closedness" of the text is an effect, not of indexical reference to predetermined meaning elsewhere, but to the text as a self-referential construct. Meaning is closed insofar as it is enclosed within textuality.

In the last passage quoted, Charles was looking for Roland as his nephew. The normal pattern was for the noble male to be sent to his maternal uncle as boy and adolescent: it was the uncle who brought him up, educated him in the responsibilities of nobility and the techniques of knighthood, the whole range of activities covered by the Old French verb "*nourrir.*" The intensity and depth of this tie is not to be underestimated: the closest to it in our own culture is the paternal bond.[12] In any case, while Charles goes forward seeking his nephew on the field of battle, it is not only his nephew he finds when he does, indeed, come upon Roland's body. Charles faints, is leaned against a pine tree by his noble companions, and, when he returns to consciousness, sees again his nephew and starts to grieve for him:

> Guardet a la tere, veit sun nevold gesir.
> Tant dulcement a regreter le prist:
> "Amis Rollant, de tei ait Deus mercit!
> Unques nuls hom tel chevaler ne vit
> Por granz batailles juster e defenir.
> La meie honor est turnet en declin." (ll. 2885–90)

> He looks at the ground, sees his nephew lying there.
> So gently he began to grieve for him:
> "Dear Roland, may God have mercy on you!
> Never did any man see a knight like you
> for planning great battles and fighting to the end.
> My realm and power have begun to decline."

Charles was looking for his nephew. He finds his nephew, and a great deal more. Charles names Roland *amis*, a term which is sometimes a diplomatic one, meaning little more than "ally" or even, negatively, one with whom the subject is not at war. But it also means the closest and most intimate of relations: "beloved" is not too strong at times. Charles has found the dear nephew he sought, but he has also found something else, specifying his nephew's corpse as the sign of his own decline. For the passage just quoted identifies Roland, not merely as the close and intimate nephew of a great noble, but as the source of the latter's military power and reputation. It is Roland's prowess as a knight and capacity

as a strategist that are identified by the lines, as well as the fact that his death
signifies the weakening of Charles's "*honor,*" a term that means both reputation
among men and the land that is the source of wealth, power, and reputation.[13]
The corpse he finds is that of his most courageous warrior and greatest general.
Men will fear Charles less, and the grief of that military and political loss will
endure:

"Cum decarrat ma force e ma baldur!
N'en avrai ja ki sustienget m'onur:
Suz ciel ne quid aveir ami un sul;
Se jo ai parenz, n'en i ad nul si proz." (ll. 2902–2905)

"How will my strength and joy now fail!
None will I have to uphold my honor now:
I think I have no ally under the sky;
though I have kin, none has such value."

Charles's complaint continues. Foreign men will come to his court at Laon
and will ask for the captain count; he will have to tell them Roland died in Spain,
and he will reign only in grief. When he goes to Aix, in his chapel, men will
come to ask for news. The disappearance of his nephew and general will lead to
the rebellions of subjugated peoples:

"Puis entrerunt mes peines e mes suffraites.
Ki guierat mes oz a tel poeste,
Quant cil est morz ki tuz jurz nos cadelet?
E! France, cum remeines deserte!
Si grant doel ai que jo ne vuldreie estre!" (ll. 2925–29)

"Then begin the seasons of pain and poverty.
My armies, who will lead them with such power,
now that he is dead, who always led us forth?
Oh, France, how you remain deserted now!
I have such grief, I do not want to live!"

Arguments which have preoccupied traditionalist scholars as to whether the
historical battle of Roncevaux was a minor mountain ambush or a major defeat
for the historical Charlemagne are irrelevant to the textual problems: here, there
is no question but that the loss of Roland is a military disaster. For Charles, his
greatest single warrior and his best general, the practical source of his military
power and the basis of his worldwide reputation as an awesome military power,
has suddenly disappeared, and he foresees the military and political effects this
subtraction of power will have.

Part of the extraordinary quality of the death scene is that Roland is not only
arranging a scene but disposing his own body and adjuvants into a message. The
sender uses himself as the signifier in order to transcend his own death, as mean-

ing to be apprehended by those who survive. There is a self-conscious semiotic manipulation of self as object that is remarkable, even if it is recounted briefly and receives little emphasis in the narration. But this mise-en-scène of the semiosic process produces an unexpected message, which, it is stressed by the text, is that of the destinator in the text, not by the text as destinator. The text, by deploying this structure, does not take it upon itself to say that Roland died a conqueror—it merely cites him as saying so:

Pur ço l'at fait que il voelt veirement
Que Carles diet e trestute sa gent,
Li gentilz cuens, qu'il fut mort cunquerant.

He did it so, for he truly wanted
that Charles should say, and all his tribe,
the noble count, that he died conqueringly.

Auerbach quite correctly emphasized the parataxis that is one of the distinguishing features of the *Roland* text when seen from our particularly hypotactic view (of language as well as of other things, politics for instance, where metonymic causation depends upon a hypotactic mental set). This emphasis has had the unfortunate effect of disguising to readers quite properly impressed with his analysis those decided examples of hypotaxis that do occur in the text, and sometimes at crucial moments.[14] As in the present case. The linguistic formulation—Roland did this because he really wanted Charles and all his people to say that he, the noble count, had died conqueringly—exactly parallels the semiotic doing the text has just described: the assertion is Roland's, not the text's.

The *cunquerant* of the death scene (l. 2363) is echoed by the *cunquerrantment* (l. 2869) of Roland's boast as remembered by Charles. That particular adverbial form is a hapax: it does not occur, to my knowledge, anywhere else in Old French. As such, by its pre-position in its syntactical unit, and by its separation as adverb from the verb it modifies by the adverb *si*—"Cunquerrantment si finereit li bers"—the word calls attention to itself. In doing so, it confirms the less emphatic, somewhat more subtle stress it receives in the death scene, coming as the final fall of a fairly complex hypotaxis, itself remarkable in a largely paratactic environment. These stylistic stresses suggest the paradoxical quality inherent in the notion of Roland's past narrative as one of "victory." What kind of a victory is it that leaves all the winning combatants dead? And, as we have just seen, when Charles discovers Roland's body on the battlefield, the emperor himself identifies that body as the loss of "honor," or reputation and power: for Charles himself, there is huge loss, even if there is admiration for the heroism that brought it about. Militarily, this "victory" looks more like an unmitigated disaster.

How can such a disaster be a victory? The text leaves no alternative to the paradoxical evaluation of the events at Roncevaux as simultaneously /disaster/

and /victory/.[15] The first significance is readily comprehensible in our cultural codes: the enormous loss of human life defines huge social loss. Nor should it be thought—as we often do in considering other societies whose codes are different from ours—that human life was merely meaningless for the Middle Ages. Life itself, its uses such as political and military power, and personal relations such as Aude's love for Roland, were valued in the texts of the period, and presumably in the social text as well: Oliver's inculpation and Charles's lament indicate as much. What is less obvious, however, is the semiotization of those events as /victory/. "How is it possible for such a disaster to be more than a Pyhhric victory?" is not at all a rhetorical question. It is a substantive one, forced upon us by the text: what are the elements in the codes of the period that enable it to evaluate such disastrous loss of human life as victorious? Taking the question literally, just *how* is such a signification possible?

One part of the answer is not too distant: the last combatant alive on the field of battle claims the victory of the encounter. But that answer merely postpones the issue: *how* can the loss of so many men be disregarded for the topographical location of a sole survivor, and one who survives for such a short time? That question, which must be answered if we are to understand the text, is not answered in the text itself. The rule is obviously present, but its significance and the manner in which it can become a rule are very much offstage. As we have seen, some aspects of the text refer to a prior and a transcendental reality; others refer to other moments or aspects of the text in a self-referentiality that is perhaps more extensive than previously thought; but this text is also a social text—as is any text—in that its significations are inevitably social significations, elements of meaning that cannot be defined within the semiosis of anything we can recognize as "the text itself." At best, we can theoretically attribute to such elements of meaning the status of "presuppositions" or "implications" and produce arguments as to whether such significations are properly part of the "text itself" or not. What experience suggests, however, is that we, as historical epistemological subjects, cannot recognize the elements of meaning so designated without extensive reading of texts other than what is presented to us as "the text itself." A practical epistemology cannot avoid an extensive study of what has hitherto been considered "contextual" information: what makes of Roland's death and the disaster of Roncevaux a victory can only be grasped on the basis of certain social and political arrangements that, while certainly operative in the text, are not specified by the *Song of Roland*. Part of what is "arranged" in social structure is use and control of land, an issue to which we will return.

The ambivalence of the events of Roncevaux, and of Roland's performance in particular, is not an invention of the twentieth century. It is incorporated in the text itself, in action as well as in words. Well before the moment of Roland's death, his behavior and comportment as leader of the rear guard was subjected to evaluation and judged wanting. It was judged wanting, not by any inimical instance, but by his closest companion on the field of battle, his friend Oliver. During the second discussion of the question whether Roland should blow the horn to recall the main body of the army under Charles, Oliver produces two evaluations of Roland's leadership. Oliver's first evaluation of Roland's action is cast in terms of an exclusive disjunction:

> "Mielz valt mesure que ne fait estultie.
> Franceis sunt morz par vostre legerie. . . . " (ll. 1725f.)

> "Measure is worth more than foolishness.
> Franks are dead by your light-headedness. . . . "

This judgment consists of an assignment of blame: it is Roland's *legerie* that is the cause of the death of so many Franks, and he bears responsibility for it. The abstract valorial alternative of the first line leads to a univocal assignment of blame. *Estultie* and *legerie* combined add up to an absence of thoughtfulness, of reflection, of prudent or sagacious weighing of alternatives and intelligent choice. As a result, Charles will never again have the use of their service or their help (ll. 1727 and 1732).

Oliver's point is a serious one. He and Roland are bound to Charles by bonds of friendship and blood, but another "role" (in the semiotic and sociological sense) is also at play. He is their feudal overlord, and it is as his vassals that they have fought and led the rear guard. Feudalism represents a major historiographical and interpretative problem to which we will return. For the moment, we note only that, as overlord and vassals, they are bound by contract. That contract defines a set of sociopolitical relations and specifies their reciprocal responsibilities or duties and privileges. Among these, the overlord can expect to receive services which include that of *auxilium*, military aid. Oliver's comments—really a tirade against his *compagnon*—amount to an indictment of Roland for making it impossible for himself, his friend Oliver, and the remainder of the *leal cumpaignie* to perform their vassalic duty toward their overlord in the future, and hence obtain the *honor* that is rightfully theirs. Oliver's comments announce those of Charles's that we have already discussed: for both vassals and overlord, power, wealth, and glory have all been lost by the rear guard under Roland's leadership.

Oliver does more than formulate a judgment of Roland's performance as captain of the rear guard. The text demonstrates the depth of his feeling in a slightly roundabout manner. After Roland has blown the horn to warn Charles—thereby splitting his own temple and causing his own death—Oliver too is mortally wounded. Pale, the blood pouring down his body, his sight is troubled: he can no longer see. Not recognizing Roland, Oliver attacks him, splitting the inlaid helmet to the nosepiece, but not touching Roland himself. Roland speaks to him, *dulcement e suef*—the only time such adjectives are used of Roland—and asks:

"Sire cumpain, faites le vos de gred?
Ja est ço Rollant, ki tant vos soelt amer!
Par nule guise ne m'aviez desfiet!" (ll. 2000–2002)

"My lord companion, do you do this willingly?
For this is Roland, who always loved you dearly!
You have not challenged me in any way!"

Oliver will recognize Roland from his voice and beg his pardon: the two will be reconciled in as touching a scene as one can imagine on the field of heroic battle. But Roland's amazed questioning is noteworthy. He raises the question of intent or consciousness: *de gred* means "knowingly, willingly, aware." He identifies himself in a slightly skewed manner, displacing the subject function into the third person: this is Roland, who has always loved you so much. And he concludes, in a manner that is inconceivable in our culture, by observing that Oliver, his closest friend, companion at arms, brother of his own fiancée, has attacked him without the challenge that would be proper according to the warrior codes both would observe, codes that define their status as subjects of the ideology that grants them identity and value within their social group. It is also a reference to the set of codes which, somewhat earlier, Oliver invoked to voice his negative judgment of Roland. There is not transcendence here, there is merely the return of the law that creates Roland and Oliver as knights, as warriors, as vassals, as fighters and followers of their chieftain Charles. In a narrative moment that has absolutely no narrative function, but which produces powerful semantic effects, Roland invokes in his own defense the law of feudalism that condemns him, as his closest friend attacks him blindly: how can one not make the isotopic transfer from Oliver's earlier anger at Roland for refusing to blow the horn to the present attack on Roland? The heartrending irony which is the audience's privileged perception until both Oliver and Roland realize what has happened is also enriched by the displaced propriety of the narrative moment: had Oliver attacked Roland when he could see the latter, one might have understood the anger that led beyond the bounds of proper vassalic comportment, but one would have had to blame the rebellious vassal. Now, blind and dying, Oliver is beyond reproach: he can attack Roland without incurring judgment and can be forgiven, by Roland as well as the audience, because of his unseeing eyes, even as the significance of the combat communicates itself to be "seen" by the audience.

In fact, in a passage quoted earlier, Oliver voiced another judgment of Roland, one that does more justice to the multiple values of the text. After the moral criticism of Roland we have seen, Oliver hypothesizes a narrative that would have occurred had Roland followed his advice and blown the horn for

Charles earlier. Charles would have come to the field of battle along with the main body of the army, they would have won the battle, and King Marsile would either be dead or captured (ll. 1728–30). As it is, Oliver pronounces a paradoxical judgment on Roland:

"Vostre proecce, Rollant, mar la veïmes!" (l. 1731)

"Your prowess, Roland, such bad luck for us!"

Oliver's judgment, here, is of a very different kind than that which he voiced earlier in terms of exclusive disjunctions. That was a simple, flat, univocal moral judgment. It implied a single scale of values, producing unhesitating evaluations of human behavior. This judgment is something else again. It asserts contradictory evaluations of the same object. I would suggest that, as against established opinion that tragedy is impossible in a Christian context, this line defines Roland's performance as tragic:[16] the definition of tragedy as disaster produced by the highest and most admirable development of human faculties and potentials strikes me as far more interesting than the simpleminded equation of moral weakness with unhappy results—that is the more usual, bourgeois interpretation of Aristotelian *hamartia*. Alternatively, one might argue that the *Chanson de Roland*, being tragic, is not really Christian, at least at the level of deep structure.[17] More important for present purposes, however, is the recognition that Oliver's judgment of Roland's actions is a paradoxical one, and that this paradox, like all paradoxes, contains a dual evaluation of its subject. It is only the most obvious comment on the *Chanson de Roland* to say that, if Roland's performance constitutes heroism, that heroism must be juxtaposed to the narrative phenomena that make of that performance an extremely costly one. This observation of the obvious rejoins the text's own repetitions as to the deaths of Roland, the peers, the 20,000 Franks of the rear guard, and the multiple dimensions that this disaster takes and which are stressed, particularly in Charles's laments: military, political, and social.

Abstracting the personal dimension of the discourse, a major social and political dimension is revealed in this line. As noted in our earlier discussion, *proecce* starts as a lexeme whose meaning is general and abstract, "value" or "profit" without any particular content. In actual historical usage it is transformed into a key ideological term which bears a loaded semantic content: all those (semantic, physical, and moral) qualities which are appropriate and necessary to a knight are precipitated into that single, *porte-manteau* lexeme, including strength, bravery, competence in the necessary manipulations of arms and horses, and finally loyalty, meaning the predictability of the subordinate in serving his superior. These are the qualities that make of an adjuvant an object of value for a noble Subject who hires him as a mercenary or engages in the exchanges that constitute the vassalic relationship (of which more anon). Returning then to Oliver's line—"*Vostre proecce, Roland, mar la veïmes!*"—and abstracting the personal element, what is left is a judgment by a particular agent, who himself subscribes to its values, of the value system of a particular social subset: the warrior class. This line defines the structure of tragedy: that structure is the structure of paradox, since the same value or set of values is stated to be both admirable and disastrous. Roland is "hero" precisely because he incorporates the ultimate values of his cultural code and does so to an extreme that makes of them a logical source of disaster. The *Chanson de Roland* is a warrior epic, and it is a poem that occasionally invokes and subscribes to Christian values: it is anything but the narrow poem of didactic moralism that an extraordinarily persistent tradition of religious chauvinism would make of it!

The text provides a surprising confirmation of this view of narrative structure and verbal texture. As I said at the beginning of this section, the dying Roland transforms himself into a complex sign. Complexity, here, is defined as the opposite of "exclusive disjunction": it consists of the conjunction of either contradictory or contrary values, hence a non-exclusive disjunction. Part of the auto-semiotization of Roland's death consists of his placement of two adjuvants, instruments that have helped him attain his moment of glory and apotheosis, under his body as it becomes his corpse: his sword and his oliphant. Both are inextricably tied with his narrative performance, both connect that performance with the code of vassality. One has been the instrument of aggrandizement, the conquest of Charles's empire, and the construction of Roland's value. The other has been at the center of the argument between Roland and Oliver, his closest friend and companion, and became, as we saw, the occasion for Oliver's complex but profoundly negative judgment of his friend, the hero. Even this brief characterization of the sword and the horn reveals the ineluctable imbrication of the two adjuvants with the narrative of which they are integral parts. Their significances can only be discussed as part of those narrative programs. Just as the parts compose the whole, the whole constitutes the parts as functions. But as we have seen, the discussion of the whole text as narrative must necessarily imply the discussion of those parts of its constitutive codes that are not "located" within "the text itself" but extend "outward" from the text into the social text. Discussion of the two objects named in the semiotization of Roland's death depends on the analysis and interpretation of the entire narrative in the history, narrative or not, of its period.

2 | The Gaze of the Other

Le signifiant se produisant au champ de l'Autre fait surgir le sujet de sa
signification.

Jacques Lacan, *Les quatre concepts fondamentaux*

The Sociological Presentation of the Self

THE *CHANSON DE ROLAND* largely tells its story from the point of view of the
Christian camp of Charles's Frankish troops.[1] Its axiology is undoubted. Its
story is narrated from a valorial position which is that of the Christians as against
the Saracens. The latter are to be converted or to be killed: there is no empathy
for alterity in this text. The opposition between Christian and Saracen is a
simple, radical one, an "us *vs.* them" as purely categorical as that between the
cowboys and the Indians in the old westerns. It is so simple and absolute an
opposition that it hardly even makes sense to consider the effects—undoubted as
they may be—of cultural "filters": their effectivity would presuppose an intent,
a desire to know the other culture, even a mere curiosity, of which there is no
trace in this text. The "Saracens" of the *Roland*, who are also called "pagans,"
are not textual figures bearing any "real" relationship to their presumed referents: they do not "refer" to the concrete, historical societies that occupied either
Spain or the Near East.[2] Those historical societies comprised cultures and a civilization that were, in fact, far more advanced, tolerant, subtle, and sophisticated
than the Christian societies of the West within which the *Chanson* was developed
and admired. The *Roland* betrays no interest in the actual characteristics of that
other society and polity. Rather than a (non)representation of that cultural
Other, what the text produces is a very slightly varied reproduction of the same
semic traits attributed by the text to the Christian self: the military organization
and tactics of the Saracens, their political organization, their decision-making
process, reproduce the same basic processes ascribed to the Frankish army under
Charlemagne. Even their religion, in historical reality monotheistic, turns out to
be a parodistic reproduction of the Christian trinity, with its pantheon of
Appolin, Tervagan, and Mahomet. In one of the paradoxes of history, it has been
suggested that it was this projection of the self on the screen of the Other, this

false and prejudicial image of the Muslims, that European knights brought with them on the First Crusade.[3] Without realizing it, the historical Crusaders would have been battling an image of themselves.

The religious difference, as inexact as it is, constitutes the solitary semantic marker strongly differentiating the "Saracens" from the "Christians" in the *Chanson de Roland*. It is entirely false as a historical representation, but the religious differentiation is the only textual trait that makes of the textual figure of the Saracens in the *Roland* something other than a faithful reproduction of the Christian social and political process within the textual diegesis.

The culture in which the *Roland* is embedded has very little real concern with human alterity. The other as defined in geographical, political, and cultural terms and the Other as existing within the same geographical and semiotic space are reduced to parodistic figures. Discussion of the possible reasons for such a cultural blindness can only take place on the level of speculation: it may well be that the space of the Other, in the Middle Ages, was entirely taken by the mystery of the divinity, so that strictly human alterity could only be recognized as a negatively marked version of the self. At least such a conceptualization for what is initially a shocking phenomenon allows for the fact that the vision of human diversity developed by modern anthropology was lacking in the eleventh and twelfth centuries. What is more difficult to mentally encompass is the ease with which modern scholars and critics, who benefit from that cultural relativism, continue to embrace without hesitation the crude, aggressive nationalism and religious absolutism which they continue to identify with the grotesque enterprise of the Crusades. There is something profoundly repugnant not only about the cultural and political ethos displayed by the text—an ethos which has occasioned the entirely admirable indignation of only one scholar to my knowledge: Jean-Charles Payen[4]—but about the *acceptance* of an ethos which was historically so grossly destructive. Such an embrace by our contemporaries who are—in principle—capable of conceptually distancing themselves from the position of the text they are studying is not without serious ramifications in the twentieth-century world. It is precisely that incomprehension of alterity, that transformation of an epistemically and culturally Other into the negative version of the self, that impedes dialectical progress by casting the Other at the other pole of a purely dyadic system. Unfortunately, the same kind of simple "ethical" binarism that we find in the *Chanson de Roland* continues to operate in contemporary scholarship and in modern political discourse. That dyadism was a necessary prerequisite for the programmed extermination of the Jews in the Holocaust, and it was equally present in the discourse that cast the Soviet Union into the role of the "evil empire." And of course, such discourses are not without their effectivity in the pragmatic world of military and nuclear decision making.

The extreme reductiveness of the category of the Other has further textual results, however. Its binary opposite is the self (not to be taken as a psychological notion). Since the Other is merely a minimally differentiated version of the Self, it therefore becomes a screen for the projection of an internal problematic of the subject. Insofar as the alterity of "Saracen" has no substantive consistency, the figure of the "Saracen" in the *Roland* becomes merely another representation of the essential problematic which is at work in (the representation and reality of) the Frankish polity.[5] We will see, in fact, that the same pattern of complex political relations and (non)fulfillment of contracts obtains within the figure of the Saracens as within the Christian camp. The reduction of alterity implies a repetition of identity *and* a repetition of the problematic of identity.

Nevertheless, there is one moment within the *Chanson de Roland* in which the structure of an epistemological alterity is broached. It is a moment in which the relative cognitive positions of alterity—the knower and the known as representing cultural and political alterities—are represented. Without giving textual reality to the historical culture of the Muslims in Spain or the Near East, it does establish the Other's cognitive position, using it as an occasion to display the self as if it were being presented to that Other.

After the opening Saracen council, that camp sends out its representative, the ambassador who is to bear the message of the contract King Marsile offers to the Franks. That is Blancandrin: wily, diplomatic, patient, and perceptive, he is an actor to whom no negative marker adheres, even though he is a master liar and as much an essential link in the chain of betrayal as Ganelon. Other than the fact that he belongs to the category of the Saracens, nothing is held against him. He is distinguished primarily by cognitive traits, those specified by the text as constituting the quality *sage*. As the king's advisor, he is the opposite number to Duke Naimes on the Frankish side. Having first performed the message to the Franks, having then brought back their messenger to his own camp, he will disappear from the narrative: neither death nor conversion is attributed to him.

Blancandrin comes upon the Frankish camp at a moment of pleasure and self-satisfaction. Having overcome Cordres, the Franks are enjoying booty and respite. As he comes upon them in a *grant verger*, they are represented in an idealized self-image that comes close to being a sociological self-portrait. In response to the gaze of a posited Other, the text presents a portrait of the self on a sociopolitical isotopy which is hierarchically organized. It starts from the top, to move down the sociopolitical scale:

> *Li empereres se fait e balz e liez*:
> Cordres ad prise e les murs peceiez,
> Od ses cadables les turs en abatied;
> Mult grant eschech en unt si chevaler
> D'or e d'argent e de guarnemenz chers.

En la citet nen ad remés paien
Ne seit ocis u devient chrestien.
Li empereres est en un grant verger. . . . (ll. 96–103)

The emperor is joyful and jubilant:
He has taken Cordres, broken the walls,
knocked down the towers with his catapults.
What tremendous spoils his knights have won—
gold and silver, precious arms, equipment.
In the city not one pagan remained
who is not killed or turned into a Christian.
The emperor is in an ample orchard. . . .

The repetition of the figure of the emperor at the beginning of the first and eighth lines of the *laisse* closes off those lines in a separate subunit, on the triple isotopies of /past/, /victory/, and /alterity/: it "describes" (or creates) the Other, in a recent position on the line extending backward from the *hic et nunc*, and it is the Other as defeated: that is the first part of the image the text produces face to face with the recounted arrival of the Other's messenger, Blancandrin. Death, destruction, booty: those are the semantemes Christianity offers the Other on his arrival to their camp.

If the text attributes the victory over Cordres to Charles, he is not alone. In the orchard with him are the great nobles of his court:

Li empereres est en un grant verger,
Ensembl'od lui Rollant e Oliver,
Sansun li dux e Anseis li fiers,
Gefreid d'Anjou, le rei gunfanuner,
E si furent e Gerin e Gerers. . . . (ll. 103–107)

The Emperor is in an ample orchard,
Roland and Oliver are with him there,
Samson the Duke and Anseis the fierce,
Geoffrey d'Anjou, the king's own standard-bearer,
and so too were Gerin and Gerer. . . .

Of these seven names (Roland, Oliver, Samons, Anseis, Geoffrey, Gerin, Gerers), six figure also in the *laisse* in which Charles, much later in the poem, will grieve the losses of the dead men of the rear guard at Roncevaux, naming them "*Li .XII. per, que jo aveie laiset* . . . " (ll. 2410): "The twelve peers, whom I had left. . . . " We will return to the question of the "twelve peers" below. With the addition of Geoffrey of Anjou, the text is naming the "greats" of the kingdom who occupy the place just below that of the emperor in its sociopolitical hierarchy. In the text, they figure primarily as military leaders and warriors commanding the major detachments of Charles's host.

After the emperor, after the greats of the kingdom, comes the third category, introduced by the text in a manner that almost disappears from some translations:

> La u cist furent, des altres i out bien,
> De dulce France i ad quinze milliers. (ll. 108f.)

> There where these were, there were also many of the others,
> from sweet France there are fifteen thousand.

"Where *these* were [i.e., the twelve peers], of the *others* there were also plenty: from sweet France, fifteen thousand of them." The king and emperor forming a class of one, the rest of the warrior society represented in the *Roland* is internally subdivided into two parts: a class of twelve, and a much larger category, the "others" who can be referred to in gross numbers, such as the 15,000 from sweet France, a kind of number that signifies the mass of lower-level knights. Indeed, as the text goes on to specify, in an idyllic vision snatched from the rigors of battle, these are the mounted professionals of war, the *chevaliers*:

> Sur palies blancs siedent cil *cevaler*.
> As tables juent pur els esbaneie
> E as eschecs li plus saive e li veill,
> E escremissent cil bacheler leger. (ll. 110–13)

> The knights sit on bright brocaded silk;
> they are playing at tables to pass the time,
> the old and wisest men sitting at chess,
> the young light-footed men fencing with swords.

After the emperor, after the "greats" of the kingdom and the feudal world, the lower-level knights play at table games while the younger among them, those not yet fully fledged as knights, engage in playful dueling.

The text of the *laisse* will close in hieratic grace, with a return to the figure of the king and emperor, seated in distinction on a folding stool rhetorically located next to other markers which, like the *verger* in which the text finds itself, indicate the idealization of the landscape:

> Desuz un pin, delez un eglenter,
> Un faldestoel i unt, fait tut d'or mer:
> La siet li reis ki dulce France tient.
> Blanche ad la barbe e tut flurit le chef,
> Gent ad le cors e le cuntenant fier:
> S'est kil demandet, ne l'estoet enseigner.

E li message descendirent a pied,
Sil saluerent par amur e par bien. (ll. 114–21)

Beneath a pine, beside a wild sweet-briar,
there was a throne, every inch pure gold.
There sits the king, who rules sweet France.
His beard is white, his head all flowering.
The body is noble, the countenance fierce:
whoever seeks him, has no problem finding.
The messengers dismounted, and on their feet,
they greeted him correctly and in peace.

So closes the brief glimpse of sociological self-portraiture vouchsafed the modern reader by a text which mostly takes itself and its sociopolitical structures for granted.

The rhetorical point of the *laisse* is the moment of respite after battle, in which distinctions of age, wisdom, and lightness of body are more overtly stressed and certainly more affecting than sociological distinctions. The moment functions, after all, not only as the deserved respite after battle, but as the idealized vision of the Franks at rest, as close to being at peace as they can while still at war in a foreign land. It is the intrusion of relaxation, of pleasure and joy at one of the rare peaceful interstices of war: it is the moment before the levered machinations of evil start them on the mountain path to destruction. The sociological distinctions, barely suggested by the text, are the structural presuppositions of the text. They are structural in textual terms because they are structural in social terms. Given that texts are also part of the means by which society reproduces itself—the ideological relay traverses what we consider the "literary" instance in the Middle Ages at least as much as it does today, and perhaps more importantly—these structures are also social because they are textual.

The question then arises, however, as to the relation of this sociological analysis to the actual social and political structures that obtained in the historical society of France around the turn of the eleventh and twelfth centuries; that is, in the social body in which the *Chanson de Roland* was embedded. This is the concrete form of the question of the relationship between text and history which is specific to this particular text. The question, for us, is not a causative one: the issue is not whether the series of "textuality" takes priority of effectivity upon the series of "history," or vice versa. The issue, as is normal for a semiotic inquiry, is not that of the efficient cause (in Aristotelian terms) or of "mechanical" causation (in Althusserian terms) but of the *signification* to be attributed to a textual characteristic. As indicated in our introduction, that signification is to be construed by the insertion of the textual series into the historical, and vice versa: the text being, by nature and by definition, a historical entity, it is as an element of the historicity of its time that it will signify. This historicality is to be attained by motivated transformations of an intertextual nature, assuming "history" to play the role of another text for purposes of semiotic analysis.

The Intertextuality of the Peerage

In the text, the figure of the "twelve peers" is a sociopolitical group of high status, associated with Roland, all of whose members are killed while serving with him in the rear guard. The membership of this group is a fluctuating one, but as the denomination recurs, it must be accepted as encoded in the text. The difficulty this figure sets for a socio-historical interpretation of the *Chanson de Roland* is that no self-evidently equivalent term can be found in the social text of the period. In the historical reality of eleventh- and twelfth-century France— as that reality has been recuperated and staged by historians—there did not exist a group of twelve men, of such exalted status that they ranked just below the king, institutionalized as equals and forming a corporate body. A first and nega- tive conclusion to be drawn from this fact is that the text is hardly a mimetic one: it is not a mirror promenaded along the route of eleventh- and twelfth-cen- tury reality! The second conclusion is more positive: if the textual actors are given attributions of traits that do not mimetically represent a circumambient historical reality, is it nonetheless possible to separate out the particular traits concerned, identify those also to be found in the social text, and then track the process of the redistribution of semantic traits so as to identify the transformative work of the text? A possible rephrasing of that awkward question would be the following: is it possible to analyze the relation between verbal text and social text so as to identify its ideological thrust or intent? The answer to this question can only be formulated after a closer examination of the relevant social text itself.[6]

An intertextual relation provides a useful link here. An epic somewhat later than the *Roland* stages a similar narrative situation. In the *Chanson d'Aspremont*, Charles leads his troops to Aspremont, which is held by the Saracens. He asks for someone to reconnoiter the enemy positions and count their forces. As in the council scene of the *Roland*, a series of volunteers is re- fused by Charles, in an obvious adaptation and transformation of the *Roland* text. Charles explains his rejection of the volunteers as follows:

"Baron," dist Carles, "ne vos voel anuier.
Jo ne voel pas a paiens envoier
Haut hom nul qui tiere ait a ballier,
Que ne l'ocient cil gloton paltonier."[7]

"Barons," says Charles, "I do not want to anger you.
I do not want to send to the pagans
any high man who has territory to govern,
lest that insolent rabble kill him."

Acknowledging his political embarrassment in a manner that the Charles of the *Roland* did not, Charles here apologizes for the potential insult in his words ("I do not wish to anger you"), and then states that he will not send to the pagans "any high man who has a territory to rule." More specifically, the verb *ballier*—it will give "bailiff" in English—implies, not only governance, but governance as the delegated representative of another, of a greater lord. Charles thus recognizes the potential danger to the messenger and refuses to risk the life of one of those who rules a territory as his delegate, his *lieu-tenant*, as it were: such a one who rules in the king's name, and represents his power, is too valuable.

The *Chanson d'Aspremont* belongs to the period of Philip Augustus, a period during which the king of France had begun to exploit his rights over his vassals. During the reigns of the earlier Capetians of the eleventh and early twelfth centuries, however, these nobles had ruled their territories in complete independence from the king, whose suzerainty remained purely nominal.[8] Within that earlier time frame, the specification of meaning added by *Aspremont* to the *Roland* intertext can only be construed as a reference to Carolingian ideology. Both during the Carolingian period and later, during the reign of Philip Augustus, the principle of devolution of power from central kingship to the territorial powers of counts and dukes holds true; it is in the intervening, properly "feudal" period that these great nobles govern their territories, not as subordinates of the king, but as potentates themselves. It is this principle of devolution that provides the isotopic identity of the two codes invoked: that of apostolic devolution from Christ that is implied by the number /twelve/, and that of political devolution of king to /peers/. Thus, it would appear to be the category of the upper nobility, a class which survived the enormous social changes of the Middle Ages with remarkable persistence, which the textual figure of the "twelve peers" seems to encode. That is undoubtedly true, but it is a partial truth only. In order to see both its truth and the partiality of that truth, it is necessary to examine more closely the structure of the social text of which the *Roland* is a transformation.

3 | Excursus I: Aesthetics, Economics, Politics

> Feudalism itself had entirely empirical relations as its basis.
> Marx, *The German Ideology*

> It is the sweat of the poor . . . that furnishes those luxuries with which the mighty sate themselves.
> Odo of Cluny (*ca.* 930), *Collationes*

Beauty, Value, Violence

THE BRILLIANT BEAUTY of noble weapons and armaments is a frequent motif in the *Roland*, especially as concerns the enemy. Preparing for battle, the Saracens display the warrior magnificence of the instruments of war:

> Paien s'adubent des osbercs sarazineis,
> Tuit li plusur en sunt dublez en treis.
> Lacent lor elmes mult bons, sarraguzeis,
> Ceignent espees de l'acer vianeis;
> Escuz unt genz, espiez valentineis,
> E gunfanuns blancs e blois e vermeils. (ll. 993–99)

> The pagans don their saracen mail,
> their armor's mostly triple thick.
> They lace on tough helmets from Saragossa
> and the swords' hard steel from Vienne;
> their shields are noble, their spears from Valencia,
> and their flags are white, and blue, and red.

The most striking descriptions, however, are not those of the weapons' beauty alone. Rather, the touch of sunlight on metal and its brilliant reflections remain in the memory:

> Laissent les muls e tuz les palefreiz,
> Es destrers muntent, si chevalchent estreiz.
> Clers fut li jurz e bels fut li soleilz;

N'unt guarnement que fut ne reflambeit.
Sunent mil grailles por ço que plus bels seit. . . . (ll. 994–1004)

They leave the mules and palfreys behind,
they mount war-horses, they ride in tight formation.
The day was clear, the sun was bright,
their equipment glitters in fiery light.
A thousand trumpets sound for beauty's sake.

The brilliant fusion of artifice and nature is functionalized in the narrative. The sounding of the horns alerts the Franks to the presence of the enemy army. Oliver, climbing a hillock, observes the enemy. The text foregrounds the description by narrative triplication, frequent in oral literature. First it has offered the narrator's description, just cited. It repeats the description in a kind of free indirect discourse (*discours indirect libre*, or "middle voice"), as the narrator's account of what the character sees (ll. 1031–35). Finally, the character himself will repeat the content of the message in direct discourse. Stressing their number, he refers to the

"Helmes laciez e blancs osbercs vestuz;
Dreites cez hanstes, luisent cil espiet brun." (ll. 1042f.)

"Helmets laced on, white hauberks on their backs,
straight spears, their smooth handles glisten."

Again, later, when Marsile attacks, leading his twenty divisions through a pass,

Luisent cil elmes as perres d'or gemmees,
E cil escuz e cez bronies sasfrees. . . . (ll. 1452f.)

The helmets shine, their gemstones mounted on gold,
and the shields and saffron hauberks. . . .

These are collective descriptions, the visual effect of a massed army of mounted knights in the sunlight. Individuals receive analogous descriptions. Turpin attacks Abisme, aiming first at the shield,

Pierres i ad, ametistes e topazes,
Esterminals e carbuncles ki ardent. . . . (ll. 1500f.)

It has stones, amethysts and topaz,
precious stones and burning carbuncles. . . .

It is especially the enemy whose appearances are gloriously limned. When Frankish armament is singled out for description, it tends to be more briefly, at the corner of a hemistich. Oliver attacks Climborin, spurring his horse *des esperuns d'or mier* (l. 1549). Roland's famous sword receives an analogously brief mention, *Durendal qui plus valt que fin or* (l. 1583). There is a general tendency to amplify the attribution of beauty to pagan armament and to observe more reserve or reticence regarding the Christian armament: does this suggest envy of Oriental wealth?

A major exception is Roland's dying address to Durendal, when a Christian weapon is endowed with the same kind of stylistic beauty as pagan armament:

> "E! Durendal, cum es bele, e clere, e blanche!
> Cuntre soleill si luises e reflambes!" (ll. 2316f.)

> "Hey! Durendal, you're bright, and clear, and white!
> You glisten and flame up to the sun!"

Even here, it will be more the sword's function than its beauty that will be stressed, as Roland lists the many lands the sword has conquered for Charlemagne (ll. 2322–34).

But when Charles and the army finally hear the call of Roland's olifant, then the Franks dismount to arm themselves. The process of arming oneself is designated by the verb *aduber*: they dub themselves, or more accurately, they dub their bodies with their armor and weapons, translating the ritual gravity of the process with reference to the ritual that transforms the postulant into a member of the company of knighthood. The standard *distributio* is rehearsed—haulberks, helmets, golden swords, shields, spears, and multi-colored flags—before they remount their horses. At that point, the sun shines on them:

> Esclargiz est li vespres e li jurz.
> Cuntre le soleil reluisent cil adub,
> Osbercs e helmes i getent grant flabur,
> E cil escuz, ki ben sunt peinz a flurs,
> E cil espiez, cil oret gunfanun. (ll. 1807–11)

> The day and the vespers are clear,
> the dubbed gear shines against the sun,
> hauberks and helmets throw off great flames,
> and these shields, painted with flowers,
> and these spears, these golden gonfanons.

The text leaves no doubt: weapons and armaments are beautiful, they are a beautiful sight to behold, on the backs of the knights and under the sun, brilliant and costly in their exotic manufactures and in their ornamentation. It is as if the weapons were the concretization of the warriors' value and contained their heroism as a precipitate. The weapons and their beauty are signifiers of the courage and the heroism of knights, ready for battle, ready for death.

Beyond the beauty of the instruments of war, the text also retains the primitive and animistic trait—in spite of its "Christianity"—of naming the most distinguished of the weapons and the mounts, Durendal, Veillantif, Hautecler, etc., suggesting the status of a personage for the instruments of war. Indeed, the anomalous presence of this archaicizing trait within a poem, which would offer Christianity as one of its ideologies, is indicative of a more fundamental level of significance. The fact that ultimately Christians and Saracens share the beauty both of weaponry and its glint as caught by sunlight suggests the bond that ties them more closely, perhaps, than the religions which separate them: they share the values of knighthood, of joyous battle, the bond of a particular, well-defined social grouping, with its telos and its ideology.

The motif of the beauty of the armor and the weapons is not merely ornamental. It signifies the class identity of warrior-knights and the qualities requisite of their calling on either side of the religious divide. And yet, the motif of the beauty of weaponry is frequently subordinated to another motif, especially in the battle scenes, that of the mighty stroke of the sword which cuts through helmet, mail, skull, chest, and horse, to lodge hard in the ground. That stroke often cracks open more than the life of man and horse: it destroys the encrustations of beauty and value on the doomed knight's armor. When Oliver, himself mortally wounded, attacks Marganice with his sword,

> Tient Halteclere, dunt li acer fut bruns,
> Fiert Marganices sur l'elme a or, agut,
> E flurs e cristaus, en acraventet jus;
> Trenchet la teste d'ici qu'as denz menuz. . . . (ll. 1953–56)

> He holds Haltecler, of burnished steel,
> hits Marganice on the high, golden helmet,
> he scatters down its flowers and crystals;
> he cuts the head right down to the small teeth. . . .

Similarly, when Roland hits the nameless Saracen who tries to steal Durendal along with the olifant, he breaks the steel of the enemy's helmet, his head and bones, knocking both eyes out of his head, and slams the enemy dead at his feet, so that the olifant's gold and crystals fall off.

At moments, the financial value of objects destroyed is continuous with the value of the body itself. When Roland attacks Grandonie, the count lays down a blow so "virtuous" that

> Tresqu'al nasel tut le elme li fent,
> Trenchet le nés e la buche e les denz,
> Trestut le cors e l'osberc jazerenc,
> De l'oree sele lé dous alves d'argent
> E al ceval le dos parfundement. (ll. 1645–49)

> He splits the helmet down to the nosepiece,
> he cuts the nose and mouth and teeth,
> right through the body and the hauberk's tough mail,

and the golden saddle's two silver knobs,
and drives on deep through the horse's back:

The helmet, the nose, the mouth, the teeth, the entire body, the halberk, the saddle, and the horse itself that bears the man and his armor to death are merely so many verbal stations on Durendal's descent separating the man from his life.

This is no less true when the archbishop exercises vassalic violence. He attacks Abisme, a vassal with much temerity (l. 1478), whose shield, as we have already seen, is covered with precious stones:

Pierres i ad, ametistes e topazes,
Esterminals e carbuncles ki ardent. . . . (ll. 1500f.)

Gems there are, amethysts and topaz,
precious stones and carbuncles burning. . . .

But when Turpin is through, little of value is left:

Enprès sun colp, ne quid qu'un dener vaillet. (l. 1505)

After his blow, I don't think he's worth a cent.

At the sight of which the Franks exclaim:

"Ci ad grant vasselage!" (l. 1508)

"Now *that's* vasselage for you!"

The theme of beauty destroyed is remarkably frequent, both in extended passages such as we have just quoted and at the turn of a cornered hemistich: *la bucle de cristal* (l. 1263), *l'escut . . . ad or e a flurs* (l. 1276), *l'oree bucle* (l. 1283), *an escut en la pene devant . . . tut trenchet le vermeill e le blanc* (ll. 1298f.), *la bucle d'or mer* (l. 1314), *l'elme . . . i li carbuncle luisent* (l. 1326), *le blanc osberc, dunt la maile est menue* (l. 1329), *la sele ki est a or batue* (l. 1331), *l'escut li freint, ki est ad or e a flur* (l. 1355), *an elme ki gemmet fu ad or* (l. 1585), all are the joyful sacrifices of value to the violence of man.

It is not only the bodies of warriors that are cut and pierced, along with their horses; financial wealth in the conspicuousness of its military displays is destroyed without regret. So frequent is the theme that beauty's telos would seem to be its conspicuous destruction in battle: it is a joy, it is a *jouissance*, to strike, to kill, to destroy both the life of the antagonist and the magnificence of his armor. As surely as Bertrand de Born, in the famous sestina "*Be'm platz lo gais temps de Pascor*," the *Chanson* displays the thirsty pleasure and satisfactions of war's destructive violence, and particularly when it engages the gratuitous fracture of aesthetic and economic value conjoined in the precious stones of knightly armor, the signs of value. An antirational economy of conspicuous consumption, of joyful destruction, of waste, of *dépense illimitée*, inhabits certain corners of the *Roland*, presumably the most primitive, those which hark back the most to nomadic beginnings. In this theme, beauty and economic value are mere indices of joyfully destructive violence.

But negation requires a prior affirmation of value. The joyful destruction of value is predicated on economic value created in a rational economy of production, imbricated with the political organization of society.

The Noble, the Knight, the Peasant

Perhaps more than at other periods, politics in the Middle Ages was an important determinant of other instances of society, including the economic: such was the opinion of Karl Marx, among others.[1] The basic form of production in this social formation was that of agricultural production by small-scale producers attached to the land and to their instruments.[2] The surplus value of their production is expropriated by the dominant noble class, numbering perhaps a bit more than 1 percent of the population and employing various methods which are incorporated in the different modes of organizing the manorial system.[3] The widespread image of small, relatively independent economic units, producing within their own limited resources most of what was required for survival and reproduction, refers to an earlier period of the Middle Ages. As the Carolingian Empire disintegrated and political power shifted from a centralized *imperium*, it was transferred first to the dukes and the counts, only to slip from their grasp a little later. As political control became ever more fragmented, and was defined as the effect of controlling a fortress and a handful of vassals; as external invasion reaffirmed the need for military protection; and as only local force and power existed to fulfill this need; so also economic production became limited to servicing the circumscribed political unit at the scale of the *châtellenie*. While trade, even on an international scale, was never completely interrupted, the disappearance of centralized authority and the powers devolving from it represents a stage in which an extreme degree of localized economic self-reliance was the norm, in which the face of France consisted of an endless series of small, independent manors whose survival largely depended on the ability of a particular castle-master to organize and hold the loyalty of a number of vassals, based in a military fortress.

A reversal of the trend toward minute fragmentation appears to have occurred toward the end of the tenth and the beginning of the eleventh centuries. First, particular lords of local fortresses tended to group themselves under the leadership of a single *châtelain*, whether one of their number, possibly of relatively recent nobility, or drawn from one of the older local noble families. At a later stage, the old nobility, represented by the dukes, the counts, and the viscounts, tended to reintegrate these independent *châtellenies* into larger, nascent regional powers. At about the same time, and without addressing the question of the priority of the two phenomena or their causal relationship, there occurs a profound transformation in the manorial, and properly economic, organization of society. The agricultural basis of society persists, but it is given a new orientation. In the earlier stage, that of extremely fragmented localism, the expropriation of surplus value took two primary forms: captation of peasant labor on the lord's land and direct contribution by the peasantry to the lord's living process in the form of material goods such as the "donations" or "payments in kind" of chickens or bushels of grains produced by the dependents and turned over to the lord. The fundamental change that occurred in the course of the eleventh and twelfth centuries is the transformation of this model into one in which money plays an increasingly important role. The agricultural production of the peasant—still the overwhelmingly basic mode of economic production—undergoes the mediating instance of money before being subject to the lord's expropriation. Both labor and material objects are transformed into species-value: rather than concrete work or material goods, the lord now, more and more, takes cash from the producers.

The political and legal form by which this extraction of mediated surplus value was obtained from a peasantry was that of the *ban*, the right to command, to constrain, and to punish; more broadly, the right to promulgate rules, to constrain their observation, and then to punish whatever contravention might occur.[4] This definition centers the *ban* in the exercise of justice; its profits seem to have been substantial. Imposed by a "seigneurial authority that was multiform and knew no limits," it was tantamount to "a form of legitimated and organized pillage, tempered only by a new morality of peace and by the resistances of peasant solidarity."[5] The variety of fines and taxes which transferred wealth from the peasantry to the pockets of the lords was extraordinary. A striking example of just how irrational—and financially productive—this right to "justice" might be is that of the *taille*, a financial imposition which was irregular in both amount and frequency: its timing and amount was determined entirely by the particular lord, who could demand payment, in any amount, at any time, from those peasants living within his domain and who were his dependents. In addition to such means of extortion as derived from the lord's judicial authority, other *coutumes* were more directly economic. Such were the taxes on flour mills, the baking ovens, the wine presses, the taverns, all monopolies likely to be owned by the local lord. Other sources of banal profits were the better-known tolls on roads and river crossings, the right of lodging (in fact, payment for a day's total living expenses for the lord's agents, their horses, and their dogs), as well as the *banvin*, the sale of wine at the end of the season when it had to be sold before it turned too bitter for consumption.

By the end of the eleventh century, the system of banal lordship was well established.[6] The system would certainly not have worked had it functioned only with the social classes so far discussed: the upper nobility, enjoying the rights of the *ban*, and the peasantry, upon whom those rights were imposed. Why should the peasant pay the multitudinous taxes and fines? Why should the peasant relinquish the small pile of *deniers* that were his only after arduous labor and conversion of the products of that labor into money? As both medieval historians have realized and as Michel Foucault argued, wherever there is power, there is resistance, and few groups are as likely to offer an effective, tactically evasive resistance to the powers employing taxation as the French peasant: this is not a social group that has ever given up its accumulated wealth, produced by the hard use of its bodies, voluntarily. Even though various documents (written by clerics in the service of lords, either secular or religious) name the payment of banal impositions "gifts" (supposedly proffered in recognition of the lord's protection), the extortion of surplus value was not achieved by the simple and free exchange of agricultural labor for military protection, as might be suggested by the clerical ideology of the three orders.

On the contrary, the expropriation of that part of the profits of the productive process that was not necessary for survival and reproduction was obtained only by means of force, actual or threatened. Banal profits were the result of constraint, exercised permanently and systematically, in a thoroughly institutionalized form of violence. Documents of the period refer to the "customs" of extortion as *malae*, *pravae*, or *injustae consuetudines*.[7] In another region, the middle of the eleventh century sees a lexical transformation: what had earlier been called *usus* or *exactiones* are called, as of 1050, *forcias*. The verbal form is even more telling: *forçar* is the term for the collections of banal lordship in Catalonia.[8] Duby somewhere characterizes banal extortion as "organized pillage."

How was this force applied? The requirements of the political situation were quite specific. It must be applied to peasants—servile or free—working in the countryside. It must be applied with sufficient frequency to ensure continuity of production, on both the lord's demesne and the peasant's own plot. It must be sufficiently permanent to ensure that the peasants remain on the lord's land. Since much of his income depended on the payment of banal fines, a regular presence was required, both to establish infringements of laws and collect payment of fines. In other words, a major "police" presence was required, remembering that the police power is not merely a repressive power but is thoroughly imbricated in the productive functioning of the socioeconomic system. The required dispersal, permanence, and mobility of police power was achieved by the readily available means of mounted professionals in the delivery of military force, the armed retainers known as *chevaliers* or knights. Their original function may well have been defensive, as claimed by the ideology of the three orders; during the eleventh and twelfth centuries, they were the source of violence rather than its control.[9] Above all, they policed the countryside. In this context, the main burden was castle-duty and the daily cavalcade, the *chevauchée* of the documents, in which part of the fortress's garrison rode out to reassert its presence and, through the semiosic mediation of the knights' and horses' bodies, the presence of the banal lord to the subject peasant population.[10] In addition to the pragmatic advantage that increased height gave these warriors mounted on their horses, the symbolic value of increased mobility and heightened stature must not be underestimated. In a semiosic process already discovered in the case of Roland, the body is transformed into a signifier: the very bodies of knight-and-horse became the mobile signs of power and of potential force, destruction, and devastation, instilling fear and submission in the peasantry even when not unleashing military violence against them. These corporeal signs were part and parcel of a larger and redundant system of ideological signification which included the very castle from which the knights rode out and the gonfalons they bore.[11] The regularity of their appearance, the rhythmic scansion of the *chevauchée*, has permitted one historian to speak of the "measured terrorism" thus exercised against the peasantry.[12]

This was the primary function of the class of knights in what is generally called "the feudal system." Feudal vassals were the agents of seigneurial oppression who, by the fear they inspired, constrained the peasantry to bend to the yoke, to fulfill the requirements of new forms of labor, of the productive labor assigned to it by existing power.[13]

The knights of the eleventh and twelfth centuries were mounted warriors first and foremost, *chevaliers*, a professional guild of elite warriors.[14] Beneath the rather grandiose ideologies produced by the various texts in which knights appear, such was the fairly simple basis of their existence, after the period when defense against external attack was their major rationale. The knight's body, as we have seen, is transformed into a sign of potential and actualizable violence in the daily cavalcade through peasant spaces, a sign whose pragmatic effect would have been fear and terror. His encoding in the social text and in the concrete text of the *Roland* is clear: both revel in the display of knightly violence, the verbal text dwelling on the sword strokes, their descent through the metal of the helmet, the skull and the brains in the helmet, and through the armor, the chest of the man, and the trunk of the horse beneath; sometimes enough momentum is left in the sword to drive it deep into the reddening ground. This violence, indeed, is the isotopic connector between the ideological text of the *Roland* and the sociohistorical text of lived experience. It is also that aspect of representation with which knights and noble in the audience could identify in glory. In the ideological text, of course, the victim is another knight, far more glorious as victim than an unarmed peasant. And in the *Roland*, the knightly opponents are of different nationalities and religions, of course, though of the same class. Ideology working through textuality can work wonders of transformation, but the intertextual connection must not be lost to sight. The oppressive function of violence, internally directed in a given society against its own productive element, is transformed into the heroic defense of religion in other lands.

The Ideology of Knighthood

"Ideology" implies another discourse, not necessarily "scientific," but at least more revelatory of something "ideology" would prefer veiled or disguised. And in spite of the powerful presence of multiple ideological components in the *Chanson*, it is remarkable how much of that "other" discourse—closer to concerns we might agree to call "realistic," without necessarily labeling them either the Real or reality—pierces through. Again and again, the text allows glimpses into the operations of its social formation that one would have thought excluded by the very presence of ideology.

As the social structure of Frankish society was presented to the eyes of its Other in the person of Blancandrin, so is the ideology of knighthood voiced, not by a knight, but by a churchman, the archbishop, who acts, however, exactly like a knight and a great noble. It is Turpin who defines the rules of the knight's life, as the enemy flees before Roland like stags before dogs:

> "Itel *valor* deit aveir chevaler
> Ki armes portet e en bon cheval set:
> En bataille deit estre forz e fiers,
> U altrement ne valt .IIII. deners,
> Einz deit monie estre en un de cez mustiers,
> Si prierat tuz jurz por noz peccez." (ll. 1877–82)

> "Bearing arms, straddling a good horse,
> here's the value a knight must have:
> In battle he must be strong and fierce,
> or he's not worth two cents,
> but should be a cloistered monk
> and pray each day for our sins."

The image of the knight, bearing arms and seated on a good horse, could be illustrated from any number of medieval capitals, illuminations, or stained-glass windows. It is an iconic image, iconic in both senses of the word: as mimetic and as deriving from a world of visual representation. It is an image stripped to its bare essentials—the knight bears arms on horseback—and the function attributed to him is equally spare and hieratic: he must be strong and fierce in the battle which is his function. That is what a knight is, that is what is expected of a knight, and his French name says as much: the *chevalier* is a man, trained to fight on horseback, who does so with strength and the ferocity of a savage animal, and does so with pride: the term for proud, *fier*, derives from the Latin *ferus*, meaning wild, untamed, as with animal and beasts.

These concrete specifications are framed by the repetition of a crucial word, one which both occurs in ordinary discourse and has its place in the most recondite discussions of philosophy, economics, semantics, and semiotics: it is such a *valor*, in the first line quoted, that the knight must have. The later verse, coming as it does as a summarizing conclusion after the specification of the expectations upon the knight, states that if he does not have these qualities, he has no value at all, he is not worth two (or four) cents. "Valor," as military virtue, connects with "value" as social concept, immediately translated into financial value, that of "two [or four] cents' worth." And the archbishop—who in other circumstances, off the battlefield, might read the clerical sociology of the three orders in the original Latin of Gérard de Cambrai or Adalbéron de Laon[15]—goes on to juxtapose the knight to his social alterity. If the knight is not going to fight with strength and ferocity, he might just as well become a monk, in one of these monasteries, and pray daily for our sins—presumably, as we go about our business of killing. The archbishop's assumption, of course, unstated but effective in his discourse, is that the choice presents itself to a noble: after all, from a more distant perspective, might not the peasantry also be an alternative to being a good knight?

Beyond that essential function, fighting on horseback, being a knight implies following certain social rules, the *lei de chevalers*, as for instance undergoing the ritual of being dubbed (l. 1143). Knighthood's origins are highly debatable, but detailed examination of the early texts indicates the knight is, first and foremost, a professional of mounted warfare. For all practical purposes, however, by the time of the *Roland*, and especially in the field of ideology, the concept of knighthood is fused with that of vassal: the content of the expression just cited, *lei de chevalers*, can equally well be rendered by *lei de bon vassal* (l. 887). Both nomothetic ideologemes require subordination, both imply service, and exactly the same services. But vassalism implies social relations that are not necessarily present, for instance, in the knight as hired hand, i.e., as mercenary soldier. And it is on the axis of vassalism and lordship—the particular historical forms of domination and subjection—that a complex ideology formed.

Knighthood and warriorhood fuse as the essentializing definition of manhood for the individuals concerned: to be another's vassal-and-knight is to be a/his man: "Hom sui Rollant," "I am Roland's man," says a certain Walter, and he defines that quickly: "jo ne li dei faillir" (l. 801), "I must not fail him." Appropriately enough, it is Roland who defines the role of knight-and-vassal experientially, one might almost say existentially:

"Pur sun seignur deit hom susfrir granz malz,
E endurer e forz freiz e granz chalz,
Sin deit hom perdre del sanc e de la char." (ll. 1117–19)

"A knight must suffer great hardships for his lord,
endure sharp cold and great heat,
and a knight must loose of his blood and flesh."

For Roland, the great chieftain of warriors, knows exactly what is needed, and he deploys all three words with which we are concerned within two verses:

Li quens Rollant unkes n'amat cuard,
Ne orguillos, ne malvais *hume* de male part,
Ne *chevaler*, s'il ne fust bon *vassal*. (ll. 2134–36)

Count Roland never loved a coward,
nor a proud and an ill-born *man*,
Nor a *knight*, if not a good *vassal*.

The mounted warriors of the *Roland* are taken universally as their lords' men, knights and vassals, in complete synonymy. The text repeatedly details the services (l. 1858) to be rendered. These are specifically the aid and counsel specified in the Latin formula of *auxilium et consilium* (ll. 168 and 379 for *cunseill*; l. 1731 for *aie*). But these services are not unidirectional. The services of the vassal imply (in the strong, logical sense of the word) a reciprocal duty on the part of the lord, one which will become exceedingly important in the text, that of "nourishment," that of "protection." Roland, dying, thinks of Charles *kil nurrit* (l. 2379). The many passages in which the lord is expected to act as *guarant* for his men, to *guarantir* them, in the function of protection, will be cited later. Suffice it to say now that, in the synallagmatic (i.e., reciprocal) contract which binds vassal and lord, the lord's function as guarantor is one major part of the exchange between himself and the vassal, as specified by their contract.

The exchange of services is the ideal material for the elaboration of ideology. Services lend themselves most readily to representation in terms of honor, glory, and the duty that devolves from birth into a particular lineage. But the discourse of ideology allows its material alterity to pierce through the text. For the fact is that these ideological values of social relations were doubled by their concretization in terms of economic or financial value. The text constructs an economic isotopy and stresses its importance through multiple repetitions. It is sometimes associated with the anthropological category of "gifts," as with the repeated details of wealth and value that accompany the description of Marsile's "gifts" to Charlemagne, in anticipation of their efficacy in helping persuade him to depart and leave Spain. But this tribute to an external, superior military and political power (since Marsile promises to pledge fealty to Charles in Aix) is not merely destined to Charles as receiver or Destinatee: the value thus transmitted, the pagans realize, will perform the concrete political and economic function of paying off Charles's soldiers:

> "Ben en purrat luer ses soldeiers" (l. 34)

> "He'll have good wages for his men who fight for pay" (Goldin, l. 34),

a message which Marsile's emissary, Blancandrin, will repeat directly to Charles:

> "Tan i avrat de besanz esmerez
> Dunt bien purrez vos soldeiers luer." (ll. 132f.)

> "And there will be so many fine gold bezants,
> you'll have good wages for the men in your pay." (Goldin, ll. 132f.)

The *Roland*'s *soldeier* is the same word as *soudoyer*: "mercenary." Is the word to be taken in its specific, technical sense, or does the text here recognize the practice of the chieftain's distribution of booty to his men? It is one of his functions as chieftain, as feudal lord, to spread the wealth among his vassals. This is one of the main economic rationales of warfare in early medieval society: war is an economically profitable enterprise, and the profitable economy of the period is a war economy.[16] When Blancandrin comes upon the French camp to discuss terms with Charles, he finds the emperor and his men happy, for the distribution has apparently already occured:

> Mult grant eschech en unt si chevaler
> D'or e d'argent e de guarnemenz chers. (ll. 99f.)

> His knights have huge spoils,
> gold and silver and expensive armaments.

For the booty is an economic aspect of war which doubles the isotopies of courage and honor without undermining or deconstructing them.[17]

Beyond the immediate booty that can be distributed as mobile wealth to troops on the battlefield, there is the other form of wealth, crucial for the Middle Ages: land. Land is what Roland has conquered for Charles, and it is his eagerness to attack all lands that Ganelon cites against Roland's recommendation of war. For part of the "real" relationship between lord and vassal is, in fact, the relationship of "real estate." More passes between the two roles of feudalism than services, booty, and even money: land—the essential source of wealth in the Middle Ages—is part of the exchange as well. Charles recognizes what he owes his men in exchange:

> "Seignors barons, je vos aim, si vos crei.
> Tantes batailles avez faites pur mei,
> Regnes cunquis e desordenet reis!

Ben le conuis, que gueredun vos en dei,
E de mun cors, de teres e d'aveir" (ll. 3406–10)

"Lord barons, I hold you dear, and put my faith in you.
So many battles you've fought for me,
conquered kingdoms, unseated kings!
I recognize it, I owe you rewards,
even from my own person, of lands and wealth."

Baligant specifies the lord's "debt" even more specifically:

Li amiralz recleimet sa maisnee:
"Ferez baron, sur la gent chrestiene! . . .
Ferez, paien: por el venud n'i estes!
Je vos durrai muillers gentes et beles,
Si vus durai feus e honors e ters." (ll. 3391–99)

The emir calls on the men of his household:
"Strike, barons! the Christian hordes! . . .
Strike, pagans, what are you here for?
I'll give you women, beautiful, noble women,
and I'll give you fiefs and tenures and lands."

Fiefs, "honors" (as already noted, the word denotes both "honor" in the modern
sense and the land whence honor derives), and lands, all synonyms: grants of
wealth, in exchange for services rendered, in the form of land which, along with
the labor to work it, is the major source of noble wealth.

Exchange is assumed as the norm of social relations, and it includes services,
money, and lands, equally and without distinction, in what may appear as an
improper syncretism to a later consciousness that associates money and real estate
with the commercial exchanges of a capitalist mode of production. In fact, exchange in the forms of barter, money, and land is perfectly normal within the
"feudal" system, as far back as one can trace it. It is simply an insufficiently
developed Marxism to not realize that money and land are merely one form of
value, more or less capable of being transmitted from one individual to another.

So thoroughly assumed and integrated are the processes of exchange that, in
multiple forms, its vocabulary is scattered throughout the *Chanson*, sometimes
quite literally, sometimes metaphorically, and often at the most intense moments:

Halt sunt li pui e tenebrus e grant,
Li val parfunt e les ewes curant.
Sunent cil graisle e derere e devant
E tuit *rachatent* encuntre l'olifant. . . . (ll. 1830–33)

High are the hills, shadowy and vast,
deep the defiles, swift the running streams.

Trumpets sound, ahead and behind,
and all *repay* the olifant.

Exchange is intertwined with the religious isotopy, as Roland urges his
knights to "sell themselves dear" in mortal combat:

> "Ci recevrums martyrie,
> E or sai ben n'avons guaires a vivre;
> Mais tut seit fel *cher* ne *se vend* primes!
> Ferez, seignurs, des espees furbies,
> Si calengez e voz mors e voz vies,
> Que dulce France par nus ne seit hunie!" (ll. 1922–27)

> "Here we receive our martyrdom,
> now I know, we've little time to live;
> but he's a felon who does not *sell himself dearly*!
> Strike, lords, with your glistening swords,
> fight for your death and your life,
> let's bring no shame on sweet France!"

Vengeance itself is part of the exchange system: it consists of an exchange of
damages for damages. Exchange is the norm; inexchangeability will be marked,
as uniqueness contrasts to the norm. Thus, Aude will die refusing exchange, and
Roland, dying, will define the uniqueness of Durendal and express the desire that
it not pass on to any Saracen, to the point of trying to destroy the sword (ll.
2312–54).

Examples could be multiplied. Enough has been said to demonstrate that
economic value, in multiple forms, is normalized in the codes of the text, without
any derogation to the courage, the honor, the glory of knightly vassals, the feudal
system as a whole, or indeed the kingship of the emperor. True, Ganelon the
traitor is accused of having sold his stepson's life for wealth: it is as a perversion
of the proper place of wealth that his behavior is criminal, not simply because he
accepts gifts. In that respect, he acts like any king, noble, or vassal: the production, donation, and exchange of wealth comprise the normal pattern of noble life
in the early Middle Ages, as well as in the burgher life after the commercial revolution of the eleventh and twelfth centuries. Indeed, the protection of his lord's
wealth is a recognizable part of the warrior-vassal's code. When Roland proudly
accepts the nomination to the rear guard, he specifies, not that he will act hon-
orably, or courageously, or as a loyal warrior—all of which he does, of course—
but that Charles will lose no thing, not even a horse or a pack-mule—animals
cited as bearers or signs of financial value—that is not first defended. (ll. 755–
59). Heroism and honor are not corrupted by contact with wealth: on the contrary, heroism, wealth, and honor are each other's signifiers.

What the text assumes and does not demonstrate, however, is the relationship between the social organization of society, the political organization of its dominant class, the function of the warrior class, and the economic organization of society.

Function, Ideology, Identity

Semiotically speaking, the "knight" is a signifier bearing the signifieds of /violence/, /subordination/ (to his noble superior), and /dominance/ (to the peasants): his meaning devolves from his sociopolitical function; that is, from his function in "context." This function is specific to the category of the knight within the social formation which created him, nourished him, and depended on his continued presence. That social order was far more complex than our sketch has acknowledged. None of its three essential terms—noble, knight, and peasant—is socially or semantically "simple": all produce complex significations. Our sketch cannot claim to represent the extraordinary variety of social types and arrangements that actually obtained during the eleventh and twelfth centuries: suffice it to say that the social and political creativity of the period can be appreciated only after extensive research in the customs of various regions as they can be reconstructed on the basis of fragmentary, lacunary, and biased documentation. One aspect of that bias is that the documents we study as "literary" concern themselves almost exclusively with the upper regions of the social structure, even though, as already noted, that part of society numbered no more than 2 percent of the population. The overwhelming majority of the population, its peasants, remains radically underrepresented in the documents. In this respect, the Middle Ages is no different from any other period: the textuality of the eleventh and twelfth centuries was the property and remained in the control of its dominant social class, that of the nobility. This control extended even to the key ideological text of the period, the Bible, whose translation was forbidden by the Church and which therefore remained inaccessible to the general population: the sacred text remained under the control of the clerical segment of the nobility.

At this point, a closer look at the nobility is necessary.[18] Satisfying God knows what symbolic yearnings for a social promotion on the part of historians, the medieval nobility has received a disproportionate amount of attention from them. To some extent, this is disciplinarily justifiable by the fact that, after the clergy, it is the nobility that has left behind the largest amount of historical documentation. In some cases, however, the "historical" character of the documentation is dubious. The genealogical literature produced in the Middle Ages was hardly based on disinterested historical research. It was oriented toward the goal of justifying a particular noble's status, wealth, and possession of a castle, which was the centerpiece of power in his social functioning; the nobiliary continuity— a version of the myth of origins that Derrida has addressed—was established through a documentation that was essentially fiction, and it is quite possible to conclude that "contemporaries were entirely conscious" of these manipulations.[19] What is behind the ideological production of meaning? What does it mask? In opposition to the peasantry, the nobility is a single, unitary bloc. Within itself, however, it is not a simple, unitary entity. On the contrary, it is riven by differentiations. The concrete reality, as one perceives it through indirect layers of textuality, appears to have been enormously varied. The major categories identified appear to have a general validity, however.[20] At the top of the secular division of the dominant class was the relatively small group of men who combined noble heritage through the blood line with effective control of fortresses and hence of land. This is the small group of princes, dukes, and counts, tracing their nobility back to the Carolingian or even Roman periods, whose political claims were regional. Recent historical research suggests that, contrary to Marc Bloch's opinion, this group was remarkably stable from antiquity through the Middle Ages.[21] Just below this group came men whose claims to nobility were less certain or especially less ancient, but who had obtained effective control of a territory through the military control of a fortress or a group of fortresses: these were the *châtelains*. While the older nobility in the eleventh century might view the latter as *parvenus*, their effective control of the region around a *château* or a group of fortresses provided them with the same banal rights over the peasantry as were enjoyed by the older nobility. Sharing the same control of the productive forces and the land through military force, and exercising the same mode of expropriating surplus value from their subject populations, the economic interests of these two groups, the princes and the *châtelains*, were identical. Below these two levels came a category that was to become more frequent in the twelfth century romances than in the epic, that of the *vavasseur*. Technically speaking, the *vavasseur* is a rear-vassal, the vassal of a vassal: his powers would be delegated either from a prince or a *châtelain*. In one region, at least, the *vavasseurs* are specified as chieftains of a household containing at least five knights, the minimum garrison of a castle.[22] Recruited either from the secondary lines of noble families or from the knights themselves, they seem then to have played the role of the captain or the *lieu-tenant*: the subaltern organization and leadership of troops.

The troops, of course, were the knights themselves. Men of modest wealth, their economic basis was typically the possession or use of a small, landed patrimony, ranging from a couple of *manses* to fifteen or so. The sons or grandsons of peasant families, their wealth was concentrated in their horse and their military equipment. Outside of combat, their general mode of life differed little from that of the peasants themselves: "The small noble of the twelfth century is a rural cultivator (*un exploitant rural*). . . . [H]is true home is in the fields, and the knightly life-style has a peasant side to it."[23] Thus, their socially subaltern status is coordinate with their mode of life.[24] We are here touching upon a fundamental ambiguity, essential both to the understanding of the knightly category and to the historical positioning of knights within the complex structure that is medieval society. As we have seen, their function, based on their character as *Träger* of actual or potential violence against the peasantry, was to assure the continued extraction of surplus value from the productive element of society, the peasants. In this sense, the *milites* could be considered an integral part of the productive process as a whole: their military and political presence played a necessary role in the optimal functioning of the economic machine of the time as established for the profit of the ruling class. The knights were that part of the necessary infrastructure in which the political dictates of the owning class were translated into the productive process itself.

Functionally, the knights were an element of the class characterized by political dominance, juridical freedom, and economic wealth. But while the knights were functionally an integral element of the dominant class, they were, in origin, and in their mode of life, much closer to the peasantry than to the ruling segments of society they served. Subject therefore to a dual ideological interpellation which could produce different and opposing subject-positions, they were constituted by a social contradiction, and their determining cathexis could theoretically ally them either with the peasantry from which they rose or with the class which they served. Here again the knights of the eleventh and twelfth centuries were typical of police forces in general: recruited from the social classes they control and punish, they serve the opposing and dominant class. The knights were thus a hinge group: essential to the reproduction of the socioeconomic order, yet susceptible to an identification with the peasantry, their allegiance to the ruling class had to be secured.

This allegiance was threatened by the effects of economic developments toward the end of the eleventh century. The success of banal lordship over the preceding century, a success in the profits of which the knights partook only indirectly, nevertheless accentuated the disparities between them and those who were its ultimate beneficiaries: the old nobility and the *châtelains*. The hinge group was also in a hinge location. The upper nobility enjoyed the right of the ban and its profits; the knights initially did not.[25] Their social and political superiors' life-style evolved to markedly higher levels of consumption thanks to the newly monetarized mode of production. The knights, however, while instrumentally essential to the development of banal lordship, remained locked into the older, less profitable economic system of production for use and barter, even as the social pressure to engage in conspicuous consumption of the signs of nobility increased. The very success of banal lordship thus weakened one of its essential links: its economic success increased the economic, social, and ideological distance between the actual ruling class and those whose political identification with the values of the ruling class was essential to its continuation, the knights.

This effect was, in turn, overdetermined by developments within the ideology that had attempted to structure identification and loyalty itself: "feudalism."[26] As noted earlier, my usage restricts this term to denote the political organization of the lay segment of the ruling class. As such, it is part of the broader ideological field, which in turn operates within social and economic frameworks. If the actual function of knighthood was to incorporate, display, and sometimes actualize the permanent potential of violence against the productive element of society, thereby assuring the peasantry's continued productivity beyond its own physical needs, its political and ideological aspect comprised a highly developed system of customary but generalized legality. The feudal contract was always "synallagmatic," a legal term denoting reciprocity. It gave recognizable form to the exchange of services and privileges on both sides: the military aid of *auxilium* and the juridical participation of *consilium* (whose enforcement might, of course, entail *auxilium*), for wealth and the status, rights, and privileges of wealth. In exchange for promised services, the superior lord granted his vassal a fief, most frequently in the form of landed property, whose income, produced by the peasants attached to that fief, supported the knight in his functions. While the ideological representation of the vassalic relationship stressed mutual vassalic and lordly loyalty as virtues and as sentiments, the feudal contract specified both the services due and the basis of profits that were the material aspect of the social relation.

This arrangement was undermined in the course of the eleventh and twelfth centuries, largely by developments which testified to its success in the organization of dominance and its economic effectivity. The eleventh and twelfth centuries witnessed striking developments in the regime of feudalism, including the syntagmatic reversal—and hence transformed signification—of the fief itself. In earlier periods, homage and sworn fidelity resulted in the grant of the fief: the homage, as it were, caused the grant of the fief, and personal loyalty constituted the center of the vassalic relationship. However, "after 1075, homage is no longer the cause but the effect of the grant of land": homage is sworn in order to obtain the particular fief in question, *pro hoc beneficio*. This process has been called the *réalisation* of vassalic homage: the transformation of the vassalic relationship from one of intense, mutual affection and loyalty into one based in the profitable grant of land, for which the services of the vassal paid the rent, as it were.[27] A further decrease in the solidity of the personal relationship of vassalism occurred in the political sphere. Not only is the vassalic submission attenuated by concrete economic interest, it is also weakened by its multiplication into a plurality of homages. This development is also based on the new status of the fief as directly economic. Since the fief produces wealth, and is seen as a producer of wealth, it does not take great economic sophistication to realize that where one fief is profitable, a number of fiefs will be even more profitable. Hence the practice of entering into vassalic relationships with a number of lords, obtaining a number of different fiefs and their profits, and the resultant plurality of homages. The plurality of loyalties and the contradictory duties implied by this plurality made the particular vassal elusive in rendering the vassalic duties owed. It allowed him to play off one vassalic bond against the other; indeed, it determined that he would do so. By the end of the eleventh century, such a plurality of homages appears to have become nearly universal. As a result, the personal commitment of the vassal is no more than a formal prerequisite to the obtention of a fief: his fidelity, his loyalty, become part of a commercial deal.

Thus, three developments loosened the earlier bond between lord and vassal: the transformation in the status of the fief, the quality of the vassalic submission, and the number of simultaneous homages sworn. While the calculus of self-interest might seem to be reinforced by overt economic dependency and the increased number of fiefs, the ideological bond cementing the adherence of the vassal to his lord and his socio-military function in support of the upper nobility was weakened. Such a loosening of the ideological cement between those who profit and dominate and their instruments could pose a danger to the continuation of this arrangement.

Three moves of an ideological nature seem to have operated in corrective reaction to this felt danger; as usual, these developments occurred according to a varying chronology in different regions of France. The first was the incorporation of a trait specific to the knightly culture into the culture of the upper nobility: the *rite de passage* whereby the postulant for entry into the profession of the mounted warrior was actually accepted by that profession, the ceremony of knighting itself.[28] The *adoubement* was adopted as a ritual to characterize the entry into full status by the nobility as a whole. As a result of the adoption of a trait characteristic of the subgroup by the subsumptive group, the latter proceeded to "identify" itself with the former. This is the second ideological move: the adoption of the name of *chevalerie* as the term including both the upper nobility and the lower ranks of knights, the social denomination of the lower class being now used to refer to the conjunction of that lower group with its political superiors, the upper nobility. Finally, however, and perhaps most tellingly, the lower class of knights, functionally nothing more than armed retainers provided with a means of economic support, the group of *milites* upon whom the exploitative structure of society depended for its functioning and continuance, was rewarded by social incorporation into the upper class through ennoblement.[29] The first two moves might be considered an exchange for the last. If the ceremony of knighting and the adoption of the term *"chevalerie"* were the incorporation of signs specific to the lower order by the upper, the process of ennoblement constituted the granting of the characteristic trait of the upper order to the lower. This semiotic promotion within social strata was not purely ideological, however: membership in the nobility carried with it the privilege of being "free," i.e., of being free of the onerous taxes that weighed upon the commonality. Thus, a fairly large-scale exchange of semiotic integers and their material implicates would serve the ideological purpose of fusing the lower, policing function of society with the class interests of the upper, profiting order of society.

Correlative with these integrative moves was the proclamation of class unity in the specifically "symbolic" domain. Such a proclamation, as obvious as it may seem from modern sociological and political perspectives, was not readily made in the eleventh or twelfth century. The very *location* from which it might be made posed a problem, taking the notion of "location" as indicating a specific cultural space. The general ideological function in this society had been preempted for centuries by the Church. Its interest, however, was peace and the protection of its own institutions and their members. The Church's holdings were a main target of the knights' depredations. In addition, those members of society who were helpless looked to the Church for protection. Its interest was therefore contradictory to that of the secular nobility and led to strategies of division and control of the secular nobility's warring potential. An alternative cultural location was required for the semiotic transactions required by the development of a fundamentally secular ideological problematic. It was found, or created, in the cultural form of the *chanson de geste*, the medieval form of the epic. The essential problematic of this textual type, in the early period of its appearance on the documentary stage, is precisely that of the unity/disunity of the nobility.[30]

To recapitulate. The period of the *Chanson de Roland* is also the period in which the social order of the dominant class undergoes certain changes in response to economic developments of major proportions, economic developments which cause certain strains in the relations between the upper nobility—which ultimately profits from the existing economic order—and the knights who serve it in the police function. The social changes result in efforts at the identification of the two segments of the feudal class, the knights and the upper nobility. This identification is an ideologeme, which functions, not so much to justify the feudal class as against the peasantry, largely outclassed and out-militarized, but to secure the profound alliance of the two segments of the feudal class and, in particular, the ideological cathexis of the knights to the existing order. This function is performed by a text like the *Roland* in a number of ways: the separated, detailed glorification of warfare; the sur-valorization of knightly qualities, in particular that of loyalty; the transposition of the object of military power from the defenseless peasant to the Saracen, ambiguously marked as an admired equal and radically marked as a negative alterity; and, finally, the identification of knighthood with the represented performance of a textual class which, in terms of the hierarchical structure of society, represents the upper nobility—the twelve peers—to which are attributed precisely those traits that make a hero out of a good and faithful knight. The twelve peers are a conflation of traits, a condensation (after Freud) of semic elements, melding in the field of ideological representation, characteristics of the upper and lower segments of the newly enlarged nobility, the castle-masters at their several social levels and the knights who perform the police function on behalf of the new nobility. This ideological melding is part and parcel of the larger historical movement which we have traced, in which various means of identifying the knightly class with the dominant order of the upper nobility are employed. The textual ahistoricity—the absence in the sociopolitical body of a historical equivalent to the textual figure of the twelve peers—is, then, understandable as an ideological construct which *does* have a historical significance. That significance is not recuperable on the basis of the traditional Marxist analysis of "literature" as mimetic of a prior social reality, but only on the basis of a semiotic text inserted into the social and historical structures of its time.

4 | The Subsystem of the Professional Warrior: Courage, Contradiction, Irascibility

> . . . there is no abstract human nature, fixed and immutable . . . human nature
> is the totality of historically determined social relations, hence an historical fact
> which can, within certain limits, be ascertained with the methods of philology
> and criticism.
>
> Antonio Gramsci, *Selections from Cultural Writings*

ROLAND IS THE hero, Ganelon is the traitor: nothing simpler than that enunciation, which will obtain universal acceptance. It is not untrue, the text itself would agree, if it could speak these words. It does speak, and it speaks as follows: Ganelon is the traitor, perhaps the necessary instrument of Roland's heroism, and Roland is the hero. That heroism may be clouded. Certain of its moments have been subject to discussion, as to their morality, their military value, their desirability: they are still the actions of a hero. Whatever else may be said regarding the *Chanson de Roland*, there is little reason to question the notion that it contains an apotheosis of heroism.

"Hero" and "traitor," however, are profoundly ideological terms. What makes for a "hero," what makes for a "traitor," is the connection of the figures bearing those labels to codes of signification solidly anchored in social codes, of their own time as well as of the reader's time. In those social codes, such typologies clearly have ideological values: the type of the "hero" and the anti-type of the "traitor" are integral parts of systems of valorial representation that function in the constitution and legitimation of social subjects, in the assertion and counterclaims that constitute ideological conflict (and sometimes negotiation), as well as in the older sense of ideology, the self-interested representations of particular social groups as against other social groups. Heroism and treachery are profoundly ideological notions in any society.

In spite of the cultural alterity which constitutes the epistemological difficulty of twentieth-century medievalism, the qualities that make for hero and traitor in the social and political text of the *Roland* are readily recognizable. These qualities, which can be called semiotically "ethical" semes, are strength, courage, technical ability in the manipulation of horse and weapons (one of the meanings of *proecce*), and loyalty. That these qualities characterize Roland as hero, that they characterize other heroic knights and nobles in the *Chanson*, will occasion little discussion. What is more pressing is to recognize that they also characterize the "traitor," Ganelon.

A repeated image stands out in the visual memory of the text. In the council of the Franks, Ganelon is nominated to bear their message to the enemy king Marsile; in the council of the Saracens, fulfilling his role as ambassadorial messenger, he is threatened with death. On both occasions, Ganelon throws off his great mantels of fur. Has it been said that this gesture is a functional one? The long, heavy fur coats that are the mark of a great noble hang over the sword at the man's side, between the pommel and the warrior hand that reaches for the instrument of his courage. Their presence and their weight impedes that hand in its swift movement toward that sword. In a society athirst for marks of distinction, a society enormously productive of various identificatory modes of signification, the coat of fur is retained as long as possible: it is discarded only when the danger of battle becomes imminent. The gesture disengages the individual's arms, hand, and sword pommel so that he is ready to fight. In throwing off that coat, Ganelon declares himself ready for battle, ready to risk his life, and the representation of the image is a striking one:

> De sun col gietet ses grandes pels de martre
> E est remés en sun blialt de palie.
> Vairs out les oilz e mult fier lu visage;
> Gent out le cors e les costez out larges;
> Tant par fu bels tuit si per l'en esguardent. (ll. 281–85)

> He throws from his neck the great furs of marten
> and stands there vari-colored in his silken tunic,
> eyes noble, his face was fierce;
> noble the body, the great chest of a lord;
> so handsome, all his peers admire him.

Gesture, description, or others' perception; narrative act, qualifying statements, transformed into a communication from narrative subject, who is also the destinator of a communicative function, to those standing nearby as recipients of the message; all corroborate the valorial terms generously scattered in the text: *fier, gent, larges, bels*, all are elements communicated to his peers. The physical, the psychological, the social, are noted in quick succession, and the net result of the description on the modern reader is confirmed by the audience of the communicative act within the text, the medieval knights who are amazed and admire Ganelon. Ganelon delivers his message to Marsile. It is a lying message, as the audience quickly learns, which angers the pagan king. Ganelon quickly turns that anger against Roland, affirming he is only acting as the emperor's messenger, affirming as well his continuing loyalty to Charles by both word and a gesture that implicates his life as the ransom at risk for his words (ll. 457–66). Throwing his coat to the ground again,

de s'espee ne se volt mie guerpir;
En son puign destre par l'orie punt la ting. (ll. 465f.)

his sword he will not throw down!
In his right fist he grasps its golden pommel.

What was only implied in the passage from the Frankish council here is specified: the gesture of throwing off the coat leads hand to sword. Both words and gesture bear the meaning of readiness for battle, hence the qualifying attribution of /courage/ to the actor. Again, when the falseness of Ganelon's message is revealed, Marsile's son asks for the privilege of despatching him, and Ganelon displays his courage and readiness for battle:

Quant l'oït Guenes, l'espee en ad branlie;
Vait s'apuier suz le pin a la tige. (ll. 499f.)

When he hears that, Ganelon brandished his sword;
he runs to the pine, set his back against the trunk.

Like any good warrior, then, Ganelon is courageous.[1] The question of his technical skill in mounted combat is not specified by the text: we never actually see him fighting. Since it is a characteristic of all the knights of the text, pagan as well as Christian, there is no reason to doubt his capacity in this regard. His loyalty, of course, will be the question considered at his trial: we will return to it then. A quick survey of secondary qualifications is in order. As we have just seen, he is qualified as fierce and proud (*fier* carries both meanings), noble and handsome, physically large and imposing (not a negligible quality for a warrior who must put his weight behind his lance and sword). When he returns to his tent after the nomination as emissary to Marsile, his men-at-arms console him, arguing that he ought not to have been nominated for that mission because he has often frequented the royal court, where men called him a noble vassal, and because he comes from a very great family group:

"En la cort al rei mult i avez ested,
Noble vassal vos i solt hom clamer . . .
. . . estrait estes de mult grant parented." (ll. 351–56)

"You've often been to the king's court;
there, men called you a noble vassal . . .
. . . you're drawn from a great family."

Thus, Ganelon comes by his courage and impressive appearance, according to the codes of his society, by familial devolution, and hence by the appropriate social status in a hierarchy whose apex is contiguous to the king at court.[2]

The point is not to glorify the traitor but to indicate that he represents and shares in the values positively valorized by the ideology of his society, values that are also those of the hero Roland.[3] It is a semiotic principle, however, that there is close interdependence between the qualitative statements that describe an actor and the narrative programs attributed to him. Quality leads to action: the semantic equivalent of the philosophical term "quality" is "value," which is also a term in ideological analysis. Thus, the assertion that a character possesses a certain quality translates into another assertion that his ideology constitutes him as an actor—narrative and historical—of a certain program of narrative action.

Ideological Value (I): The Constitution and Destitution of Subjects

Two isotopic parameters are essential for the constitution of the initial narrative syntagm. One is the play between individual actors and the collective actants. The text attributes to Charles the narrative program of *fraindre Saragosse* (*laisse* 1); by implication, Marsile's program must be "garder Saragosse." But Charles and Marsile are not simply individuals. The narrative subjects are rather the collectivities to which each belongs, and in which each is *primus inter pares*. These collectivities are simultaneously the ultimate narrative subjects and their own destinators: the two kings are delegated destinators. The two destinators, $D1$ and anti-$D1$, deal with each other, negotiating contracts. The overall pattern of the first narrative sequence has the following shape. The anti-destinator (Marsile) offers a contract the audience knows to be deceptive, though the positive destinator (Charles) and the subject (Roland) do not. Contractual guarantees are demanded and offered; again, the audience is privy to their deceptive character when they are offered; again, the positive agents are not. As a result of these negotiations, the initial narrative program of the destinator is abandoned: Charles abandons his goal of "*fraindre Saragosse*." Instead, he will return to France, expecting that the anti-destinator Marsile will rejoin him at Aix, to submit personally as his vassal and to hold Spain from him as a fief. At this point, then, the actor Charles changes narrative programs: abandoning the original objective of breaking Saragossa, he chooses instead to return to Aix. Feudally speaking, the appointment of Roland to head the rear guard is a delegation of authority; semiotically speaking, it is the installation of the narrative subject by the destinator. The subject is assigned an instrumental program of a military nature, that of protecting the main army's rear. Whether that program is carried out successfully or not depends on an evaluation of the values at issue in the text.

The overall narrative structure outlined in the preceding paragraph is military in nature. The values implicit in the verbal and narrative evenementiality, however, are political and, in a larger sense, social in nature: the nondistinction of these categories is characteristic of the social text of the period. The presence of these values is produced by subordinate narrative events. Specifically, these semantically crucial events are the selection of agents of the destinator, who is the leader of the military expedition on the positive deixis. Both Ganelon, as messenger to the anti-destinator, and Roland, as chieftain of the rear guard, are technically speaking the "lieutenants" of Charlemagne, the *lieu-tenants*, i.e., those who hold his place and act in it. They perform their functions only by devolution of authority from Charles. Yet each acts, in fact, with some degree of independence from that authority: neither is merely an instrumental automaton. It is in the two aspects of their implementational performance—their selection and their actual performance of the assigned narrative goals—that the essential values at stake in the narrative are produced.

Another isotopic parameter essential to the initial narrative sequence is the pragmatic distinction between the cognitive positions of the audience and the narrative agents. In spite of the appearance of structural simplicity, the *Roland* incorporates a kind of rhetorical triangulation we have come to think of as characteristic of more "advanced" and "sophisticated" narratives. The fundamental cognitive relation of the audience to the narrative diegesis is that of (dramatic) irony: the audience knows more than the narrative agents. That the contract offered by the Saracens is deceptive is unknown to its communicative recipients but entirely patent to the audience, which has witnessed the preceding Saracen council: we have observed the Saracens define the deception of their contract. Indeed, that is the function of the initial position of the Saracen council. Because we have observed that initial narrative segment, we know that the ensuing offer to Charles is false, we therefore understand that Ganelon is wrong in arguing for its acceptance during the Frankish council and that Roland is right in urging its refusal. It has nothing to do with preferring holy war to peace; it is entirely a matter of the cognitive position into which the text triangulates the audience in a form of pragmatic manipulation. The text's specification of Ganelon as traitor is merely the concretization at the level of manifestation of what is already implicit in the epistemological structure of the text: that Ganelon is wrong and that his argument leads to loss and defeat.

Ganelon wins the argument, but it will prove a Pyrhhic victory. The Frankish council of war decides to accept Marsile's offered contract, but to require specific hostages as guarantees. An emissary therefore must be found to represent the Frankish demands to Marsile. Charles poses the question in general terms: "Lord barons, whom shall we send to Saragossa, to King Marsile?" (ll. 244f.). Four members of the council offer themselves for the dangerous mission in turn: Naimes, the elder advisor; Roland, the impetuous warrior who has spoken against accepting the offered contract; his friend Oliver; and the archbishop Turpin. Each is rejected in turn. Charles says of Naimes that he will not send so sagacious (*saives*) a man so far from himself; Roland and Oliver are excluded on the basis that none of the twelve peers is to be nominated for the mission; and

Turpin is simply ordered to sit still on his white carpet, without further explanation. The mission bears a high degree of risk: messengers are easily killed. What the discussion produces is a class of men too highly valued by Charles and the Franks to be hazarded in such a high-risk mission. By implication, therefore, there is another class of individuals, of lesser value, for whom that risk is acceptable to the collectivity, to the destinator. Being of lesser value, they are expendable. Once that class is established, even by implication, any further nomination implies that the individual nominated belongs to that class of lower value.

To nominate Ganelon under these conditions is therefore to designate him as a "second-class citizen," as one who, being of lesser value, can acceptably be sent on such a mission at the risk of his life. Even though the assembled Franks combine their acceptance of the nomination with signs of approbation (ll. 278f.), the implicational structure of the enunciatory act is such that the act of nomination constitutes a derogation, a subtraction of the value that Ganelon had assumed existed: an insult, in short.

What is only implicit at first is made overtly and aggressively explicit in the next segment, as Ganelon is directly insulted. Showing due regard for the niceties of a situation that is simultaneously personal, feudal, and diplomatic, he warns Roland that his nomination must be expected to have repercussions: a further narrative hangs from the act. His warning is phrased with odd delicacy, given the brutal character of the warriors involved: "I will do you great harm, such that it will last all your life long," warns Ganelon, "I will do something playful in Saragossa, to clear this great anger of mine" (ll. 290f., 299ff.). What reads like veiled threats to us constitute, in the legal codes of the period, a proper legal warning to an adversary, a warning of non-peaceful intent that has legal implications.

This observance of juridical niceties, however, has disastrous results. Punctilious observation of legal codes is greeted by derision:

> Quant l'ot Rollant, si cumençat a rire. (l. 302)

> When Roland heard it, he started to laugh.

The text does not specify the semantic content of what must be considered an act of enunciation. That can only be implied from Ganelon's reaction:

> Quant ço veit Guenes qu'ore s'en rit Rollant,
> Dunc ad tel doel pur poi d'ire ne fent;
> A ben petit que il ne pert le sens. (ll. 303–305)

> When Ganelon sees now Roland laugh,
> he has such grief, his anger nearly splits him;
> he's close to losing his mind.

The psychological nicety, in a crude and brutal warrior culture, which traces anger back to pain, sorrow, or grief, has not been noted to my knowledge.[4] The causative structure indicated is

$$\text{pain} \quad \rightarrow \quad \text{anger} \quad \rightarrow \quad \text{split subject}$$

which, by apposition, is equivalent to "losing one's reason."

The radical effects of Roland's derisory laughter may seem excessive to the modern reader, accustomed to register such events as a discrepancy between public opinion and internal conviction of value. For Ganelon, however, the sense of his real value is attainted. In a society founded upon "honor," the value of the individual is not detached from the judgments of his peers. Whether he retains his value or not depends directly, unmediatedly, upon the good opinion they have of him. That Charles allows his nomination where he had impeded others; that the assembled Franks endorse the nomination; that his pride as a warrior punctiliously observant of the legal proprieties of his society is ridiculed publicly; all cumulate to contradict profoundly the status and attendant value devolving from lineage, status at court, and previously received marks of respect. The image of "splitting" (*pour poi . . . ne fent*) is quite precise, whether it implies schizoidal division or not: one side of the individual retains the sense of value, the other registers its withdrawal. No wonder "he nearly split with anger"!

This sense of honor is one that is generally shared by the actors of the text, as is its contrary, shame.[5] It is the same sense of honor that impels Roland to act as he does. It is a collective sense of honor, one that each individual shares with his specific collectivity. It is the value that will be the basis of Roland's determination to avoid the derogatory public songs that might follow a less than honorable death; that will be the basis of his refusal of additional reinforcements for the rear guard offered by Charles; that will impel his refusal to blow the horn when Oliver reports on the great number of Saracens massed to attack the rear guard. It is even the same value Oliver will invoke, in the second discussion regarding the blowing of the horn, and it is the value recognized by Turpin when he finds a compromise for the two companions regarding the blowing of the horn. For all these actors, feudal, noble vassals all, honor is the social and objective valuation of the individual by the society of his peers, the valuation that constitutes him as both a social object of value and as the narrative subject of actions attributed to the noble. Honor is the ultimate value in that set of values that constitutes the noble ideology of the *Chanson de Roland*, taking ideology both as it constitutes the Subject by interpellation and as it provides for the lived relation of the men to their real conditions of existence.[6]

But the value of honor is not merely a punctual value, floating alone and above life even in its preeminence. It is imbricated in complex presuppositions, enablements, and potential narrative programs. For members of this class,

/honor/ is a value that, once acquired, can be lost through cowardice, disloyalty, and the acceptance of injury or insult. Any of these acts can lead to the lessening or withdrawal of the value previously attributed by the collectivity. To accept loss of honor without an effort to recoup that honor is termed *recreantise* (Vulgar Latin: *se recredere*, to give oneself up), the worse state imaginable for an actor in this socio-historical field. Its alternative is to undertake a course of action that will disprove the denegation of value: a concrete, physical demonstration, that the actor is of higher value than his detractor, putting into play and into danger both of their lives. The exemplary model of this course of narrative action is singular combat, the duel, in what the period considers the Judgment of God. It implies what we can call, thinking back on the issue of the *Oresteia* and *Raoul de Cambrai*, the problematic of vengeance.

The private contract established between Ganelon and Marsile calls for the presence of Roland in the rear guard. Thus, when Ganelon moves to have Roland assigned to the rear guard, his act bears the sense of inevitability. It is implicit in the earlier narrative act, the contract with Marsile. Besides being the narrative implicate of that contract—itself determined by the yet earlier derogation of Ganelon's value by Roland himself—Ganelon's nomination of Roland to head the rear guard is a direct pendant to Roland's earlier nomination of Ganelon as ambassador to Marsile, both formal and structural. As acts of enunciation, the two nominations are parallel in their syntax, latinism, and rich rhyme echoing across nearly five hundred lines that separate the two verses—a marked feature in a world of assonance:

Ço dist Rollant: "Ço ert Guenes, mis parastre." (l. 277)

Roland said: "That will be Ganelon, my stepfather."

Guenes respunt: "Rollant, cist miens fillastre." (l. 743)

Ganelon answers: "Roland, this stepson of mine."

In each case, one term on the stepfather/stepson axis nominates the other to a dangerous mission. Each does so publicly, in the presence of the collectivity which includes the emperor and the assembled Franks. Nor is the parallelism formal only. It is structural in that, within the feudal code, the second nomination is a precisely appropriate response to the first. Each of the two speech acts places the nominee in mortal danger. As well as being a parallel linguistic response, each is also an "ethical" response: the second is a vengeance for the first within the codes of its society.

Thus, Ganelon's nomination is a precisely proportioned response to Roland's earlier nomination of Ganelon on a number of semantic axes: formal, structural, legal, and ethical. It is perhaps partly a horrified perception of that complex proportionality that is incorporated in, and produced by, Charles's reaction to Ganelon's nomination of Roland:

> "Vos estes vifs diables.
> El cors vos est entree mortel rage." (ll. 746f.)

> "You are a living devil.
> Deadly rage has entered your self."

Charles's reaction is one of indignation. Roland's reaction is more complex. Indeed, the reaction attributed to Roland by the manuscript Digby 23 in successive *laisses* can seem contradictory. The first reaction contains the following lines:

> "Sire parastre, mult vos dei aveir cher:
> La rereguarde avez sur mei jugiet!
> N'i perdrat Carles, li reis ki France tient,
> Men escientre, palefreid ne destrer,
> Ne mul ne mule que deiet chevalcher
> Ne n'i perdrat ne runcin ne sumer
> Que as espees ne seit einz eslegiet." (ll. 753–59)

Lord stepfather, I have to cherish you!
You have had the rear guard assigned to me.
Charles will not lose, the king who rules France,
I swear it now, one palfrey, one war horse—
while I'm alive and know what's happening—
one he-mule, one she-mule that he might ride,
Charles will not lose one sumpter, not one pack horse
that has not first been bought and paid for with swords."

The first two lines are perhaps to be read as one of the warrior ironies that occasionally dot the stylistic landscape of the *Roland*. Contrasting these two lines with Charles's reaction in the preceding *laisse* suggests the speaker is inverting a possible negative reaction to being nominated into an expression of gratitude. The remainder of the speech is characterized by an impressive formality. At the level of content, it produces the semantic effect of totalization by its comprehensive listing of the beasts of burden to be defended. Even more impressive is the syntax: its hypotaxis is a marked feature by contrast to the parataxis which has been asserted as the dominant stylistic feature of the *Roland*.[7] Rather than a mere paratactic series of assertions, the syntactical kernel of the sentence—Charles will not lose an animal that is not first defended—is itself hypotactic and provides a syntactical frame from which to hang more modifications. Implicit in both the semantic exhaustiveness and the grammatical principle of differentiation between subordinate and superordinate levels of syntax is the principle of control by the enunciator of his enunciation, and hence of his self-control. His speech is according to rule, and that is exactly what the text specifies:

> Li quens Rollant, quant il s'oït juger,
> Dunc ad parled a lei de chevaler. . . . (ll. 751f.)

> Count Rolland, when he heard himself designated,
> then he spoke according to the law of the knight. . . .

The next two *laisses* present quite a different reaction, so different, indeed, that earlier scholars, bound by classical presuppositions regarding the psychological unity of character, proposed to consider these *laisses* an interpolation into the manuscript of the text.[8] Whereas in the *laisse* just cited, Roland speaks according to the professional knightly code, now he reacts with great anger, *ireement*:

> "Ahi! culvert, malvais hom de put aire,
> Quia le guant me caïst en la place,
> Cum fist a tei le bastun devant Carle?"

> "Dreiz emperere," dist Rollant le barun,
> "Dunez mei l'arc que vos tenez el poign.
> Men escientre, nel me reproverunt
> Que il me chedet cum fist a Guenelun
> De sa main destre, quant reçut le bastun." (ll. 763–70)

> "Ha! you nobody, you base-born, evil man,
> did you think the glove would fall from my hands
> as the staff fell from yours before Charles?"

> "Just emperor," said Roland, the baron,
> give me the bow that you hold in your hand.
> No man here, I think, will say in reproach
> I let it drop, as Ganelon let the staff drop
> from his right hand, when he received it."

Whereas the first response was characterized by the implementation of the knight's code, with the controlled dominance over self that is bespoken by content and syntax, the second response is characterized on the contrary by the successive exclamations of the first line, which could equally well be punctuated "Ahi! Culvert! Malvais hom de put aire! . . . " to emphasize their parataxis; and by the aggressive sarcasm of the rhetorical question that is continued in the following *laisse*—"Did you think that the symbol of the mission which the emperor accords his *lieu-tenant* would fall, as you let it fall in from your right hand?"—thus presaging the negative outcome of the mission and the incompetence of the appointed *lieu-tenant*. As a rhetorical question, it signifies: the glove will not fall when Charles hands it to me. In turn, that signifies: my mission is not negatively valorized in the order of things, as was yours. In turn, that signifies: I am of greater value than you. The complexity of the mediating sequence of implications is worth noting: as brutal and "primitive" a war epic as the *Chanson de Roland* contains subtle and complex structures of signification.

As witness this group of three *laisses*, containing Roland's reaction to his nomination. The first signifies self-control, the domination of accepted social codes over the anger of the individual. The second and third signify the opposite, the loss of that control and the expression, both directly and indirectly, of verbal aggression, with the resulting devalorization of the interlocutor. Two directly contradictory semantic reactions to the same impetus are given by the text and attributed to the same textual actor. This is neither error nor evidence of compositional incompetence. It merely indicates that the text is not structured by the same set of codes as determine the reaction of modern readers. Specifically, the text does not assume a unified, cohesive human subject as the entity to be represented. Indeed, one may raise the question whether the representation of individual human subjects is its function, as opposed to the representation of the contradictions of human society. In that case, the topic of the text is precisely the contradictory reactions which a specific actor has to a given impulse. The subject is momentarily a split subject, collected and self-controlled one moment, angrily lashing out the next. This duality of character is not only attributed to Roland, however. It is equally characteristic of Ganelon, who, as we saw, was also caught in the simultaneity of contradictory impulses: to carry out a narrative program producing the semic value of loyalty to his king and emperor, to obtain vengeance for the public slight of *his* nomination and the derogatory derision that accompanied it: that was the form of content of the *angustia* in which he was caught. In each case, the actor undergoes a derogation of value simultaneously individual and social in character. As a result, each of the two actors must attempt to correct the devalorization to which he has been subjected, the devaluation of his social "currency": that is the economics of honor, the rationale of vengeance. Both Roland and Ganelon incorporate the fundamental value of their social codes: their narrative programs, for all their ideological differences, attempt to carry out social imperatives of an "ethical" and political sort. And for all these differences, those narrative programs assert exactly the same social value: honor.

Ideological Value (II): From Subject to Traitor?

At this point in the narrative trajectory, we still remain within the categorical parameters established by the text early on: Roland as hero, Ganelon as traitor. In the next narrative syntagm, matters become more complex. Not that the hero is dethroned; rather, the costs of heroism—its implications—are displayed.

Roland has been installed as commander of the rear guard. The goal of his narrative program is military: to protect the main body of the Frankish army as it crosses the mountain passes back into France. He refuses Charles's offer of supplementary troops—up to half his army—to bolster the rear guard: that refusal is read as a statement of heroic courage, a promise of superb performance of his mission:

> "Jo n'en ferai nient.
> Deus me confonde, se la geste en desment." (ll. 787f.)

Bedier translates as: "*Dieu me confonde, si je démens mon lignage.*" This is not incorrect, of course: *geste* often does mean/lignage/. But it also, and even more frequently in this text, means the written work, prior to the present oral performance, in which the heroic story of Roland and the twelve peers at Roncevaux is contained, and to which the text of the oral performance makes frequent (fictive) appeal. In addition to rejecting the (further) degradation of his lineage, Roland in this interchange also refuses to give the lie to the story of his own heroism: he rejects the possibility of undermining the myth which the present text, the actual *Chanson de Roland*, is retelling by the reinvention characteristic of the oral epic with its simultaneous identity and self-diffraction. While the text does present him as "flawed," it is not a moral flaw such as is attributed to Aristotle's theory of *hamartia* in a bourgeois interpretation of his *Poetics*, but in the ontological sense in which we speak of a split subject today: Roland insists on the identity of his Subjectivity with its legendary constitution. He thereby demonstrates the public nature of subjectivity in medieval codes.

Nevertheless, the concept of lineage is important. Roland invokes it a number of times, though without using the word itself. He defends his *parastre* against Oliver's accusation (ll. 1026f.), and he twice refuses to sound the horn to call back Charles and the rest of the army, on the grounds that his parentage would incur shame and reproach:

> "Ne placet Damndeu
> Que mi parent pur mei seient blasmet. . . . " (ll. 1063f.)

> "May it not please God
> that my kin should be shamed because of me. . . . "

And again in the following *laisse*:

> "Ne placet Deu," ço li respunt Rollant,
> "Que ço seit dit de nul hume vivant,
> Ne pur paien, que ja seie cornant!
> Ja n'en avrunt reproece mi parent." (ll. 1073–76)

> Roland replies: "May it never please God
> that any man alive should come to say
> that pagans—pagans!—once made me sound this horn:
> No kin of mine will ever bear that shame."

This reason is associated with the potential loss of personal reputation: Roland would lose *"mun los"* (l. 1054) and endure *"huntage"* (l. 1091). Need it be stressed that these are variations on the concepts of value and honor?

In the initial discussion of whether or not the horn should be sounded to recall Charles and the army, Oliver takes the opposite position: he argues repeatedly for Roland to call back the reinforcements Charles would bring. In doing so, he appeals to a very different concept than did Roland. It is the concept of number. The isotopy of quantification is the most frequent one in his discourse. No man on earth ever saw more of the pagans (l. 1040); there are 100,000 of them (l. 1041); they have great forces (ll. 1049f., 1050), as opposed to the Franks, of whom there are few; the valleys and the mountains, the hills and the plains are covered with them—the host of the foreigners is great whereas the company of the Franks is very small (ll. 1080–87). Thus, while Roland's appeal is to feelings of familial pride and the isotopy of shame and honor, Oliver—who is no less proud than his companion—appeals to the concept of the number of the enemy. Is this appeal to the principle of numeration to be associated with the great change in mental practices noted by one historian, the turn toward a more intense search for terminological and numerical precision both, the substitution of a concern for efficiency and profitability for the earlier preoccupations with power and prestige? Occurring in the last decades of the eleventh and the first decades of the twelfth centuries, this change in mentality is coordinated with major changes in the economic domain, by which the strongest and most powerful members of society will tighten their domination of the poor and the weak, extending the power of the ban and renewing the basis of the manorial economic system.[9] In any case, the numerical principle is a principle ideally suited for the subordination of men in the service of another power constituted precisely as power: the State, which will in turn eventually be born of the impossibility inscribed by the *Chanson de Roland*.

In the second scene of the horn, the tables are turned. Now, it is Roland who acknowledges the quantitative isotopy. It occurs now, not in a comparison of the troops brought to the field by Saracens and Franks, but in association with the dead lying on the field of battle. Speaking to Oliver, he says:

> "Bel sire, chers cumpainz, pur Deu, que vos en haitet?
> *Tanz bons vassals* veez gesir par tere!
> Pleindre poums France dulce, la bele:
> *De tels barons* cum or remeint deserte! . . . " (ll. 1693–96)

> "Lord, companion, in God's name, what would you do?
> All these good men you see stretched on the ground.
> We can mourn for sweet France, fair land of France!
> A desert now, stripped of such vassals."

As Roland goes on to ask how they can get the news to Charles, it is Oliver's turn to invoke the value of shame:

> "Jo nel set cument quere.
> Mielz voeill murir que hunte nus seit retraite." (ll. 1700f.)

> "I don't see any way.
> I would rather die now than hear us shamed."

It is now Roland who speaks of sounding his horn to recall Charles *as porz passant*, and Oliver who invokes the shame to be visited on him and Roland and their lineages:

> "Vergoigne sereit grant
> E reprover a trestuz vos parenz;
> Iceste hunte dureit a lur vivant! . . . " (ll. 1705–1707)

> "That would be a great disgrace,
> a dishonor and reproach to all your kin;
> the shame of it would last them all their lives! . . . "

The formal inversion is clear—as clear as was the inversion in which Roland's nomination by Ganelon paralleled Ganelon's nomination by Roland. Here the arguments *against* blowing the horn and those *in favor of* the same act are repetitions of the same arguments in the earlier scene of the horn, merely being attributed to the opposing actors: the arguments remain the same, the enunciators are switched.

Again, however, the inversion is not merely a formal one. The inversion itself signifies, and the text specifies the semantic content of the inversion. After Oliver has rejected Roland's proposal to sound the horn repeatedly, and has added that, should they survive the present occasion, never will Roland lie in Aude's embrace—it is the first mention of Oliver's sister and of her being affianced to Roland—after these exchanges that occupy three consecutive *laisses*, Roland finally asks his companion in arms:

> "Por quei me portez ire?" (l. 1721)

> "Why are you angry at me?"

The question names the essential dynamic of the interchange between the two men. It is anger that drives them, just as it was anger that drove the earlier exchange of insults between Roland and Ganelon—just as it was anger that kept Achilles in his tent before Troy. Injury produces anger, and anger produces counteraction equally injurious.

Ganelon transgresses the limits of acceptability pragmatically; Oliver transgresses cognitive norms in his commentary on Roland's actions. Oliver is characterized by the text as opposed to Roland, as *sage* is opposed to *preux*. While the exact semantic content of *sage* is difficult to identify—wise? prudent? sagacious?—it clearly designates a value that is primarily cognitive, while Roland's is primarily pragmatic. But Oliver recognizes Roland's great value, his value in terms of the system of values within which both of then operate. In a verse quoted earlier, he recognizes Roland's value even as he acknowledges its cost: "Vostre proecce, Rollant, mar la veïmes" (l. 1731).

The word for Roland's value—*proecce*—is etymologically a word that means value: Low Latin *prodis*, meaning "profit." Its concrete meaning, at the time of the *Roland*, is both broad and precise:/vassalic value/, i.e., that complex of semes that together constitute the ideological value system of the mounted warriors as vassals. *Preux* is the frequent adjectival form, *proecce* the more abstract noun. That quality is the one which leads to the performance of the "*exploits courageux*" which are one of the meanings attributed to the term by the dictionary (Greimas). Roland, the highest imaginable embodiment of his class, bears that value into combat as his signified. As Oliver's double vision recognizes, it is this value that is the cause of the debacle of Roncevaux. In other words, Oliver's perception is that it is precisely the highest value of the warrior class that determines the extraordinary devastation he and Roland behold on the field of battle. That paradox, that irony, is what we call tragedy:

> "Cumpainz, vos le feïstes,
> Kar vasselage par sens nen est folie;
> Mielz valt mesure que ne fait estultie.
> Franceis sunt mors par vostre legerie.
> Jamais Karlon de nus n'avra servise.
> Sem creisez, venuz i fust mi sire;
> Ceste bataille ousum [faite u prise];
> U prist u mort i fust li reis Marsilie.
> *Vostre proecce, Rollant, mar la veïmes!*
> Karles li Magnes de nos n'avrat aie.
> N'ert mais tel home des qu'a Deu juise.
> Vos i murrez e France en ert hunie.
> Oi nus defalt la leial cumpaignie:
> Einz le vespre mult ert gref la departie." (ll. 1723–36)

> "Friend, it is your doing.
> Reasonable service is not madness,
> measure is worth more than foolishness.
> Franks are dead by your light-headedness.
> Never again will Charles have our service.
> Had you believed me, our lord would have come,
> we would have won this battle, taken the enemy;
> Marsile would be dead or taken.

Your valor, Roland, it's our bad luck to know it.
Charles the Great will have no help from us.
There'll be no man like him til the judgment of God.
You will die, France will be shamed.
Now our loyal company takes its end:
Before nightfall, parting will be grief.

The double opposition of reason and madness, of measure and foolishness, implies two narratives, one hypothetical, one the actual narrative of the text. In both cases, the narrative trajectory is interdependent with qualities of the actors. The first indicates the possibility of carrying out one's vassalic responsibility according to sensible, reasonable principles, which are equated to the faculty of counting numbers, of measuring quantities and proportions: this is opposed to the ardor and madness of battle, to the harsh, violent temerity of haughty, overweening pride (I am combining the two etymological senses of *estolt*: Germanic *stolz* and Latin *stultum*). Concretely, a narrative program according to the values of *par sens, mesure*, and *sage(sse)* would have implied blowing the horn earlier, causing Charles to return to the scene, the Franks staying alive, winning a victory over Marsile, who is taken prisoner or killed, so that the Franks can remain in Charles's service, Roland stay alive, and France remain proud. The alternative set of qualifications—*folie, estultie, legerie*—have determined the actual program in which, the horn not having been sounded, Charles remained absent, the Franks have all died, their side has endured a striking defeat, Marsile remains alive and free, Charles will never again have the service of his men, including Roland, who is to die shortly, and France is to be shamed: "Vos i murrez e France en ert hunie" (l. 1734).

What is remarkable is that, even after this detour through an external valorization of Roland's actions, a valorization which clearly perceives the negative aspects of that behavior, Oliver still returns, at the end, to the value system which he shares, in fact, with Roland: that system of honor and shame which valorizes loss as shameful. Shame and the pride of honor are the ultimate values for Oliver as well as for Roland. It is only in the narrative instrumentalities by which that value is to be reached, and its opposite avoided, that Oliver differentiates himself from Roland. His perception of Roland's tragedy does not transport him outside the value system that brings about that tragedy: his cognitive extra-vagation leaves him within the system that is going down. In semiotic terms, Oliver's perception may constitute the contradiction of Roland's value, its negation: it does not place him in the position of contrariety, the assertion of another value. That will be left for the later section of the text.

The persistence of the value of/honor/is reiterated by the resolution of the pragmatic problem: to blow the horn or not? The resolution is brought about by a figure who might be thought to hold the promise of a possible transcendence of the endless cycle of destruction determined by/honor/and the class that honors it: the Archbishop Turpin, who accompanies the Franks in battle. The potential for transcendence is implicit in the eminence of his religious status. But that potential is aborted: Turpin, who transgresses the rules of his religion by bearing arms and mounting a horse, turns out, in fact, to be merely another knight in religious guise. The historical fact is that most churchmen were members of the aristocracy, and many continued to behave as nobles even when wearing the cloth.[10] He argues for blowing the horn now, on the basis that it will be of no practical use to them (they will be dead by the time the main body of the army arrives), and two positive reasons: it will assure them of proper burial and of vengeance:

> "Ja li corners ne nos avreit mesters,
> Mes nepurquant si est il asez melz:
> *Venget li reis, si nus purrat venger*;
> Ja cil d'Espaigne ne s'en deivent turner liez.
> Nostre Franceis i descendrunt a pied,
> Truverunt nos e morz e detrenchez,
> *Leverunt nos en bieres sur sumers,*
> *Si nus plurrunt de doel e de pitet,*
> *Enfuerunt nos en aitres de musters*;
> N'en mangerunt ne lu ne porc ne chen." (ll. 1742–51)

> "Sounding the horn could not help us now, true,
> but still in is far better that you do it:
> *let the king come, he can avenge us then—*
> these men of Spain must not go home exulting!
> Our French will come, they'll get down on their feet,
> they'll find us here, dead, cut to pieces.
> *They'll lift us into coffins on the backs of mules,*
> *and weep for us, in rage and pain and grief,*
> *they'll bury us in the courts of churches;*
> and we will not be eaten by wolves or pigs or dogs."

The only "religious" note in this speech is touched when the archbishop foresees the French dead buried in churchyards; even that note is motivated by avoiding the eating of the corpses—their carnal remains—by wild animals. Not only does the archbishop infringe the rules of the Church against bearing arms, mounting horses, and fighting: his Christianity is a singularly un-Christian one. His thought is entirely that of a member of the same class as the warriors before him. His thought is that their common death requires the exchange payment of vengeance. No more than Roland or Oliver does the archbishop deny the value system of his class: the opposition of honor and shame. The only thing that is in question is the issue of instrumentalities: how shall we best serve that value in the present circumstances?

Structure of Structures

We have traced two dual structures operating in the first half of the narrative, that part of the text which can unhesitatingly bear the title "The Song of Roland": that of nominations, and that of the sounding of the horn. Each is textualized as a binary subsystem. The nominations are those of Ganelon, and then Roland. The sounding of the horn presents first Oliver asserting the desirability of the act, with Roland opposing it, and then reverses the roles between the two companions. In each case, the second syntagm in the sequence is both the reversal of the first in its distribution of narrative and semantic traits and its result: the nomination of Roland by Ganelon results from the nomination of Ganelon by Roland, and the reason Roland has to consider sounding the horn the second time around is that he refused Oliver's injunction to do so the first time. Finally, the recurrences are recursive: the same set of logical and semantic operations is valid on the higher analytic level as pertains to the lower levels of analysis. The "sounding the horn" sequence is the result of the "nominations sequence": it is only because of the narrative determinations set in motion, first by Roland's nomination of Ganelon, then by Ganelon's nomination of Roland to head the rear guard, that the overwhelming discrepancy between the pagans and the Franks occurs and poses the question of whether or not to summon Charles. But the two major sequences are also opposed semantically, as the contradictions of the feudal system are seen to function within that subset of the feudal vassalic class that is entirely admirable, the heroes who die on the field of battle at Roncevaux, rather than merely between the hero and the traitor in the preceding sequence. These complex, superposed relations may be represented graphically:

(A)   (B)

nominations   *sounding the horn*

(a)   (b)   (a)   (b)

vs.   *vs.*   *vs.*

(Roland→Ganelon) → (Ganelon→Roland) → Oliver (+) → Roland (−)

Roland (+) → Oliver (−)

Parallelism has long been recognized as an essential technique of narrative composition in the *Chanson de Roland*.[11] What this analysis reveals, however, is a semantic persistence under a complex, hierarchized, and recursive system of oppositions. The first half of the narrative saturates its representation of the entire class of professional mounted warriors with patterned recurrences of the same set of semantic oppositions and redundancies, demonstrating the recurrent doubling of its pattern throughout the subcategories of the class. This, while threading these differentiated recurrences along a narrative linearity which relates them as cause to effect. The whole sequence is a work of binary composition, held together with extraordinary coherence both as narrative and as textualization of the values of a particular social class.

All the major participants are members of that particular social group in the textual diegesis. As individuals, they deploy specific roles, forming a distributional grid: hero, hero's friend, positively valorized warrior (Turpin), negatively valorized warrior (Ganelon). All, however, are knights: they share, and narratively demonstrate, the same system of knightly values: strength, courage, ability in the use of horse and weapons, loyalty, and the ethical value of honor. Roland and Ganelon share the same fundamental characterological trait: an irascible touchiness when the point of honor is disturbed. That irascibility is associated with the performance of mounted warfare, in which the warrior's life is always at risk. But these individuals are not merely repetitions of the same: they represent and set into play a social system. Their relatively superficial individuation (taking that term as the recognition of differentiating textual traces) is just adequate to cast them into the separate roles required by the operation of a true system. It is as a system of relatively differentiated actors that Roland, Oliver, Turpin, Ganelon, and the cohort of the other knights of the text perform their roles, their text: it is a knightly system of repetition and difference that they perform, in this first part of the *Chanson de Roland*. And it is their specific systematicity, that degree of identity and diffraction of the same set of values, that brings about the disaster at Roncevaux. It is knighthood, that social complex of strengths and weaknesses, that spells out the annihilation of the flower of knighthood in the Frankish rear guard. The structure of the structures of the narrative recursively repeats Oliver's analysis of Roland's tragic pattern: it is the strengths in question that lead to disaster.

5 | The Destinator's Multiple Roles: Syncretism or Contradiction?

> ... le discours n'est pas simplement ce qui traduit les luttes ou les systèmes de
> domination, mais ce pour quoi, ce par quoi on lutte, le pouvoir dont on
> cherche à s'emparer.
>
> Foucault, *L'ordre du discours*

WHEN BLANCANDRIN ARRIVES at the Frankish encampment, his gaze includes
not only the subject but the destinator as well. King and emperor, uncle and feudal overlord, Charles is so readily identifiable even by a stranger entering the
Frankish camp, he needs no identification. The destinator assigns narrative programs and goals: he determines value, both in its introduction into the narrative
text and in its final judgment. For few texts is the identification of the function
of the destinator so clear and self-evident as in the case of the *Chanson de Roland*. Nevertheless, a problem does inhere in the semiotic interpretation of the
figure of Charlemagne, a concrete problem with sizable theoretical implications.
Any one of the properly semiotic roles assigned to Charles—uncle, feudal overlord, king, emperor—could provide the social, political, and historical basis for
the performance of the *actantial* role of destinator. How then to evaluate the fact
of the multiplicity of the roles that we have already identified? Should this multiplicity merely be considered an example of overdetermination, in which each
role reinforces the ultimate actantial performance of the destinator? Or is it the
differences from one role to another that are to be examined, and their potential
contradictions stressed? I will discuss the political roles of Charles in ascending
order: feudal overlord, king, and emperor.

The Culpable Guarantor

Oliver climbs to the summit of a hill. He sees the assembled Saracens, ready
to spring the trap set in collaboration with Ganelon upon the Frankish rear
guard. Highly concerned (*mult esguaret*, l. 1036), he comes down the hill as
rapidly as possible, to inform the Franks of what he has seen: the great number
of pagan troops, their readiness for combat, the awesome brilliance of their armament: "You will have battle such as has not been seen heretofore," he tells his
comrades, and he implores God's help. His speech concludes with an impera-

tive—an order, a recommendation, an entreaty?—one would have thought su-
perfluous in such a heroic poem:

> "El camp estez, que ne seium vencuz!" (l. 1046)

> "Remain in the field, that we not be conquered!"

Does this syntagm imply a possibility that the Frankish troops would abandon
the field before the overwhelming numerical superiority of the enemy?

Roland, in command of the detachment, decides not to call for help, in spite
of Oliver's urging. He encourages his men, as is appropriate to the role of military commander, promising the Saracens "martyrdom" and his men rich booty.
Oliver disculpates both Charles and their comrades, those absent and those present, and then turns to the latter:

> "Kar chevalchez a quanque vos puez!
> Seignors baruns, el camp vos retenez!" (ll. 1175f.)

> "Now ride as hardy as you can!
> Lord barons, take your stand in the field!"

In both instances, the word *camp* means *champ*: "battlefield." Oliver is telling
the *baruns* to remain in the battlefield. One would have thought this recommendation, or order, or entreaty, unnecessary in a narrative poem of epic combat. It
presupposes the possibility that those addressed might react in the manner opposed to the sense of the utterance: they might leave the field of battle, when
battle is offered. How much weight should be attached to the possibility, now
repeated in the text, of an evasion of combat so out of line with what we have
been taught to expect of the Frankish heroes of Roland's rear guard?

The presupposition is not lost on the text. Each time it appears, it is countered by assertions of the Franks' eagerness for battle and loyalty to their leader.
The first occurrence of Oliver's imperative noted above is immediately answered
by his comrades as follows:

> Dient Franceis: "Dehet ait ki s'en fuit!
> Ja pur murir ne vus en faldrat uns." (ll. 1047f.)

> The Franks say: "God hates the man who flees!
> At the cost of death, not one of us will fail you!"

This answer verbalizes the presuppositions: it is flight, retreat, that Oliver fears.
He sees the possibility of what is often referred to as the most shameful abandon
of vassalic loyalty: *recreantise*. A comparable response occurs in the second instance of Oliver's recommendation quoted above. He amplifies his themes: think
of striking blows, he urges, both taking and giving them, and let us not forget
Charles's *enseigne*:

A iceste mot sunt Franceis escriet.
Ki dunc oist Munjoie demander,
De vasselage li poust remembrer. (ll. 1180–82)

At this word, the Franks cry out.
Whoever heard that shout, "Mount Joy,"
could well remember vasselage.

The Franks shout out Charles's "sign": the text specifies the value of vassalage in their reaction.

Oliver, after Roland's decision not to call for help, concludes that serving in this rear guard is an occasion for grief: whoever participates in this battle will not live to fight another. Roland reacts:

"Ne dites tel ultrage!
Mal seit del coer ki et* piz se cuardet! [*misprint for *el*?]
Nus remeindrum en estal en la place. . . . " (ll. 1106–1108)

"Don't speak such outrage!
Shame on the heart gone coward in the chest!
We'll remain standing in this place. . . . "

A third time, then, the presupposition of an assertion elicits a direct response by the text, a denial of that implication, an assertion that the Franks will stand and fight.

Would flight from the field of battle imply cowardice or disloyalty on the part of those fleeing? The "obvious" may be misplaced trust in our own values and in the inveterate twentieth-century habit of allegorizing medieval texts. That habit reveals our own idealistic tradition, our own obsession with "higher levels of meanings" than those guaranteeing the coherence of text. Medieval society, in whose codes the early epics functioned as revelation of historical contradiction and as ideological assertion, was perhaps closer to the fundamentals of social life, to the basic relations that enable any society at all to survive in spite of its fundamental social conflicts.[1] The association of the notion of contract in our codes with the domain of commerce, along with the idealization and romanticization of personal relationships, tends to disguise the fundamental role played by interpersonal contracts, often presupposed and unverbalized, in defining social relations. Our identification of such contracts in medieval texts is rendered even more difficult by the cognitive reversal that obtained in the original historical context of these texts, where the importance of such contracts was so self-evident, and their content so well known, that they received little stress in the texts themselves. What is both quantitatively and rhetorically minor in the text— because so obvious—may nevertheless constitute a major structural component.

The operative contract in question is that which defines the respective *roles* of the lord and the vassal within the feudal relationship.[2] The assumption by any individual of the role of feudal lord is marked by a specific ritual, essential to the establishment of the feudal contract and, indeed, performative of the contract. The ritual begins with the act of homage: the concrete gesture comes first, the vassal placing his two hands within those of the lord: total submission of the one actor, acceptance of responsibility by the other. Only after this dual gesture, figuring precisely the synallagmatic, i.e., reciprocal, character of the contract, is the oath of fidelity sworn on the Bible or on relics: the verbalization, the specification of the *signifié*, can only follow the enactment of the corporeal signifier.[3]

In accounts of the content of the contract, stress is usually placed on the duties of the vassal, *auxilium et consilium*: concrete service, both military and other, as well as attendance at the lord's court for councils and especially for the judgment of legal cases. The lord's obligations are parallel to the vassal's and provide the very reason for which the vassal is willing to accept submission to the lord. Fidelity works both ways: if the vassal is to provide military service, the lord has the responsibility of providing the vassal with the means of doing so. The provision of armor and a mount are normal parts of the lord's responsibility. The grant of the fief is originally rationalized as providing the knight with the wherewithal to support himself and obtain the necessary accoutrements of warrior service. The general welfare of the knight is also his superior's obligation. This includes providing education for the vassal's son and finding appropriate spouses for vassalic offspring. Negatively, the lord is to refrain from damaging the vassal in person, property, or honor: to a large extent, the feudal contract is little more than a peace treaty, both signatories agreeing not to do each other harm. More positively, the lord owes the vassal positive protection, both judicial and military.[4]

It is this central element of the *role* of the feudal lord that is at play in the passages we have been discussing. The presupposition that the Frankish troops might decamp before the numerically overwhelmingly superior force led by Marsile is explained by the fact that their suzerain lord, Charles, is not in a position to fulfill that clause of the contract binding him to the men of the rear guard, which calls for the protection of the vassals by their lord. As a result, it is implied, these vassals might reconsider the contract between themselves and their feudal lord and think it null and void. They might consider themselves relieved of their obligations under that contract, in particular the obligation to fight for the lord in question.[5]

This connection is specified by the Archbishop Turpin, in response to the boasts of two pagan kings. Oliver has urged on his comrades. The Franks respond by bravely joining the Saracens in battle and calling out Charles's battle cry *Montjoie*! The Saracens, however, receive the attack without fear. Combining the speeches of Aelroth (Roland's opposite number, the nephew of Marsile) and Corsablix, the importance of the geographical disjunction between Charles and the rear guard, and the incidence of that disjunction on the contractual relationship between them, becomes plain. Charles is called *fols*, France will lose her pride and Charles the right arm of his body, because

"Traït vos a ki a guarder vos out." (l. 1192)

"He betrayed you, who was to warrant you."

He whose role it was to protect you has betrayed you by his absence. The semantic reciprocal of this perception is that the Franks can be viewed with disdain. They are few:

"Cels ki ci sunt devum aveir mult vil.
Ja pur Charles n'i ert un sul guarit:
Or est le jur qu'els estuverat murir." (ll. 1240–42)

"Those who are here, they're worth contempt.
Not even one is warranted by Charles:
This is the day they'll have to die."

The absence of the lord means the vassal's abandonment. The result is the social and moral degradation of the vassals, since they are deemed unworthy of protection. Honor and its source were comprised in the same notion: the fief granted by the lord and the resultant glory were fused.[6] Analogically and hyponymically, the lord's protection was part of the honor and glory associated with the fief that was its social and economic support.

As in the previous cases, the accusation is recognized as grievous by the text, and it is answered. Roland answers first, denying each clause of the accusation point by point:

"Ultre, culvert! Carles n'est mie fol,
Ne traisun unkes amer ne volt.
Il fist que proz qu'il nus laisad as porz,
Oi n'en perdrat France dulce sun los." (ll. 1207–10).

"Go on, you serf![7] Charles is not mad,
he never was a man who treason loved.
He acted right to leave us guard the passes.
France will lose no praise today."

The second inculpation of Charles, that of Corsablix, is answered by Turpin:

"Culvert paien, vos i avez mentit!
Carles, mi sire, nus est guarant tuz dis;
Nostre Franceis n'unt talent de fuir." (ll. 1253–55)

Pagan serfs, you're lying through your teeth!
Charles my lord is still our warrantor;
our Franks have no desire to flee."

The last line seems at first supererogatory. Corsablix has said nothing about the possible flight of the Franks. The line is not the denial of a specific accusation. On the contrary, it seems almost an element of proof for the preceding lines: Charles remains our guarantor, argues Turpin, and the fact that the Franks are not fleeing shows it. Again, the presupposition of Turpin's speech is that, were they to think themselves abandoned by their guarantor, the Frankish troops could justifiably be expected to flee the battlefield. It is only the assertion of the contrary, that Charles has *not* abandoned his role as guarantor and protector, that prevents a debacle at this point in the narrative.

Oliver would seem to have ample reason to feel *mult esguaret* as he scouts the opposing forces from his hilltop. He not only perceives the enormous disparity between the Frankish forces and those of the Saracens: this disparity leads semantically to an implied abrogation of the feudal contract as a result of the feudal overlord's inability to provide "protection" for his vassals, to carry out his responsibility as their *garant*. For the sociopolitical contract that binds Charles and his men, which functions as the juridical destinator of Charles's army, is a feudal contract, not a national one between the State and its citizens. Because it is as Charles's vassals that the Franks are at Roncevaux, they have no reason for remaining there once the contractual bond between them is broken. Once the lord is incapable of fulfilling his side of the contract, why should the vassal risk his life to uphold his obligations? Indeed, the normal feudal code provided for the *diffidatio*, in which the failure of the lord to fulfill his side of the contract binding him to the vassal allowed for the abrogation of that contract by the affected vassal. Under the circumstances in which the vassals of the rear guard find themselves, flight, retreat, a total debacle, is a clear narrative possibility.

In fact, the debacle will occur, though somewhat later. Along with Roland, 20,000 men die on the field of battle, along with their ruling leadership elite. Such a debacle is not an accident of nature, in twelfth-century textuality any more than in the twentieth. The losses of men, of their captains, the non-observance of a political and military contract—these are not narrative events that can occur with impunity: they leave a residue to be dealt with. That residue has personal and emotional aspects, as the brief encounter with Aude will indicate; it has political and legal aspects as well. The *Chanson de Roland* deals with that residue, repeatedly and in complex ways. Unfortunately, modern scholars have not heeded these textual moves. Extensive discussions have focused on whether Roland is to be considered a hero in truth, on whether he is not guilty of a *démesure* that condemns his men to death even as it guarantees him the glorious fame that is the ultimate value in the warrior ethic. What has not been generally recognized is that, rather than concerning itself with any potential culpability of Roland's—the evidence cited above suggests that that is fairly patent within the frame of reference of the text—the text is concerned with parrying potential accusations asserting Charles's culpability.[8]

Certain textual maneuvers in this direction are narrative. Thus, Roland insists on retaining the normal number of men in the rear guard—20,000—in spite of the strong possibility of surprise attack, when Charles, in implicit recognition of this possibility, offers major reinforcement: half the army. Roland's refusal demonstrates his heroism or his foolhardiness: it also shifts the burden of responsibility to him, because Charles will have offered him the means by which the debacle might have been avoided. Another such maneuver is Roland's refusal to blow the horn at Oliver's suggestion when it still might serve the practical purpose of recalling the main body of the army in time to aid the rear guard: again, the issue of culpability is shifted from the feudal lord to the vassal.

These narrative moves deal with the issue of Charles's potential culpability by implication. The text, however, also formulates the issue directly and with a frequency all the more remarkable for not having been noted by the general run of modern scholarship. When Oliver refuses to speak to his companion after Roland's refusal to sound the horn, he disculpates both Charles and the Franks of the rear guard:

> "[Charles] n'en set mot, n'i a culpes li bers.
> Cil ki la sunt ne funt mie a blasmer." (ll. 1173f.)

> "[Charles] knows nothing about it, the great man has no
>   guilt for it.
> Those who are here are not to be blamed."

This is not in response to any textual accusation of Charles. At the most, it is part of an attempt to inculpate Roland, who has just addressed his troops in the manner typical of an epic leader (ll. 1165–68).

The fact that the Saracens are portrayed as feudal lords and vassals makes them reliable judges of feudal obligations. When, in passages already cited, the Saracens inculpate Charles for not protecting his men, for abandoning them to their enemies, in abrogation of his feudal role (ll. 1192ff., 1240ff.), such remarks are not to be taken lightly. Indeed, the text does not take them lightly. On the contrary, these accusations are specifically and righteously denied each time they are made. The repetitions of the point in our text repeat those of the Roland-text, ignored as they have been by modern scholarship. Roland is the first to engage in denials (in a passage already quoted) that, with the hindsight borne of rereading, we know are wrong:

> "Ultre, culvert! Carles n'est mie fol,
> Ne traisun unkes amer ne volt.
> Ii fist que proz qu'il nus laisad as porz.
> *Oi n'en pedrat France dulce sun los.*" (ll. 1207–10)

> "Go on, you serf! Charles is not mad,
> he never was a man who treason loved.

> He acted right to leave us guard the passes.
> *Sweet France will lose no value here today."*

It does not help that only two lines later occurs the famous line:

> "Nos avum dreit, mais cist glutun unt tort." (l. 1212)

> "We have the right, these swine are in the wrong."

For in spite of this judgment, with which both the text and the Christian God presumably concur, the rightful Franks will be decimated. The same must be said of Turpin's words in the following *laisse*, when he denies pagan accusations of Charles. He claims that the Saracens lie, that

> "Carles, mi sire, nus est garant tuz dis." (l. 1254)

> "Charles, my lord, is our warrant still and always."

In fact, in spite of all these disculpabilizations, the king and emperor will not perform as "warrantor" of his men at Roncevaux: they will die without the protection due them from their feudal lord.

At this point it is appropriate to recall that proper nouns such as "Roland" and "Charlemagne" do not refer to creatures of flesh and blood but to semantic networks of value spread throughout a particular text which precipitate into the kind of figure we call an actor or a character. Narrative invariably implies an anthropomorphic level of representation, but that fact should not license the categorical mistake of textual figures for people. This is not an argument for the moral evisceration of "literature": it is, however, an argument for separating the issues of value and interpretation from that of the representational function of language, without discarding either. "Roland" and "Charlemagne" do not designate people: they are proper nouns that index a particular kind of textual figure, the precipitate that combines a variety of semic investments in the simulacrum— always marked by its textuality—of an actor or character.

I have already referred to the one form that the previous discussions of culpability have taken: that of Roland's guilty heroism. The text makes the same assumption regarding Roland as it does regarding Charles. To the men of the rear guard, Roland is their guarantor: they expect from him the protection to which the vassal is entitled from his lord, and which Roland might expect from Charles (l. 1161). The issue of Roland's innocence or culpability is inversely related to that of Charles's innocence or culpability. The innocence of one implies the culpability of the other. The culpability assigned to one actor absolves the other. Precisely because of the repeated disculpabilizations of Charles, the issue remains alive. Indeed, it is possible to interpret the remainder of the poem as being elaborated precisely in order to deal with the issue of residual culpability.

The question of culpability is to be considered in the context of the combats that compose not only the second major sequence of the narrative but the first sequence as well. In particular, the comportment of Charles during the successive councils of the Franks requires examination. In the first council, when Blancandrin is heard to deliver Marsile's first offer, Charles's reaction is cautious and circumspect:

> De sa parole ne fut mie hastifs. (l. 140)
>
> With his word he was not hasty.

Having mulled over the Saracen offer, he asks on what basis he might trust its words (ll. 143–45). Again, when Charles transmits that offer to his council, he states the terms proposed by Marsile but is careful to add:

> "Mais jo ne sai quels en est sis curages." (l. 191)
>
> "But I don't know what his [real] feelings might be."

As the court's presiding officer, Charles takes his time, asks for guarantees of verbal offers, and points out that an offer of future performance is not automatically to be trusted. Similarly, when the question of the identity of the Franks' ambassador to Marsile is raised, Charles takes an active and thoughtful role in the proceedings, refusing the nominations of the twelve peers: it is exactly that performance, of course, which is the basis of Ganelon's anger when he is nominated by Roland, as it implies his expendability by comparison to more valuable nobles. Because the nomination is made by Roland, it is at Roland that Ganelon's anger can be vented. But that nomination would not have had the meaning for Ganelon it does have, had it not been preceded by Charles's exclusion of the peers. It is Charles's active narrative role in the deliberations that produces the insulting meaning of Roland's nomination of his stepfather.

Charles's performance in the second council is different. The political sagacity, the active thoughtfulness displayed in the first council scene, is absent from the second, when the leader of the rear guard is to be chosen. When Ganelon nominates Roland, that nomination is accepted. Charles's speech registers a negative perception of Ganelon's action—we will look at it shortly—but there is no effort to impose the kind of reflection and consideration that was typical of the earlier decisions. Once again, textual structures assist the avoidance of the issue. I have already noted the parallelism between Ganelon's nomination of Roland and Roland's earlier nomination of Ganelon, a parallelism which, on the level of both language and narrativity, produces a sense of poetic justification that adds inevitability to the narrative proceedings. These structures thus tend to deflect the issue of Charles's role as enunciative referee ("the chairman of the meeting" function), which he played so effectively earlier, as well as the political referee between his vassals.

In spite of this deflection, the text does not allow the issue to drop out of sight. During the night preceding the second council at which Roland is named to the rear guard, Charles had already experienced annunciatory dreams, dreams whose allegorical integument is so thin as to hardly disguise the proleptic reference to future events. In the first dream, Ganelon seizes Charles's lance and shakes it so fiercely that its slivers fly to heaven. In the second dream, located at Aix, two wild animals fight, one attacking Charles, the other defending him. The metonymic conjunction of these dreams with the second council scene leads to metaphoric identifications. Indeed, the suggestion of the text is that Charles does make the connection. When he hears Ganelon's nomination of Roland, Charles exclaims:

> Quant l'ot li reis, fierement le reguardet,
> Si li a dit: "Vos estes vifs diables.
> El cors vos est entree mortel rage." (ll. 745–47)

> Fiercely the king looks at the one who spoke
> and said to him: "You are the living devil.
> Deadly rage has entered into you."

What explains this verbal reaction but a cognitive awareness of the meaning of Ganelon's act, a meaning entirely overt to the audience? And if that awareness is present, why is there no evidence of the caution and sagacity that were displayed earlier?

As the theme recurs under the system of epic foreshadowing, the question also recurs. Charles and his troops come into sight of Gascony and the *Tere Majur*. The "suspicion" that might have been produced by the dreams sent to him by the divine world from which they originate seems to turn to more definite "foreknowledge." In two parallel *laisses*, the first of which is poetically resounding and the second of which is telling, Charles reveals his concern and his thoughts:

> Halt sunt li pui e li val tenebrus,
> Les roches bises, les destreiz merveillus. . . .
> Sur tuz les altres est Charles anguissus:
> As porz d'Espaigne ad lesset sun nevold.
> Pitet l'en prent, ne poet muer n'en plurt. (ll. 814–25)

> High are the hills, the valleys shadowy,
> the cliffs are gray, the gorges strike with awe. . . .
> Above all others Charles is feeling cornered:
> He's left his nephew in Spain's defiles.
> Sorrow takes him, he cannot help but weep.

When Duke Naimes asks what weighs on him, Charles is precise:

> "Tort fait kil me demandet!
> Si grant doel ai ne puis muer nel pleigne.

Par Guenelon serat destruite France.
Enoit m'avint un'avision d'angele,
Qu'antre mes puinz me depeçout ma hanste:
Chi ad juget mis nés a rereguarde.
Jo l'ai lesset en une estrange marche.
Deus! se jol pert, ja n'en avrai escange." (ll. 833–40)

    "He does me wrong who asks!
Such grief I have I cannot help but groan.
France will be destroyed by Ganelon.
Last night there came to me an angel's dream,
that in my hands he broke my spear:
he named my nephew to the rear guard.
And I have left him in a foreign land.
God! If I lose him, there will be no exchange."

In this speech, there is no question but that—at this early point in the narrative, before the battles have begun—Charles already connects Ganelon's nomination of Roland to the rear guard with the potential loss of Roland and the destruction of "France."

The text does more than merely adumbrate Charles's cognition of Ganelon's betrayal. It operates the equation of the heaven-sent dreams with the narrative of the text, and Charles's own responsibility in the latter. This consciousness of the significance of the dreams and the implications of the earlier narrative exchanges are generalized in the following *laisse*:

Carles li magnes ne poet muer n'en plurt.
.C. milie Francs pur lui unt grant tendrur
E de Rollant merveilluse poür.
Guenes li fels en ad fait traïsun. . . . (ll. 841–44)

Charles the great cannot help but weep.
A hundred thousand Franks have great tenderness for him
and awesome fear for Roland.
The felon Ganelon, he has betrayed him.

In this case, the consciousness is textualized without being assigned to a particular actor. Alone, it might count simply as the shared consciousness of the audience and the text. Coming as it does right after the preceding *laisse*, in which Charles is shown as making the conscious connections that doom Roland, it also must be counted a repetition of the isotopies of the earlier *laisse*.

Thus, the text keeps the issue alive, disculpating Charles and in doing so insisting upon the question the disculpation should resolve. The text is continually responding to an implicit accusation; it feeds that implicit accusation continually. No narrative function is served by that accusation, by the foreknowledge that is textualized, as far as overt narrative operations are concerned. From the point of view of narrative structure, the issue of Charles's consciousness here is gratuitous. From a broader semiotic point of view, however, the cognitive dimension of the text raises questions that relate to its deep structure, to its fundamental value-conflict.

The text implicates Charlemagne repeatedly: it thematizes his absence in the exchanges among the Franks and between the Franks and the Saracens, before and during the battle, even to the extent of specifying that Charles has "betrayed" his men. The text repeatedly defends Charles against such accusations. It does so by verbally asserting that he *will* protect his men. The narrative of the text, however, demonstrates the falsity of that assertion. In its very narrative structures, and in their interplay with its discourse, the text develops Charles's responsibility, by the difference in his comportment during the two council scenes, and by the developed disjunction between the patent meaning of the annunciatory dreams he receives and their non-application to the surrounding narrative, even when Charles has made explicit his cognitive awareness of their significance. The fact that the earthly destinator receives communications from the supernatural destinator whose cognitive content is not shown to have any effect on the development of the narrative line is noteworthy. Particularly in a historically determinate type of textuality such as the epic, within which the hierarchical predominance of the pragmatic aspect of narrative is evident, the disjunction between the cognitive and the pragmatic is remarkable. One would expect the cognitive trajectory from the supernatural destinator to the earthly and collective destinator to be continued by a transmittal of the cognitive message from the destinator to the destinatee and subject, who could then, in turn, transform that cognitive communication into a pragmatic course of action. But the fact is that that trajectory is interrupted at the instance of the text's narrative destinator, and that interruption is anomalous, both in semiotic terms and in feudal terms. If Charles is not overtly inculpated; if there is never a suggestion that he is to be considered in the same category as Ganelon, *cil ki la traïsun fist*; nevertheless the text plays on unresolved ambiguities, ambiguities which, among other things, allow for the assignment to Charles of the narrative program "avenging Roland" and the resolution of the legal issues left by his death. The ambiguity of the text, its semantic irresolution, is necessary in order to allow it to bring about the transformations required by an ideological program, one of whose functions is to override the question of Charles's culpability by a historical and dialectical *Aufhebung*.

Has too much been made of the isotopy of culpability? Charles himself seems to recognize its pertinence. Enough evidence—in the sense the term has in legal proceedings—has been amassed to legitimate our taking the term of *seigneur* in the legal sense it has in the feudal code, along with the specifications of duties and responsibilities assigned to the role of the *seigneur* as contractor in the synallagmatic exchange of the feudal contract between lord and vassal. This technical sense of "lordship" should be retained when Charles's self-judgment, performed upon the discovery of Roland's corpse in the field of battle at Roncevaux, is conjoined with his mourning of his nephew:

"Ami Rollant, Deus metet t'anme en flors,
En pareïs, entre les glorius!
Cum en Espaigne venis a mal seignur!" (ll. 2898–2900)

"Friend ⎫
          ⎬ Roland, may God place your soul among flowers
"Ally ⎭

in paradise, among the glorious!

          ⎧ *bad* ⎫
What a ⎨   ⎬ *lord you followed to Spain!* . . . "
          ⎩ *evil* ⎭

From Individual to Role

In spite of his preeminent position in the *Chanson de Roland*, the issue is not one that affects Charles as an individual. As we have seen, the political system attributed to the Saracens replicates the feudal system as it operated in the ideology of northern France and England. The same code governs the relations between lords and vassals on the two sides. The same narrative competences and performances are coded into the representation of Saracen relationships as are operative in the Frankish camp. The Saracens comment on the relationship between Charles and his vassals; inversely, the Franks comment on these categories as they play in the field of their opponents. Thus, the Saracens will have no protector against death, as Roland informs Oliver during their dispute about whether or not to sound the horn (l. 1081), and as another knight informs a Saracen after having despatched him on his horse (l. 1303). The Saracens pursued by Charles after Roland's death are said to have no guarantor immediately after they invoke the god Tervagant for help at the river Ebre, in which they promptly drown (l. 2471). Saracen discourse naturally and repeatedly employs the vocabulary of *guarant*, *garir*, *guarison*, etc., in structuring relations among each other and their Gods. Individuals do or do not have a guarantor (the negative being more frequent than the positive as they go into battle: ll. 1277, 1418, 1440); they invoke their gods as guarantors in battle (ll. 868, 3271); one wise Saracen (Naimes's equivalent) informs Baligant that his Gods will not protect him in battle against Charles's Franks (ll. 3508–19); and Baligant's messengers to Marsile inform the latter that Baligant will be his protector (l. 2726).

For as the theme is concretized around Charles in the Christian camp, so is it concretized around Baligant among the Saracens. While perhaps less frequent there, it is just as telling. When the text introduces the distant feudal lord of Marsile in *laisse* 189, it explains that the latter sent word to his protector Baligant when Spain was first invaded by Charlemagne seven years earlier, entreating his superior to come to the rescue. If he did not come, Marsile threatened to abandon his Gods and idols, convert to Christianity, and find peace with Charles. The reaction to danger attributed to Marsile is different from Roland's: the Saracen king has no hesitation in calling for help when faced with a dangerous enemy. The difference makes no difference, however: whether the vassal requests help or not, it does not come on time. Marsile learns that a distant lord is slow to come:

[Baligant] est loinz, si ad mult demuret. (l. 2622)

[Baligant] is far, and has delayed a long time.

Even in view of the distance between Spain and the Near East, seven years is a long time. Baligant's delay allows for cutting irony. When Baligant arrives on the Spanish shores, he sends messengers to his vassal, his instructions accompanied by a sign of vassalic devolution comparable to those which Charles gives Ganelon and Roland when they accept their missions from him: a glove, ornamented with gold, to wear on the right hand, as a sign of the emir's determination to fight Charles "if I find him" (l. 2676). When the messengers arrive at Saragossa, however, it is to hear from the townspeople in the streets that Marsile lost his right hand in battle to Roland's sword, a story repeated by Marsile's wife Bramimonde (*laisse* 195). The messenger complains that the Lady talks too much; he notes the great forces encamped nearby and explains that Baligant is ready to chase Charles in France. She responds ironically. Don't bother, she says, you needn't go that far, he's closer by:

"Mar en irat itant!
Plus pres d'ici purrez truver les Francs:
En ceste tere ad estet [Charlemagne] ja. VII. anz! . . . " (ll.2734–36)

"Why, you needn't go that far!
You can find Franks closer by:

[Charlemagne] has been in this land seven years
  already! . . . "

The verbal irony duplicates the double narrative irony. The offer of protection comes after the need; the promise to go seek out the Franks in France comes after their long presence in Spain; both offer and promise are thus rendered nugatory by the narrative context.

In spite of the delay, Baligant intends to perform as protector (l. 2726). In the field of battle, the emir rides through the enemy, cutting down one after another count, Guinemant, then Gebuin and Lorant, and also the lord of the Normans, Richard the Old. The pagans cry out:

"Preciuse* est vaillant!   [*Baligant's sword]
Ferez, baron, nus i avom *guarant*!" (ll. 3471f.)

  "Preciuse is worth much!
Strike, barons, we have a *warrantor*!"

A little later, Baligant himself raises the question of protection, albeit at a supposedly higher level. After he invokes the Gods, he learns of the losses on his side, including those of his son and his brother (ll. 3495–99). He bends his head (as did Charles in thinking about Roland's death), the pain is such he thinks to die. He calls Jangleu d'Outremer and asks his opinion as to the Franks and the Arabs. Jangleu answers:

"Morz estes, Baligant!
Ja vostre deu ne vos erent *guarant*. . . . " (ll. 3513–14)

"Baligant, you're dead!
Never will your gods *warrant you*. . . . "

Not only is Baligant incapable of protecting his vassals: the gods to whom he is a vassal fail him in turn.

The failure of the *garant*, the absence of protection from the feudal superior, in spite of the vassalic contract, is thus not a personal phenomenon but one that is generalized: it is not just a particular actor who is aimed at, it is the role (in the semiotic sense) that is inculpated. Roland, Charles, Baligant, all fail to fulfill their contract of protection with their social and military subordinates: Roland does not protect his men in the rear guard; Charlemagne does not protect the twelve peers and the rear guard; Baligant does not protect Marsile, his vassal; and the pagan Gods do not protect Baligant. Lords both Christian and Frankish as well as lords who are Saracen and pagan fail equally in their fulfillment of the vassalic contract. It is not one side or the other, it is feudal lordship *per se*, the semiotic role of the feudal superior, that is charged with malfunction, or more precisely, with malfeasance. The question thus arises: to what extent are the culpability and the malfunction not the characteristics of individualized actors only—even though narrative fiction must by its nature negotiate all general statements through the bearers (*Träger*) of individual actors—but systemic in nature?

The *Chanson de Roland* establishes the general rule of the unreliability of the feudal lord as *garant*, as protector of his sworn vassals. In the case of Charles in particular, the narrative "lets him off the hook" by making Roland bear a large share of responsibility. A symmetry is thus established between the two synallagmatic terms of the feudal contract: both are made to bear negative markers in this text. As the vassals engage in an endless round of self-destructive behaviors, so do the lords repeatedly fail to prevent the destruction of the subordinates who had placed faith and the expectation of protection in their hands. It is thus not merely the category of the vassals that is inculpated by the text: the lords as well do not function according to the codes of expectation. If neither vassal nor feudal lord perform properly, however, then it is both terms of feudalism that are at stake, and it is the total system of feudalism itself that is questioned. The *Chanson de Roland* is an intensely political poem, not only because it focuses intensely on the political relationships that constitute the social diegesis of its textuality. It is also intensely political in dealing with a political *system* rather than just its actors, taken either as individuals or as individual classes. It is furthermore intensely political in a specific sense: not only does it deal with the systematicity of the political relations that constitute its social diegesis, it does so in a specifically structuralist manner, by a binary analysis of that systematicity. The representation of that systematicity demonstrates both the characterological dynamic by which the vassalic component of feudalism is impelled to destroy itself, and the unreliability of the hierarchical relation based on mutual trust, loyalty, and the observance of the contract. In other words, the *Chanson de Roland* is intensely political in its focus on systemic relations, and that focus is a critical one.

6 | Excursus II: The Play of Absence and Presence in Medieval Kingship

> Il y a des variables d'expression qui mettent la langue en rapport avec le
> dehors, mais précisément parce qu'elles sont immanentes à la langue.
> Deleuze and Guattari, *Mille plateaux*

WHEN BLANCANDRIN COMES to the camp of the Francs, he finds the hieratic
figure of Charlemagne:

> La sied li reis ki dulce France tient. (l. 116)
>
> There is seated the king who holds sweet France.

The semantically "heavy" words are three: the two nouns—king, France—and
the verb—*tient*, or holds. The verb's literal meaning should not be overlooked:
one "holds" a land—or a fief—with a number of implications, one of which is
to hold it so that it can be squeezed: to hold a land or a fief is to hold a source
of productive wealth, to which—as the one who legally "holds" it—the king or
vassal will be entitled, as the one who "holds."

That, in a sense, is the easiest word of the line. The nouns, both of which
can readily be "re-cognized," are highly problematic. The proper noun "France,"
which we unhesitatingly identify with the "hexagon" of contemporary geogra-
phy, is a term whose reference is most elastic in the eleventh and twelfth centuries, and in the text of the *Roland*. It may signify an entity much smaller than
the hexagon, or one much, much larger: a feudal principality, or the empire.

If the geographical entity over which the king holds sway is ambiguous, so
is the notion of kingship itself. Indeed, it is unclear whether Charles should be
considered a "king" or an "emperor": from the very first line of the poem, he
is called both, and it is quite unclear whether the two terms had clearly distin-
guishable meanings at the time of the *Roland*:

> Carles li reis, nostre emperere magnes. . . . (l. 1)
>
> Charles the king, our great emperor. . . .

Is it that he holds two titles, syncretically and cumulatively combined in one individual, or is it that the two terms are considered roughly equivalent, and that
he is merely blessed with titular synonymy?

Carles li reis, . . .

The disintegration of the Carolingian Empire, the effective disappearance of those institutionalized organs of empowerment and control we call the State, the ensuing devolution of power to ever smaller and more local levels, left the situation of the medieval French kingship in a peculiar tension between absence and presence. What was "absent/present" was not the corporeal body of the French king: the Capetians were remarkably successful in producing a continuous string of heirs to the throne. Nor was it the "spiritual" king that, after the corporeal body, made up the other half of the "king's two bodies," to use the title words of Ernst Kantorowitz's famous study:[1] the presence of the spiritual can always be manufactured in the ideological domain. Indeed, the ideological presence of the king appears always to have been recognized and respected by the kings' contemporaries. Even in the depths of material or moral degradation, he remains a sacred chieftain, anointed by God. His aura has its effect, and no one, not even his most dangerous rival, the duke of Normandy, dreams of dispossessing him.[2] The play of absence and presence, in which a place for the king was always felt effectively to be present, was rather between that ideologically encoded "place" and the actual exercise of power in the performance of those narrative programs felt to be normative according to the king's semiotic "role." The absence/presence of kingship played in the discrepancy between encoding and enactment.

That play occurred within the framework of a larger contradiction, however, the fundamental difference between the two modes of social and political organization, kingship and feudalism. Their diachronic relationship is clearly sequential: feudalism follows upon the disappearance of the centralized power and authority of the Carolingian Empire. In turn, the resurgence of kingship under the twelfth-century Capetian kings is based on their ability to use the feudal mode of organization to their advantage, both in imposing control upon their own principality and in manipulating relations among their vassals and peers. A temporary melding of the two occurred under what has been labeled, with appropriate hesitation, the "feudal monarchy," an inherently "unstable amalgam."[3] Two fundamentally different and contradictory models are at work. In one, power, legitimacy, and authority are located in an exclusive, central instance, a political centrality from which all other exercises of power devolve to lower levels which in turn, explicitly or implicitly, appeal to that one, higher authority as the source of legitimation. Given the geographical dispersion of the Carolingian Empire, this devolutionary step was essential, and a strong, publically recognized hierarchy of powers and authorities was extruded from the center in an administrative and military armature of imposing stature. The disappearance of the center brought into being a completely different model of sociopolitical organization. At first, the qualities of the state—power, authority, legitimacy—fell onto the shoulders of those who had been the primary agents of the one, central-ized instance, the counts and the dukes who had represented the first level of devolution. Then even that reduction of sovereignty was too ambitious, and the effective level of the government of men (taking "government" in its etymologi-cal sense of "directing," "piloting": leading, forcing, determining) fell lower, far lower, to whoever in a given locality controlled suffcient military force to impose his will upon those of that locality. The essential semes of this system are /force/ and /space/: whoever could muster, control, and apply the requisite military force upon a subject population, assert his exclusive control within a given territory, was *ipso facto* its political leader. The essential elements in that military force were a fortress-castle and military dependents, who, for whatever reason, ac-cepted the leadership of the one individual. Certainly, the prestige of nobility and aristocracy, as well as the habit of leading and commanding men that ac-companies such status, was helpful in establishing effective military domination and leadership over military dependents; so was the wherewithal which supplied horses, weapons, a coat of mail, and a helmet. The conjunction of these qualities explains the remarkable genealogical persistence of the nobility from Roman times into and through much of the Middle Ages. Nevertheless, these qualities had to be predicated of individuals who functionalized them as castle-masters, the *châtelains* who wielded the only effective power for a period which until recently was unhesitatingly called "the feudal period." As one historian has put it, "the 11th century knight lived in a society which was dominated by force and in which competition by means of force was almost completely untrammeled."[4]

The fortress-castle was the centerpiece in this form of social organization based on effective military power. Most of the elegant and large constructions that have survived postdate the period of feudal fragmentation. But on the aver-age, one might expect to encounter a castle every twenty kilometers or so. Once that is said, one has defined the effective diameter of the exercise of power. The fundamental *circonscription* was a territory of some twelve miles across, ruled from a fortification which could house the available military force and its leader. This fact determines the basic social relations of the social formation. Those who ride in and out of that fortification are the ruling class of society, its dominant element, whether old blood or new, whether aristocracy whose origins went back to Roman times or new, aggressive muscle shoving into the sphere of dominance. Aside from this small population devoted to force and its exercises, the over-whelming preponderance of the population consisted of peasants who worked the land of the territory outside the castle, under the watchful eyes of the fortress. These are the polities, scattered by the hundreds and thousands across the face of France, which were the sole effective form of political organization. A *reductio* of government *ad absurdum*, certainly, to the irrational surds of force, rapine, and pillage which were the only forms of protection and security available, or, at least, the necessary implications of what protection and security were available, given the character of the men on horseback whose force shadowed the peasant territory around the central fortification.

The reason for the irreconcilability of the two models—the monarchical and the feudal—is a very simple one.[5] In both cases, force must be exercised at the local level, in a form and frequency effective both to protect the local territory and to intimidate the subject peasantry. In the monarchical model, that force is directed and determined from the center and serves the interests of the center. In the "feudal" model, that force is fragmented and scattered across the countryside, responding only to the interests, the character, the practices, of that handful of men and their lord who ride in and out of the fortresses. They know and accept no superior instance: they are responsible to themselves, that small knot of men whose relations mingle and fuse those isotopies separated into differentiated institutions by the state: military, political, lineage, family, household (*maisniee*), marriage, whoring, and *compagnonnage*, all revolving around each other to the point of confusion within the walls of the single castle and its master's manor. Outside that surcharged and overdetermined world, there is nothing but Others who are, by definition, enemies: the peasants, who are to be forced to labor in order to produce the requisite surplus, and then forced to abandon that surplus; the monasteries, whose efficient productivity regularly accumulates a surplus that is ineluctably tempting; and the more distant Others, for the more adventurous bands seeking distant and rewarding booty from Eastern lands, the slaves to be captured in raids on the Slavs, dragged back to "civilization" and sold for noble profit. The slave trade, the pillage of the monks' patient labor, the extraction of surplus value from the sweat of peasants born to labor— these are the forms of primitive accumulation of capital. Their control, the claim upon these profits, is very much at stake in the military, political, and social organization of society.

The historical evolution with which we are primarily concerned consists in the slow recuperation of political sovereignty at increasingly higher levels of hierarchy, from what has sometimes been described as the "anarchy" of feudalism, but which needs to be understood primarily as the ways men found to cope with the *ad hoc* contexts of survival to which they were delivered by the disintegration and disappearance of centralized authority and police power. The ever-greater fragmentation of the territory we call "France" today had as its obverse the progressive weakening of the French kings. While the signifier *regnum Franciae* was quite popular among twelfth-century chroniclers, its signified had been greatly watered down as the power and authority of the successive kings disintegrated during the tenth century.[6] The range of the king's power was effectively limited to his domain as a feudal noble, roughly equivalent to the rather small province called the Ile-de-France. Its outline can be traced by a quadrilateral figure touching on Laon, Compiègne, and Beauvais in the north, running through Mantes, Dreux, and Rambouillet in the west, across Orléans, Le Moulinet, and Sens in the south, and following the rivers Yonne, the Seine, and the Oise back toward the north, including centers of population at Soisy, Gonesse, Senlis, and Soissons.[7] Even within this limited domain, the king's power was not everywhere effective. The region included enclaves ruled by nobles who controlled the rights of justice as well as both administrative and financial powers. The king's effective domain was that over which he exercised unmediated power: this consisted of tracts that were frequently minuscule, "a dusting of incomes" as one historian has put it—*"une poussière de revenus"*—which might include entities such as part of a pasturage, one share of a toll, a split percentage of a tenant's harvest. Even the king's own personal domain was no more than the debris of the Merovingian domain, "an agglutination of a multiplicity of particular, local rights."[8]

In addition, the king exercised a protectorate over a variety of ecclesiastical institutions. This protectorate included monasteries, abbeys, and bishoprics in a far larger geographical area than the domain sketched out above: it stretched from Therouanne and Tournai in the north through Burgundy and into Provence.[9] This "protectorate" was also quite profitable, adding substantially to the king's financial resources. Nevertheless, this collection of financial and military resources provided a limited base of power with which to exert influence in the larger "kingdom." Indeed, even in the twelfth century, the king did not attempt to exploit his theoretical rights over the major vassals in the country at large: he intervened very rarely in fiefs which were probably no longer thought of as devolving from the king.[10] So great was the decline in royal authority that what existed in political reality was the limited, regional power of a Capetian principality, rather than a kingdom.[11] In this context, what is most striking in the juxtaposition between the historical reality of French kingship and the representation of French kingship in the text of the *Roland* is without question its discrepancy.[12]

The decline of the monarchy extends into the beginning of the twelfth century. It is pointless to attempt to define a specific "nadir," since this decline is mixed in with signs of recovery associated with economic and political renewal throughout France. Indeed, the very weakness of the French monarchy may paradoxically have been one source of its renewal.[13] It is possible to chart the descent of the respect with which the French kings are held by the gradual disappearance of the nobility from their court.[14] Attendance was both a sign of respect for the kingship and a practical matter. From the very year of Hugh Capet's accession, royal diplomas must be signed, not only by the king's chancellor, but by whatever notables happen to be at court at the time: royal authority alone is insufficient to support the royal decision. In later reigns, the status of these countersigners continually falls as fewer and fewer of the kingdom's nobles attend the king's court. Under Philip I, almost no counts or dukes appear at court: instead, one finds increasing numbers of local *châtelains*, castle-masters from the Ile-de-France who experience the king's power directly. One also finds members of lower classes such as town mayors. Monarchy increasingly depends on small people for the exercise of diminished power.

If the high aristocracy, both lay and clerical, abandons the royal court, this determines the necessity of a new development to parry the absence of the nobility. A cadre of major administrative officers develops: the *seneschal*, the *connetable*, the *chambrier*, the *bouteillier*, whose titles indicate their origin as personal functionaries of the king, become the central personages in an incipient royal administration, concerned with major political, judiciary, and financial decisions, even including relation with the Church. The absence of the nobility led to the development of the central cadre of what would eventually become the centralized bureaucracy of a renascent monarchy. They were the beginning of a permanent government, dependent on the king and answerable to him alone. As the documentary records show, this group of men became more and more important. Originally drawn from the lower nobility, they tended to come more from the ranks of the leading châtelains in the Ile-de-France toward the end of the eleventh and beginning of the twelfth centuries: men possessing sources of power within the king's dominion, but nevertheless dependent upon the king. In that complex situation, they formed a permanent core of royal administrators and provided a continuity and a source of strength that would be instrumental in the further development of the monarchy.

That was a long-term prospect, however. The successful elaboration of the monarchy depended on a prior base of power: it was first of all as a noble that the king of France had to assert himself. The crucial turning point of this process of self-assertion appears to have occurred during the reigns of Philip I and his son Louis VI, whose conjoined reigns extended from 1060 until 1137: as was customary for the Capetian kings, the son and heir presumptive was associated to the father's reign before the latter's death, assuring the inheritance and incidentally providing "basic training" in kingship to the future king. Philip I received "an almost uniformly bad press" in his own time, being renowned primarily for "personal turpitude," largely as a result of his defiance of ecclesiastical sanctions and moral norms when he put aside his wife Bertha and carried off the wife of a vassal in order to live openly with her: Bertrada of Monfort was her name, and her attractions must have been intense, for he continued to live with her even after repudiating her in an effort to reconcile himself with the Church! In addition to such moral and marital peccadiloes, Philip seems to have sold Church office, thus further displeasing the episcopate.[15]

It was to Philip's son, however, that fell the grueling task of establishing effective domain over the king's domain, the Ile-de-France. This was Louis VI, surnamed the Fat: he had to be lifted to his horse by beam and pulley. Greedy and gluttonous (like his father; these seem to have been family traits), he could seem "saintly" only by contrast with Philip I.[16] It fell to him to wage a ceaseless war against the savage and violent castle-masters of the Ile-de-France, in the endless, mounted assertions of presence, prerogative, and military domination. It was a life dedicated to the subordination of the "rebellious barons" (to use a phrase from literary history) by dint of military force. Subjugating these ferocious warrior-chieftains, subordinating them to his overlordship, building new fortresses in a variety of locations so as to make permanent the control over the countryside—these were the means by which Louis VI increased the power of the French kingship. As a result of his solidified power base, it became possible for powers elsewhere in France, both lay and ecclesiastic, to appeal to the king for help, providing him with occasions for military and political interventions farther afield in the kingdom, in the Berry, in the Auvergne, for instance. Louis was able even to take on—with appropriate caution—the noble leaders of other great principalities, such as Normandy and Flanders, though Blois, even before its junction with Champagne, remained beyond him.

Along with this decided increase in political power within his own feudal domain—in turn the basis of economic wealth—and the resultant ability to interfere in farther regions of the kingdom, Louis also had the great good fortune to become the subject of an idealizing, adulatory, and self-serving biography by his friend and counselor, the Abbot Suger of St. Denis. In an epoch and a culture in which economic wealth and political power were inextricably mixed and interdependent, in which therefore the manipulation of symbols and ideology were a major source of both power and wealth, the political benefit of Suger's ideological developments can hardly be overestimated. Partly out of friendship for Louis, partly out of self-interest as the abbot of a major ecclesiastical institution, Suger repeatedly insisted on the association of the French monarchy with the Abbey of St. Denis, with the ideologically charged mytheme of Charlemagne, and thereby laid the basis for the rituals and theory of a "sacral kingship."[17] Louis VI and his friend the abbot thus managed to simultaneously develop the military, political, economic, and ideological bases of the French monarchy.

Louis VI's reputation with modern historians is largely based on Suger's chronicle. His successor, Louis VII, benefited from no such friendly chronicler or biographer, and his modern reputation—as a largely pale, colorless, and ineffectual leader—is due at least in part to that absence of enthusiastic documentation. Nevertheless, his contemporaries found much to praise in him, and modern, balanced surveys of his reign conclude that there was more to praise than to condemn.[18] Furthermore, what is to be praised at the level of practical politics is the largely unsung work of patient administration and alliance-building, characterized by silence and prudence. A large part of his success lay in the financial administration which made of the king of France the wealthiest noble of the country.[19] The production of wealth from various sources is obviously a crucial element in the development of political rule. It may be, however, that Louis VII's crucial achievement lay in another domain, that of symbolic and ideological representation, the accumulation, that is to say, of ideological capital. To some extent, it was his very weakness as monarch that allowed for such accumulation.

Louis was born to Louis VI as his second son. As such, he was not groomed for the succession, destined to his older brother Philip. Instead, the young Louis was sent to the cathedral school in Paris, probably to fit him for an ecclesiastical career. As a contemporary noted, he was so pious, Catholic, and benign that one might mistake him for a man of religion rather than a king. Not only a man of piety, he was known as a just man, with simple tastes and high expectations of the institution of the monarchy. His personal characteristics announced those of his great-grandson, Louis IX, also known as "Saint Louis." In his own time, John of Salisbury would dub him *"rex christianissimus."*

In the realm of moral qualities and ideology, where the social capital of symbolic value is accumulated, it did not hurt also to be the first French king associated with a crusade, even if it was to result in a personal and political disaster. Louis VII married Eleanor of Aquitaine the year of his accession, 1137. The granddaughter and heiress of William the IX, the troubadour duke of Aquitaine, had been left in the custody of William's feudal suzerain, Louis VI, by William's death. The marriage between his custodial charge and his son was an immense political achievement, uniting France with the enormous duchy of Aquitaine: few marriages so precisely exemplify the diplomatic nature of medieval marriage. During the crusade, which began ten years after the marriage, conflict within the royal couple was rumored, as was an attraction of the queen for her uncle Raymond of Antioch. After a brief reconciliation by the pope, the final rift occurred in 1151, and the marriage was declared null and void in the following year on grounds of consanguinity. The bad part, however, was yet to come. Within a few months Eleanor married Henry Plantagenet, Duke of Normandy, who became king of England two years later in 1154. As a result, benefiting from the lands Eleanor brought him, Henry, king of England, became "the largest single landholder in France. His vast conglomeration of lands stretching from Durham to Dax entirely overshadowed those of his suzerain the French king."[20]

Politically speaking, this was a disaster of the first magnitude. Symbolically speaking, however, Louis's incompetence in the politics of a political marriage itself emphasized the spiritual isotopy, the ideological and symbolic value of Louis's historical figure. Again, weakness paradoxically turned into Capetian advantage. In spite of occasional ferocious episodes, like the campaign against Theobald of Blois which ended with the burning of the church at Vitry, 1,500 people caught in the flames, the most lasting contribution of Louis VII's kingship may have been outside the military and political sphere. His remarriage to Adèle of Champagne not only was part of an extended noble exchange of diplomatic women—Theobald and his brother, Henry the Liberal, both married daughters of Louis VII from his marriage with Eleanor—it also united the king with a direct descendent of Charlemagne. If an essential part of monarchy and the modern state is the achievement of legitimacy by consent of the governed, the production of ideological value conferring such legitimacy is a crucial element of governance.[21]

Louis VII's reign from 1137 until his death in 1180 occupies the center of the twelfth century: that is the crucial period of cultural and especially textual development. Even though the political space of the French royal court played next to no role in the development of literature—most of the action occurred in noble courts outside of Paris and the Ile-de-France—that development occurred within a political time frame which is also that of royalty, undergoing important development: the conjunction is perhaps not entirely accidental.

A small change in diplomatic terminology can suggest the accomplishment of the three Capetians discussed here. Following the Capetian custom, Louis VII's son, Philip Augustus, was crowned king during his father's lifetime and reign, in 1179. As early as 1181, the title changed from *rex Francorum* (King of the Franks), which it had been under Louis VII, to *rex Franciae* (King of France), suggesting the progress of royal authority over a geographical area and the first bases of renewed national unity accomplished under Louis VII.[22] Inheriting a well-ordered principality, Philip was able to extend the royal lands from the small domain of the Ile-de-France north, west, and south. Philip Augustus, less attractive personally and morally than his father, managed to take Normandy and Anjou from the English, and to restrict English power to the single province of Gascony, thus largely reversing the losses incurred by his father's divorce. The battle of Bouvines in 1214 was a "major and resounding victory which . . . secure[d] his massive territorial gains, and . . . rapidly became the symbol of revived royal power."[23] It sealed the results of the slow progress of royal power during the twelfth century, during most of which the French king had been eclipsed by the king of England. It is with Philip that the combined military force, political power, and accumulated symbolic capital of the French king enabled him to affirm, not only his predominance among the princes of the principalities, but a truly monarchical preeminence: with Philip, an effective kingdom of France exists, and while its apogee is still centuries in the future, its political, economic, and ideological bases have been established. Although not yet effective in the entire geographical region indicated today by the term "France," the king, by the end of Philip's reign, is far more present than absent, far more anchored in the economic and political realities of the kingdom than the largely ideological investment already effective under his forefathers. As one modern historian of Philip's reign concludes,

> From a feudal principality, somewhat more eminent than the others because of the fact that its leader had the benefit of the royal title, Philip Augustus had created a State, France, and he had definitively given it a capital, Paris.[24]

The crown of the king of France in the twelfth century was hardly a monosemantic sign. Its meanings were complex and contradictory. The king's economic independence—a major source of strength and respect—was based on his feudal status as the noble chieftain of a principality. On the ideological isotopy, the king's preeminence is not put into question: his sacral status is respected even when it has little practical significance, documents drawn up in distant regions where he has little effective power are dated nonetheless according to the year of his reign, and a theory of divine kingship is in the process of being elaborated which will have resounding success in later European history. At the beginning of our period, the king of France is politically one of the weakest of the five or six aristocratic leaders of principalities located in his kingdom; his weakness determines a permanent political strategy to secure such alliances with these other princes as will prevent their rallying together against him. By the end of our period, the king has established effective suzerainty over even the greatest of those princes, he has a preponderant role in those areas of the kingdom not yet under royal control, and his economic base within his own principality and feudal domain provides him with the means to regularly employ mercenaries in the service of his policies. Perhaps as important, a permanent and independent bureaucracy, answerable to his exclusive interests, has been developed on a feudal basis. Well established within his personal domain and principality, he is once more respected in the larger kingdom and can undertake policies that require the presence and support of great nobles from that larger realm. In other words, the bases for the institutionalized State have begun to reappear in the geographical space we call France.

Interestingly enough, the question of conscious intentionality, so crucial to contemporary literary theory, seems most dubious here. While the general development of the French monarchy throughout the late eleventh, twelfth, and early thirteenth centuries follows a rational path, while its successive stages bear logical relations to each other, it is not at all clear that the successive kings of France—Philip I, Louis VI, Louis VII, and Philip Augustus—were following a consciously developed strategy. Was there such a plan, such a "positive intention of consolidation"? At least one historian of the Capetian royal family doubts it. "Successful as they were in annexation and expansion, the Capetians never had any intention of extending their domain over all France." They merely desired a domain of a size and organization to sustain them in appropriate pomp, surrounded by clustering fiefs held from the crown, directly or mediately, "by vassals prepared to respect their feudal obligations." As far as historical evidence of a general strategy is concerned, "There is no evidence of any sort to suggest that the Capetians had any clear idea of the course they were following, beyond a general conviction that no occasion of possible aggrandisement should be neglected."[25] The practice of aggrandisement, however, was undertaken in a complete absence of theory, of preconceived planning, by a practice of kingship that never defined itself.[26] Even at the end of our period, in the reign of Philip Augustus, the concepts of *regnum* and *imperium*, of "kingdom" and "France," remain unarticulated and cannot legitimate Philip's military conquests.[27] It might be objected that, if the kings did have such a strategy, then keeping it under their crown might be the most effective strategy in view of the potential fear and jealousy of the other nobles of the realm. Such a subtlety might have been beyond the individuals concerned; in any case, the hypothesis, though attractive, is entirely speculative. Neither right nor wrong, it is inherently indeterminable. Exactly the same conclusion is appropriate for the conscious strategies and intentions of the individuals producing the texts we study: they presumably had some thought of what they were doing, but those thoughts, and those of their contemporaries regarding the texts they produced, are quite lost to us, and irrecuperably so.

The contradictory isotopies of the kingly code developed independently of each other. Oddly enough, the ideological advanced before the material.

> Although royal power in the twelfth century remained limited in terms of land and resources, the reputation of the king as overlord, lawgiver and protector was beginning to revive quite widely, well before the great conquests of the early thirteenth century. So too was the image of the French king as the holder of sacral powers and as the defender of the kingdom.[28]

The relation between this development and the production of a text like the *Roland* will occupy us later. For the moment, it is important to underline that the *Roland*, belonging to the ideational sphere, develops in tandem with the ideological isotopy of kingship, rather than the material institution of kingship.[29] What this asserts is the unity of the ideological domain as against its dependence upon material developments, even at the expense of semiotic cohesion.

The course of historical development in the twelfth century, from this perspective, will be to unite the symbolic "value" generally accorded the king of France with real and effective power based on a control of a limited but well-organized territory—the Ile-de-France—and the husbanding and deployment of the economic surplus this principality produced.

. . . nostre emperere magnes

The first line of the poem qualifies Charles not only as king but also as emperor. A heritage of the two antiquities, the classical and the Carolingian, the notion of "empire" leads two forms of existence in our period: "real" and "ideological."[30] In the codes of the "real" military and political history of our period, the "empire" plays a very limited role. The anecdote told by Suger about the offensive of 1124 is both indicative and remarkable: insofar as the "empire" enters into the encodable of northern France of the twelfth century, it is as an external power. Furthermore, it is another power at the same level and of the same type as "France": when it enters into the purview of matters "French," it is primarily as an enemy power, one which is to be opposed. That, it turns out, is not so difficult to do. In 1124, once the "French" troops were assembled on the field of potential battle outside Metz and the German "emperor" could see them, he turned tail and went home. At the level of the military and political issues facing the king of France, the "empire" was an external power that could occasionally threaten his sphere of activities, and not much more. It was far from the superior and subsumptive power of its claims.

In a way, the play of "empire" takes place above and beyond the problematics of French kingship. Christianity is bi-cephalic, as Jacques Le Goff has put it: its two heads are the pope and the emperor. The medieval history that depends on these two actors is more a matter of opposition than of agreement: "l'histoire médiévale est plus faite de leurs désaccords et de leurs luttes que de leur entente."[31] In fact, however, it is not of their conflicts that medieval history is made. The emperor's political hegemony over Christianity is more theoretical than real. Combatted in Germany, contested in Italy, the emperor is generally ignored by the more powerful princes. In particular, and as early as the Ottonian period, "the kings of France do not consider themselves in any way subordinate to the emperor," and canonists of various countries deny that their kings are subjects of the emperor and his laws.[32] If the conflicts between pope and emperor "occupy stage front, [that is only a] theater of illusions, behind which will take place the serious matters."[33]

The real issue is not between the pope and the emperor, but between the pope and the king or, as the traditional formula has it, between the *sacerdos* and the *rex*, the priest and the king. This opposition, of course, had been the structural heart of the Investiture Controversy. While this led to the assertion of greater independence of the Church from secular power, it did not lay to rest their syncretisms. On the contrary, the opposition of *sacerdos* and *rex* did not result in their permanent separation, but in renewed efforts at their fusion: "each attempted to make real in himself the unity of the *rex-sacerdos*," of the priest-king.[34] This explains both the total absence of the Papacy, either as reference or as sememe, from the *Song of Roland*, and the fundamental ideological content of Charlemagne-as-emperor. As ideologeme, he represents the fusion of divine devolution and the military component of kingship in the narrative of the poem. It is this fusion of the religious and the secular that also explains the puzzling absence of the Papacy—a power as important on the political stage of the time as on the religious—from the text: if the text incorporates the fusion of the two functions, then there is no room for the institutionalized incorporation of either as separate element. In the dialectic of ideological values, the centrality of Charlemagne as *rex-sacerdos* leads to the exclusion of the Papacy. That exclusion is his *raison d'être*, or, rather, it is in response to the enormous *faille* marked by the absent existence of the papal institution that the figure of Charlemagne is composed.

This consideration has led us out of the domain of the "real" to that of ideology, which is the most important domain of the "emperor" and his "empire." If the political consistency of the empire is in fact a fairly weak one, and if, as a result, the empire impinges little upon the political development of France in the twelfth century, the imperial idea is not absent from the ideological space around the French kings. In particular, the incorporation or subsumption of the idea of empire by the figure of Charlemagne is particularly valuable to the strategic writings of Suger in support of the French monarchy. The *oriflamme* which Louis VI went to take up at St. Denis before going to Metz in 1124 was reputed to be Charlemagne's own standard: deposited at the abbey by Hugh Capet, it took on the character of the royal banner in a semiosis linking the Capetian kings with the Carolingians. The ideologeme of "Charlemagne" became an object of value over which struggled the German emperor and the French king. If one chronicle identified the emperor rather than the king as Charles's descendent, the French could point to the repeated association of Charlemagne with France in the *chansons de geste*, as well as the fact, already noted, that Louis VII's wife, Adèle de Champagne, was a direct descendent of Charlemagne. If Fredrick Barbarossa had the great emperor canonized in 1160, poems and genealogies under Philip Augustus stressed the descent of the kings and their mothers from Charlemagne.[35]

If the memory of Carolingian Charlemagne, with its biblical and Augustinian antecedents, was turned into the object of a cult, and became the object of different narrative strategies, each intent on claiming the ideologeme for the symbolic use of one European power or another, it was because the figure of Charles, in the cultural codes of the twelfth century, performed that fusion of values representing concrete, materially based institutions which, in fact, were growing ever farther apart in their interests and goals. The ideological syncretism of the sign papered over a fissure which most of the subjects of that culture were not ready to recognize, since it was a fissure in the ideological field which constituted them as Subjects. The ideologeme of Charlemagne as emperor fused the political value of supreme military commander with the religious value of priestliness: it asserted the unity of the political system with the religious. As ideologeme, it operated in a field which is simultaneously ideological and semiotic: it was therefore the object of competing narratives and interpretations. Its fusion papered over the growing fissure between the religious establishment and political developments. Ideology exists, among other things, to disguise contradictions, even as it constitutes subjectivity by and within those contradictions.

This ideological analysis of the relations between the codes of kingship and the empire is confirmed by the manner and time of their fusion. A phrase that was to know a major fortune in the development of the "political theology" which transferred symbols and slogans from the religious to the political sphere was that which described the king of France as "emperor in his own kingdom."[36] The earliest use of that phrase occurs in 1190, after the first decade of the reign of Philip Augustus. It transforms the universal absolutism of an emperor's reign into the concrete powers of a king in a specifically and geographically limited *regnum*, a specific kingdom. That phrase, by itself, stands as the sign of the ideological functioning I have attempted to sketch out.

The Carolid ideologeme was made to function by association with the historical figure of the king. That association is first of all a fact of contiguity: as such, it is a metonymic or synecdochic relation that is established between the /king/ as a ruler of a kingdom and the /emperor/ as universal ruler. Like a metonymy, that synecdoche functions as the basis for a further metaphoric identification of the two terms in contiguity. The king, ruler of a *regnum* subordinate to the empire of the emperor, becomes identified with the emperor himself. The emperor, figuring in the ideological realm the fusion of two semantic traits felt to be growing further and further apart, /sacrality/ and /kingship/, turns into the figuration of the ideological ideal of Suger—whose institutional interests were served by such ideological fusion—that of a sacral kingship.[37] As noted above, if one actorial figure can be made to incorporate both semes of religiosity and politicality, what need is there to recognize the independent institutionalization of either seme? Indeed, it would be illogical, given this ideologeme, to present the Papacy as an independent narrative existent.

The linguistic study of the lexeme "emperor" produces analogous results. The original meaning of *imperator* is that of a general, a commander-in-chief. The meaning is then transferred outside the strictly military realm and acquires significations such as leader, chief, director, ruler, or master; even, in some cases, that of manager. Its applications are as an epithet of divinity, of Jupiter in particular; to designate the winner, in a game of chess; it is, finally the title of the Roman emperors. Other semantic traits were added in the course of time. The Carolingian thinkers, and after them the Germans, will develop the theme of the *dominium mundi*, the universality of the emperor's domination, especially after the return of Justinian law.[38] This universalism, however, can be modified, perhaps in reaction to the recognition, most immediately, of the Eastern empire that quite obviously did not enter under the dominion of any Western emperor. The empire can be conceived as a unit of a politico-religious nature, one of several, each claiming to represent the essential, central world, surrounded by other, peripheral worlds which are considered merely secondary. Thus there is lodged, within the *Chanson de Roland*, an assumption of the rightness of expansionism as policy and as strategy. The pagans are wrong, the Christians are right, and Charles's right to invade and subordinate Spain is not only never questioned: it requires no justification.

This universalism, even if modified, implies the subordination of the other rulers within the territory of the empire, the *reguli*. The emperor is a ruler under whose domination rule the kings of more limited territories. Again, the condition is one fulfilled by our text: Charles is described as having subordinated—with the help of Roland—the countries of the ancient Carolingian empire, and this at a time when the essential task of rulers was dominating their own feudal principality—the geographical equivalent of a modern province! Not only has Charles subordinated these princes, he also leads them into battle, in spite of the geographical distance and regional differentiation which opposed themselves to such subordination. Finally, the text assures the three elements of *actio* in Roman manner: *potestas, auctoritas,* and *imperium:* material force, moral and legal superiority, and the supreme power of military command, which are unhesitatingly attributed to the Charles of the text. The *Chanson de Roland* excludes broadly contemporary characteristics essential to the current conception of the emperor. Instead it reproduces (with some additions to be noted in a moment) the essential components of an earlier theory of emperorship, partly Roman, and more completely Carolingian. It would appear that the ideology survived, largely untouched by the shifting conflicts that preoccupied the Papacy and the claimants to the throne of emperor. The dualism of the empire and the Papacy institutionalized the Augustinian theme of the Two Cities, which is radically absent from our poem.

Religion is present in the poem, but never as an institutional alternative to the secular. Quite to the contrary, it is the highest figure of secular power which communicates both directly and indirectly with the Deity. The Church is represented in the narrative by the Archbishop Turpin, who—as we have seen—does pray for the assembled corpses of the Franks. Above all, however, he is characterized as a noble warrior, wielding his lance and sword with the best of them, on horseback like any other military hero, loyally subordinate to his feudal superior. To mount horeseback, to bear arms, to accept subordination to secular authority—normal encodings of vassalage—are "normal" only insofar as a secular code of values and behavior subordinates the clerical values of the time, as in the case of Roland, of Turpin, of Charlemagne. Insofar as religion is present in the narrative—and it is present only at selected moments which have little to do with the central political problematic of the poem—it is present as a secondary characteristic of the one and only sociopolitical organization functioning in the text, a syncretically unstable meld of feudalism and monarchy.

Reis and *Emperere* Textualized

A yet different picture arises when the two words *reis* and *emperere* are looked at within the strict textual context. In fact, in most uses, the two are interchangeable, without noticeable differentiation of meaning. The test comes in the commutation of terms in successive lines with analogous contents. Thus, to cite one case in which the two lines are, respectively, the last line of one *laisse* and the first line of the next, the switch between the two terms seems innocent of all semantic difference:

> Li *reis* li dunet e Rollant l'a recut. (*laisse* 62, l. 782)
> Li *empereres* apelet ses nies Rolland. . . . (*laisse* 63, l. 783)

> The *king* gives [it] to him, and Roland received it.
> The *emperor* calls his nephew Roland.

A stronger example is Charles's reaction to Aude's death:

> Quidet li *reis* que el se seit pasmee;
> Pited en ad, sin pluret *l'emperere*. . . . (ll. 3724f.)

> The *king* thinks she has fainted;
> he is moved, and the *emperor* weeps for her.

Such variations are determined more by variation of the signifier for /Charles/ or by formulaic structure than by a semantic difference attributable to the two words.[39] These examples suggest a rule to the effect that when "*rei (s)*" and "*emperere (s)*" occur within two lines and refer to the same actor (thus excluding a possible reference of "*emperere*" to Charles and "*reis*" to Marsile, for example), the meaning of the two terms is synonymous. Certain other uses confirm such an observation. In an expression such as "*(li) reis magnes*" (ll. 3611, 3622), the adjective is transferred, as in the very first line of the poem, from "Charlemagne," more readily associated with "emperor" than with "king." More telling yet, when the two terms recur in the same line (again as in the first line), the particular way in which they occur reinforces the same interpretation: "Carles li reis, l'emperere des Francs" (l. 2658). Here, "Charles" is directly qualified by "*reis*," and the term "emperor" is syntactically in apposition to it, implying equality of signification. Even more telling is the fact that "emperor" is in turn qualified and limited: Charles is termed "emperor of the Franks," a far more limited emperorship than was claimed by the emperor of the Holy Roman Empire, or the Carolingian emperor, Charlemagne.

In spite of these suggestions of fundamental equivalence, some differences in usage do exist which suggest, if not a great difference in denotation, at least variation in connotation. There is only one "king" besides Charles among the Christians: that is Vivian. But the pagan ranks number quite a few "kings," including those of Capadoce and of Niniven, kings who are qualified as *leutiz* or *leutice*, or *persis*, and kings who are granted the privilege of proper nouns: Almaris, Canabeus, Corsalis, Dapamort, Florede, Flurit, Malcud, Maltraien, Marsile, Suatilie, and Torleus; Marsile alone is referred to some thirty-five or more times, in different morphological forms of his name, as "king," either in direct address or in reference. A further distinction is strictly syntactical: *rei* seems to occur more often as object than does *emperere*. Thus, while no exact differentiation either in semantics or in usage can be drawn between the words "king" and "emperor," some shading does seem to distinguish them. In the absence of a specific distinction, either semantic or ideological, one may well think that, while its specifiable semantic content is more or less identical to that of "king," the term "emperor" is suggestive of a broader realm of domination: it reinforces the content of "king," it stresses that content, it perhaps means something like "very king," or "king to a superlative degree."

Given the very limited efficacy of the empire as a political reality, or of the emperor as a political agent, in the Francophone domain of the *Song of Roland*, one must ask where to locate the textual figure of the emperor-king of the *Roland* within the competing political and institutional forces of the time. The fusion of the religious and the secular in the figure of the *rex-sacerdos* contravenes quite directly the aims of the Gregorian reform, intent on controlling the secular by separating from it the ecclesiastical institutions and guaranteeing their independence. This reform represents a strategy in which the Church attempted to adapt itself to a new Christianity in the context of the enormous movement of forest-clearing, of the wave of the construction of churches and castles, the growth of towns, the development of long-distance commerce and of a monetary economy.[40] The earlier period had reacted in two opposed manners: integration within the world and its complete refusal. The Gregorian reform attempted a *via media*: to disengage the Church from the world, that is to say, secular society, in order to enable it better to dominate the new world. This middle way requires a separation of powers or realms precluded by their identification in actors such as Charlemagne and Turpin. The goals or interests of the Church are not represented by such ideologemes. On the contrary, the separation required by the Gregorian reform is directly contradicted by the syncretism of the Charles-figure, and by that of Turpin, representing a far earlier and more primitive fusion of the military and the religious.

Our textual-semantic study of the comparative uses of *reis* and *emperere* suggests the kind of narrative and political strategy which best functionalizes those findings. One explanation has the added advantage of readily fitting into another recognized technique specific to the *chanson de geste*. That is the entirely normal procedure of promoting a given figure to a higher actorial role: knight to lord, lord to king, and—in this case—king to emperor.[41] Both the semantic study and this encoding technique of rank promotion indicate the following simple equation: emperor = king +. This is particularly true in view of the ideological campaign noted above, to endow the Capetian kings of France with the efficacy of a "sacral kingship," a campaign whose success would both resound across centuries of French history and cause continued difficulties in the relations between the kings and the Church. In the context of a poem whose major concerns are political in nature—the distribution and control of military force and the hierarchical ranking of political instances—the captation of a sememe uniting the ideological values of /preeminence/, /religiosity/, and /universality/ is a potent move befitting the actor concerned in the accumulation of cultural and ideological value. In the first line of the poem, *Carles li reis, nostre emperere magnes,* the four syllables of the first hemistiche identify the actor concerned: the second hemistiche is an amplification, supported in numerous textual and narrative ways, of the basic actantial role set into play, that of the king. If this reading is correct, then the representation of this only apparently syncretic figure as a political agent is quite consonant with the realities of late eleventh- and twelfth-century French kingship, up until the second half of the reign of Philip Augustus. As one scholar primarily concerned with political thought has put it:

> The king's authority was not indeed questioned but it receded to a further remove. The kings themselves, imbibing the contemporary atmosphere, came to think of themselves not as monarch of Roman or Byzantine type but as lords at the head of a pyramid of personal loyalties. In the great French eleventh century epic poem, *The Song of Roland*, the king's chief vassals are "the peers of France" and Charlemagne in the poem is little more than the chief among them. France in the tenth and eleventh centuries offers the extreme example of the composition of royal power in favor of the great dukes and counts, though the Capetian dynasty of kings (from 987) clung to the prestige and aura of the old monarchical tradition and kept it alive against better days.[42]

Indeed, the hierarchical and rhetorical promotion we have studied is part of an effort to strengthen the monarchy on the basis of the recognition of the new social, political, and economic facts of the twelfth century. One feature of this new world was the extension and generalization of vassalic customs, which continued to spread since the time of Charlemagne. Although there was an element in the relation between king and subjects radically different from all other political relations, nevertheless that relation too was increasingly conceived of as a form of vassalic subordination: the bond between king and subject was seen as the result of a reciprocal commitment establishing an intimate bond and subordinating the subject's fidelity to the king's loyalty. As a result, the king ended by being confounded with a feudal lord.[43]

This confusion of royalty with feudal nobility was only one example of a phenomenon generalized throughout society. All social relations were transformed by a general current in the process of creating a new type of society: not even the bishops were exempted. Interestingly enough, neither was the historical emperor. In sequence, the Ottonians attempted to construct an emperorship based on the general support of the bishops, the creation of subordinate *regna*— an archaicizing effort which failed. This was succeeded by an effort at a *renovatio mundi* piously synthesizing various elements: installation in Rome, creation of a senate, the extension of courtesies to the kings. It was only at a third try that the "classic path" of feudalization was chosen: controlling fiefs and castles, having one's own bishops and vassals, controlling men and money, and being able—thanks to these means—to make oneself feared and obeyed.[44]

The actorial figure of "Charles" is highly syncretic, combining semantic elements of /feudal lord/, /king/, and /emperor/. The narrative performance of the figure, particularly in the council scenes, is very much that of a feudal lord; in the very vagueness of his preeminence, as well as in the geographical territories which are attributed to him, he "is" very much the king of France; and in his name, qualifiers, and superordinate status over the assemblage of troops from the distant regions that formed part of the Carolingian empire, he is quite identifiable with the figure of an "emperor." As lexeme and actor, then, "Charles" is a sliding signifier, producing vague and ambiguous significations. The ideological syncretism of the figure enables the text to produce the multiple significations implicit in the narrative text and to make their limitation quite difficult. What is a semiotic conundrum for the modern semiotician, however, is only the price to be paid for the text's performativity.

7 | Funerary Rituals

> . . . le langage ne peut jamais que tendre indéfiniment vers la justice en
> reconnaissant et en pratiquant la guerre en soi. Violence contre violence.
> *Economie* de la violence.
>
> Jacques Derrida, "Violence et métaphysique"

THE BALIGANT EPISODE interrupts, in its various segments, narrative developments whose coherence is defined by a common theme: not only do they come
after Roland's death, these narrative syntagms are concerned with problems
posed by that death.[1] As is well known, death is a problem for the living, not the
dead. Anthropologically speaking, the crucial problem is the reintegration of the
members of the social group into its unity after the disappearance of one of its
crucial members. Vis-à-vis the fact of death, the social group performs its rituals,
the means by which the disappearance of the dead is acknowledged and the social
reconstitution of the living achieved. The values of the group define the individual who dies a "hero," and his actions become the idealized narrative representation of at least one ideological potential in the group's semiotic universe.
Issues of responsibility and culpability, problems of the figuration of value in a
mode transcendent of the quotidian, the radical incommensurability between the
survivors and the human gap facing them—all are social and ideological fissures
obsessing the survivors, not those who are gone. The group's task is to knit again
the web of its social unity, to reintegrate its members into the collectivity.

The Unreintegrated Mourner

While portraying the generality of the surviving Frankish troops as grieving
their losses, the narrative focuses on the figure of Charles as survivor. It is Charles
who is cast into the textual figure of the consciousness of loss. The rhetorical
charge of this aspect of the figure is not to be denied.[2] It is perhaps that aspect
of the Roland-text which remains the most accessible to the poetic taste and values of the typical reader of our time: an academic reader, haunted by the nostalgia for an imagined past of wholeness and integration. The continued effectivity
of this emotional charge, however, must not be allowed to mask the fact that the
poem is here performing an essential operation. The section in question changes

things, it performs a transformation upon those materials which, at its beginning, are givens because they are the product of the earlier sections of the poem. In doing so, of course, it functions like any narrative syntagm: it constitutes a transformation of its narrative materials.

The essential moments of this transformation are three:[3] the lament for the dead; the revenge upon the retreating Saracens; and the discovery, collection, evisceration, and burial of the heroes' bodies. These three moments imply successive locative displacements: Roncevaux, the River Ibre, Roncevaux again. They also are constituted by different types of textualizations: as implied by the noun that designates it, the lament is a purely verbal textualization; the revenge, though it includes some dialogue, is primarily a narrative moment; the complex "burial" of the heroes is composed of a particular combination of the verbal and the narrative.

The lament takes the form, somewhat surprising, of a classical topos in an oral text: it is the first use of the *ubi sunt* theme in vernacular French poetry. The appearance of this poetic theme from the classical and written tradition in the oral text of the *Chanson* presents clear evidence of the mixed character of the *Chanson de Roland*. It is "mixed" not only in its ontological status but also in its socio-historical and ideological content. Its form as a rhetorical question— Where are the dead?—is "empty" in the sense that the question is not a real one: the answer is not open to question. In this case, the inevitable answer to the rhetorical question is, after each naming of a hero, that he is dead, dead on the field of battle, where the protection he had a right to expect from his feudal lord was not forthcoming—a feudal lord who is the one intoning the lamentation for the dead. Whether the *laisse* in question does name all the twelve peers or not, what it does accomplish is the presentation of a situation of tragic irony: an actor faces the disastrous results of his nonperformance of a contractual obligation. This cognitive moment is only narrativized here: it is verbally made explicit somewhat later.

Although "empty" in this sense, the lamentation in the form of *ubi sunt* does perform essential narrative structural roles. It presents itself as the expression of emotions, a theme textualized a number of times in this syntagm.[4] This textualization is a necessary precondition of the following narrative program. It is only once the emotions of Charles and his men have been given socio-textual existence that they provide the content of a qualifying statement justifying the revenge obtained against the fleeing Saracens. Duke Naimes intervenes upon the expression of the emperor's great grief, pointing to the fleeing Saracens:

"Veez avant de deus liwes de nus,
Vedeir puez les granz chemins puldrus,
Qu'asez i ad de la gent paienur.
Car chevalchez! Vengez ceste dulor!" (ll. 2425–28)

"Look, two leagues ahead of us,
see the great dusty roads,
there is the mass of the pagans:
Ride on! Avenge this pain!"

Vengez ceste dulor! provides the link between the emotion and the succeeding action.[5] The grief is experienced as an impermissible trespass upon the survivor, a damage done him for which legal reparation can be claimed. That reparation is the basic narrative stuff of the *chanson de geste* as a whole, in particular that which is known as the rebellious barons cycle: there, revenge is taken upon the feudal lord whose treatment of the vassal is unjust. Here, it is revenge against those who by definition have no moral or juridical status before a strictly Christian law, the nonbelievers. In any case, the survivor experiences his grief as an injury done him for which the appropriate mode of treatment is the exaction of vengeance, conceived as a legal mode of compensation. The expression of grief here transforms what a twentieth-century consciousness would consider pure interiority into a social and semiotic fact that is the basis for narrative action.

That narrative action is collective: "*tuit en sunt cummunel*" (l. 2446). In fact, it is so collective that it requires the intervention of God in a new mode. In the Roland-text, God intervenes by saintly interposition, either cognitively (as in the dreams brought to Charles by the Angel Gabriel) or pragmatically (to collect Roland's soul as his ultimate destinator). Here, however, God is presented as directly interfering with the operations of Nature: at Charles's prayer, God stops the flow of time to allow the Franks to catch up with the Saracens. It is thus a miracle, a type of grant of a magic adjuvant that had not been awarded Roland. As in the Roland-section, Charles is endowed with the power to receive privileged communication from God in the form of proleptic dreams. In this second major half of the *Chanson*, Charles will once again be visited by annunciatory dreams. His communicative competence with the Divinity extends to the point of being able to request and obtain a change in the fundamental assumptions, not only of human life, but of narrative per se. The suspension of the flow of time, the ability to perform narrative actions that would otherwise be prevented by something as fundamental as the passage of time, changes the very conditions of possibility of narrative itself. What would be impossible for any normal /human/actor becomes possible for Charles. The miraculous interference of the Divinity in the workings of Nature foreshadows the perhaps equally miraculous solution that will be achieved in the final trial scene of the epic.

At this occasion, "religion" makes a striking entry into a text which is anything but religious or Christian in its fundamental content. In view of this limited import, the form this religiosity takes should be noted. It constitutes a direct grant of power to Charles as king and emperor, utterly disregarding (as the poem does in general) the historical institutions of religion: the medieval Church in any of its forms. It may well be that the pope and emperor are mutually defining binary opposites in the historical, extra-textual domain:[6] in this concrete text, the pope and the institution he heads simply does not exist. All the ideological power associated with the pope and the Church in contemporary cultural codes are attributed to the figure of the king of France who is also the emperor of Christendom. Within the economy of the text, this "extra" ideological valorization is of the same order and function as the Baligant episode: the extraordinary investment of ideological value in this particular figure is functionalized by the need to enable him to perform certain narrative acts that might otherwise prove too difficult for an ordinary human agent. The character of these acts, the specific isotopy on which they will occur, is indicated by the third Moment.

Having despatched the fleeing Saracens by drowning and the sword, Charles and his men return to Roncevaux. This a/b/a structure marks the revenge wrought upon the Saracens as necessary, but also as a necessary interruption of the basic business of this section, namely the enactment of the rituals of the dead. Before their performance, however, the weary Franks take their rest and sleep for the night. Charles lies down as well, but he does not fall asleep immediately:

> Carles se gist, mais doel ad de Rollant
> E d'Oliver li peseit mult forment,
> Des .XII. pers e de la franceise gent
> Qu'en Rencesvals ad laiset morz sanglenz.
> Ne poet muer n'en plurt e nes dement
> *E priet Deu qu'as anmes seit guarent.* (ll. 2513–18)

> Charles lies down, but his grief for Roland
> and Oliver weighs upon him heavily,
> for the twelve peers and the Frankish army
> whom he left, bloody and dead, at Roncevaux.
> He cannot help but weep and lament,
> *and pray to God He may protect their souls.*

As at the moment of Roland's death, when he surrenders his glove to God as a sign of final and ultimate fealty, so here as well the relation of the individual to his God is figured by the feudal metaphor, the divine assumption of dead souls and hope for their salvation being figured by the relationship of feudal protection: Charles implores God to enact toward his dead vassals precisely that relationship he himself was unable to perform and which, as a result of his failure, caused those vassals' death.

When Charles, wearied by grief, does fall asleep, it is to encounter annunciatory dreams that parallel those of the first part. In terms of the twentieth-century reader, these proleptic dreams "make sense," i.e., carry specific meaning, only on the basis of a retrospective reading: one must have read the *Chanson* to the end at least once before in order to understand that these two successive dreams refer first to the impending battle with Baligant and second to the trial scene at Aix, with an allegorical representation or pre-presentation of Ganelon, his thirty relatives, and both Thierry and Pinabel. Reading, for us, is a punctual, datable event, whose cognitive function is clearly delimitable. But the cognitive conditions of the medieval audience were quite different from ours. For the medieval audience, there is likely never to have been a "first" time: the *Chanson de Roland*, from what we know of it, was a popular text, and is likely to have been performed by *jongleurs* repeatedly, albeit in different forms. As a result, the events of the poem have an identity under the specific variations characteristic of any individual performance: they exist in some field of permanence external to the particular performance. Functionally speaking, they exist in a sphere that is analogous to the neo-Platonism typical of medieval aesthetics descending from Philo and St. Augustine. As a result, the meaning of these proleptic dreams, definable for the modern reader only on a linear dimension of temporality, are extra-temporal for the medieval audience of the oral performance *and* immediately accessible. That audience, even illiterate, will always already have known the story and its outcome: even though this was obviously not true in any one particular case (even a medieval individual biography had to contain a "first" time hearing of the text), it is nevertheless an ontological condition of the oral medieval text that its basic narrative pattern has to be construed as always already known.

Thus it is that the proleptic dreams that come to Charles, ambiguous as they are if taken in a unidirectional successive temporal sequence that permits them to be semantically informed only by a retrospective look upon the narrative, must be considered as endowed with the semantic content that, for the modern interpretant, derives from a forward look to the later narrative events. In this respect, the dream-text is "closed": its meaning is determined by its narrative insertion. The first dream sets Charles in a battle accompanied by multiple "natural" signs of terror—thunder, winds, and ice, storms and tempests, fires and flames falling upon his army; lances and shield take fire, weapons and armor twist, and the army is in great distress. It is attacked by bears, leopards, serpents, vipers, dragons, and demons—a plethora of the supernatural, to which are added 30 million griffins! The battle is general, until Charles himself is attacked by a great lion filled with rage, pride, and courage. There is little reason to hesitate in identifying the proleptic narrative referent of this *laisse* as the later battle between the Frankish army, led by Charles, and the troops of Baligant, a battle which will find its conclusion in the individual combat between the two emperors. The second dream, localized at Aix, sets into the dream scene one chained bear and thirty more claiming to be his relatives and demanding that he be returned to them. At this point, a hunting dog arrives, a greyhound to be exact, who attacks the largest of the thirty bears. The emperor witnesses a miraculous combat, but, as in the preceding dream, does not know in his dream who wins. Again, there is little reason to hesitate in juxtaposing this dream with the combat between Pinabel, representing the thirty relatives of Ganelon at his trial who are also his hostages, against Thierry, the lean and unheroic knight who will, in fact, win against Pinabel.

The structural import of these dream syntagms is not their allegorical significance, which is so patent as not to require "interpretation" in any serious sense at all, but rather their function within a narrative structure. They occur at the hinge point between two larger syntagms: the narrative of the funereal rituals of the survivors and the beginning of the Baligant episode. Whether they are to be considered a part of the former or of the latter is not an issue for the present reading, which accepts the presence of the Baligant material along with a conviction of its later and additive nature. For these proleptic dreams, the meaning they bear and which is demonstrated to Charles by the Angel Gabriel, who brings him the dreams themselves (*senefiance l'en demustrat mult gref*, l. 2531),[7] rejoin a general semantic level of the text. They demonstrate the connection of the present narrative moment with a later one, by "re-telling" the later diegetic and narratively "real" event ahead of time, before its actual occurrence in the narrative. The establishment of the semantic connection produces the meaning that both the funereal rituals and the Baligant episode have to be seen in relation to the later syntagms they announce. In particular, the funereal rituals and the reintegration they operate lead to the ultimate narrative sequence of Ganelon's trial. They *lead to it* in that they perform a function that is prerequisite to the later narrative syntagm. The reintegration of the living must be performed before the final judgment of the cause and responsibility for the dead can be passed. Ganelon's trial could not occur unless its actors retrieved their full standing as subjects within the social group.

This suggests, rather profoundly, how far outside the circle of the social group is the present position of the actors, and of Charles in particular.

After the Baligant episode stages the encounter of Baligant's messengers and Marsile, and then between Baligant himself and his vassal, the text shifts back to Charles at Roncevaux. The third moment of the funereal syntagm is the essential one. It is constituted by a compound of verbal and narrative subsections, including both Charles's search in the battlefield with 20,000 dead and the speech we have already examined, in which he laments Roland's death. We have already seen Charles recall his nephew's arrogant boast of knightly prowess— that he would die farther forward than any of his men or peers—in a reminder of the traits which made the knightly class so problematic for their lords and for society at large. The political isotopy is doubled by the familial bond, reiterated several times.[8] The "regret" for Roland is identical with the earlier *plainte's* invocation of the *ubi sunt* theme: like the *ubi sunt* theme, it looks backward and stresses the absence of the dead. Charles's lamentation, however, does the opposite. The absence of the dead is presented in a proleptic framework, looking forward to a future point in time and presentifying the effects that Roland's death and absence will have in the future. Recommending Roland to God's mercy, Charles touches on his uniqueness as a warrior and concludes the first brief speech: "La meie honor est turnet en declin" (l. 2890). Literally, "my 'honor' is turned toward its decline." The strangeness of the word "honor" has already been noted. What is restricted to the valorial field for us moderns—"honor" for us is strictly a matter of opinion, either internal or that which others hold of an individual—is simultaneously material in the medieval language.[9] "Honor" can indeed have the same meaning it has for us, the credit or esteem in which a given individual is held by his fellows; but it also has the meaning of the complex of land and social organization which produces wealth and power and which often takes the specific form of a fief. Indeed, the ambiguity of the word (an ambiguity which exists only for us, since we—unlike the medievals—separate the material base from its ideological value) suggests the interdependence of the two semantic components: one is not "honorable" unless one has a certain material base of power and wealth; and possessing such a base produces the credit and esteem of one's fellows, unless one acts in such a way as to lose that respect. In certain ways, the Middle Ages were far more materialistic than we are; or perhaps their materialism was simply more self-evident.

Charles's *honor* is then his reputation, and that complex of geographical territory and sociopolitical organization is the base of that reputation: his fief, his kingdom, his empire. All three are profoundly weakened by Roland's death.

Charles's *plainte*, complexly turned toward the past and the future, retrospective and proleptic simultaneously, will touch upon a number of themes. Grief is not the only emotion textualized. In the second of five *laisses* in which Charles mourns Roland, he recapitulates a number of these themes, and he associates grief with culpability:

"Ami Rollant, Deus metet t'anme en flors,
En pareis, entre les glorius!
Cum en Espaigne venis a mal seignur!
Jamais n'ert jurn de teie n'aie dulur.
Cum decarrat ma force e ma baldur!
N'en avrai ja ki sustienget m'onur. . . . " (ll. 2898–2903)

"Friend Roland, may God place your soul among flowers,
in paradise, among those of glory!

What a { bad / evil } *lord you followed to Spain!*

Never will a day pass I do not grieve for you.
How my force and my joy will decline!
None will I have to sustain my honor. . . . "

In these speeches, Charles more often refers to Roland on the familial isotopy, naming him as nephew repeatedly.[10] The feudal isotopy is specifically evoked only once, in the line in which Charles refers to himself as Roland's lord. And of course, it identifies him as a *bad* lord. In the one occurrence of the feudal isotopy, it is connected, as we have learned to expect from the earlier discussion, with the issue of culpability.

The necessary dualism of funereal ritual—"letting go" and reaffirming the unity of the social group, assertions of absence and presence as simultaneities—is thus laid over, by Charles's own complaint, with the specifically political form which is the ultimate isotopy of the *chanson de geste* in general. That dualism is restated in the most primitive moment of the ritual, in the burial of the great majority of the dead, the extraction of the hearts of the heroes—Roland, Oliver, and Turpin—and their enclosure in marble sarcophagi, well washed with spices and wine. The hearts are to retain for the survivors the strength of the dead, even as their (ultimate) burial is to recognize their departure. Presence and absence both, the anthropological ritual has a complexity that the political does not. Where the funereal ritualization of loss affirms a duality against the brutal fact of death, the political isotopy allies itself with that brutality. There is nothing in this *plainte* about the inspirational value of the legend and *chanson* to be told and sung about Roland and his peers. In Charles's political evaluation of the meaning of Roland's loss, there is room only for loss, for the resulting political and military weakness of his reign. His personal grief is doubled by a political issue that overrides the personal. Indeed, the personal must be expressed, indulged in perhaps, in order to allow for the movement toward the political. For the personal loss is not resolved but met by the funerary rituals of the text; the political loss, and its implications, must yet be met and resolved, more directly and more brutally.

Finally, the syntagm of funeral ritual has as narrative function the (re)statement of this dual valorization of the loss of the hero, the personal and the political. It does so with an internal organization of closure. I have pointed out that the first Roncevaux syntagm is verbal, the Ebre syntagm is narrative, and that the second Roncevaux syntagm is both verbal and narrative. That second Roncevaux syntagm, however, is internally organized in a pattern that is recursive of the overall organization of the ritual syntagm. Its first "move" is to discover Roland: as we have seen, that takes a predominantly verbal form as Charles recounts Roland's earlier boast at Aix. That is followed by another verbal syntagm, Charles's long lamentation. These two verbal syntagms are followed by the concluding syntagm, narrative in nature, in which the dead are buried, the heroes have their hearts extracted and are both shrouded and encased in sarcophagi. This recursivity, recapitulating in the final narrative subsection the pattern of the whole, thereby gives closure to the whole. That closure marks the fact that one moment of the narrative has ended and another begins.

The Death of Aude, or the Refusal of Exchange

The major burden of the text after the conclusion of the Baligant episode is to deal finally with the issue of culpability for Roland's death, as well as the sociopolitical development of a way to prevent the recurrence of what led to the disaster at Roncevaux. In the Oxford *Roland*, the syntagm concerned with these issues—Ganelon's trial—is preceded by a brief, two-*laisse* passage that returns to the isotopy of the funeral rituals. It also initiates another isotopy, that of exchange: the brief episode is a narrative isotopic connector between the funeral rites and the trial.

The emperor has returned to Aix. Aude, Roland's betrothed, comes to the court to ask for her man. She asks, and the manner in which she asks and the manner in which her demand is received indicate that what she asks for is her right. Charles acknowledges Roland's death; he offers instead his son Louis as substitute. The text asserts the advantageous character of this offer: Louis would inherit Charles's reign. Nevertheless, Aude rejects the offer, and does so radically: she dies on the spot. Her corpse is turned over to nuns in a convent, who bury her properly, alongside an altar:

> Mult grant honur i ad li reis dunee. (l. 3733)

> The king gave [the convent] very great honor.

The syntax suggests what the text does not specify: that the "honor" is financial value.

The syntagm is framed by two lines that seem to announce something else. The two *laisses* of the Aude syntagm are *laisses* 268 and 269. The last line of *laisse* 267—preceding the Aude-syntagm—announces a different topic:

> Dès ore cumencet le plait de Guenelun. (l. 3704)

> Then begins Ganelon's trial.

Then, in *laisse* 270, the theme of the return to Aix is restated (l. 3734) and developed, and in the following *laisse*, the beginning of Ganelon's trial is announced once again:

> Dès ore cumencet le plait et les noveles
> De Guenelen, ki traïsun ad faite. (l. 3747f.)

Then begins the trial, the arguments, and the charges
of Ganelon, who committed treason.

Thus, both before and after the Aude-syntagm, Ganelon's trial is announced. It
is patent that the Aude-syntagm is not Ganelon's trial, or any part thereof. Nevertheless, the repeated assertion of the text suggests a connection between Aude's
death and Ganelon's trial.

The genetic explanation for both the discrepancy between the topic announced in l. 3704, and the succeeding syntagm, and the isotopic continuity between the earlier section, which deals with the funeral rituals of the dead of
Roncevaux and the Aude-scene at Aix, is fairly obvious. In an earlier stage of
the *Chanson de Roland*, the episode of funereal ritual and the death of Aude were
two subsidiary parts of the same narrative syntagm whose topics were the collective and individual griefs and the rituals of reintegration and exclusion that
follow upon the death of the culture-hero, the icon of the warrior society. It is a
syntagm whose topic is the reconstitution of the collectivity after a disaster which
calls its very values into question. The present state of the evolution of the oral
epic contains an additional syntagm, inserted between two subsidiary parts of
the earlier stage, in which an outsider and his troops come and interrupt the
collective ritual of grief and reconstitution. The Baligant episode, in other words,
interrupts a narrative unit which had a unified production of meaning dealing
with social emotions after a great disaster, intervening between the narration of
the great defeat itself and the legal and political fallout that succeeds it. The new
episode interrupts the sequence: (loss) + (mourning) + (adjustment), each of
these terms occurring on both the individual and the collective isotopies.

The present syntagm adds new elements to the textual production of signification; it also introduces a new cultural and valorial logic of coherence into the
world of textuality. Insofar as social contracts determine the exchange of social
value, Charles does more than merely discharge his responsibility as a social
agent: his offer contains a valorial supplement, a surplus value which might have
been expected to determine, even to overdetermine, an acceptance by the recipi-
ent of the communicative exchange. The surplus value here is the difference between the value of a great noble, even a culture hero, and the king's son. More
determining than cultural values, the political value, and the implicit territorial
and financial values, is expected to assuage the damage to her own value that
Aude has undergone in her grief and the loss of her betrothed. Aude's refusal is
all the more striking then, because it not only rejects the proposed exchange and
the supplementary surplus value it contains: in her death, she also refuses any
further social intercourse and verbal exchange with the destinator.

To the modern reader, the notion of the substitution Charles proposes seems
absurd: how shall one man be accepted as the substitute for another in a romantic relationship which consists precisely in the election of one individual as the

unique cathexis of certain emotions? Here again, twentieth-century codes are inappropriate. Marriage, far from an expression of the romantic election of another person as the primary cathexis of the individual and the announcement to the collectivity of the couple's desire to make their union permanent (perhaps, at this point on the edge of the twenty-first century, already a somewhat old-fashioned view of marriage!), marriage in the Middle Ages, at the social level with which we are concerned, is a dynastic and diplomatic affair generally more concerned with the aggrandizement of dominion over lands and other forms of property than with tender emotions.[11] Not that tender emotions do not exist in this text, or in the epic in general: they do, and this particular syntagm is only one example of such emotions in the *Chanson de Roland*. Others are the not infrequent references to wives and women who wait for the warriors in *dulce France*, to whom they are eager to return; the equivalent is stated of the Saracen warriors. The text recognizes such attachments as normative and refers to them without hesitation. But the text is a warrior epic, and such topics are not the topics which are developed within its frame; in this respect, the Old French epic is poorer than the Greek. On the other hand, while the Greek epic may be more inclusive, the French is more intense and perhaps accomplishes social transformations that remain unthought of in the *Iliad*. While the tender emotions do exist at the edges of the *Roland*, however, they are not the basis of the politics of marriage, nor are they a major concern of the text. The theme of individual fidelity is touchingly deployed here, but it masks another operation that is of more moment to the achievement of this text.

The two *laisses* that deal with Aude are more than a romantic interlude (the way they have most frequently been taken by traditional criticism), and more than a textual supplement incorporated into the text itself. They have a function, they perform a transformation. First of all, the narrative syntagm provides an isotopic connector, incorporating the theme of death, and of Roland's death in particular, within a textual space that also places the action at Aix, where the trial takes place. It does more than merely state these two themes of death and the trial simultaneously, however. The funerary theme, as we saw, was meant to achieve the reintegration of society as a whole after a crucial loss, and in particular the reintegration of the primary grievant, Charles. That reintegration is not achieved yet, however. Charles's effort to set things right, as feudal overlord, as monarch, as uncle, is unsuccessful: the issue of compensation for Roland's death is still unsettled.

That issue is as foreign to the modern reader as that of the values actually involved in noble marriage. Whether because of a religious heritage that can be taken to assert the sanctity of human life or because of a tradition of individual subjectivity which represents each person as a unique phenomenon, our ideology does not allow for the principle of compensation to be recognized overtly in cases of death.[12] Both the Judaic and the Germanic traditions are more sensible. Acknowledging that perhaps there are emotional components in such a loss for which compensation is literally unimaginable, both traditions recognize that the dead person was also a social value, and that compensation for that aspect of the person can be arranged. A system of exchange, in which the social being of the individual is recognized as a social value for which other forms of social value can be exchanged, is elaborated in both traditions. It is probably the Germanic tradition which was most determinative in shaping medieval attitudes. The tradition of a fixed tariff of equivalencies—the *wergeld*—of compensation, even in the case of the unemendable *morth* (murder), was a characteristic of archaic German law which continued into the period of the *Chanson de Roland*.[13] Such legal compensation is an extension of the principle of exchange into the domain of law, even as law governs the most extreme disruptions of social relations. The principle of exchange is at work, then, in Charles's offer, which is neither unfeeling nor crude: it is a recognition both of the reality of loss and of the limited nature of the compensation that society, as an entity, is capable of providing its members. The offer is an entirely appropriate enactment of social and conventional codes and bears with it a surplus of valorial supplementation that signifies generosity or, in medieval terms, *largesse*.

Nevertheless, the offer is absurd, even in Charles's own terms. Charles's offer refers to Roland as an *hume mort*. In a line already quoted, he says to Aude:

"Jo t'en durai mult esforcet eschange." (l. 3714)

"I will give you a highly augmented exchange."

Aude's response, by its very rhyme within an assonanced text, stresses that it is the notion of exchange she is rejecting:

Alde respunt: "Cest mot mei est estrange." (l. 3717)

Aude answers: "This word is foreign to me."

What is *estrange* (L. *extraneum*; foreign; the term belongs to the same semantic family as the Greek *barbaroi*) is exchange. Aude takes the position that no exchange is possible for Roland: it is an anomalous position in the codes of her society. It is also a costly position to take: it costs her her life. The beloved's death implies an absolute cathexis on one individual. What may strike the post-romantic reader as a literary cliché is, in the textual and cultural context of the end of the eleventh and the beginning of the twelfth centuries, quite remarkable. That anomalous character, rather than the romantic associations, is what is textually most functional.

Oddly enough, Aude's refusal of the principle of exchange in connection with Roland had been prefigured in our text, and prefigured by none other than Charles himself. It was Charles who, speaking of Roland to Naimes, said earlier:

"Deus! se jol pert, ja n'en avrai escange." (l. 840)

"God! if I lose him, I'll never have an [equal] exchange for him."

It was Charles himself, then, who established the principle of non-substitutability in Roland's case, well before he offered a substitute for Roland to Aude. Aude's refusal is merely a reiteration to Charles of Charles's own understanding: it is his own cognition that comes back to haunt him. No man can be a substitute for Roland. Roland was unique, but as soon as that is said, it is crucial to specify what that adjective comports, lest our conceptions of the uniqueness of the individual flood into the receptacle of the waiting signifier.

Roland's uniqueness, at the actorial level, is specified so frequently that it is hardly necessary to cite those bits of the text in question. It is military, and hence political. Not only is there no trace of a unique interiority in Roland—one might make a better argument for Oliver, Charles, or Ganelon in this regard—but his uniqueness is entirely constituted by the social qualities which are those of his social class carried to extremes: both his warring abilities and their character-ological implications are those of the knight as a social type. Simply, he has a far greater allotment of the specific traits than the ordinary knight. In terms of the inner/outer dichotomy, Roland's uniqueness, like his individualism, is entirely "external." What counts is not some hidden and unique subjectivity, but the fact that, as a Subject, Roland is capable of undertaking narrative programs—and carrying them out successfully—that no one else can.

Aude's refusal of Charles's offer, and the implication of Roland's uniqueness that it bears, has as its meaning a reassertion of the momentous loss that is Roland's death. It reasserts that the issues implicit in that death, and in the nar-rative syntagms that lead up to it, have not yet been resolved, especially as they attach themselves to Charles's person. Not only is the sequence of funerary ritu-als undergone ineffective in reintegrating Charles as survivor into the social group. Insofar as Aude is in her rights in demanding of Charles her betrothed, his inability to produce Roland causes her death: another element of culpability is added to the unresolved issues of the text.

Not only is the ideal hero of the society dead and its ruler and Destinator inculpated: the basic principle of social organization—that of exchange—has been interrupted and suspended. This is the ultimate significance of Aude's re-fusal. If the normal pattern of exchanges encoded in the laws and conventions of the society no longer hold; if the damage to the social fabric is so grievous that its system of compensatory awards is refused by those whom it should benefit; then the very principle of sociality has been suspended. What is at stake is not a romantic attachment, nor even the justice to be accorded heroism, betrayal, and contractual responsibility: because of the characteristics of the textual actors involved, what is at stake is the continuation of society. The subject as hero has died in spite of a contract of protection between himself and the ruler of the society who is the destinator of the subject's narrative. The stakes that are set into play by the *Song of Roland*—as by any great work, from the *Iliad* and the Greek tragedians to Samuel Beckett—are the ultimate values of the society in which it is embedded. That "setting into play" is also a "setting at risk": each time textuality "plays" with the values of its social structure, it not only takes the risks of an aesthetic adventure, it also risks the survival of the social text, the social fabric, the social body.

The Transformative Performance

These risks, these stakes, are now the burden of Charles. That simple statement of the obvious defines the essential transformation that has occurred during the preceding segments of the narrative. That transformation lies on the actantial level. During the Roland-sequence, Charles is cast as the destinator of the narrative. As such, he is also the source of both legitimacy and values for the narrative program undertaken by the subject. It is a truism of semiotic theory that any subsidiary actor can also be the subject of his or her own narrative program: we have found ample evidence that this was so even for Charles as destinator in the Roland-sequence. What is at stake here, however, is quite a different matter. It is not a question of being the subject of a particular narrative program that can be subsumed by the overall narrative trajectory: it is a question of becoming the subject of that overall narrative trajectory itself. What has been achieved by the syntagms of ritualized lamentation, burial and evisceration, collective revenge and valorization, is the transformation of Charles the destinator into subject of the narrative text itself.

Charles does not thereby cease his performance of the role of destinator. Rather, the actor Charles now performs both roles simultaneously in a syncretism that, curiously enough, is typical, not of any genre of eleventh- or twelfth-century narrative, but of the twentieth-century novel. The effect of this syncretism is to bring into play, and to put at risk, the fundamental values of the social group. The destinator is the repository of these values: indeed, the "destinator" is merely an anthropomorphic designation of the textual instance from which those values are deployed. It is from the destinator that those values are forwarded to the subject, that they may be deployed in narrative action. It is from that instance equally that an ultimate judgment is emitted: that is the function of sanction. The separation of the two fundamental actantial functions—that of the destinator and that of the subject—allows for the possibility that the latter's narrative tests only his individual ability to enact the destinator's values, not the values themselves. The transformation of the destinator into narrative subject is therefore fraught with profound significance: it is the fundamental values which the social group invests in the test that will be called into question by the narrative of the destinator-turned-subject, not merely the performance of those values by a subject who may or may not be up to their enactment. Turning the destinator into narrative subject ineluctably brings into question, not how individuals may act out the values of society, but the values themselves.

8 | Textual Coherence and the Dialectics of Ideology

> Narrative discourse often presents itself in the form of a circulation of objects of value; its organization can then be defined as a series of transfers of values.
>
> Greimas and Courtés, *Semiotics and Language*

WHAT HAS COME to be known as the "Baligant episode" is awkward to deal with. Both its intrinsic problematic and the scholarly bibliography that attends it are imposing. The latter, however, is largely cast in terms which are of dubious relevance today. The argument of philologically inspired scholarship was cast in terms of the "authenticity" of the Baligant episode, this "authenticity" being determined by the scholar's opinion as to whether the syntagm in question was part of the "original" *Roland* or not. The epistemic framework of this scholarship recognized only graphic text: written signs inscribed on some kind of permanent material. Discoveries first centered on Homeric epic, then on continuing traditions of popular, recited narrative on the European continent, led to the recognition of a category, necessary for the students of a wide variety of texts (including the medieval), previously categorized as "literature" in the philological sense, of "oral literature."[1] What originally appeared to be an oxymoron has now gained general acceptance. Homeric epic and medieval epics such as the *Chanson de Roland* are strong indicators of the effective existence of a tradition of oral composition, performance, and reception, all three moments being instantaneously present in the moment of performance. Such a tradition consists of the continual recomposition of the oral text in all the varieties of concrete social situations that are appropriate to oral performance within a particular social formation. That process of recomposition includes a wide spread of textual variability, affecting all levels of the text, from the phonic elements of language to the large narrative syntagms such as the Baligant episode. Major elements in what would have been considered the "plot" of a story are added or subtracted quite normally in the context of oral tradition, even where the text in question is a highly admired and respected one. Value, here, is not associated with self-identity but with a supple adaptability to new contexts and potentials of signification.

Empirical research on both oral field materials and inherited written texts has affected the more general theory of textuality as directed toward medieval problematics. The recognition of orality as a cultural phenomenon and its incorporation in a large number of medieval texts has led to substantial modification in the posing of interpretative issues. The problem is no longer whether the Baligant episode is authentic or not. The normal path of textual development in an oral culture is through a process of textual accretion.[2] As a result, the notion of "an original text" is recognized as an ideologeme belonging more to nineteenth- and early twentieth-century problematics than to the Middle Ages, and the issue of "authenticity" disappears: the Baligant episode is authentic precisely because it is a later addition within an ongoing and continually developing process of textual creation, conceived as an endless process of invention, modification, and transformation.[3]

In this as in so many other areas, the fluid, ceaselessly energetic and inventive process of textual and social creation of the Middle Ages has been cast into the rigidifying molds of modern categories. Not that this should be considered morally blameworthy. The fact is that modern scholarship of the nineteenth and twentieth centuries is held prisoner by its own modes of perception and conceptualization. These include the "material" facts of empirical data. Not only most of the entities that are addressed by our "literary" scholarship and criticism but even the very texts that represent oral traditions come to us prepackaged in stable, permanent, supposedly unchanging form of print publication. The written text, whether of a manuscript, print, or xerographic culture, is inherently antagonistic to the oral tradition. The written text is the transformation—more or less exact—of speech as orality into language as graphic inscription, and it is a transformation that kills the orality. It is only in their betrayal that we can perceive these "texts," it is only through their contraries that we can enter the process of constructing models to account for their existence and functioning.

One approach would be to consider these written texts more or less accidental incorporations and indexes of larger, more fluid and permanently shifting entities, the realms of "meaning" that might have been apprehended at the performance of a particular moment of the epic story as broad, vague, and nonlimitable nebulae of semantic refulgence—somewhat similar to Saussure's conception of the world of ideation prior to the introduction of language.[4] Writing up the results of such a research program might require the talents of a poet in addition to those of a scholar, but the goal would certainly be worthwhile. Another approach—which I make mine—is to accept the "texts" we inherit as texts in the strong, semiotic sense: as coherent processes of signification and, more important, as signifying processes that are transformational in nature. While such a "take" on the texts we inherit is a limiting one of only partial legitimacy, it is one which our epistemic dispensation enables us to enact with interesting and valuable results.[5]

The particular manuscript—Digby 23, in the Bodleian Library at Oxford—freezes one instant of a fluid, ongoing oral tradition. That instant occurred in specific circumstances that are also lost to us: possibly a performance in the great hall of a feudal castle-master; possibly before a more popular audience in a town marketplace; possibly in the halting and continually interrupted dictation of an illiterate jongleur to a more or less distracted cleric inscribing what he heard (possibly not exactly what was being said, chanted, or intoned) on the parchment before him; possibly a jongleur himself, literate this time, inscribing on parchment what he thought he would have sung at that moment had he been in a performance situation, or perhaps what he would have liked to sing had such material been acceptable to any potential audience; or possibly some other social circumstance I have not thought of. Any one of these modes of (re-)performance might well have been accompanied by elements of intonation, musical effects, gestural mimicry, even broader stage or dance movements, providing both ornamentation and quite possibly additional semiotic elements of signification, that are— again—entirely lost to us as twentieth-century readers.[6]

All that remains of the eleventh- or twelfth-century performance is an incomplete aspect of the total performance situation we would like to examine, were it only possible.[7] It is not possible, and its impossibility determines that we examine only that trace called "textuality," which is only a partial aspect of the semiosis of the original event inscribed in the text. With one additional element. The concrete social situation of performance, and the date of performance, are lost, almost certainly irretrievably. What is not lost, however, is a general temporal frame, and a general social context within which the text is to be located. The social and historical parameters thus established allow for a verification of semantic investments, as well as an understanding of the individual text as part of the larger social text of the period. In this manner, the particular problematics of an oral text rejoins the general problematics of a socio-historical semiotics.

Textual Coherence: The Narrative

In its internal narrative structure, the Baligant episode poses no difficulty: its narrative is quite coherent. It begins with a reference to the second verse of the very first *laisse* of the poem, invoking the seven years that Charles has spent in Spain (l. 2610), and then introduces a major new actor in the text: the Emir Baligant, older than Virgil and Homer. Baligant has never been mentioned in the text before. According to *laisse* 189, Marsile had sent word to Baligant at the beginning of the hostilities between himself and Charles, requiring his aid and threatening to abandon his idols if Baligant fails to provide such help. That was seven years earlier. What reasons may be alleged to explain the seven-year delay are not mentioned. Arriving in Spain, the emir sends messengers to Marsile, demanding that he come to Baligant *pur reconoistre sun feu*, to acknowledge his fief (l. 2680). The messengers' arrival in Saragossa is surrounded by lamentations. In extensive discussion with the messengers Marsile rehearses his defeat in the preceding encounter with Charles. The messengers then remount and return to Baligant, communicate the sad news to him, as a result of which Baligant rides to Saragossa with his *paien d'Arabie* to receive the fief of Spain back from his dying vassal (ll. 2827–44). At this point the narrative of Digby 23 is interrupted to allow for the rituals in observance of the Frankish dead.

After the interruption, both pagan and Christian forces form their order of battle: first Charles and then, in less detail, the emir organize their forces. As in earlier battles, there is a movement from the general to the particular, from the lesser knights to the greater: the final combat is between the ultimate incorporations of the two sides, their leaders, Charles and Baligant. Although the emir lands a blow on his opponent's head that goes through his helmet and reaches his head, making Charles waver and nearly fall, the Christian emperor receives divine aid:

> Mais deus ne volt qu'il seit mort ne vencut
> Seint Gabriel est repairet a lui,
> Si li demandet: "Reis magnes, que fais tu?" (ll. 3609–11)

> But God does not want him killed or vanquished.
> Saint Gabriel returns to him,
> and asks: "Great king, what are you doing?"

The angel's voice reinvigorates Charles, who quickly despatches the emir and thereby puts to flight the remaining pagans. The section concludes after noting that Charles has now conquered Saragossa, thus completing the narrative program indicated in the first *laisse*. The city is turned over to Charles by Marsile's widow Bramimonde, who will undergo conversion to Christianity shortly.

From the perspective of a modern reader, the major content of the Baligant episode—the battle narration— follows the basic epic formulae without quite achieving the intensity of the earlier Roland battles. It is fairly tiresome: I know few readers of the text who reread these descriptions with any pleasure. Nevertheless, the impact of this section upon the text as a whole is major. One scholar wrote that with the Baligant episode, the poem is far more ambitious and noble, producing a political and religious signification which makes of the text "l'épopée d'un monde et d'une époque."[8] The ideological investment in such an aesthetic judgment is worth noting: that comment repeats the gesture of the epic poem itself in eradicating both the textual Saracens and their historical allegoremes, the Moslems of the Middle Ages, by constituting the poem that eradicates them as the "epic of a world and an epoch." It would seem that, after the Second World War, it would be appropriate to take one's distance from the totalitarian implications of an aggressive expansionism, even one that existed eight centuries ago, as well as from the genocide that it implied. More nuanced is the judgment of Joseph Duggan, who writes:

The duel between Charlemagne, emperor of Western Europe, and Baligant, supreme lord of the Arab world, transforms the poem from the account of a battle in the Pyrénées between French and Saracen fighting men, brought about by the personal resentment of one Christian chief for another, into an almost cosmic struggle of good and evil wherein right triumphs over all that is culturally and religiously strange.[9]

Both the grandeur of conception implicit in the Baligant episode and its problematic relation to a late twentieth- century historical awareness are more delicately inscribed in this phrasing.

Putting aside the subjective reaction to the "literary quality" of the Baligant episode, which has to do mostly with language and motif deployment, what are the major transformative effects of the Baligant episode to the text of the *Roland*? There are three, responding to basic semiotic categories: narrative programs, actants, and ideology. These three categories are obviously profoundly interrelated, particularly from the perspective of the signification produced. But it is valuable to take them individually, and in the order named.

Narrative Programs

The question before us is no longer the "authenticity" of the Baligant episode but rather the difference it makes to the poem. That difference is substantial and should be approached by the classic procedure of commutation. In so doing, we address the major narrative syntagms of the text, not its verbal or stylistic details.

La Chanson de Roland *without "Baligant"*

Minus the Baligant episode, the *Roland* tells the story of the tragically successful reintegration of a subordinate entity into the realm of Charles. The narrative program announced in the first *laisse* is successful, but at the cost of losing the major military might of the realm: its outstanding general (who is also Charles's nephew); the peers of the realm who are also its political and military leaders; and a sizable contingent of armed warriors. Aside from the question of the importance of the historical battle of Roncevaux—minor skirmish or military disaster?—the text defines the narrative event as a devastating blow to the power and the person of the emperor.

Although the event is explained—as it usually is in epic—as the effect of a traitor's betrayal, an issue of culpability hovers about the edges of the narrative, as an isotopy repeatedly broached without ever being definitively resolved, until the final trial scene. Although that episode strikes any reader as fairly definitive, we will see that even that does not quite settle the issue. In addition to the issue of individual culpability, fused with a problematic of revenge, revenge must also be taken against the collective agent constituted by the army of Marsile. As a result, a dual response is determined: pursuit of the fleeing Saracen troops and punishment of Ganelon.

When this dual sanction is performed, a new order is established, one that is of importance especially to Charles. In a peculiar way, the manner in which this new order is established performs a deconstruction of certain ambiguities, pervasive earlier in the text and necessary in order to enable the text to perform its transformations leading to that new order. While this last moment will be discussed in the next section, I beg the reader to accept its assertion for the time being.

This analysis produces the following sequential structure:

1. [Conquer Spain]
   a. take Saragossa
   b. kill Roland, peers, troops
2. Resolve culpability
   a. assign culpability
   b. punish actor
3. Establish new order

The narrative logic is evident. Roland and associates are lost in the process of achieving the major military goal announced at the beginning of the text. Events unfold with the sense of inevitability of a tragedy. Hero and traitor are members of the same social category, and the traitor enacts the same social and characterological values in his narrative program as the hero. At the level of collective actants, the *Roland* is not so much a narrative of betrayal of one group by a single individual, although it is given as such: at the level of the collective isotopy, it is the class or social category depicted and represented by all the actors named that self-destructs: as we have seen, it is indeed the same socio-categorical dynamic that is at work in both Roland and his stepfather Ganelon. The self-destruction of the class in question both clears the ground for and necessitates its replacement by a new political order (to be examined in the next section).

A major shift in conceiving of narrative was performed by the Russian Formalists, whose work has influenced narrative semiotics. Rather than being explained in terms that are both psychological and temporally sequential according to a pattern A $\longrightarrow$ B $\longrightarrow$ C, which is the pattern of explanation characteristic of mimetic and realistic fiction, Formalism, and after it semiotics, conceives of narrative as a textual process oriented toward achieving certain ends. As a result, the pattern of explanation is no longer psychological or mimetic but operational: actors, actants, narrative programs, all the paraphenalia of narrativity are selected and deployed in such a manner as to achieve certain predetermined ends. As a result, it is the end which explains the beginning, rather than the other way around (C $\longrightarrow$ B $\longrightarrow$ A), the proviso being, of course, that the A/B/C sequence still adhere to the principle of the inescapable verisimilitude, much broader than an earlier sense of psychological *vraisemblance*.[10] In this context, the end of the *Roland* may be conceived of, not as mopping up the sorry state of things left by earlier narrative events, or even a perfectly recognizable pattern of crime, punishment, and vengeance, but as the goal of the text itself. And it is not only the "end" as the last, or next-to-last, narrative syntagm which may be the goal: certain earlier episodes which appear, at the surface of a reading, as unfortunate occurrences may in fact function as fundamentally necessary instrumental goals within an overarching program. If the end of the narrative is to install a new political order, then the earlier sections may be read as preparatory to that establishment. In other words, what are given as the regrettable results of unfortunate maneuverings may be necessary prerequisites for the state of things proposed by end of the text. The regrettable loss of Roland, Oliver, the peers, and 20,000 Frankish troops, and even Ganelon, valiant warrior that he was, may be requisite for the establishment of Charles's new order at the end of the *Roland*. If so, it may be the social category of the feudal warrior which is necessarily sacrificed, with all the ambiguity of the notion of sacrifice.

In such a reading, the narrative outline given above may be rewritten:

1. Discard feudalism
2. Assign culpability
3. Punish culpability
4. Establish new order

This version of the narrative dynamic may help explain why the issue of culpability—which ought to be taken care of simply by the presence of the traitor Ganelon—is so inexplicably tenacious: in the dialectic of historical power relations, as we can see them from our retrospective perspective, the locus of power that benefits from the disappearance of what the French call *la féodalité* is the king: Charles himself.

La Chanson de Roland *with "Baligant"*

In a sense, the import of "Baligant" has been recognized by traditional criticism without the benefit of semiotic analysis: indeed, I have already quoted such recognition above, in citing first Maurice Delbouille, then Joseph Duggan, regarding the "cosmic" dimension introduced into the far smaller, more local and personalized narrative of personal resentment. The insertion of this narrative syntagm into the prior narrative is one of the most striking examples of a technique I have called "upping the ante": the additional syntagm, exemplifying the accretive mode of composition typical of oral textuality, produces the signification that far greater stakes are implicit in the narrative than were heretofore suspected.

While the initial syntagms remain the same, the insertion of the later episode retroactively produces new significations. The defeat of Saragossa, completing the reintegration of Spain into the Carolingian empire, remains a narrative task to be accomplished, but acquires the signification of the local exemplification of a worldwide conflict: the localized problem (the resubordination of a rebellious subject kingdom) is transformed into the instantiation of a universal conflict. What was originally an issue of political subordination within a political hierarchy doubled by a religious differentiation now becomes the cosmological opposition between "Christianity" and the Other—to cite Joseph Duggan's words, "all that is culturally and religiously strange" and, being strange, is turned inimical. But that very strangeness is suspicious: as noted above, while touches of exoticism are rampant in the names and descriptions of the textual "Saracens," the fundamental political and even religious structures are remarkably similar to those of their "Christian" opponents, to the extent that, at this structural level, elements of identity are far more present and active than elements of difference. As must inevitably be signified by the play of mirror images, the Other—here portayed as profoundly hostile—as our self-image is largely an introjection of the image others, or the Other, communicate to us. Only enough difference is allowed the figure of the Other to justify the transformation of Us into an Other who is inimical: it is the religous isotopy that justifies the hostility that leads to disaster.

As a result, the narrative outline of the new entity "*Roland* with 'Baligant'" can read as follows:

1. Discard feudalism
2. Resolve culpability
   a. assign culpability
   b. punish culpability
3. Universalize conflict
4. Establish new order.

The insertion of the new episode is thus revealed as functional in a fairly recognizable manner. The universalization of the conflict, raising the stakes involved, is tantamount to carrying the conflict outside the borders of the known world relevant to the earlier conflict, the world of the European continent. If "*Roland* without 'Baligant' " posits the lands of France, Germany, and northern Spain as the relevant topography, "*Roland* with 'Baligant' " expands the topographical reference to a geographical totalization: it is the domination of the entire known world that is at stake.

External dangers and enemies have always legitimized internal political processes. What is remarkable in the case of the accreted Baligant episode is that the degree to which the stakes are upped is extreme: nothing less than "everything" is wagered in the previously limited, local conflict. Two possible "explanations" occur: the implicit significance of the conflict in the A-structure noted above may have begun to surface, and it may require further legitimation; or the textual transformations operated by the text may have become, not perhaps more likely, but less improbable, in the course of historical development, so that the increased possibility of a "real" enactment of the textual process may have required more urgent legitimation. In either case—and the two are perhaps not exclusive—the function of the Baligant episode is to provide further legitimation for that process that was already at work in the earlier text lacking "Baligant": it may be that the text's addition responded to semantic pressures developing in the sociopolitical world, affecting the interpretability of the *Roland*.

Actants

The qualifications accorded the figure of Charles as a narrative actor at the very opening of the textual world—king and emperor—persist. But it is erroneous to consider his narrative program in and through the Baligant episode to be constituted by the single function of obtaining revenge for Roland's death. Both his actantial status and its ideological outplay change fundamentally.

In "*Roland* without 'Baligant,' " Charles's actantial role is that of destinator, the initiator of action, source of value, and performer of the final sanction upon the subject's performance. It is Charles who gives the subject Roland his mission, signaling that grant of a mission by the gesture of handing Roland the glove or bow as symbol of the devolution of authority (*laisses* 60–62). Through that legitimate devolution flow the social values at work in the narrative program of the subject. These values, such as courage, skill in combat, loyalty, are occasionally represented by specific qualifying statements in the verbal level of the text; more important, they are incorporated in the narrative action of the text. Charles even provides the subject with the adjuvant, of magic character in Propp's fairytale pattern: both the 20,000 troops of the rear guard and the grant of the legitimizing bow are agents to sustain the subject's efforts. The sanction is performed in a number of ways, direct and indirect. Charles's *plainte* for his lost nephew and general defines his huge military and political loss, and thereby conveys an implicit evaluation and sanction. The attempt to recompense Aude for her loss is another valorization of the dead subject. So, finally, is the revenge wreaked upon the actor considered responsible for the loss of Roland: the performance of revenge itself is a valorization and hence an indirect sanction. The one element that is not sanctioned, oddly enough, is the specific performance of the mission assigned the subject: Charles does not approve or disapprove of the narrative performance which the reader, in fact, knows better than Charles himself. While this central element is not weighed and judged, it is implicitly ratified by the other sanctioning gestures named.

The narrative program of obtaining revenge for Roland's death and reestablishing his justice within the diegesis of the narrative retain Charles in the original actantial status as destinator, with the same values as he had then. The fact that he has to enact that program himself, however, already represents a shift toward subjectivity. Far more telling is the appearance of the new antagonist Baligant, along with his troops: an entirely new conflict is engaged, with a new order of battle. And in the moment when Baligant and Charles face off against each other in individual combat, as well as in the trial scene of Ganelon, where Charles maneuvers to obtain the results he himself desires, there is no more room for doubt. The actor who, in the first narrative syntagms of "*Roland* without 'Baligant,' " performed primarily as destinator is transformed, in "*Roland* with 'Baligant,' " into an independent narrative subject, not only the source of value and goals, but the primary enactor of the narrative transformations. From a somewhat clouded and ambiguous position as Destinator, Charles is "promoted" to narrative centrality as the Subject of his own narrative. This promotion stresses the performance of God as Charles's destinator: more affirmative in the Baligant episode, the Deity intervenes assertively in the level of narrative action itself.

As we have seen, in combining the actantial roles of destinator and subject, Charles resembles one of the essential actantial traits of the modern hero who is his own destinator. It is undoubtedly this duality that allows a specially modern sensibility to resonate to the vibrations of Charles's performance. What is taken as a given by the modern syncretic actor, however, is the result of grievous loss for Charles. While this syncretism may look additive to the twentieth-century semiotician, it is the result of subtraction in the context of medieval codes.

In addition to his function as individual Destinator, however, Charles represents a collectivity as well. Roland, Oliver, and Ganelon can be taken one by one as subject, adjuvant, and traitor. As we have seen, however, all of them belong to a category composed of another syncretism—that which combines the traits of the warrior knight and the great feudal noble. These figures, and the others of the same kind, appear in the world of the text not only as individual actors but also as instantiations of some collective entity, drawing on the social codes of their time in defining the signification they produce. In the "objective reality" of the time, or what is presented as such in works of history, warrior knights and great aristocrats inhabit different positions in the same social formation. In the text in question, these two positions are fused, and the result is that these actorial figures, taken together, put into play in the textual diegesis what the tent presents as a unity: that of a "feudal class." "*Roland* without 'Baligant' " sets into action a collective Subject that is eminently recognizable as "feudalism": its rules, values, and typical patterns of action are determining in the first half of the poem. What of the figure of Charlemagne, then? The ambiguities with which he performs his multifaceted roles as feudal overlord, king, and emperor constitute a close allegory to the situation of the king of France at the beginning of the twelfth century: respected as king, he was nevertheless hemmed in by those who, though lesser in noble rank, were more powerful, militarily and politically, than the king.

It is, then, that peculiar conceptual category that the figure of Charles represents, the class of one, the type with only a single token. There is no reason to doubt this semantic investment: it merely records what has been generally recognized and is indeed textualized by the *Chanson de Roland* itself. Charles is king of France, and emperor too, whatever that may mean. What has not been as thoroughly grasped, however, is that the transformation of semiotic actants to which we have pointed in our earlier discussion represents a momentous change in the domain of political history. To say that the figure of Charles syncretizes the actantial roles of destinator and subject means that the king is now able to act independently of his barons, free of the restraints imposed by a realistic evaluation of relative forces. It means that the French monarchy, whose main necessity and virtue, for a long time, had merely been to survive, now became an independent narrative agent on the stage of history.

This promotion of kingship on the scene of politics is not a simple, single event. It implies a change of relations between this class of one and the remainder of the dominant social and economic class of the time. That change consists of transforming what had been a purely symbolic hierarchical superiority on the part of the kings of France—the refusal to be another noble's vassal, to bend the knee before another aristocrat, even a man of the Church, and the implicit and almost totally unfulfilled claim to rule a (undefined and nonexistent) kingdom of France—into narrative reality. It means taking the effect of refulgence, noted earlier, and giving it military form. And it means subordinating the other *détenteurs de force* to the rule of the monarchy. It means coping with the implicit conflict that cast the monarchy and the feudal system as antagonists. In coping with the anarchy of fragmentation as the fundamental political fact of its age, feudalism elaborated structures of value and personal relationships that in turn confirmed and reinforced the dispersal of force and control, the social and political fragmentation that had brought it into existence. When the monarchy was able once again to begin its assertion of centralization, its desires and interests set it into conflict with the feudal organization of fragmentation. The opposition of fragmentation and totality was not a theoretical matter in the twelfth century, it was the very stuff of political conflict.

In other words, the rise to a greater level of eminence reveals an opposition that had always already been there: feudalism and monarchy, as modern historians recognize, deploy different and opposing modes of social organization. That opposition can readily be phrased in terms of the distribution of political power: one power center or many. Feudalism, of course, was the regime of the many, the regime of the endless dispersal and diffraction of power. (For contemporaries obsessed with horrors of totalization and hence athirst for fragmentations, it should be noted that fragmentation is not inherently democratic!) Each of the feudal nobles, at the head of a territory and with his clutch of subordinate warriors, lording his power over a submitted peasant population, would undergo infringement upon that power by the development of an effective kingship asserting its centrality and gathering to itself the reins of power dispersed now for centuries. Within the field defined by the combined isotopies of military force and political power—hardly separated in our period—the conflict between the two models of political organization was patent and could only be temporized by an unstable compromise such as that of the "feudal monarchy."[11] In such a co-text, the *Roland* readily figures as a transitional model between feudalism and monarchy.[12]

That field, combining the military and the political, is the field of the *Chanson de Roland*, which takes a grimmer view of this opposition than did the historical process. The latter operated by a process of progressive subsumption stretching over centuries—the defeat of the Fronde in the seventeenth century marked the end of the process—which frequently obtained the collaboration of those being subsumed. The text performs this subsumption more quickly, radically, and surprisingly. The *Roland* sequence eradicates the elite of the feudal class, along with a strong component of its subordinate fighting warriors, producing as well a crippling loss for the king and emperor: his army decimated, he foresees an enfeebled and pitiable future. Now, along with Baligant, a huge contingent of enemy troops arrives in ships from the east. The emir has convoked the people of forty kingdoms, and the armies of this hateful people are great (ll. 2623 and 2630). His army corps are counted by the tens and the dozens, the numbers of men by the tens of thousands. The concrete details of the battles between Charles and the pagans will amply demonstrate the very large number of the latter.

Clearly, this poses something of a military and a narrative problem. With Charles's army weakened by the disappearance of the brightest and the best, with his own feelings of having been radically weakened by the disappearance of those who died at Roncevaux, how shall the emperor face this major invasion from the East? With what forces will he encounter this external invasion? As we have seen, even the earlier part of the text is perfectly aware of the numerical principle in the opposition of combatting armies: see the discussion of Oliver *vs.* Roland.[13] Granting that the medieval principles of verisimilitude are different from our own, a problem subsists: in terms of the representation of the text, it is a military problem; in terms of its textuality, it is a problem of a narrative and an ontological sort. By ample redundant repetition, the text stresses Charles's estimation that the loss of Roland and his troops renders him and his empire weak and helpless before strangers as well as when confronted with the potential revolt of subjugated peoples. The textual battle is a disaster for Charles as a military power. Repeatedly, he portrays himself as not only personally aggrieved but as profoundly weakened militarily and politically.

Not only are these losses not discussed as the emperor now faces the entire contingent of *escheles* arrived from the Orient under Baligant's leadership: his weakened position is not even mentioned in passing. Instead, in *laisse* after stately *laisse*, Charles forms his ten army corps, composed of "Franceis," Bavarians (led by Ogier the Dane), Germans, Normans, Bretons (thus presumably the vassals of dead Roland, though he is not even mentioned in passing), Poitevins and Auvergnats, Flemish and Frisians, those from Lorraine and Burgundy: finally, the tenth division is composed *des baruns de France* (l. 3084). As far as this section of the text is concerned, it is as if the conflict and the losses of the earlier battle had never existed: neither is it specifically referred to by the text, nor do its events have any impact whatever on the narrative of the Baligant episode.

The textual discrepancy must be recognized as a discrepancy, and yet the text must be accounted for and interpreted as it really exists in the Oxford manuscript. Taking the text as text, we note that Charles is terribly weakened by the battle of Roncevaux, and that he nonetheless fields an extraordinarily large—even mythical—number of troops against Baligant. No description is given of any levy or call to arms, from previously unmentioned allies, or from new corners of the empire. No narrative account whatever is given which would explain the sudden availability of troops where devastation and desolation reigned but a short while ago. On the contrary, rather than give a narrative account, the text merely records the words spoken and the present presence of the required troops, organized according to their *escheles* and fielded to face the enemy in appropriate military formations. The transformation from weak and helpless, *sans* troops, to powerful, militarily resourceful, and endowed with ample military might is entirely a matter of words: the words of the text transform one state of Charles's military power into another, not any narrative invention. The words of the text, the words of Charles, produce the troops, create them, and field them against the enemy.

There is no reason not to recognize the analogy with divine creation: the topos of the analogy between the poetic word and the divine word of creation is hardly new. There is no reason not to recognize the analogy, though the text does not mention it; but before that, it is important to note that any word, taken to create a thing or state of things that did not exist previously, is a *performative* word. The words of the text, the relevant words of the emperor, which field the tens of thousands of troops that previously did not exist, perform the (bringing to) existence of what they describe and signify. The new troops exist only because of those words: hence their performativity.

That performativity is repeated, albeit at a different ontological and theological level, when Charles is wounded by the emir. As we have seen, the Angel Gabriel descends and merely asks "What are you doing?" These words, in turn, enable the wounded hero to fight again and kill his opponent. The Baligant episode in particular is far from a mimetic text whose *"vraisemblable"* is coded according to some "realism" otherwise not known in the Middle Ages. On the contrary, the essential narrative "reality" is created and produced by a kind of ontological linguistic performativity. We will see in the conclusion of this chapter that such a performativity in fact inheres in the relation between the *Chanson de Roland* as a whole and later historical developments.

For the moment, let us note the third major semiotic category affected by the accretion of the Baligant episode. Not only are new narrative programs developed; not only is the previous destinator transformed into the narrative subject; the text performatively creates an entirely new set of adjuvants required by the new narrative programs. This is not an inevitable performance. God will interfere in support of Charles's combat against the emir: the individual duel is also a *judicium dei*, and the transcendental destinator will see to it that his terrestrial emanation and representative subject wins in His, the Christian Deity's, court. By commutation, one can imagine a single combat between the emperor and Baligant so impressive that, by itself, it turns the tide and turns the field of battle over to the Christians, however few and ragged they may be: the verisimilitudinary principle then would be the demonstration of God's greater power.

These newly created adjuvants, granted little of what we like to call "literary depth" by the text, nevertheless perform according to complex textual parameters. On the one hand, they are to perform as substitutes for the troops despatched by the Roland-sequence: functionally identical to those who died at Roncevaux, they are to fight on horseback and with total fidelity to their overlord, incorporating the same combative traits as did their predecessors. On the other hand, while performing their functional identity with those earlier troops, they are also to differentiate themselves markedly from their predecessors. Their difference is coordinate with the difference incorporated in their leader, in the narrative subject. That subject is no longer given the textual marker and identified with the semiotic role of "feudal lord" alone. Charles remains a feudal *seigneur* but his textual definition, as we have seen, is doubled and tripled by the additional roles of "king" and "emperor." It is part of the *Roland*'s political codes that it recognizes, implicitly, the difference.

That difference can best be identified indirectly, through the mediation of another reader of the *Roland*. Another scholar, engaged in a very different kind of reading, nevertheless spots a textual moment of importance for our interpretation. Implicitly confirming our notation that Charles is now transformed into subject, he writes: "The emperor is now clearly leading his men in person, acting as his own field commander." He parades before the enemy and invokes God; the Frankish army is ready for combat:

> Now Charles does something that may appear strange at first glance but is natural under the circumstances. He names two men, called Rabel and Guineman (not otherwise known as great warriors), to take the places of Roland and Oliver as leaders of his vanguard. He gives them a sword and the hero's horn. This is not some insult to the pair's memory, but a recognition of the fact that Charles must count on the best men he has. Both Rabel and Guineman are, if

not fabulous palladins, at least willing and competent knights, and that is what the Christian cause needs.[14]

I might wish to quibble about the use of an ideologically loaded phrase like "*natural* under the circumstances": it is not "nature" which is at work, but a highly performative artifice. But Rabel and Guineman are not "the best men [Charles] has": such phrasing endows them with what they do not have, a previous textual existence. It is not the case that Rabel and Guineman are "not otherwise known as great warriors," but rather that they are not previously known at all. Rabel and Guineman are invented by the text at the moment they are endowed with the signs of the earlier heroic pair of peers, in a perfect example of "unnatural" artifice. Those signs, the sword and horn which textually resound to the echoes of the earlier Roland-sequence, and most particularly to Roland's death-scene, establish Rabel and Guineman in a "typological" relation to Roland and Oliver, asserting simultaneously the identity and the difference of this new pair. Repetition and even substitution do not imply identical value. Rabel and Guineman, like the rest of Charles's troops, are invented, created, and performatively textualized for the purpose, for the circumstance that the text also creates.

When appointed, these two knights have no previous textual existence. Their appointment and their creation are simultaneous:

> Carles apelet Rabel e Guineman.
> Ço dist li reis: "Seignurs, jo vos comant,
> Seiez es lius Oliver e Rollant:
> l'un port l'espee e l'altre l'olifant,
> Si chevalcez el premer chef devant. . . . " (ll. 3014–18)

> Charles calls on Rabel and Guineman.
> So spoke the King: "Lords, I order you,
> be in the places of Oliver and Roland:
> Let one bear the sword, the other the oliphant,
> and ride forward, first in the front line. . . . "

Unknown, they are to bear the markers of their predecessors, in their predecessors' "places." The use of *lius* (= modern French *lieu*) is exactly the same as in the word *lieu-tenant*: one who holds another's place. Does the fact that Rabel and Guineman occupy the same narrative space as Roland and Oliver before them signify that the four are to be (con)fused? Hardly. Placing two actors defined by their anonymity in the place of Roland and Oliver, refulgent with the semes of heroism, comradeship, and anteriority, endowing those two anonymities with the signs of the earlier types, can only underline all that differentiates the two pairs. The anti-types, Rabel and Guineman, are to ride with Roland's sword and horn, and in Roland and Oliver's places in the advance guard, but will hardly be confused with Roland and Oliver. It is precisely nonidentity, or discrepancy, which is the major semantic charge of the passage. In spite of their syntagmatic substitutability for Roland and Oliver, the two present knights are unmistakably marked by the lack which differentiates them from those in whose places they ride: the total absence of prior existence, of *honor* either in the sense of fame or fortune, reputation or land, and hence independent power. Assigned to Roland's and Oliver's places as they are given textual existence, created *ex nihilo* by Charles's performatives appointing them, they are, ontologically, functionally, militarily, and politically, entirely Charles's creatures. It is the absence of "priority" that makes them what they are: nothing but Charles's creatures.

Rabel and Guineman are not alone in this double status of identity and difference. As we will see, they are just as much "new men" as Thierry de Chartres. One wonders about the shape of earlier scholarship, whose focus on the heroism of Roland and Charles so blinded it to other semantic components that even so insistent a repetition passed unnoticed. In any case, the text accumulates repetitions of the narrative discrepancy and displays them overtly: there is no attempt to diminish and disguise the difference between the diegetic universe of the Roland-sequence and the Charles-sequence for the sake of an anachronistic form of textual unity. The structure and the significance produced by the juxtaposition of the two major narrative sequences is precisely the difference between the two types of actors and the sources of their social being. Here, as in so many other passages, the point in medieval text construction is not smooth unity but the combination of textual identity and difference that produces signification.

The changes wrought so far by the Baligant episode suggest something more than a mere vengeance for the deaths of Roland, his peers, and the mounted troops. The transformations of narrative programs, narrative subject, and adjuvants—major categories of semiotic analysis—suggest a new narrative order, and a new political order as well. So much so that one wonders if the ultimate *raison d'être* of the Baligant episode, if the reason for its insertion into a text that certainly possessed its prior coherence, was not to stress some semantic element already present, if only by implication, in the prior text, something already there, which needed to be emphasized by the structural innovation allowed by oral technique. Was the political meaning of a prior state of the *Roland* so obscured by its epic heroism as to require the insertion of a narrative sequence whose heroism was so transparently a matter of textual artifice as to reveal that signification more openly?

Such artifice would also be understandable as a suture to the plane of a futurity toward which the text imprecisely tends. An anticipated renascence of monarchy, without a "realistic" indication of how this might be brought about in the social text, a monarchy which prefigures the creation of the nation-state, here takes the form, less of an "imagined political community"[15] than a mythological and ideological protopod, in which an image of the past serves to limn a tropism toward the future, in a kind of pre-textual stage of a desired object. If the *Roland*'s vision of a new political order is dim and imprecise, it does grasp the essential point of the "nation," from its own historical perspective, which is its syncretism of different and even opposing groups: its subsumption of feudalism by the monarchy anticipates Ernest Renan's understanding of the nation as a collection and fusion of different races.[16] In this sense, the Carolingian mythology invoked by the *Roland* is a form of the classical topos of the golden age, prefiguring a future polity felt as undefined necessity rather than concretely imagined.

9 | Ganelon's Trial, or the Monarch's Revolution

> [H]istorical enquiry brings to light deeds of violence which took place at the origin of all political formations, even those whose consequences have been altogether beneficial.
>
> Ernest Renan, "What Is a Nation?"

WITH NO OTHER syntagm does the shock of alterity between modern presuppositions and the medieval text explode with such clarity as in the case of Ganelon's trial.[1] The issue of justice—which the trial would seem intended to establish—is so intimately imbricated with the reader's ideology and utopian aspirations (utopianism and ideology, if not identical, are also not independent of each other) that the contrast between our own conceptualization of its forms and those of another epoch, another culture, cannot help but involve us in the most difficult acts of reading. The minimal requirement here is appropriate attention to the forms and structures of the text, the ways in which its codes —semiotic and juridical—command its performances. Beyond that, the recognition due to those encodings that it could presume as normative, and that may have to be recovered in part through the study of other texts of the period, or the researches into those other texts by the specialized readers we call historians, becomes all the more crucial. Twentieth-century presuppositions as to the form, purpose, and fairness of judicial procedure are obstacles to apprehending the operations of this text. Two major characteristics of contemporary judicial procedure are quite beside the point: its formal impartiality, and the assumption that its cognitive dimension is the primary one. Courtroom drama is most frequently, for modern readers, a cognitive program designed to answer two questions: what happened and who did it, recognizing that those two questions are, in fact, often answered by the same program of inquiry. The (supposed) impartiality of our judicial procedures is meant to secure ground rules by which that cognitive adventure can procede with the greatest chances of success. The adversarial character of prosecuting and defense attorneys is perhaps the only trait of modern Anglo-Saxon procedure that retains a strong resemblance to the medieval practice.

In the trial scene of the *Chanson de Roland*, almost none of the characteristics of our judicial codes can be found. Here, the guilt of the accused is announced at the beginning of the proceedings—which do nothing but repeat the same assertion announced upon the actor's first entrance onto the scene of the text (ll. 178 and 3748). What happened and who did it, the standard questions in modern courtroom drama, are known ahead of time in oral literature: if no one ever heard the *Roland* for the first time, if its fundamental moments were always already known to the audience, then no fundamental cognitive discoveries of that order could be produced. Hence, while suspense may exist in limited ways for the actors of the text, the text itself is unlikely to be structured according to the principle of suspense. There is no cognitive dimension to Ganelon's trial: his guilt, and even his eventual punishment, are known from the very beginning. His guilt is a given of the narrative; what is interesting, what was a question for the original audience, as it is for us, is how this known narrative outcome and information are given meaning by those elements that are not simply givens of the text. The issue is not what happens or who did it, but rather "what does it mean?" The challenge of that question is: how do we proceed to determine the meaning?

The answer, as always, is: contextually and structurally. The issue is not cognitive; it is distributive and, at least on the surface, the distribution would appear to be one of exclusive semantic traits. The semantic stakes established by the preceding analyses are the issues of /culpability/ and /innocence/, as distributed between two actors, Ganelon and Charles. The natural assumption is that the /culpability/ of one determines the /innocence/ of the other, and vice versa: the determination of one actor as /innocent/ would imply the /culpability/ of the other. An exclusive disjunction is the normal assumption. But as we have seen in our discussion of Aude's death, it is more than two individual actors whose integrity (in a logical sense) and survival are at stake. In spite of the funerary rituals deployed by the text, in spite also of the imposing monumentality of the Baligant episode with its attendant cosmic implications, the very basis of sociality has been thrown into question: the principle of exchange has been grievously demonstrated to have become inoperative. Both of the two major actants— the Subject of the present narrative (formerly the Destinator) and its Traitor—and the very collectivity which, one would have thought, constituted them as actors, are being questioned by the structures of the text, and in particular by its concluding trial.

Charles is the plaintiff in the case. This immediately poses the question: what recourse is available to the plaintiff? Within the codes of the society in question, the answer of available legal recourse is determined by the social status of the individual actor. As a noble, Charles is free to avail himself of that mode of recourse which, in the textual evidence at least, is the most frequent one employed by men of his noble status, namely vengeance. Charles is a noble who has been injured in the familial isotopy: it is his nephew—a proto-son—who has been killed. In the political isotopy, it is his vassal who has been killed. In some vague but larger sense, perhaps as a "potentate," as one who wields great power, it is his major military source of might that has been killed and subtracted from his strength. On any of these noble bases, Charles might initiate a private war of personal vengeance that would be recognized as rightful within the codes of his society and its texts.

The difficulty is that private war and the vengeance it affords are part of the sociopolitical system that is itself at stake. We have already seen the text discard the feudal class at Roncevaux and substitute for it the ordered divisions with which Charles fights Baligant. The right to private war and noble vengeance is a characteristic of that class, and hence, metonymically, it is that right which Charles must also destroy. It is the right to vengeance by private war which rationalizes the reaction of injured honor, the irritability of noble pride, which is a theme from this very text to Corneille's *Horace*. It is precisely the legitimacy of the nobility's claim to wreak its private vengeance that has caused it to destroy itself: Ganelon's and Roland's actions both are to be interpreted as exemplary of this pride, this irascibility, this assertion of legal right and justice. It is precisely the fact that both incorporate the same value in their respective and complementary narrative programs that has caused the disaster at Roncevaux and the devastation of Charles's military force. Hence the rejection, implicit in the choices Charles does make, of this noble recourse: to claim and enact a private vengeance would merely continue the same cyclical dialectic initiated by Ganelon and Roland and transform the text into one of the epics included in the rebellious barons cycle, whose dialectical impetus is precisely that Oresteian and Jacobean revenge pattern. In fact, for Charles to claim that right and to act upon it would both continue the intolerable feudal patterns against which he acts and invalidate all claims to a superordinate legitimacy.

To act as a feudal noble would be to assert not only that one is a feudal noble—a fact undoubted by the present text—but that the specific status of being one noble among others is the basis of the legitimacy of one's act. It would imply equality with his antagonist, an admission that his rights and legitimacy extend as far as those of his opponent, and no farther. In the political codes of the period, this is an equality of juridical nature, which, as we have seen, the kings of France, even at their nadir, never accepted. That is the significance, long purely symbolic, but increasingly significant in the practical politics of the twelfth century, of the kings' refusal to swear homage to any other power, lay or clerical, for any holding whatever. Symbolic ideological practice, purely "fantastic" in relation to actual political power in the realm of reality, was a performance in lieu of, and perhaps preparatory for, the acquisition of actual political power.

Charles's narrative program, at this point, is oriented to discard the questioning which haunts him throughout this text: the question of responsibility in Roland's death, of culpability for the death of his nephew and vassal, and along with Roland, the death and disappearance of the twelve peers and the 20,000 men of the rear guard. But the figure of Charles is limited in the means by which the assertion of its own innocence, and the assertion of Ganelon's culpability, can be accomplished. It cannot be done in a way that implies Ganelon's right to the revenge on his stepson: a narrative program that attempted to discard Charles's culpability by assigning it to Ganelon and yet proceeded by implicitly asserting Ganelon's right to act as he did would be self-defeating. That would be the implication, if Charles acted as a feudal noble entitled to vengeance by means of private war: asserting the right of the noble class to enact revenge by private war, it would justify not only Roland's action at Roncevaux but also Ganelon's in his embassy to Marsile. Charles's goal must be to disculpabilize himself, assign /culpability/ to Ganelon, and to do so without justifying the latter by recognizing the traditional right of his class.

Charles, with some help, is about to enact a political revolution by a juridical *coup d'état*. As is inevitably the case, the revolution—any revolution—must proceed by employing existing social forms and groups to achieve its ends: that is the paradox of revolution, the mortgage of revolution, and the reason revolution so rarely succeeds. Its constitutive act relies upon what is to be overthrown. Charles's revolution is no exception. The means by which his revolutionary transformation of medieval political structure is achieved relies upon older forms, upon even older forms of judicial procedure than those of his own time (locating that time as extending from the beginning to the middle of the twelfth century). In relation to the juridical codes of the period, the trial of the *Chanson*—as is the case with other features also—is archaicizing. In its refusal of compromise; in its reliance upon a champion using military force; in its reliance upon the *judicium dei* itself; the *Chanson* calls upon forms of judicial structure that are largely outdated, though still of recourse. The text takes one or two steps backward in order to perform a very broad jump forward.

It would be a profound misunderstanding of these pages to interpret them as ascribing to Charles a deviousness and hypocrisy that betrayed his nephew and vassal, Roland, along with the latter's peers; of a cold, calculating, and manipulative intentionality oriented to aggrandizement of his power as monarch. Such a misinterpretation would stem from the traditionalist assumptions of "mimetic realism" which constitute "character": the textual figure is presumed to reflect a prior person living in reality, or is considered as such, and hence is judiciable by both legal and moral judgments. "Charles," in this discussion, designates not a person but a personage, not a moral being but a textual figure, and an "actor" in the semiotic sense: a collection and systematization of semic traits which, taken together, constitute a textual operator within a larger textual system.

The Actorial Level: Inexorable Structure

Like many medieval texts, including the *Chanson de Roland* itself, the trial's structure is bipartite. It tells first of a failure, then of a success. The inexorability of the narrative syntagm results from the conjunction, and more, from the identification of the two levels of structure: that of narrative syntagm and that of the judicial procedure it recounts. Rarely in a narrative syntagm as long as this is the distinguishing feature of the older epics—the functional discreteness of the *laisse*—so evident. The *laisses* are not only discrete, they are relatively brief: the longest, at 22 lines, is *laisse* 277, in which Thierry outlines Charles's case.

The major subdivisions of the text are three: the qualifying test, the main test, and the sanctions.

The Qualifying Test

The structural features of the first section are the following: the principals represent themselves, presenting oral argument directly to the assembled court, which, after due deliberation, returns a recommendation that Charles declare Ganelon "quits," that Ganelon serve him loyally henceforth, and that Charles recognize the impossibility of recovery. Charles's response (l. 3814) and the text's paraphrase (l. 3815) show that he considers this judgment a betrayal, that his court has failed him: he himself has failed in the attempt of his narrative program.

In establishing his court according to feudal custom, Charles convokes "men from many lands" (*humes de p[l]usurs teres*, l. 3743). They include Bavarians and Saxons, the Poitevins and the Normans, those from the Ile-de-France, the Germans and the northern Germans, as well as "the courtliest of all," the Auvergnats (ll. 3793–96). While Petit de Juleville may have exaggerated slightly in his statement that this high court consists of "*l'aristocratie de tout l'empire*,"[2] it is clear that the court is a representative one, drawn from different sections of the empire: in some sense, it is the totality of the empire that sits in judgment. In spite of these imperial associations, however, the court is convoked and proceeds as did any normal feudal court, constituted by the suzerain lord as a convocation of his greatest vassals.[3] The lord convokes the court and delegates to it the function of judging a particular case: he demands vassalic *consilium*. The advantage of such delegation is that it implicates the members of the sitting court in the eventual enforcement of the judicial decision. The great vassals, in passing judgment, commit themselves to defending the judgment by their own military power if that becomes necessary.

It is with *laisse* 271 that the veritable trial of Ganelon begins:

> Dès ore cumencet le plait et les noveles
> De Guenelen, ki traïsun ad faite. (ll. 3747f.)

> Now begins the trial, the arguments, and the charges
> of Ganelon, who committed treason.

The text here recombines the phrases of two widely separated syntagms: the initial introduction and identification of Ganelon in the first council scene of the

Franks as *Guenes i vint, ki la traïsun fist* (l. 178), and the first announcement of the beginning of the trial, just before the Aude syntagm: *Dès ore cumencet le plait de Guenelun* (l. 3704).

One characteristic of Charles's (and the *Roland*'s) revolution is to observe punctiliously the details of legal procedure. Both the words of the episode and the sequence of steps followed are those of a judicial trial. It begins with Charles's formal complaint against Ganelon, and the latter's formal response. Charles specifies that Ganelon took from him the 20,000 men of the rear guard, his nephew, Oliver, and the twelve peers. Charles suggests as motive the desire for gain: *traït por aveir*. Ganelon's response is entirely consistent with the demonstrations of courage and bravery displayed during the embassy to Marsile. He answers first by asserting the truthfulness of his response (*"Fel sei se jol ceil,"* l. 3757) and paradoxically acknowledges a motive for which the text gives no evidence—Roland damaged him in gold and property: this would suggest the possibility of revenge in the material domain, but nowhere else does the text breath a word of this.[4] In any case, Ganelon immediately acknowledges that he did indeed seek Roland's death and ruin—that fact is agreed upon—but absolutely denies the legal characterization of these facts, i.e., their legal significance. Once again, there is disagreement, in an early medieval text, as to the meaning of an event. In spite of the repeated assertions by modern theoreticians, following on the heels of traditional scholars, to the effect that medieval signification is unitary, composed of exclusive disjunctions only, the texts continue to assert the ambiguity of human evenementiality.

Ganelon does not seek to hide the fact of his responsibility for Roland's death, but he denies categorically that, in doing so, he committed treason:

"Mais traïsun nule n'en i otrei." (l. 3760)

"But treason, no—I'll grant no treason here!"

The paradox will be repeated and amplified in the next *laisse*, in which the accused admits the facts of the case against him and merely refuses the legal category employed by his accuser. As was the case when Ganelon risked his life before Marsile in the latter's court, to assert his loyalty to Charles and taunt the pagan king before him with the imminent danger of having to share the kingdom of Spain with Roland, so too now, the text praises the heroic traitor:

Devant le rei la s'estut Guenelun.
Cors ad gaillard, el vis gente color;
S'il fust leials, ben resemblast barun. (ll. 3762–64)

Before the king, there stood Ganelon.
His strong body, the noble color of his face—
had he been loyal, he really would have resembled a
    noble man.

The ambiguity of the personage as presented by the text is concisely displayed. The text does not hesitate to take a position: Ganelon was not loyal, there is no question; within the framework of the text's own axiology he acted as a traitor. Nevertheless, he stands courageously before the king, "every inch" a baron, a great feudal noble of heroic stature. That he belongs to the same category as Roland, the great, irascible race of warriors, is unquestioned by the text.

Ganelon's response and defense is an extraordinary demonstration of the capacity of truth-saying to admit perspectival effects. With the sole exception of the concluding line, no assertion of the speech can flatly be claimed to be false. Even where there is some departure from the perception that the audience may have had of the earlier narrative events of the text, as in ll. 3370–73, these divergences can readily be accommodated as the moral perception that Ganelon would have had of his own acts, motives, and situation. There is in this defense no statement which can be called a "lie" by reference to a narrative "truth." All that is in question is the proper interpretive category to bring to the events being discussed:

> "Pur amur Deu, car m'entendez, barons!
> Seignors, jo fui en l'ost avoec l'empereür,
> Serveie le par feid e par amur.
> Rollant ses niés me coillit en haür,
> Si me jugat a mort e a dulur.
> Message fui al rei Marsiliun;
> Par mun saveir vinc jo a guarisun.
> Jo desfiai Rollant le poigneor
> E Oliver e tuiz lur cumpaignun
> Carles l'oïd e si nobilie baron.
> *Venget m'en sui, mais n'i ad traïsun."* (ll. 3768–78)

> "Barons, for the love of God, hear me!
> I was in the army with the emperor
> and served him well, in love and loyalty.
> His nephew Roland began to hate me,
> and designated me to death and pain.
> I was the messenger to King Marsile.
> I used my wits, and I came back alive.
> I defied Roland, that great fighter,
> and Oliver, and all of their companions:
> Charles heard it, and his noble barons.
> *I took revenge, but there's no treason here."*

The recital of the facts that will remain close enough to the audience's memory of their original recounting much earlier in the narrative to obtain essential assent is followed by a subtle *distinguo* that has an effect of surprise after so much agreement between the telling and its original narrative referent. The *distinguo* itself is one that obtains equal assent, since it merely incorporates a distinction encoded in the norms of medieval law. It is important here to reassert that Ganelon's trial scene, if not a "courtroom drama" comparable to daytime television serials, is without any question informed and structured by concepts, codes, isotopies, and practices of medieval judicial practices.[5] It exists as the confrontation of two contradictory legal codes, both of which are imbricated in fundamentally different distributions of power: each, that is, implies a different polity. Furthermore, it is in the trial scene that the latent conflicts we have traced at the margins of the text come to the surface of the text, are defined, and, in a paradoxical way, are settled. To disregard the technical and historical legal content and structure of this syntagm, by recategorizing it as a "moral tale within another moral tale"[6] is in fact to beg the historical and textual questions posed by the concrete text in order to substitute the modern critic's inveterate moralism, far less trenchant than the conceptualizations of the twelfth-century text. Indeed, the medieval sense of justice was far removed from our abstract moralizations. Quite the contrary, "justice" was a noble practice that was exercised for lucrative purposes, as a means of domination, and which, as a result, was frequently identified with pain and suffering.[7] Even this "justice's" purview was "singularly limited" by the right of private vengeance, a right which was one of the marked traits of the nobility,[8] and a characteristic of the nobility as an anthropological social grouping. Vengeance was one of the primary retaliatory instruments available to the lineage in its self-perpetuation as a "corporate aggregate," a solidarity mechanism constituted as "a structure maintained through time where the presence of individuals more than their personality is material to the functioning of the system."[9] Vengeance, as a narrative structure, is thus incorporated both in the general social and legal system and in its anthropological, quasi-familial structures. This overdetermination helps explain the unreflective, automatic quickness with which it is undertaken. The first gesture of the eleventh-century knight who feels himself to be injured is to wreak vengeance upon his aggressor.[10] Efforts at establishing modalities of compromise would be made: they are the direction of the future and are inscribed in the effort of the jury of Ganelon's peers' initial recommendation to Charles. Nevertheless, if the violent and agitated world of the noble manor was not anarchic, as the early feudal period is sometimes depicted, its inhabitants were not men adept at restraining their passions and covetousness.

Far away from any moralizing and religious idealization, the knight does not fight, most of the time, to protect his peasants, or men of the Church, or perhaps more abstract values. He fights to avenge his lord, his relatives, his friends, or himself: "For that purpose, he fights often." Mounting a horse, bearing arms, and both their semiosic display and actual use in creating and disseminating violence are a complex of noble privileges that characterized the noble class for a very long time.[11] Even in the thirteenth century, the legitimacy of private war remained an exclusive apanage of the nobility. Provided that war had been openly declared and that both parties were willing to fight, such armed conflict was as legal as a trial.[12] It is hardly appropriate scholarly practice to cite an author on Germanic law, characteristic of the small tribal warrior band called the *comitatus*, as applying to the large-scale armies attributed to Roland and Charlemagne, while disregarding the same author's comment, later in the same paragraph, that "it was . . . not until the middle of the fourteenth century that war against the monarch constituted treason and that misdeeds of this type were officially considered political crimes against the state."[13] However irrational or undesirable it may seem to twentieth-century moralisms, the autonomous violence of the nobility, amply attested in historical documentation, was an inherent trait of its self-definition:

> The autonomy of the nobility was, above all, a military autonomy; and any impingement upon the free exercise of arms was an impingement upon political power as well.[14]

Not only, then, was autonomous violence a practice and a privilege to which the nobility cleaved: there was no juridical reason to abandon it. Private vengeance quite normally led, through the *faida*, to private war, which the nobility considered a perfectly legitimate recourse, a recognized procedure, and an incontestable right. In the context of historically contemporary codes, this practice and privilege did not conflict with the principle of the monarchy. The feudal nobility considered private war a perfectly legitimate recourse, an entirely acceptable procedure, as well as an unarguable right, *which did not call into question the principle of the monarchy*.[15]

The noble has right to vengeance, to private war if necessary to carry it out; thus, in admitting vengeance, Ganelon does not admit to any judiciable offense. The quality that makes of vengeance—or any killing—a judiciable offense is that of being covert and not preceded by adequate warning: that is the quality that constitutes both murder and treason. In the original council scene, after being nominated as messenger to Marsile, Ganelon openly challenged and defied Roland, Oliver, and the twelve peers. Specifically to Roland, Ganelon said "*Jo ne vus aim nient*"(l. 306), a statement to be understood as the equivalent assertion, in the discourse of modern diplomacy, of a declaration that relations between two sovereign states are "unfriendly"; i.e., it is tantamount to a declaration of war. More generally, Ganelon had spoken to Charles when the latter ordered him to come forward, to receive the stick and the glove that signified his mission:

> "—Sire," dist Guenes, "ço ad tut fait Rollant!
> Ne l'amerai a trestut mun vivant,
> Ne Oliver, por ço qu'il est si cumpainz.

Li duze per, por ço qu'il l'aiment tant,
Desfi les ci, sire, vostre veiant."(ll. 322–26)

Said Ganelon: "Lord Roland did all this.
In all my life I'll never love him,
or Oliver, because he's his companion,
or the twelve peers, because they love him so.
I defy them here in your presence, lord." (Goldin, ll. 322–26)

Can one imagine a more dramatic reversal, or a more telling defense, than calling upon one's accuser as witness?

Neither Charles nor Thierry will argue this point: both the principal and his representative will grant the distinction to Ganelon. Nor will any question regarding this point be raised in the deliberations of the court. Indeed, one must conclude that the text, in all of its specificities—its actors, its narrative or descriptive syntagms— grants this point totally. On the basis of the evidence provided by this text, one could conclude that Ganelon, the feudal noble, has acted entirely within the rights granted him by the feudal code of law in taking his revenge upon his stepson Roland. Ganelon has punctiliously observed the necessary caution, that the adversary be advised ahead of time of one's ill intent so as to avoid the possible accusation of murder and treason, characterized by covert, unannounced enmity. With only one dissenting voice, the court recommends to Charles that he announce that Ganelon is "quits," that Ganelon serve him *par feid e par amur* (l. 3810): the same words used by Ganelon in his own characterization of his own behavior toward Charles (l. 3770). Ganelon, after all, is a most noble man, and the dead cannot be brought back to life even at the cost of further death.

This *laisse* (276) concludes, and the next begins, with Charles's recognition that his narrative program—to obtain justice by means of a recognizable feudal court—has failed (ll. 3814–17). Yet what else could have been expected but that a feudal court composed of feudal vassals would return a verdict in feudal law which recognizes feudal privilege? No matter how strongly modern readers—as well as the original audience—may *feel* the wrong done Roland, Oliver, the twelve peers, the rear guard as a whole, and Charles as their potentate, the machinery invoked, so firmly anchored within feudalism as it is, can hardly produce a non-feudal result! The form of justice specific to feudalism can hardly be expected to overturn the interests of the class whose interests it represents. Indeed, this will remain true, even though the mode of resolution here presented is, in historical fact, one that is relatively "up to date." Earlier periods tended to have recourse to the "judgment of God" more frequently; it is a relatively "modern" trend to submit cases for mediation by authority outside of the field of contention itself, the *judicium dei* having too often been perceived as a Latin phrase in fact meaning the determination of right by might.[16] Peaceful settlement of disputes by compromise becomes more frequent in a period which perceives economic return on property as more valuable than familial or tribal honor. Thus, even the more advanced form of feudal justice, represented by the performance of this court, does not bring the desired form of justice.

Charles thus fails in his first narrative program within the judicial framework. More broadly, however, this is the second attempt to establish the principle of exchange. The first was, of course, the exchange of living Louis for dead Roland in response to Aude's demand for her man. In this case, Charles's attempt was to obtain the death of the culpable in exchange for the death of the victim. In both cases, the principle of exchange is refused by the text. If the first rejection of exchange by Aude put into question the principle of sociality, how shall one measure the semantic effect of the second refusal of the same sort? Charles considers the members of the court to have behaved toward him in a criminal manner ("*Vos estes mi felun*," l. 3814); but as he suffers the reaction to this effort of his, he experiences such pain *si se cleimet caitifs* (l. 3817). Bédier translates the last word as *malheureux*, Moignet as *infortuné*, and Goldin as "wretched man." None of these is wrong, of course, but it is worth looking at the word's etymon. *Caitiff*, which in modern French becomes *chétif*, comes from Latin *captivum*. A captive, like Ganelon, for instance, is one who is presumed to be guilty: hence he is to be put into chains and to be beaten and whipped as well. The suggestion of culpability tags along with the unhappiness of a man called a "captive."

The Main Test

The second half of the bipartite judicial structure begins with the notation of Charles as *caitifs*, but then proceeds to introduce a new actor, one who has been noted only once before in the text, a few lines earlier (l. 3806).[17] There he is announced simply as *Tierri, le frere dam Geifreit* (l. 3806), that is as the brother of Geoffroy of Anjou. As he actually steps forth on the scene of the text to speak and perform his narrative, the text endows him with the narrative space of a physical description normally granted those whose presence really counts in the narrative: Charles, Roland, Ganelon, and now Thierry de Chartres. While the *form* of preceding dialogue and action with a description is followed, the conventional content is not. The figures of the greater warriors of epic are imposing in aspect: large, strong, prepossessing, their musculature is equal to the tasks imposed by combat with lance, sword, and shield, and their hair blond, presumably in recognition of their descendance from the conquering Germanic tribes. Thierry is something else again:

> Ais li devant* uns chevalers, Tierris, [*Charles]
> Frere Gefrei, a un duc angevin.
> Heingre out le cors e graisle e eschewid,

Neirs les chevels e alques bruns le vis;
n'est gueres granz ne trop nen est petiz. (ll. 3818–22)

Behold before him a knight, Thierry,
brother of Geoffroy, an Angevin duke.
Skinny he was, thin and slight,
his hair all black, his face rather dark;
hardly a giant, but not too small.

If epic heroes are preternaturally tall and imposing, one can hardly imagine a less heroic portrait than Thierry's: the three adjectives in l. 3210 all contain the seme /thin/, and the etymon of the first suggests it is from hunger! Dark of hair: medieval heroes tend to be blond; swarthy of complexion: epic heroes have clear faces; neither tall nor too short: just average, one might say—an odd figure to have appear at a momentous occasion, championing the cause of king and emperor! The implications of his social status are similar. He starts simply as "*a* knight," one who has not been heard from before. As the text develops, he is a knight who has no particular place of his own in the world: his identity is merely that of the brother of one of the great ones, Geoffroy the Duke of Anjou. Thierry, brother of Geoffroy, is presumably a younger brother, the scion of a noble house perhaps prevented from marrying and establishing an independent status and property lest the noble heritage be split and splintered among the competing establishments of a noble progeny.

In spite of the family connection, then, Thierry de Chartres is not one of the greats of this world: he appears as the younger son who has turned professional but undistinguished warrior, one of that large social category, the *chevalers* who formed the class of professional mounted warriors. It is an odd choice to represent as champion of the emperor and his interests in a judicial combat to the death, but there it is. One might add that he is not, in fact, anyone's "choice": he is self-elected to the function. But it is the text, finally, that places him in this position. Odd as it may be, Thierry de Chartres figures as a lowly textual entity representing the highest level of interest, the highest stakes in the text. Paradoxically, in opposition to the feudal codes normative in feudal epic, it is the antihero, looking rather like Mr. Average Frank, *un de chez nous, quoi*! who is charged with the highest value by the poem.

His speech is equally puzzling. It begins with a rhetorical introduction which is perfectly adequate and would fit into any feudal address:

"Bels sire reis, ne vos dementez si!
Ja savez vos que mult vos ai servit.
Par anceisurs dei jo tel plait tenir. . . . " (ll. 3824–26)

Good lord king, do not torment yourself!
You know I have served you a long time.
On account of my ancestors I must speak as I do. . . .

The invocation of service is that of a dutiful vassal, and the theme of the ancestors of one's lineage is well known as typical of noble and knight in this text. Thus, Thierry begins as a loyal vassal, a knight who performs his service to his lord. But the heart of his speech is something else again. In the brief compass of four lines, Thierry de Chartres enunciates a theory whose political reverberations will continue until the end of what Marxist historiography calls the feudal period, namely the end of *l'ancien régime*, with the Revolution of 1789. Indeed, in the political and legal context of his time, the theory Thierry enunciates— in a manner whose rhetoric is as unprepossessing as his person—is properly revolutionary:

"Que que Rollant a Guenelun forsfesist,
Vostre servise l'en doüst bien guarir.
Guenes est fels d'iço qu'il le traït;
Vers vos s'en est parjurez e malmis." (ll. 3827–30)

Whatever wrong Roland did Ganelon,
being in your service, that was his protection.
Ganelon is criminal, in that he betrayed him.
Toward you, he's perjured in bad faith.

Thierry does not present any counter to Ganelon's argument that Roland had done him harm in gold and property. Thierry implicitly grants that Roland had acted wrongly, even criminally, toward his stepfather. *Que que Rollant a Guenelun forsfesist*—whatever it may be that Roland had done bad to Ganelon: the breadth of the concession is unlimited. There is no defense, the point is ceded absolutely. Nor does Thierry counter the claim that Ganelon had defied Roland, Oliver, the peers, and the men of the army, properly and openly: that too is granted, and Ganelon is thereby acknowledged to have met the requirement of the only limitation upon the noble's right to vengeance and private war. Nor, finally, is any argument presented directly against feudal law allowing feudal nobles to exact noble vengeance through such private warfare. In fact, almost no element of Ganelon's case is touched by Thierry's argument. The element that condemns Ganelon is one entirely outside his argument, outside the world he inhabits. It is presented so simply, so briefly, that with very few exceptions, it has passed almost unnoticed. The key declaration is a simple sentence:

"Vostre servise l'en doüst bien guarir." (l. 3828)

"Your service ought to have protected [Roland] from it [i.e., from Ganelon's attack]."

In feudal terms, this line makes no sense whatever. Any noble had the right to defend his honor against any other noble: it was the ignoble that were excluded from the system of honor. It is not because Charles is a higher level of nobility than Ganelon that being at his service ought to have afforded Roland protection:

it is because he is a different category of person. It is not Charles's nobility but his status as king/emperor that places him above the fray of noble vengeances. In this, the argument is analogous to that which the Capetians offered against doing homage as anyone's vassal: the king does not submit as inferior to anyone. He is of a different kind, and if he is the only one in his category, then he is a class of one. The king, Thierry claims, is super-ordinate: as the peasantry is forbidden to participate in the game of feudal hierarchization, so is the king not to be sucked into it. Charles is not only—as is frequently the case in the *Roland*—the one before whom the nobles stand: he is above them, of another order. Thus his person, and the service of his person, convey a special protection unique within the kingdom.

Semiotically speaking, Ganelon's assertion is that of an exclusive disjunction between noble vengeance and treason. Against this, Thierry asserts the position of nonexclusive disjunction, the position of *both/and*. While it is true, implicitly, that Ganelon had exercised an undoubted right to personal vengeance, it is also true that that exercise constitutes treason:

> Guenes est fels d'iço qu'il le traït;
> Vers vos s'en est parjurez e malmis. (ll. 3829f.)

> Ganelon is criminal, in that he betrayed [Roland];
> he has perjured and forsworn himself toward you.

Ganelon's act was *both* legal as noble, feudal vengeance *and* criminal, because treasonous toward the king. In other words, two rules of law are competing here: the rule according to which nobles continue to enjoy an established privilege of private war and the rule, of dubious status, which claims that certain occasions, at least, in which that first rule is exercised are nonetheless treasonous. These two codes are contradictory. They cannot both operate at the same time. Indeed, it is hard to see how they can both "stay on the books" simultaneously.

The answer to the conundrum, of course, is the principle of hierarchy. Thierry does not abrogate the principle of feudal war, he subordinates it within and under the claim of a higher rule that claims priority over the rule of feudal law. That is monarchical law: where the law of the nobles and the law of the king conflict, the latter will have priority. An act that is perfectly legitimate according to feudal rule will nonetheless be considered criminal if it infringes on kingly prerogative. Not only his own person but the person of those in his service will be covered by a veil of protection during the time that they are in the monarch's service. Rather than the destruction of the earlier form of sociopolitical organization by the new political dispensation—which would have implied the replacement of fuedalism by absolute monarchy—Thierry's argument proposes a subsumption of feudalism by monarchy, not its replacement. This subsumption will lead, in historical evenementiality, to what will later take shape as the "feudal monarchy," represented in the figured shape of the feudal "pyramid."

This is, in fact, the shape of future history, announced here in reduced form—as a model, one might venture. At this point, however, the most that can be said for Thierry's argument is that it represents a first, an innovative, and perhaps a somewhat tendentious step toward the development of the State.

While the content of the new law enunciated by Thierry may be defined as fantasy by contrast to the "real" social, political, and legal world contemporary to the text—in "the social text"—the proposed law appears to produce a gross injustice for Ganelon. Having punctiliously observed the niceties of the appropriate feudal codes in his narrative behavior toward Roland, the peers, and Charles, he sees both his juridical observance and his courage—employed under the rule of the law that is current at the opening of the text, and that is upheld by his society—come to naught. That punctiliousness is rendered pointless: it is beside the point, the point now being constituted by the point, the apex, of the newly instituted pyramid. For having punctiliously observed the details of the law in force at the time of his actions, Ganelon will now be judged in terms of a new law that has just been formulated by a textual nonentity, a Thierry who has no genealogy in preceding textuality. That new law renders nugatory his efforts to observe the old, replaced by a new political dispensation.

Judicium Dei

The single combat between Thierry and Pinabel is clearly stated to be performed under divine aegis: God knows its end before it starts (l. 3872), and Charles implores God to shed light on the issue of law at stake ("E! Deus," dist Carles, "le dreit en esclargiez," l. 3891). The "judgment of God" is an archaic form of judicial procedure, already known in the Merovingian epoch, employed when all other judicial means do not work or are absent, but remaining the favorite of the warrior vassals who crowded the count's court. The ideological fusion of legal process, however brutal, and divine benediction had, as its rationalization, a belief in the immanence of supernatural powers working through natural processes: because everything in Nature incorporated God's intent, justice was always divine will temporalized. Such a practice and ideology fit readily into the post-Carolingian disappearance of centralized power and the resultant privatization of power, law, and justice. In fact, however, the inadequacy of the method was early recognized. The Church always opposed itself to judicial combat, even though some monasteries occasionally had recourse to it. Part of the renewed period of peace included a lassitude with war and the "brutal and incoherent" forms of "justice." In fact, conciliation, arbitration, and mediation became increasingly frequent in lay society: the tendency, already present in the eleventh century, becomes increasingly frequent in the twelfth.[18]

While there is no question that the combat between Thierry and Pinabel constitutes a *judicium dei*, faith in the utter fusion of divine intent and natural process is not perfect. Twice, the divine interferes in the natural process in a manner that is therefore no longer "natural." First, Pinabel lands a blow of the sword on his opponent such that sparks fly out and set the grass aflame, hitting the forehead, the face, the whole right cheek, and opens the hauberk right to the chest (*ventre*). The narrator comments:

Deus le garit, que mort ne l'acraventet. (l. 3923)

God protects him, he is not struck down dead.

Then, when Thierry kills Pinabel, the assembled Franks, who have wept at the sight and whose reactions have been stressed throughout the description of the brief duel, react sharply:

Escrient Franc: "Deus i ad fait vertut!" (l. 3931)

The Franks cry out: "God has made a miracle!"

The proceedings are placed under the sign of God.

Nevertheless, that sign is given no manifestation comparable to the interventions in the natural order of things that attended either Roland's death or Charles's own battle with Baligant. No angel comes down to remind the warrior of his divine debt or mission, no interruption in the normal course of time and event occurs to allow the performance of a divinely ordained task. While the text *asserts* a divine presence through the mouths of Charles, the Franks, and the narrator, it does so only through the medium of words, the level of manifestation, through the metadiscourse of commentary, not through narrative, the level of surface grammar. It is only the level of the *verba* that is affected, not the evenemential level of the *res*. Why is this the case? Perhaps the answer lies in the description of the actor. What is miraculous, after all, in Thierry's killing Pinabel? Only the fact that he is protrayed as so much thinner, and hence weaker, than his opponent. Thierry himself seems to make allusion to the discrepancy between them:

Ço dist Tierri: "Pinabel, mult ies ber,
Granz ies e forz e tis cors ben mollez;
De vasselage te conoissent ti per. . . . (ll. 3899–3901)

Now Thierry spoke: "Pinabel, you are noble,
you are big and strong and your body is well formed;
your peers know your qualities as vassal. . . . "

Thierry's assertions regarding Pinabel define his own appearance and stature *a contrario*. In spite of physical characteristics which define him as weaker than his opponent, he nevertheless wins against the latter, and this defines the divine intervention, the demonstration of God's strength (*vertut*).

At the level of narrative event, the text stresses the same aspects as in the trial: the strict observance of proprieties and the sociality of the event. Pinabel presents himself before Charles, asserting his denegation of Thierry's argumentation. Both combatants submit their gloves to the emperor, Pinabel warranteeing the justice of his claim with thirty hostages; that warranty, apparently, is made to satisfy the court, which frees Thierry of the same obligation. The text stresses the punctilious observation of proprieties:

> Ben sunt malez, par jugement des altres. . . . (l. 3855)

> The others judge they have been duly summoned. . . .

This is a *social* judgment that is invoked, not a divine one. But part of the preparation for the combat will be religious observances: confession, absolution, and benediction are part of the process, as are great offerings. Returning before Charles, the combatants put on their accoutrements one by one, and those assembled to watch, the hundred thousand knights, weep out of pity for Thierry on account of Roland:

> Idunc plurerent .C. milie chevalers
> Qui pur Rollant de Tierri unt pitiet. (ll. 3870f.)

> Then wept a hundred thousand knights
> who on account of Roland pitied Thierry.

The battle itself is rather quickly despatched. One *laisse* describes the mounted combat which ends with both knights knocked off their horses (*laisse* 281). In the next, they jump to their feet, having at each other with swords on helmets, arousing the anxiety of the assembled Franks and Charles (*laisse* 282). More emphasis is given, in the middle of the battle description, to the argumentation between the two, an argumentation that parallels that, earlier, between Charles and Baligant (there is no equivalent in the *Roland*-section). This argumentation is, in fact, an effort at negotiating the differences within the framework of ongoing combat. Each is as generous as possible, within the limits of his role as champion and representative of another's cause. Pinabel offers to become Thierry's vassal, if only he will reconcile Ganelon and the king. Thierry, recognizing Pinabel's physical stature, promises to reconcile him with Charlemagne (one of the rare occurrences of the emperor's full name), but insists that Ganelon be punished so that "no day will pass that men do not speak of it." Pinabel's response is a familiar one. As against the regalian right claimed for Charles by Thierry, he asserts the familiar obligation to feudal lineage:

> "Sustenir voeill trestut mun parentet;
> N'en recrerrai pur nul hume mortel;
> Mielz voeill murir qu'il me seit reprovet." (ll. 3907–3909)

> "I will uphold my lineage,
> I will not desist for any mortal man;
> I'd rather die than be reproached for this."

One might be hearing Roland speak: the same identification with the value of the extended family that is the lineage, the insistence on upholding that value against any counterclaim, the resolute choice of death in preference to the reproach that might come as a result of *recreantise*, the feudal surrender that is cowardly by definition. This is the last time the feudal order's claim will be formulated in the poem: Pinabel is the last surviving representative to take the narrative stage in its defense within this text.

After this thoroughly consistent and sequential argumentation between the two champions of opposing claims to justice, Pinabel and Thierry return to sword play. Thierry is wounded first, but protected by God (*laisse* 285). Then he lands the mortal, deciding blow on Pinabel in the following *laisse* (286), leading the witnessing Franks to the conclusion:

> Escrient Franc: "Deus i ad fait vertut!
> Asez est dreis que Guenes seit pendut
> E si parent, ki plaidet unt pur lui." (ll. 3931–33)

> The Franks cry out: "God has shown his strength!
> Now it's right that Ganelon be hanged,
> and all his kin who stood for him in court."

The conclusion regarding the hostages is reconfirmed (*laisse* 288): they will all be hanged. Ganelon too, of course, will die, but in another manner. What I would stress now is the communal, social, and political character of the text. The imposition of punishment on the traitor and the hostages is not effectuated by monarchical decision, but by the decision of the assembled Franks: it is the Franks—warriors all, and with rare textual exception, warriors of the knightly class—who ratify the *judicium dei*, and who thereby decide their own submission to a new legal modality, rather than the one which obtained at the beginning of the text. Without any exception noted in the text, the council of the assembled Franks accepts the result of the combat as semantically charged by Thierry's earlier definition. Functionally, this is tantamount to the election of the emperor by his troops. Here, as in the narrative modality of the *judicium dei* itself, the text archaicizes, calling upon an older code of political and judicial procedure. That archaicizing is the one step backward that allows for the two steps forward. It is by calling upon a code marked by the authenticity of ancient age that the text achieves its revolutionary goal: the establishment of monarchical prerogative over the feudal.

The Traitor's Death

The extraordinary quality of Ganelon's death has been noted by modern scholars: it is indicated by the text itself, which describes it both as "miraculous suffering" (*merveillus ahan*, l. 3963) and as "terrible perdition" (*perdiciun grant*, l. 3969). It is anomalous in its cruelty, and it is natural that modern readers should react with dismay and repugnance. The traitor is drawn and quartered before the barons of the empire. The description of the effects of the torture on his body does not attempt to mitigate these:

> Puis sunt turnet Bavier e Aleman
> E Peitevin e Bretun e Norman.
> Sor tuit li altre l'unt otriet li Franc
> Que Guenes moerget par merveillus ahan.
> Quatre destrers funt amener avant,
> Puis si li lient e les piez e les mains.
> Li cheval sunt orgoillus e curant:
> Quatre serjanz les acoeillent devant
> Devers un' ewe ki est em mi un camp.
> Guenes est turnet a perdiciun grant;
> Trestuit si nerf mult li sunt estendant
> E tuit li membre de sun cors derumpant:
> Sur l'erbe verte en espant li cler sanc.
> Guenes est mort cume fel recreant.
> Hom qui traïst altre, nen est dreiz qu'il s'en vant. (ll. 3960–74)

> Bavarians and Alemans returned
> and Poitevins, and Bretons, and Normans,
> and all agreed, the Franks before the others,
> that Ganelon must die, and in amazing pain.
> Four war horses are led out and brought forward;
> then they attach his feet and hands.
> These battle horses are swift and spirited;
> four sergeants come and drive them on ahead
> toward a river in the middle of a field.
> Ganelon is brought to terrible perdition,
> all his sinews are far stretched,
> and his body's limbs burst apart;
> on the green grass flows the bright blood.
> Ganelon dies a criminal renegade.
> When one man betrays another,
> it is not right he should live to boast.

As is typical of early epic, the structure of the *laisse* is simple, categorical, straightforward. First, the unanimity of the court's decision and its content are stated; second, the decision is enacted and described in ecphrastic detail; third, the narrative and juridical principle incorporated by the tortured death is specified. The unanimity is important for two reasons. First, the court, composed of the barons of the empire, is the repository of truth and custom, as representative of the community as a whole, in which ultimate legal power resides; in addition, its participation in the decision also binds it to defend that decision in case it is questioned, or in the case—likely in epic—that its enactment lead to the frequent pattern of the *faida*, in which the lineage of the accused enters into a narrative program of revenge.

There is another significance to this unanimity, one which derives, not from the common cultural codes embedded in the narrative action, but from the very specific context and content of this particular narrative syntagm. It is essential that the adhesion of the great feudal nobles be secured in the establishment of the principle that is at stake: the predominance of regalian rights over noble rights. An unwilling subordination of the nobility, an enforced domination by the king, would have little chance of leading to the peace that might result from a centralized polity set up over warring nobles. Only if the subordination of the warring class is a willing one, an accepted submission to superior authority, can the new social compact and its new political order have a chance at success and survival. The court is delivering one of its own, who has made its own case as a social class, against an opposing locus of authority and form of governance. Only if that act of social sacrifice is a willing one can it be a successfully performative one.

What is most shocking to the modern reader is the combination of the graphic detail with which torture is wreaked upon the body of the condemned man and the fact that this torture is publically enacted.[19] The victim's sinews are torn apart, his limbs burst asunder, as the horses pull in their four different directions. The green grass flows with brilliant blood, in a public display of torture that includes as audience the modern reader along with the Bavarians, the Germans, the Poitevins, the Bretons, the Normans, and above all, the French. Shocking as they are, these narrative details are not new to the modern consciousness. Spectacular torture, recounted in detail, is the stuff of the opening of Michel Foucault's most famous book, translated as *Discipline and Punish*. The opening pages quote, at grisly length, the historical documents which tell of the public torture of the regicide Damiens, in Paris, in the year 1757. What is perhaps most troubling to the reader of the *Song of Roland* who rereads the penultimate *laisse* of the poem with this chilling, eighteenth-century scene in mind is, in addition to the pure horror of the description itself, the shiver of recognition attendant upon the uncanny juxtaposition of the two scenes of torture.

In both episodes, common traits of gross "inhumanity" are spectacularly displayed to as broad a public as possible. The detailed ecphrasis, repugnant to what we take as basic human decency, is broadly flaunted to the horror of a fascinated gaze. In addition to these stylistic similarities, the two recounted tortures perform similar functions. In both cases, the individual's body bears the mark of subjection to the power of authority. We have seen, in more than one place, the *Roland* inscribes its messages in the very corporeality of its personages, as these bodies are turned into the signifiers of the semiosic processes. In both cases, the torture is far from a senseless rage: it deploys selected techniques geared to inflict an appropriate amount of pain—Foucault notes that the technique of quartering is one designed to carry pain "almost to infinity." The judicial punishment, carrying out the decision of the feudal court, is a ritual, a social and political ritual, in which "the very excess of the violence employed is one of the elements of its glory . . . it is the very ceremonial of justice being expressed in all its force." For it is not merely a question of punishing a criminal and re-establishing the reign of justice: "The public execution did not re-establish justice: it reactivated power." The purposeful and differentiated production of pain inscribes in the subjected body the signifying economy of power. And—in both cases—the power that is (re)activated is the power of the State over and against its assembled subjects.[20]

Across the five or six centuries that separate the two events, the equivalencies we have identified are equally shocking and puzzling. So emphatic are the repetitions that we might almost be reading a case of biblical typology, with the earlier event already announcing its repetition, completion, and fulfillment in the later case. And so it is, a typological relationship, albeit in the political sphere rather than the theological. Foucault, describing the effect of the later event, writes of "*re*-establishing" justice and "*re*-activating" power. The execution by torture of the regicide Damiens had as its function to set back into a prior order of existence a system of justice and a semiosis of power that had existed and had been temporarily interrupted by that act of regicide. A few decades before the revolution that would end the justice and the power of the *ancien régime*, the retribution wrought upon the perpetrator of the crime allowed for a *re*-statement of its domination.

The typological relationship between the torture of Damiens and the torture of Ganelon juxtaposes a nearly terminal assertion of royal power against a sign of its inception. For what torture *re*-asserts on the body of Damiens, it established and constituted on the torture of Ganelon. I do not mean, of course, that no torture had been known before that inflicted on Ganelon. I do mean, however, that far from the torture being a regrettable afterthought, or an archaicizing shard or trace, the transformations of the narrative text of the *Chanson de Roland* are geared to lead to the torture of Ganelon as the final transformation of the text. Upon the body of the victim is inscribed the ultimate (in)justice done Ganelon, who had the system of relevant justice switched on him in mid-course. The distension of his body and the explosion of his limbs become the means by which the new dispensation is established and constituted. His execution is the ritual which ushers in the transformation of the feudal system of justice and the politics of power dispersion of which "feudalism" is the name. Ganelon, the last surviving member of the feudal class as represented by the actors of the first part of the narrative, is the necessary means and sign of the transformation of feudalism into the monarchical dominance which was the subject matter of dispute in his trial. Limiting ourselves to the givens of the text, and of the "literary" text at that (disregarding therefore the political and administrative texts to which we have alluded earlier), we must, in truth, limit the assertion produced through the torture of Ganelon's body to that of a monarchical predominance and priority. But that truth, established by a hindsight that stretches across the intervening centuries, includes in its purview some major moments of retrospection: the reign of Philip Augustus that ends perhaps 120 years later than the earliest dating of the *Chanson de Roland*; all the peripeties of the *ancien régime* until the establishment of the absolute monarchy of the seventeenth century under the *roi-soleil*, and its reinstitution in the torture of Damiens; the Revolution of 1789; but also beyond and into the more recent incarnations of the ambiguous monster loosed on history by the medieval foundations of the modern political structure that is ours. The intervening history of torture is not without connection to the structure of the State, which became routinized as a police technique and in the Inquisition together with the initial elaborations of the foundations of the State.[21] From the framework of these later perspectives, we understand that Ganelon's torture serves to establish the basis of what will become the modern nation-state we inhabit.

Let us be quite clear about just what is meant by that statement. The establishment of a principle of monarchical priority which will lead to the further developments of the nation-state is purely "symbolic," of course. *La Chanson de Roland* is nothing but a narrative poem, after all, hardly the stuff of which political structures and constitutions are made. The vivid description of Ganelon's death by torture is nothing more than a brilliant example of poetic figurality, an example with a particular name based on Greek antecedents: *ecphrasis*. And yet, there is room to wonder. If I have been right to suggest, indeed to argue, that the textualities we call "literature" are not some secondary, epiphenomenal, and reactive imaging of an anterior social or political reality; if such texts are first and foremost, and from the very beginning, always already social entities, parts of the social fabrics and patterns of political negotiation of their time; if the texts we reduce to the category of the "merely literary" are, in often strange and unexpected ways, performative of their own content and structures; then there is room to wonder indeed. Within the domain of vernacular culture, if we accept the dating of the *Roland*, proposed by Joseph Bédier, around the year 1100, give or take some twenty years or so in either direction—then the text is far from a specular reflection of anything in the world of social and political "reality." The *Roland* is the very first sign of that principle of monarchical priority, annunciatory of the eventual development of the modern nation-state, the very first sign to be found in the vernacular body politic of its signification. The ritual trial of Ganelon, requisite for the performativity of the text to take effect, is a ritual sacrifice whose (in)justice is blatant. An individual, innocent within the codes of his performance, must be slaughtered for the foundation of a new (in)justice, no less violent than the old, but with displacements that could seem desirable in the course of the twelfth century.

The Actantial Distribution

This reading incorporates two radically different narratives as occurring simultaneously within the same text. One is fairly close to the traditional reading. In this first narrative, Roland is the subject and Charles his destinator; when this subject dies, the earlier destinator is transformed into a narrative subject himself. At this second moment, the function of the destinator is syncretically incorporated within the same actor as the subject, but it is also lodged in a textual actor whose presence is more stressed in this second narrative sequence than in the first: God, whose interventions are more assertive, decided, and determinative in the second sequence than in the first. In this reading, the second sequence performs several functions. It wreaks appropriate vengeance for the first subject's death upon various traitors: Marsile, Baligant, Ganelon, Pinabel, and the thirty hostages. It thus reestablishes that first subject's value within the codes of his society and his lineage: Charles, avenging Roland, acts both as uncle and feudal lord in wiping out whatever negative value might attach to the status of Roland's reputation as a result of his partially ambiguous death. This first reading thus retains a continuity, in terms of cultural and semiotic codes of value, between the two narrative sequences and their respective subjects: revenge for injury and lost social value operate in both. The special sense of retrospective sadness and loneliness that unusually sensitive commentators have found associated to the figure of Charles is readily explicable here in terms of the destinator's loss of his subject and the necessity henceforth of continuing to perform heavy narrative programs as a survivor.

This reading is not wrong: it remains correct, though incomplete. Its semiotic limitation lies in the reduction of the actantial level to the actorial: subject and destinator remain merely the representational anthropomorphs who have been the subject of so much good and sensitive traditional discussion. As we have seen, however, the issues raised and played out by the text go well beyond the actorial level. This is a realization which cannot occur except *after* a first, full reading of the text. Its terms are not given *ab initio*, as are those of the actorial level. It is only a full first runthrough of the narrative development that allows the terms of the deeper structures to begin to appear. What are only—and have been presented by our analysis only as—suggestions and adumbrations by the text do not receive major functionalization by the narrative until an adequate account of the text's juridical issues and resolutions are detailed, including the final punishment of Ganelon. In other words, the appropriate actantial distribution (as distinguished from the actorial) is enabled only by the conclusion of the first reading. That is when it becomes possible to speak of the *Chanson de Roland* as incorporating a fundamental and constitutive non-exclusive disjunction: it bespeaks *both* a generalized celebration of warfare *and* a desire for peace impeded by the latent conflict between the feudal class of great warring nobles, fused with their irascible vassals, on the one hand, and, on the other, that class of one which is the monarchy. Where the actorial level presents these relations as trusting and collaborative, as positively contractual, the actantial reading shows them to be engaged in profound and momentous conflict. In this second reading, the monarchical class is the subject, God is its destinator, and the *féodalité* its antagonist, its anti-subject. Paradoxically, the entities which, figuring as enemies on the actorial level of the narrative grammar—Marsile, Baligant, and their troops— function as adjuvants on the actantial level, both in pragmatically helping to decimate the feudal class which is the anti-subject, and in ideologically providing further justification for the need to increase monarchical power. It is a truism of politics that external enemies can be the most useful allies in dealing with internal opposition.

The basic narrative pattern at the actantial level can then be summarized as follows. The subject (monarchy) must dispose of the anti-subject (feudal class) with the least possible overt acknowledgment possible. The text disposes of the anti-subject (*féodalité*) by employing precisely those characteristics which make it a danger to the collectivity; those characteristics—which are also the characteristics which make it socially useful—lead that feudal class to destroy itself: embedded in the epic *Chanson de Roland* is the tragic structure of that band of heroic warriors whose very qualities lead to their own destruction. That destruction fulfills the necessities of the monarchy by removing from the scene of narrative its political and military opponent. The battle of Roncevaux, a defeat on the actorial level, is a triumph on the actantial level, in that the decimation of the peerage of France, along with their military forces of the warrior knights under them, leaves the field of force open to the monarchy to occupy. After the necessary rituals of social reintegration—only partially successful, as we have seen; after the development of a heightened ideological necessity for increasing the power of the monarchy—the external, universal if not cosmological threat represented by Baligant and his forces; after the demonstration of divine support for Charles; the issue between feudal nobility and monarchy can be joined again on the concrete, actorial level, charged as it is by new semantic components. The individualized equivalent of the new troops created by Charles out of apparent thin air in his fight against Baligant is Thierry de Chartres, a creature of the king, whose subordinate nature is defined by his nonheroic stature.

The final act of the narrative must be the ratification of a new rule of law, of the rule of the new monarchical law embodying monarchy's new superordination. That ratification is obtained with the approval and in the presence of the subordinated population, at least the population which, up until now, has constituted the anti-subject: what is left of the feudal class. That is the transformation operated by the final *judicium dei* and the execution which follows. The *de facto* dominance of the (textual) monarchy since Roland's death is thus legitimized by various archaic, judicial maneuvers which ironically triumph by employing the feudal class's own structures.

These valorial oppositions can be displayed in the form of the semiotic square. The essential problematic of the square is to establish relations between two (logical) classes, monarchy and what the French call "la féodalité": the "feudal class" and its practices. The issue is that of dominance and subordination, of dependence and independence:

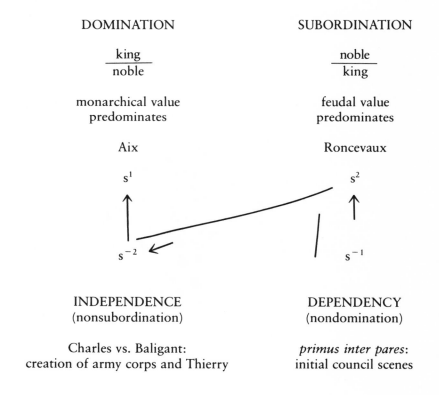

DOMINATION   SUBORDINATION

$$\frac{\text{king}}{\text{noble}} \qquad \frac{\text{noble}}{\text{king}}$$

monarchical value   feudal value
predominates   predominates

Aix   Roncevaux

s^1 s^2

s^{-2} s^{-1}

INDEPENDENCE   DEPENDENCY
(nonsubordination)   (nondomination)

Charles vs. Baligant: *primus inter pares*:
creation of army corps and Thierry   initial council scenes

The sequence indicated by the arrows traces the essential Moments of monarchical progress through the narrative: $S^{-1} \rightarrow S^2 \rightarrow S^{-2} \rightarrow S^1$. From the ambiguous, sometimes helpless "chairman of the meeting" role of the council scenes, the text moves to the ultimate eradication of the "feudality" in its ordinary and heroic incorporations. At the point of Roland's death, the value of monarchy, its interests, are subordinate to the values of the feudal class, to the semiotic and future oriented display of its *virtù*. The predominance of feudal values is negated by the Baligant episode, with its creation of subordinate troops *ex nihilo*, that is to say, out of the breath of Charles's words, in an act of pure performativity. That subordination of feudal value—of the value of "feudality"—to the value of monarchy is theorized by Thierry de Chartres at Ganelon's trial. In spite of the attempt of the noble council to acknowledge contemporary practices of judicial compromise, the text finally refuses accommodation in order to clearly assert the domination of monarchical value over the feudal.

10 | Conclusion

There is no document of civilization which is not at the same time a document of barbarism.

Walter Benjamin, "Theses on History"

War is father of all, and king of all; he renders some gods, others men; he makes some slaves, others free.

Heraclitus

The *Chanson* Ends with the Indeterminacy of Non-Exclusive Disjunction

I HAVE BEEN at pains to explore the concept of a putative medieval mode of signification, producing unitary, monological, and assured meaning, as the characteristic of the world of vernacular culture (the issue in Latin, ecclesiastical culture is more complicated and acquires the Derridean subtleties of theological discourse). Repeated instances of plurivocal structures cast such monologism in doubt: pluralities of perspectival shifts built into narrative structures, the polysemanticities of crucial value-terms, and non-exclusive disjunctions occurring at the most fundamental levels of the text already undermine the notion of a flat, untroubled monologism ensuring textual closure in the *Song of Roland*.

No place in narrative is more crucial for this issue than the end of the text. Narrative closure, while not an absolute indicator of semiotic closure, bears a strong connection to it: it is difficult to imagine a text of semiotic closure with an open, indefinite narrative ending. Indeed, the penultimate *laisse* of the poem contains a narrative move which might lead to a conclusion of such monosemanticism. The emperor calls upon his bishops and has them baptize Bramimonde, the widow of Marsile. Her baptism is performed at the baths of Aix—what could be more fitting!—and she is renamed Juliane:

Chrestienne est par veire conoisance. (l. 3987)

She is Christian, by knowledge of the Truth.

The unity of Church and State, the conversion of paganism to True Faith, the re-identification of the individual thanks to a new name characteristic of Christian latinity, the religious ritual baptism associated with the nobility of her god-mothers—all these would seem to fit readily into a significatory closure, at the end of the narrative, which would top off both text and narrative, and round it off. And so it does, momentarily.

The *laisse* of Bramimonde's conversion is the penultimate. The last word goes to Charles, a figure characterized throughout by ambivalence, by ambiguity, by duality of value and meaning. The text stresses the conclusive nature of the final *laisse* by rehearsing the immediate past: Charles has obtained justice, his anger is dissipated, Bramimonde has been Christianized. The day passes, night arrives, the king lies down in his vaulted room. It is time to rest: whatever one's ethical or political opinion of the proceedings—they do shock a modern sensibility in a number of ways—the king and emperor is entitled to a rest. Perhaps, but it shall not be. Charles is summoned by the Angel Gabriel to a new mission: he is to relieve King Vivian, at Imphe—both proper nouns new to the text, of uncertain reference—the Christians there call and cry for him. Nevertheless,

> Li emperere n'i volsist aler mie:
> "Deus," dist li reis, "si penuse est ma vie!" (ll. 3999f.)

> The emperor would have wished not to go.
> "God!" said the king, "the pains, the labors of my life." (Goldin, ll. 3999f.)

The translator's struggle with Charles's expression is obvious: *si penuse est ma vie* is, indeed, ambiguous. Both of Goldin's meanings—"pain" and "labor"—are part of the semanticism produced by *penuse*. But I would add a third seme, the etymological one, especially justified in an early text that so often is archaicizing and appears to allude to the Latin which hovers just behind the Old French. The third seme is that of /punishment/: *penuse* comes from classical Latin *poena*, including a broad semantic field of labor, suffering (especially associated with martyrdom), and punishment: as we still speak of a "punishing" task.

The verbal isotopy here rejoins the narrative: after his exertions, Charles deserves a rest. The assignment of another mission cannot help but produce the signification of yet another exhausting and punishing task. It is punishing, it is a punishment: apparently, and again, in spite of the enormous narrative machinery we have traced, the issue of culpability is not settled yet. For if punishment there is, culpability must hover about. In spite of the textual maneuvers to put that question to rest with the finality of closure that attends on Ganelon's execution and Bramimonde's conversion, the ambivalence that has characterized the Charles figure throughout remains with him beyond his end. The irresolution of the text regarding its answerability in the matter of Roland's death indicates that the issue has found no solution within the terms of the social code available to the text, those of a shame culture which opposes *honor* and *honte*. The guilt culture, however, which will take religious form in the practices of repentance and confession, has not yet become effective in the diegesis of the text. Between the two, the nomothetic code of polity functions: the fundamental contract between the two halves of the ruling class has been breached, by the figure which figures as its guarantor and which claims succession to central power. Insofar as the French nation is being founded, its founding is an aporia of (un)consciousness. Hence the text's irresolution, hence the ambivalence that haunts the figure of the king and emperor beyond the termination of the text.

This ambivalence is doubled by the ambiguity of the very last line of the poem, to which the translator's version responds with appropriate semantic scattering:

Ci falt la geste que Turoldus declinet. (l. 4002)

Here ends the song that Turold composes,
paraphrases, amplifies.
that Turold completes, relates.
Here ends the tale that Turold declaims, recounts,
narrates.
that Turold copies, transcribes.
Here ends the *geste* for Turold grows weak, grows
weary, declines.
Here ends the written history. . . .
Here ends the source that Turold turns into poetry. (Goldin, l. 4002)

The translator's exemplary decision to display what, according to normal expectations of translation, remains untranslatable, is admirable. Insofar as all commentary, interpretation, and analysis consist of "translating" from one language into another, from one mode of discourse into another, the text's unrepresentability in English demonstrates something of the text's inherent indeterminacy—even in its incompleteness. If the (non-)translation of the second half of the hemistiche demonstrates its indeterminacy, its admirable effort does not quite reach justice in dealing with the verb of the first hemistiche, *falt*. It assumes a single meaning, and hence provides semantic closure, where only more indeterminacy reigns. For *falt* could just as well mean "is missing," "defaults," indicating an incompleteness of an earlier manuscript. Or it could mean that the manuscript simply "stops," without really ending the narrative. Or it could equally well refer to an earlier oral version, which is missing, defaults, or simply stops, at this point, without an indication of a meaning for that final, non-clotural gesture.

Is it possible that the ending of the *Roland* is the beginning of that long line of "accidentally/intentionally" uncompleted texts from the Middle Ages, of which the next major example might be Chrétien's *Perceval*? Is it possible that medieval textuality so clearly rebuffed modernism's readings of "the closed medieval text," and that modern scholars missed the point for so long, preferring rather to invent cheap and sentimental narratives to "explain" such medieval openness, whose proper recognition might upset so many critical and ideological applecarts? Is it possible to imagine a more obvious demonstration of non-cloture, of textual and narrative indeterminacy, than is offered by this last and profoundly inconclusive line of the *Song of Roland*? How such a termination allows a conclusion of closure, of monosemanticism, of exclusive disjunction, on the part of modern theoreticians is beyond semiotic comprehension. Only the urgent rhetorical necessity to find a defining opposition for the indeterminacy supposedly characteristic of modernism can explain the refusal of critics and theoreticians to open their eyes before this text. It should be fairly obvious that, whatever the *Roland*'s virtues, it cannot be pressed into service for this cause. Only the politics of interpretation allows for such unmapped misreading!

The *Chanson* Produces Limited and Specifiable Significations

The *Chanson de Roland* provides neither narrative closure nor semantic closure, in spite of the brutalities with which its component narrative programs conclude. This does not equate the poem with Mallarmé's "*Un coup de dés jamais n'abolira le hasard*," or *Finnegan's Wake*. Its narrativity is taken seriously enough to preclude the kind of semantic scattering for which the texts of the end of modernism reached. That narrativity, taken seriously, implies a minimal level of anthropomorphism that is the *sine qua non* of narrative's potential for transformation, hence of textual performativity.

The textual codes that inhabit and define the narrative trajectory of the story element rejoin, at the most fundamental level, the codes of the circumambient "social text." That text, like any text, is constituted around an oppositional problematic: the "axiology" of a text is defined by values set into polemical relations, relations of conflict. What our (post)modernist episteme constitutes as a "literary text" operates within the cotext of its own culture as a mediation and negotiation of an epochal conflict of values, a valorial conflict imbricated in all the different segmentations our episteme imposes on social life: politics, economics, social structure, and the conjunction of those fields we call culture, literature, and secular philosophy/theory—the field of ideology, in other words. All are connected to the conflict between two fundamentally irreconcilable worlds of encoded values. One is a world of social fragmentation, parcelized territorial power, and face-to-face relations of both close, specular relations of identification and conflicts of social alterities so profound they can be taken as a categorical so absolute as to be undermined or deconstructed by the texts that formulate them; its primary mode of communication is oral, even as it incorporates vague references to distant written texts. Its primary mode of (oral) textuality is the epic, of which the *Song of Roland* itself is the greatest medieval token. The other world is that of a dimly perceived future, imagined in terms of a mythological and ideologized past, bearing a hypothetical and putative centralization of power capable of imposing political control over its own subjects by a radical, brutal, and archaicizing violence, subordinating the precedent pluricentrality by a fantastic verbal re-creation of its personnel, and by verbal reformulation of common-law relations between subject and ruler, as founding political acts.

These two worlds meet around the crux of violence. The essential problematic around which crystallized the text of the *Chanson de Roland* is the social use of force against the functionings of social violence. The text negotiates a narrative out of and in response to this problem, not in intellectual or theoretical discourse, but in the anthropomorphic allegory that constitutes the semiotic negotiations of all narrative texts. The anthropomorphism of the text is entirely historical: it is not as a work of philosophy that the text negotiates the problem of force and violence, but as a historical problem, with the shape and contours that the organized use of force had at a certain time, in a certain cultural context, within a particular social formation. The codes of that culture, as with so many others, exclude direct consideration of the economic issues hovering in, behind, above, or below the military heroism, as well as any direct statement of the political issues implicit in the narrative. Indeed, it is only insofar as the economic and political issues are excluded from direct representation that the text exists at all.[1] Its verbal and narrative discourses repeatedly exemplify different aspects of that problematic without naming it, under a variety of circumstances which give differentiated significance to the various moments of the narrative. Narrative is an encoding of unnamed issues: that is why it is a negotiated allegory. The process of unraveling that encoding is the only way to understand the text, if by understanding we mean something beyond the projective identification which, while emotionally satisfying, may not yield a critical analysis accounting for the existence of the text, the significations it produces, and its survival.

Military force plays a profoundly ambiguous role in the society of the *Roland*. On the one hand, it was felt to be essential for the effective functioning of the political and juridical functioning of society upon which its productivity was based: Marx himself recognized the priority of the political over the economic in the Middle Ages. Both the continuation of the peasantry upon the lord's land and the continuing rake-off of surplus value, in kind or in the form of cash, harvested as fines and taxes, seemed to depend on the continued presence of the means of delivering force: the knights, their continuous semiosic display of potential force, the continued threat of its use, its occasional exemplary employment, guaranteed the continued slaking of the noble thirst for *deniers*, for sumptuary display, for capital accumulation, for territorial expansion. This dependency was equally characteristic of the secular and the religious sections of the dominant class. At the same time that the organization of society was felt to depend upon this crucial presence of force, however, the character of the men who wielded that force was such as to result in the enormous social waste of precisely those values which the force was supposed to produce: knighthood, the essential police link between the upper nobility and the great mass of the productive population—the Repressive State Apparatus, operating primarily over and against the peasantry—was given over to continual internecine violence, destroying social life, the material conditions of production, and the produce of the countryside itself, as well as stored accumulated value and the conditions of capital accumulation. Thus, simultaneously and interdependently productive and destructive of social value, knighthood, and to some extent the nobility itself, presented a conundrum to their culture, in both its narrative and its political dimensions. Knighthood was both the lynchpin and the crucial aporia of the feudal formation. How to conceive of, how to deal with, a class of men and what they signified, equally necessary to social life, and also deeply harmful to it?

The conundrum was difficult both for the lay nobility and for the clericality—who were often, especially in the upper reaches of ecclesiastical administration, blood relations of the lay nobility. To a large extent, the clericality, in town episcopates and in rural monasteries, relied on the same direct or implied use of force for both the productivity of their establishments and the particular form of taxation assigned them, the tithe. As the religious institution of society, however, it performed an ideological function—the only institution in that society with a specifically ideological function—conjoined with a theoretical function that rendered its performances delicate. Hence the complex development of its "sociology" traced by Georges Duby in the *Three Orders*. Attempting functional description of society while protecting deeply lodged institutional investments, it was partly propaganda, most often produced by the clericality in an attempt to suppress social change, in particular the efforts toward upward mobility of the low-born. Its doctrine was in part a reaction against the distinction between commoner and noble. "The persistence and spread of the doctrine attest the persistence and spread of the threat."[2]

Given the various shifts dictated by the historical evolution of the institution in its sociopolitical context, one element that remained permanent in its "theoretical sociology" was the continued and necessary submission of the peasantry. How could it theorize otherwise, when its own existence depended on that submission? If gratitude for charitable works accounted for some part of the social value turned over to the Church by the peasants, it would be a rosy view of the world indeed that considered such warm feelings to be the sole reason—to the exclusion of the use and threat of force—peasants turned over their hard-won *deniers* to clerical overlords! And of course, that gratitude would be even more striking issuing from peasants also subject to the oppressive exactions, penalties, and punishments meted out to them by knights in the name of the secular seigneurial lord, his interests, and the sociopolitical system that legitimized his hierarchical position.

The knightly class performed a key role in this social formation. Riding out in the *cavalcade* from the fortress-castles that were society's centers of power and culture—the phrase "power containers" fits the fortress with remarkable precision[3]—the knights insured observance of the "customs" consisting of the various exactions customary at the time: the "totality of extortions" with which the powerful oppressed the poor.[4] The avidity of the warrior class intensified rural labor, the economic basis of what modern scholars are pleased to call the "twelfth-century renaissance." The specific relations between the subaltern warriors and the lords they served were highly varied: from paid servants no better than mercenaries and issuing from the adjacent class of serfs to richly recompensed and honored vassals in the "feudal system," which it is time to recognize as the internal organization, functionalization, and formalization of economic and political distribution within the dominant class.

The ideology of the knightly class evolved markedly during our period, from armed retainers defined by their function of transmitting violence, to the order of knighthood called "chivalry" with its fully developed rituals and formalized ideology at the end of the twelfth and especially during the thirteenth centuries. That this changed their economic function in society is open to doubt: ideological pretensions alone do not a social transformation make. The more overt functioning of the earlier period, in which the knights were the "agents of manorial oppression," persisted even under the later ideologizations, and it continued to be true that "in chivalry, oppression was incarnated." Not as a moral stance of the modern consciousness over against a supposed medieval immorality, but as an awareness of the interdependency of various instances within a given social formation. The noble mode of life depended on "what the knights had forced the peasants to give up to them": as a result, within the mechanisms of a manorial economy, the knightly class constituted "the center piece, the axis of the system of exploitation."[5]

The shift from an earlier economy of war and booty to the later one of productivity, first agricultural and later of the production of goods for trade, contextualized the knightly character and practices in new ways. The warfare that had earlier been productive activity for the society of the warriors (whatever its effects on the societies victimized by their raids) began to take on a different coloration, particularly when the narrative of these characteristics was played out, not against some externally located society to be victimized, but against sectors of the warriors' own society as their aggressivity underwent a process of social internalization.[6] Economic productivity is enhanced by peace and stability, and when the knightly depradations came to be turned, not against some foreign tribes considered merely as the source of slaves and booty, but against the productive assets of their own society, the more sophisticated sections of the dominant class began to understand that these depradations were damaging to their own interests. These sophisticated sections of the dominant class were, first of all, the well-organized monasteries, whose productivity was the economic avant-garde of their time, and the bishops in towns where artisanal production, commerce, and trade were already beginning to increase. In addition, some of the leading members of the lay nobility, whose own dependencies had begun to enter the phase of greater economic productivity, also realized that their interests were better served by a more peaceful policy than by military adventurism. Hence the movements of the Peace of God and the Truce of God conjoined these two segments of the dominant class with a peasantry that was the ultimate victim of that warring adventurism.

Hence also the changes in the ideology and social status of the knightly class, changes whose political import is profound: it has to do with the organization of society itself. As we have seen, the general movement toward fusing the subordinate knights with the dominant nobility entailed several moves: the adoption of the ritual of knighting by the upper nobility, the latter's self-identification with "chivalry," and the accession of the knights to nobility as well as the social status and freedom from onerous taxation that implied. I would suggest that the spread of feudalism as the representation of relations between these two levels of the dominant class—so highly differentiated in wealth and power—is itself part of the systemic effort to knit together these two elements of society. Feudalism is itself the ideology of the dominant class.[7]

The *Chanson de Roland*, however, is not merely the expression of the ideology of a particular class or even a class segment. Without lodging any claims to transcendence, the cultural artifact, operating within the social sphere, performs its programs in a larger space than such a narrowly propagandistic view. The text achieves the ideological fusion desired: the peers of the realm, on whom the first part of the text focuses, perform the narrative programs of knights while bearing the qualifying statements of the upper nobility. The text sings the praises of force, of military display, the brilliance of armaments. It gives voice to the rhetoric of mutual dependency, vassalic duty and the lord's protection, singing the virtues of the warrior and the social cohesiveness of men at war for common ideals according to a common code of value and behavior. It *also* depicts the specific mechanisms by which these very virtues are turned into ghastly destructiveness, in which lived and sung ideals of courage, loyalty, and group identification turn into betrayal, somber death, and collective loss. The relation between the assertions of the dominant class ideology and the performance of its narrative programs can only be termed tragically deconstructive.

The actual functioning of the fused nobility as a totalized class is detrimental not just to a larger social whole (the original complaint about the savagely destructive rapacity of the violence-prone *milites*), but to its very own existence. Heroism brings destruction. Feudalism in the *Roland* self-destructs according to the principles of its own existence and makes way for the political system that will replace it: first a "feudal monarchy," a temporary syncretism to be replaced in turn by a more coherent form of monarchy. In the text, even "feudal monarchy" remains a dimly felt and feared representation, whose integers continue to resemble their forebears even as the latter's fundamental status is overturned. Feudal heroes are replaced in their functions by the figures of social, political, and military anonymities which, while endowed with proper names, have no independent existence. Creatures of the king, they accept subordination and bring no qualifying or narrative opacity, no intertextuality which generates social independence, in opposition to or support of his commandments. In the person of Thierry de Chartres, even knightly appearance changes, from that of the great epic statures of heroism to the small, thin, swarthy type, readily recognizable as Mr. Average Frenchman. Not only in its origins but in its social and literary standing, the new knighthood is cut (down) to size, created *ex nihilo* to represent the norm, the average, the unheroic necessities of its performances in the service of the borning State.

The monarchical instance that benefits from this self-destruction of feudalism and its replacement by the creatures of kingship is neither pleasant nor heroic. It performs its combat requirements against Baligant with divine help but without the pleasure and pride in the manipulation of arms and the hazards of battle that inspire a Roland and even, in their moments, an Oliver and a Turpin. It flounders helplessly, not so much under the burden of a personal guilt as with a necessary historical and political culpability. From the self-destruction of the vassals it was supposed to protect, the monarchy inherits the burden of political and military power. Far from a personal guilt, its culpability is the necessary accompaniment of political devolution. If the State is established with unaccustomed savage cruelty, it leads, not to triumph, but to the unhappy recognition of the endless burden to be borne in ensuing battles.

The Subject of Violence

> Un sujet est ce terme qui, asservi à la règle qui détermine un lieu, y ponctualise cependant l'interruption de son effet.
>
> Alain Badiou, *Théorie du sujet*

The subject—the subject that will be the subject of the nation-state—is born *of* the *Song of Roland*, but is not yet portrayed or constructed in that text. The subject to be born of the *Roland* does not bear the subjectivity extensively documented by Michel Foucault's last researches, posthumously published under the overall title of the *History of Sexuality*; in particular, it does not derive from the efforts of early Christianity described in the last volume of that series.[8] In these publications, Foucault's key terms are two. The first is sexuality: it is as sexual subjects that Foucault's subjects exist. The second key term is that of consciousness. Foucault's is a subject whose consciousness of self is already established, and which is therefore capable of constituting itself, in a process described as "paying attention to oneself, deciphering oneself, recognizing oneself, and acknowledging oneself as subject of desire. . . . "[9] Because this internal structural division is taken for granted, the process of the self-constitution of the sexual subject can be taken as a "truth-game," in a project of "studying the games of truth in the relation of the self to itself and the constitution of oneself as subject, taking as the realm of reference and the field of research what might be called 'the history of the man of desire.' "[10]

That psychic structure of nonidentity of the self, the disjunction of the subject with itself, is not an eternal given of human "nature." It is a historical product, appearing at a particular moment of European civilization. The appearance in question here may be a *re*-appearance, in certain ways: if so, "it"—the subject—reappears in a very different format than in Foucault's pages. Its eventual structure will be that of nonidentity with self, precisely because that structure is elaborated in conjunction with, and because of, a political structure that does not yet exist, and that will not exist for centuries, in the periods examined by Foucault: that of the nation-state. In this respect, Foucault's teacher, Althusser, was correct in the specificity of his conception of the subject, as contemporary with the state and essential to it: the subject, constituted by the historically specific ideology of a state at a given stage of its historical development, derives its existence from its integration in the social and political structures of its co-texts. It is this subject, created by and for its integration in a historically specific polity, which the *Roland* calls for.

The subject to be born, however, is a subject not yet there. It is a subject required by a historical situation, and called for by the text, rather than being directly and extensively constructed in the text. It remains a subject in the future anterior: a subject who will have been there—or the deictic "here" of the enunciating text—at some point in the future. Neither the polity nor the subject it requires yet exist. Both are indexed, suggested, pointed to, by the *Song of Roland*, rather than produced in it. As inexistent objects of their complex signs, objects whose existence lays only in some futurity, they are imprecisely limned by the text. Rather than constructing the subject required, the text gestures, points, and says: "Here build!" At most, it provides—in graphic, ecphrastic detail—an event that is a moment in the development of what is required: the narrative event that signals a series, that participates in that series of moments far too graphically and precisely to be called a "symbol" in the literary sense. That moment is the one by which the will of the One (the royal personage whose personal rule will precede collective rule in the displacement of elected representation), the One as subject-agent and destinator will be inscribed in the bodies of the collective as subject-victim, in the torture Kafka will figure as the "harrowing": the subject's body as the material for punishing inscription of the law.

Ganelon, noble traitor to the future state, is a far cry from the anonymous victim of "In the Penal Colony" . . . and yet there is a family connection, a connection of "lineage," one might say.

What actually is there, in the *Song of Roland*, is for the most part something quite different, that to which the subject to be born is a response. The call for a new subjectivity that issues from our text does so as a response to the old subjectivity displayed in the text. It is the subject to be discarded whose representation is foregrounded in the *Chanson*. It is a curious subject, answering perfectly to the description against which an earlier period of modern thought struggled so vehemently, with its repeated announcements of the death of the subject. The subject in question is that of self-identity, a subject of total integrity, an integrity which is total because it need not be totalized, i.e., because there is no prior, internal dissension requiring (re)constitution. It is a subject of perfect coherence with itself, without hesitation, doubt, or inner conflict or even tension. It is a subject which embraces its narrative trajectory without a moment's self-doubt, even when it has to contradict itself.

It is precisely because of this absence of self-interrogation that the subject in question falls short of the hypothetical subject, posited by Kant, ascribed to Descartes, and ever after erroneously assumed as the type of subjectivity fielded by Western civilization.[11] There is no self-interrogation, even when events require the subject to change course by 180 degrees: does one blow the horn or not?. There is no self-questioning, no self-doubt. There is no necessity for consciousness, there is no function for a questioning self-consciousness. There is only the hero perfectly adequate to his task, that of carrying out the requirements of his narrative trajectory, so that his very death becomes the ultimate moment of his life, the very incarnation of his heroism. There are traces of a contradiction, as when temper erupts against self-control, but they are local contradictions, and not constitutive of the actor: they do not lead to the trait which founds a contemporary theory of the subject—its cleavage, its felt contradictions, its nonidentity with itself, its subsistence in and against the trace of the other.[12] That constitutive fissure is completely absent in the seamless heroism of the epic actor who meets the demands of his own legend so perfectly as to turn it—and himself—into myth.

For this hero—I am speaking, of course, of Roland himself—there is no question as to the source or origin of his ideology, its function, its validity. It is there, with self-evidence, to be lived, faithfully and unhesitatingly, to the hilt—quite precisely, the hilt of the sword as it plunges through the opponent's armor and into his flesh. Roland is the subject before the subject, the subject who enjoys to the utmost limit available to man—up to and including the moment of death as the concluding moment of life—an integrity which is the perfect identification with the system of values imploded in him by and as his constitutive ideology. Roland is the absence of the *faille*, of constitutive self-differentiation: Roland is the creature of might and courage who is entirely and totally constituted in the image of his ideology. There is no gap between "him" and his ideology: he states it, clearly and succinctly, he lives it, and never varies from it. What earthly need would the Roland of the *Song of Roland* have of consciousness, what use could it be to him? Consciousness is for the creature haunted by contradiction, by remainders, by margins, by inexplicabilities that become essential. There is none of that in Roland: he is dedicated, entirely and totally, by his ideology to its fulfillment in action. Even when a contradiction appears in that ideology, as in the argument about blowing the horn, even when the narratee must recognize that contradiction, Roland's adhesion to that ideology remains complete. Roland is the perfect caricature of the vulgar misunderstanding of "Althusserian" theory, a subject constituted completely and perfectly by the ideology of his time, by vassalism as the Repressive State Apparatus for an as yet inexistent state. He serves an idealized *res publica*, under Charlemagne, king, emperor, *rex-sacerdos*, as that Other which brings a totalizing legitimation equal to the hero's absolute and independent violence.

It is this perfect fit between act and deontology which makes of his death-scene confession such a tawdry, clichéd, and mawkish performance. His confession, required by death's proximity, is perfectly ritualistic. There is nothing really to confess: all his acts have been completely determined as deontological incarnation. Insofar as this fit is perfect, Roland is the most terrifying example of the destructive potentials of total legitimation. Confession is a ritual act, and nothing else: it can be nothing else unless and until the subject is differentiated from the subject. That individualizing function of confession is nonexistent in Roland's confession.

The absence of constitutive self-consciousness, of a critical, self-reflexive structure, in the narrative subject, is not identical with a similar absence at the level of the subject of the text, that of the narrator or the enunciating subject. Potentials of reflexivity and critique, of a subjectivity closer to what will later be posited as the "Cartesian subject," do exist in the text. Charlemagne's connections with the beyond, the imprecise boundaries of his self with the Other whose divinity hovers beyond the effective narrative of the text, to erupt into the diegesis on essential moments in the form of dreams or miracles, suggest repeatedly an awareness not shared, and perhaps unshareable, with others of his diegesis. Oliver, cast as the more prudent of the two buddies, demonstrates the ability to manipulate the contradictory ideologies of rationality, as embodied by the count of armies, in alternation with the heroism he shares with Roland. Ganelon above all, thrown into the role of traitor by Roland's disdain of the desire for peace voiced at the councils of the Franks, lives the passion of desubjectification by public torture before living its death. Actors embodying a divided and contradictory subjectivity do exist in the text, and one of them—Charles—replaces Roland as Subject in the second half of the narrative. But Roland, heroic warrior that he is, the perfect inversion of the academicians who ponder his narrative today, who admire in him precisely their lack, knows no moment of self-differentiation, of self-deferral. Roland is himself, entirely, with the perfect fit of his own integrity.

The nascent necessity for the subjugation of violent individualism finds no purchase in Roland, no catch-hold, no *faille* by which to enter. His integrity itself blocks any adaptability to the new order aborning. Others—Charles, Oliver, Ganelon—are in some ways closer to that new order, but none of them is ready to enter that new order, except for Charles, equally its leader and its sacrifice. And yet, somewhere within the text, in the interstices of its verbal and narrative structures, there is a point from which to view the text, a point from which the necessity of Roland's replacement within a new order, is perceptible. The cognitive position of the text is far from identical with that of its narrative subjects: on the contrary, the text takes its distances from both, in different ways. The text (re)presents a narrative, a heroic narrative, it does not endorse a static sytem of paradigmatic values. On the contrary, the text presents and transforms the terms and conditions of possibility of a moment of subjectivity.

The "new world order" in question is not one to be imposed upon a distant world from a point of centrality external to its victim, but a new sociopolitical order (re)organizing the socius itself, the very socius within which the text is performed. Its first priority is to establish its own priority, its domination of those violent, rapacious, and independent mounted warriors who circle the land and ravage its increasingly effective production of wealth. The actor Roland dies so that the *Song of Roland* can perform the delicate and brutal insertion of discipline into the role of knighthood. The *Song of Roland*—an ongoing project that traverses the culture of orality and that of writing, one moment of which was recorded in Digby 23—creates and kills Roland, the peers, Ganelon, the 20,000 troops of the rear guard, in order to perform the subjection of the warrior class, its subjection to a monarchy which does not yet exist, which awaits in the wings until the scene is set for its entrance. That entrance cannot be performed until those who are to be ruled are in a position for constitution as subjects to the not yet existent power that waits for the moment to rule. The performativity of the *Song of Roland* is to set the scene for the event.

The subjection of the subject is thus performed by the *Song of Roland* as a *desideratum* for an ulterior purpose and moment, as a future anterior. In order for the king to come, in order for the monarchy to arise which will be capable of ruling, the subjectivity of the ruled has to be asserted first, indeed performed, in the ideological field. The major operator, in that ideological field, whose effectivity is guaranteed precisely because of the narrative subject's monstrous integrity, is the *Song of Roland* itself. More than any other text of its period and its "type," it performs the ideological task for its social formation, of producing a perfect model of the subjectivity to be discarded. That model is produced in order to be discarded, in order for the model of its replacement to be sketched out. That replacement, indeed, is hardly even "sketched." It is "indexed," perhaps, but its structural role is clearly limned. The replacement subjectivity is one that is created in subjection, by imperial *fiat*, in a discourse of pure performativity: its violence is entirely at the disposal of the reigning monarch, the One in whose divinely warranted image the state will be created.

That indexical sketch of the new subjectivity is presented by the skinny, swarthy Thierry, who briefly argues its theoretical principle without providing the existential experience of the structure he proposes. His presentation, however, has this remarkable about it. The speaker's enunciation derives from his right to participate in an assembly of nobles: it is his and their common subjection to the monarch he argues. If the "lived experience" of the complex structure he proposes is not reproduced in the fiction which bears him and his discourse as an ultimate narrative moment, Thierry de Chartres announces a myriad of future Western European authors, in telling the contradiction of simultaneous independent agency and submission to the state in which the enunciatory subject lives.

The *Song of Roland* does not initiate the European tradition of "literature" in the twelfth century. It makes more sense, perhaps, to view the text as the "big bang" in which the correlative images and partial discursive accounts of subjectivity, in specific historical forms, and the state, in the limited form of feudal subordination to monarchy, are simultaneously (re)presented in their interdependence. Emblematically, it can stand as the first text of a European post-classical textuality: its inaugural value is not in question. Indeed, its inaugural value may be stressed, but not as "literature": that is a label and a category bestowed on the texts—and others of its period—by the nineteenth and twentieth centuries, in a perfect example of the reverse historicizing promulgated under the label "hermeneutics," rationalizing the subjugation of the past by the present. The *Song of Roland* performs an inaugural, ideological function in the social text of its time, it does so brilliantly, and we revere its sacrifice from the safely distant vantage shore constituted by its ritual scene of horror: our vantage point called "literature" well beyond that scene, within the polity of the nation-state. Performed as brilliant ideology, it is enshrined in the memory of our collective archive as the beginning of our "literary" tradition. Its sequence of narrative images are telling, and what they are telling, in the quasi-theoretical discourse of ideology, is the foundational gesture of the political binarism that subsists today.

The *Song of Roland* sacrifices an image of heroism on the altar of subjection, in order to clear the way for a lesser breed, those who are born into subjection, those who submit the potentials of violence to the discipline of the new "governmentality," its "disciplines" and "persecutions."[13] The potential for violence is to be retained, but delivered to the instances of government and control as required. Where the *Song of Roland* fails—as it could not but fail, being, like all the works of man, a historically bounded work, leaving unregistered the implications of its discovery or production—is in the recognition of a prior condition of possibility for this transformation. This transformation, of the violent, collective independence of warrior knighthood into the subjected soldiery of royal armies, requires the establishment, in the subject, of a new psychic instance. It is an instance dedicated to the control of violence within the self, an instance which decides when violence is to be suppressed, which violence is to be suppressed, which deployed, and when the violence is to be enacted, under proper discipline and direction. The potential of violence is to be retained, but submitted to the discipline of rule, a rule operating within the subject of violence, in the location of a specific instance. That instance, of course, must function independently of the violence to be controlled.

Charlemagne, Oliver, and Ganelon bear traces of the split subjectivity required: the process of transformation of the individual subject is elided, however, and will not be examined until Chrétien de Troyes does so.[14] And yet, the *Song of Roland* produces one theme, and returns to gnaw at it repeatedly, that will be essential to subjectivity and its ulterior developments, from the thirteenth century to Freud. That is the theme named "culpability," a nomothetic, proto-legal term bound to the hypothesis neither of a shame culture nor a guilt culture. Most of the text modelizes fairly obviously the codes of a shame culture, in which "honor" and the possibility of measuring compensation in material terms dominate. Nevertheless, the manner in which the text returns again and again to the theme of Charles's "culpability" suggests far more the operation of a guilt culture, in which the element of guilt cannot be purged and remains unresolvable. Is it possible that, as part of the transformation required to install the nation-state, a sense of profoundly individual guilt is required to replace the public honor-shame dichotomy, whose terms can always be exchanged for material value? If so, it is of more than passing interest for any effort which seeks to conflate psychoanalysis with a materialist view of the polity, that guilt—if that is what "culpability" really means in the *Song of Roland*—is attributed to the paternal function in the Oedipal relation, rather than the filial. For it is the father-figure to which the text repeatedly hangs the nomothetic responsibility for the death of the son. The inauguration of the nation-state would be attended by a willed death of the favorite filial figure, as a result of which endless guilt is lodged in the monarch who is phallocentrically equated with the One, to which the figure of the son must be sacrificed. The nation-state is always already installed with a guilt inherent to its structure, and distributed among its subjects.

In the meanwhile, the *Song of Roland* signals the necessity of a subjected subject, under the disciplinary rule of the new, monarchical dispensation, as the *sine qua non* for the negotiated circumscription—not annihilation—of violence. That subject is a historical product, and it is with the shape of that history that we conclude.

Nomadic Violence, Sedentary Economics, and the Birth of the State

The conclusion to the textual analyses of the preceding pages, so insistently focused on narrativity and its operations, can only take the form of another narrative, one of those forms of narrative fiction called "history" in our episteme. That is one of its bonds with the text discussed, considered as the *chanson rerum gestarum*: the song of deeds performed. The form of this narrative is that of history, "the western myth."[15] To identify it as a myth does not erase or cancel out its utility or its necessity: where is the individual or the collectivity acting entirely without a "myth," charged with values that constitute subjectivity?

Late antiquity, the Dark Ages, the Middle Ages—these were periods that not only lived violence: they knew it as a norm.

In contemporary thought, as the twentieth century turns into the twenty-first, violence figures as the exception, that which is to be explained: the absence of violence is assumed as a norm. Peace and stability are the general, the universal, to which war is an exception. This is the structure of our ideology, a symbolic imaginary. The gross falsity of this ideological fabrication, its gross falsity in regard to our own history, makes no difference: war and violence are the exception, peace and stability the norm. No matter the height and breadth of the burial mounds and burrows radiating away from the charnel house in all directions, overflowing with the bloody carcasses of our wars, the homeless dying in the streets, the sick dying in indigence, the defenseless civilians of other societies as well as our own who are suddenly turned into "our enemies" through geopolitical sleights of hand, as earth turns into a giant catafalque. In the increasing disjunction between the gross realities of indirect human cruelties and the continuingly inflated, idealized visions of our ideology, holocausts, world wars, ecological violence against a necessary environment, social violences against women and children, as well as men without armor, count as nothing. Peace and stability are the norm, violence and the devastations and depradations of the war-machines mere occasional transgressions of that happy norm, transgressions which may even turn functional as a spice of life, an interruption of the humdrum and quotidian lives of a bored and satiated middle class, its intelligentsia included. Not to mention the internal violences of men and women at war with themselves, in lives increasingly distanced from social and cultural ideals, hence increasingly alienated, not just from the social and the familial, but from themselves. The allegories of the spirit written in the Middle Ages do not hold a candle to the psychomachias of contemporary subjectivity.

Nor do the medieval epics hold a candle to contemporary destructiveness. If "medieval" denotes a chronological slice of history, its connotations in common parlance are those of barbarism, ignorance, and superstition. In respect to the practices of violence, **modernity is medieval**: it continues the practices of the Middle Ages, differentiating itself primarily in the amount of violence produced, and in its hypocritical disguisement. The violence with which the Middle Ages struggled still ricochets across the historiographical surfaces of modernity. Indeed, modernity is largely shaped by the efforts to continue and supplant the modes of struggling with the heritage of violence first elaborated by the Middle Ages. It is the genealogy of modernity that the gaze of medievalism encompasses, and in particular of the repressed component of that genealogy.

The forms of violence are multiple. More, there is strong suspicion that its different forms are not independent of each other. The violences internal to the individual, produced by inner psychic divisions; the violences we call domestic, affecting spouses and intergenerational relations; the violences of the streets, responding either to local interests such as turf or economic competitions in the restricted areas left available to the poor and the subsocial organizations of gangs; the violences of the states and of the state, exported as often as possible, yet often enough suffered by the very populations the state is supposed to serve—it is increasingly felt, rightly I think, that these different forms are interdependent, feed each other, help each other reproduce in cyclic dynamisms beyond ordinary means of social control. In the waning of the twentieth century, the general subjective experience in advanced, liberal democracies—those nations whose structure would most have been able to avoid violence, in theory—is that of living in a fear of increasing violence. Until recently, the concrete experiences of the streets and an increasingly stressed and torn domesticity was doubled by the geopolitical fear of a demonized antagonist, itself doubled by the terror of thermonuclear warfare. As the formerly antagonistic empires of East and West seem on the way to settling their differences by negotiation, as the former Soviet Union and its allies gravitate closer to an agreement to allow the "new world order" free play in areas formerly beyond its purview, it is unclear whether the quotients of violence will diminish or increase. The Soviet Gulag is on the way to disappearing, but former ethnic animosities, suppressed by communist state violence, have increasingly free play. If the developments in Yugoslavia are an indicator, the triumph of the West has the dialectical effect of allowing free expression to destructive potentials held in check by the dicatorship of a One such as Tito. As the nation-state implodes, the contradictions it subsumed flare up again in the form of ethnic holocausts. What the effects of this dialectic on domestic and psychic violences will be is unclear. What is quite certain is that the West has little reason for self-satisfaction or contentment at its triumph. The political form it created, beginning in the Middle Ages, and which now covers the surface of the earth, seems increasingly fragile, as does the psychic structure of subjectivity on which a livable nation-state depended.

Or is the historical recurrence of violence to be taken as a sign of its domination of human life, its apparent centrality to all forms of the socius, the inverted double to all forms of sociability devised by and imaginable to humanity? This is the lesson suggested by a growing number of modern thinkers, across widely varied fields stretching from psychoanalysis to political theory and historiography. In addition to those whose purport is to assert aggression, cruelty, and violence as primary drives within the human psyche (Freud, Lacan), there are those who take the further step of attempting to consider means of curbing that violence, religiously (René Girard), politically (Jesse Byock), or through the mental structures of anthropology (Pierre Clastres), as well as those who, in reaction to modern hypocrisy regarding violence, assert its continuing presence and perhaps necessity as one mode of political action (Georges Sorel and Walter Benjamin).[16] Along with these intellectual traditions, the reader of these pages must also include reference to the modern invention of the world war, twice indulged in, and the form of holocaust invented during the second of those world wars, taken as a model for the experience of all those who feel their whole people and their form of existence threatened with eradication.[17]

This is not the occasion to attempt either a summary or a solution. It is necessary, however, to indicate the power of the issues with which the medieval imagination was required to cope. In domains as varied as the social and political, the cultural and textual, the Middle Ages was marked by its millenial struggle to confront the problematic of violence. It did so with an extraordinary social inventiveness, of which its politics and ideologies, its cultures and ideational constructs, were major components. In some ways, the medieval effort was more to be admired than the modern: it dealt with its heritage of human violence more directly, less hypocritically, and with greater recognition of the need to integrate violence within sociopolitical structures, rather than make believe it didn't exist. We will not begin to make headway with our own versions of the issue until we grasp the continuity between those contemporary versions and the bases laid down in the Middle Ages upon which our struggles with violence are founded. However grim the issues and the facts, the historical perspective offers the most optimistic view of violence. Insofar as the issue of violence is correlative with social, political, and economic structures, so far can the subjects of (post)modernity engage in its struggles with some hope of success. In this project, a critical semiotics is essential, addressing the plays of textual signification in its multiple relations to the other instances of society, in full cognizance that those forms are always already inhabited by some degree of "writing," of ideological investment.[18] Such a critical semiotics must be historical, in full recognition of the constructed character of history. It is therefore to a partial, sketchy, and historical overview of the medieval problematic of violence that the concluding pages of this book are dedicated.

Violence comports its own aesthetics. Its forms are all-important. Clearly the period knew psychosocial violence against minorities, whether these were Jews, heretics, homosexuals, children, or women.[19] The form of violence which haunts the pages of medieval history, however, is the more brutal, overt, corporeal violence, continuous or repeated, of a particular form of combat, born by the sword or the mace in the hand of a mounted warrior, who finds joy, profound personal fulfillment, and a ratification of his own value in the delivery of violence, whatever its target, as he turns the corner of a forest path, charges as part of a squadron of companions, or enters the peasant yard. That physical, immediate, insistent violence; its actual performance in mounted combat, by individuals or the relatively small hordes of men scattered across the countryside; or merely its permanently present threat, as well as the incessant wars between small local powers, completely entitled to their right of "private" war (i.e., war not waged by an as yet inexistent State); and addressed most insistently to the overwhelming majority of the population, the *inermes*, the "unarmed," be they peasants, men, women, or children; that is the medieval phenomenon which will be the non-exclusive focus of the following pages, as it is the focus, in somewhat disguised form, of the *Chanson de Roland*.

Late antiquity, the Dark Ages, the Middle Ages, these were periods that not only lived in a climate of violence: they knew it as a norm. It would be a mistake, however, to think that violence entered a peaceable European kingdom with the invasions from the east which marked the end of Rome's military domination of the continent. One need not wait for the arrival of invading outsiders: Rome itself was a predatory organism, an archaic empire, subsisting on rapine, pillage, and confiscations.[20] The Roman Empire had achieved relatively subtle control of violence, not only in its military form, but also in the socialized and ritualized semioses allowing for sublimated participative violence in circuses, theater, and crucifixions. In principle, at least, Roman violence was controlled, organized, and operated in the service of a centralized state. It was a violence which did not threaten the self-identity of the empire.

Violence was always already inscribed in the European psyche: the *Iliad* and the story of the Atreiades—not to mention that of Laius and his descendents!—are merely the most obvious indicators that what we call "classical antiquity" was obsessed with its own violence. And yet, as Fernand Braudel titled a section of a recent book, "Let's not forget the barbarian invasions."[21] They brought something new. The violence of the nomadic tribes, whose invasion of Europe may have been a response to population pressures in the "orients" from which they came, was a violence of a different type than the Roman. They seemed "barbarous," because their cultural alterity included a joyous dedication to adventurous warfare and rapacious killing, combined with a readiness to take, kill, or destroy on uncalculating impulse. In the early fifth century, a coalition of more recently arrived tribes—Vandals, Alans, and Suevi—defeated the earlier Franks, crossing successively the rivers Main and the Rhine, invading Gaul as far as the Pyrénées, bringing down even the walled cities of Trier, Arras, Amiens, Paris,

Orléans, and Tours—an extraordinary accomplishment for nomadic warriors. Others followed in their wake, including the Allemani and the Burgundians.[22] Turmoil and disaster ensued, for nearly half a century, as the West lay open as a victim of choice. In 451, Attila the Hun in turn attacked Gaul, accompanied by Germanic vassals, Gepids, Ostrogoths, Thuringians, Rugiens, Sciri, Heruli, Burgundians, and Ripuarian Franks. Sacking Metz, moving first toward Orléans, turning then toward Troyes, he was met finally by the troops under the general Aetius, whose Visigoths turned back the attacking Huns at the toponym Mauriacus, of uncertain reference. The victory spelled the end of the eastern invasions of Gaul, widespread economic crisis, and the instauration of a new period of history on the western surfaces of the Eurasian landmass, that of the Middle Ages.

But Rome itself was no longer Rome, having already incorporated barbarian troops and generals deemed essential to the military infrastructure of the empire. In addition to the sudden incursions we call "invasions," both peasant societies and aristocracies were touched by the slow, continuous, peaceful infiltration of individuals and groups. How many were they, and into how large a demographic pool did they enter? As against earlier attempts to reduce the quantitative dimension as much as possible, Braudel suggested the possibility that, if a million "barbarians" were perfused into Roman Gaul at a time when its own indigenous population numbered 10 million, nearly one-tenth of the resulting mixed population would have been "barbarian."[23] As he pointed out, such minorities are often the yeast of society, modifying social outlines and surfaces. By both "invasion" and "perfusion," barbarians entered a new society, transforming its values, its mores, its ethos.

Their ability to enter Roman military organization, their ability to meld into the societies they initially victimized but whose cultural mores they accepted to a large extent, indicates that, whatever their character at their distant points of origin in the Orient, they no longer represented a purely nomadic and tribal state of sociopolitical organization by the time they entered Europe. On the contrary, while retaining total mobility—no "base" was left behind to return to in their major wanderings—they possessed internal organization and leadership that enabled them to make pacts among each other as well as with the Romans. If a binary typology of pure models be elaborated, with /tribal nomadism/ at one end and the /state/ at the other, neither was an actually existent from during the "barbarian invasions."

The very success of the Merovingian period in integrating invaders and the autochthonous populations suggests some degree of preparation on each side. The Merovingian period, the two centuries ensuing upon the end of the invasions, laid the bases for many of the social and political forms that would characterize the Middle Ages.[24] It had as its essential historical task "the slow, silent process which entails the fusion of the Gallo-Roman and the Frankish societies"[25] mixing in court, at the centers of counties and bishoprics, and throughout the countrysides. The sign of the fusion is simple: after the Merovingian homogenization, tombstones in the cemeteries no longer distinguish between the Gallo-Roman and the Frank. Equality in death is the sign of a successful fusion of cultures!

If the eastern invaders spelled the end of Rome and the domination of its empire—a strange blend of the archaic empire and the state—the later hordes from the northern areas of Europe produced their own terrors, revived residual fears and apprehensions from the earlier epochs, and reinvigorated existing propensities to violence. Sailing and mounted warriors without attachment, without fear, without restraint, embracing the pleasures of violence as a divine enthusiasm or rapture, added to the cultural treasure now shared with the autochthonous inhabitants of the continent those of subtle, endless torture and the harshest of calculated punishments.[26]

As with the earlier invaders, the Northmen also would enter the society they found in the spaces they entered, fusing with the local populations, their customs and mores. Reiterated invasions, however, left a legacy which had to be incorporated into the new civilization: the presence, on the continent, of the habits, mental, social, and cultural as well as military, of a largely self-reproducing war-machine, perhaps nomadic in origin, but resonating with Eurogenic potential always already ensconced in the autochthonous European psyche.[27]

As an exteriority, a historical given, characteristic of certain peoples at certain times, the nomadic war-machine is fundamentally opposed to the sedentariness associated with both city and state.[28] Its individuals are connected by familial lineages and "a spirit of the body," an *esprit de corps*, which constitutes them as "a swirling body in a nomadic space."[29] The nomadic war-machine is the contrary of the state, identified as a stability enclosed within set borders, obeying a hierarchy whose internal relations are stable even if its address is not. How could such a body—mobile, unpredictable, of uncertain consistency and outline—"settle in" anywhere, in any stable social body? If the state signifies self-identity, stability, permanence, and established borders, how could it cohere with the violence of the nomadic war-machine, with its potential for the sudden, unpredictable swoop or swirl across an agricultural countryside? How could the joy and glory of spontaneous, unmediated, mounted attack, destruction, gore, and blood resplendent under the brilliant sun—as sung, for instance, by Bertran de Born in the south, and the *Chanson de Roland* in the north of France—cohabit with the drab accommodations required by the orderly hierarchization of the state?

It is not the case that the oriental or northern nomads brought to an otherwise peaceful European countryside something otherwise unknown called "violence."[30] It is rather that the particular cultural and anthropological or political forms of the violences concerned—that which was already there, ever since the beginning, and that which the nomads brought—are different forms of violence which would seem to cohabit only with difficulty. The question is partly rhetorical, partly meditative. The fact is that reiterated invasions of nomadic warriors entered the western spaces of the Eurasian landmass, settling into societies inhabiting these spaces, to the point of fusion, mutual transformation, and reciprocal functionalization. They brought with them habits of violence which define all stages of the later development of these societies, an essential, constitutive permanence which hovers between two poles: that of the nomadic war-machine, and that of the State, which makes every effort, when it is capable of doing so, not so much to eradicate the violence, but to capture its potential and its use.[31] This capture, which continues as the necessary foundation of the modern state, is one of the essential elements of the problematic that defines the process we call "the Middle Ages."

The "passion for war and adventure," as Marc Bloch phrased it,[32] was an open, proud, joyful violence, to be distinguished, for instance, from the sly and hypocritical violences of modern societies, and their institutions such as the university. Christianization itself did not suppress or displace their violence: "the deepest faith in Christian mysteries was associated without apparent difficulties with the taste for violence and booty, indeed, with the most conscious exaltation of war."[33] The force of lineage, its confusion with the forms of feudalism, their imposition of the duty of blood-revenge leading to the reciprocal pattern of the *faida*, continued to produce incessant private warfare among competing kinship groups,[34] whose mortal reiterations are repeatedly represented in the so-called rebellious barons cycle of the Old French epic. After centuries of the "true" religion, after complex economic and political socializations, during the economic, social, and cultural resurgences of the twelfth century, instability, violence, and a superficially pointless traversal of dangerous spaces was still a necessary moment for noble youth.[35]

Violence is not merely an individual moment. It ricochets across the face of society, crossing all imaginable social and political boundaries.[36] It reproduces itself at all social levels, among individuals and collectivities, in towns and in the countryside, aimed at the destruction both of persons and property, continuously and constantly.[37] The experience of violence by its victim, even in relatively peaceable individuals and groups, can (re)awaken unexpected slumbering potentials. Violence spreads as a social contagion, even into unexpected areas. We may think language a substitute for violence,[38] but the medieval world of "gestural semiosis" is inhabited by brutality and violence, even in the absence of infringement of the law.[39] Violence, in this cultural world, is not transgression. It becomes normalized as the way in which a particular society handles its conflicts in the absence of a generalized jurisprudential system[40] of daily life. Its multiple repetitions in a literary text like the *Chanson de Roland* are merely another documentary instance available to the social historian of the particularized forms of social and military violence.

In spite of their apparent exclusiveness, the two forms of violence—that of the nomadic, that of the state—folded into each other. Their epochal syncretism constituted the complex sociopolitical system called feudo-vassalism, at the service of a manorial economy, producing a form of proto-state violence whose ideology would have a wondrously fabled history. This syncretism, however, required modifications in the process of capture and integration, transformations which marked the beginnings of its incorporation into the state. From the perspective of its nomadic antecedence, the political structure of feudalism may be considered a compromised form of nomadism; from the perspective of its future devolution, it is an *appareil de capture* by which nomadic violence is tamed and integrated, a system of seizure for an as yet inexistent state, as well as the imposition of state power at a local level, well before the State emerged as a fully existent form.

The form of the state comports three elements: the bureaucratic component of administration, the claim to the monopoly of legitimate force, and the deployment of that force within a territory defined by the exercise of that force.[41] Max Weber introduces this definition, classical in modern times, by the statement that defines its epistemological limit: "Since the concept of the state has only in modern times reached its full development. . . . " The state is defined according to its modern form, which definition is then generalized backward to all preceding occurrences.[42] One major difference between the medieval occurrence and this definition is that of territoriality: it would be a long time before "France" acquired the hexagonal shape and dimensions which now provide a metonymy of the country. More important, Weber largely takes for granted the character of the population over which authority and force are exercised. He mentions the "members of the state, [its] citizens," and he encapsulates his definition in a memorable phrase as "a compulsory association with a territorial basis," without addressing the issue of concern to both more recent theory and the *Song of Roland*: the character of the population as subjects of the state. The initial step in forming the subject of the state, as its citizens, is their subjection. The fully developed nation-state—"a power-container whose administrative purview corresponds exactly to its territorial delimitation"[43]—lies far in the future, though its origins in the Church, "as a political, institutional body," are immediately contemporary.[44] Nevertheless, an essential step in its formation, the process of subjection, is performed by feudalism's capture of nomadic energies.

Topologically, nomadic "swirling" is adapted to feudo-vassalism. The properly nomadic function of spatial traversal is retained, but in a new form: it is anchored to the fortress, and—as important—it is functionalized economically. The genius of the transformation was to retain the nomadic performance of the mounted spatial trajectory, while anchoring it to a particular geographical point of reference and return. This topology then allowed for economic functionalization and for ideological legitimation.

Two topological points, in fact, are in question. One is the individual warrior's economic base: his fief, the personal source of personal wealth as a field of agricultural and human exploitation, and the necessary condition of his power, in replacement for the booty of nomadism. The other is the fortress of his lord, at which the warrior performs regular castle duty. Entering the fortress for a set period of time, the mounted vassal issues forth in a group that rides outward in patterns required by the actual lay of the land. The effects of the *chevauchée* are several: to defend the fortress when necessary, to attack neighboring cells of identical power organizations occasionally, but especially to impose servitude on the sedentary agricultural populations submitted to the lord of the castle. The violence proper to the nomadic warring group is retained as a mounted mechanism of functionalized violence, for purposes of defense, offense, and local domination and extortion: that is the transformation which marks the "beginning" of the knighthood which would become a fabled ideology from Beaumanoir on.

The great and faulty genius of the millenial epoch which culminated in the European Middle Ages was to capture a force that might have destroyed the exhausted fragments of European civilization in the aftermath of the invasions, to incorporate it and give it form for "internal" political purposes, without ever establishing effective control over its performances: a violence which remained both the bane and the basis of its existence.[45] Its genius was faulty, because aporetic. The violence, even if it had been possible to suppress and discard it altogether, seemed indispensable for governmental rule. But the economy based upon captured nomadic violence could be sundered and destroyed by that very violence. Violence was seen as simultaneously the necessary instrument and the devastation of the new economy. This is the aporetic basis of European civilization, as well as its American offshoot, incorporating an ideal of peace guaranteed by the State while remaining inexorably grounded in the incomplete control of and by violence. Ideologies twist and turn in the skeins of this aporia, justifying State violence in the name of national and international peace.

The first major impulse for the control of the violence came from the Church, aided by some of the more advanced secular lords. Christianization, however, did not succeed in establishing that control. The forms of desired control were the successive Peace of God and Truce of God movements, which attempted, during the tenth and eleventh centuries, not to eradicate violence, but to limit its times and its victims. These peace movements failed. One reason may have been simple. Remaining on the exteriority of history, we may conclude that ideology simply could not measure itself against the pleasures and perceived necessities of violence. We may go further, however. The economic base of the Church was the same socioeconomic system as that which produced the life, property, and profitability of lay manors. Its institutions reproduced the selfsame structure of production, control, and abduction of surplus value from peasant forces of production, even when the latter were renamed "lay brothers." The Church itself was caught in the aporia of producing an ideology of peace while depending for its existence upon a system of production that required violence. Peter the Venerable, taking charge of the administration at Cluny, complains that his predecessors had stripped the abbey's treasury in recruiting and paying mercenaries.[46] The major advantage of the Church derived from its hegemonic specialization in intellectual labor.[47] It became aware of its own contradictions earlier. Its writing and bookkeeping practices allowed it to become aware of both the economic profitability and the devastating effect of violence before most secular lords.

Along with the peace movements of the tenth and eleventh centuries, the efforts of the clericality to establish ideological hegemony over the other orders of society failed as well.[48] The failure to dominate mobile, self-reproductive violence by primarily ideological means is retrospectively inevitable: the violence was incorporated and supported by kinship and economic self-interest, and it possessed its own ideological legitimation. It constituted a self-nourishing cycle stronger than religious ideology, whose claims were so obviously countered by the very existence of the institution which promulgated it. The longer-term economic rationality, which designated peace as a more reliable basis for economic development than war, may have been visible to the abbots and bishops who studied accounts and pondered barely visible new forms of economic life, as well as the chancellors of a few lay nobles. Men of religion and religious administrators, as well as some of the more perceptive secular lords, came to understand the shift from an economy based on the surplus value garnered from externally gathered booty to an economy of locally produced surplus value. They understood that this new economy translated into money which could in turn be used as a medium of exchange for goods offered on an international commercial market, as well as to live and maintain mercenaries in addition to more traditionally enfeoffed vassals. Finally, they understood that this shift required peaceful conditions.[49] Peace could be more profitable than rapine and booty. These were a minority, however. The control of violence would have to wait for the development of a greater and more centralized power, with greater violence at its disposal.

The repeated failures of the Church to establish effective ideological hegemony and thereby to control the self-reproductive systematicity of a socioeconomic and political order founded on violence led to an impasse. The historical experience of European civilization with its own violences is summed up by René Girard's terse formula:

> Il n'y a qu'un seul problème: la violence, et il n'y a qu'une seule manière de le résoudre, le déplacement vers l'extérieur.[50]

One single problem exists: violence, and there is only one way to resolve it, displacement toward the exterior.

This was precisely the thinking of Urban II, preaching the first crusade in 1095.[51] Since the reproduction of violence could not be staunched on the continent, the solution to the problem was its exportation in an ideologically approved form, promulgated by the central ideological instance itself, the Papacy. The production and reproduction of violence was accepted as inevitable, but it would be addressed elsewhere, outside the continent and economy of Christian Europe, to an "outside" that was negatively marked by the reigning ideology, that of Christianity. Even in the sharply divided ideological world of the crusades, however, the "inside" and the "outside" could not be kept watertight. Exported violence was destined for delivery to Jerusalem, to be loosed on the "barbarians," the "Saracens" who occupied the sacred precincts of the holy city. The exported form could not be aimed that precisely, however. It reproduced the self-perpetuating nomadic war-machine, unaccustomed to precise delivery of its violence as export merchandise. Not only were European Jews massacred on occasions, so were foreign Christians. In fact, the crusades, legitimated as the liberation of the holy city, could turn into unremitting attack upon alterity in any form—Muslim, Jewish, and Christian alike. Indeed, one effect of the violence is the fragmentation of categories such as "self" and "other." Even Christians in the south of France, with lands valuable enough to be desired by their northern counterparts, could be attacked with impunity, once they were labeled "heretics" and made the object of a crusade such as the Albigensian.

This violence, a permanent feature of social life from one end of the Middle Ages to the other, did not remain self-identical in an absolute state of being. Its very instrumentalization within the seigneurial system of exploitation suggests potentials of modulation, of adaptability, of modelization, as a potter modelizes the clay on the wheel before her. Nomadic violence, and the nomadic war-machine that is its social form, entered into a Faustian contract with their opposite number, with the feudal apparatuses of capture that preceded the form of the State. Feudo-vassalism was the name of the syncretic conjunction of local governance with a barely attached nomadic violence. One major form of attachment was the economic itself. Not that nomadism was without an economy: it depended on the profits of booty, and this remained, indeed, the economic form characteristic of early feudalism.[52] But the application of force was turned "inward," upon the peasant populations working the ground of the European continent, in a political internalization of violence analogous to the internalization of violence performed by the super-ego. The violence originally turned outward, against a territory such as Poland which yielded its population as "slaves" (*esclaves*, from "Slavs"), was now directed against the local agricultural producers from whom surplus value could be gathered. Was the economic the prior means by which the violence of mounted men-of-war was to be captured and managed, or was the economic developed—in part—so as to enable the socius to encompass and establish some partial control over the preexistent violence?

Never absent, but relatively rule-bound for a period of time, vassalic violence seemed suddenly to increase at a given point in history. At a certain moment, the historical documents begin to be filled with expressions that inscribe the operation of harsh extortions of labor and value from those submitted to vassalic violence.[53] The moment was that of money. There was probably no time during the Middle Ages when absolutely no money was in use, and no time when commerce, both local and international, was completely interrupted. The use of money, however, and its cultural and ideological importance, increased markedly, in conjunction with the system of banal lordship. An earlier phase is characterized by the surrender of goods themselves for the supposed services of the knights and their lords—peasants surrender a portion of the grain or legumes grown, the eggs or chickens produced, in a system where values and services are exchanged directly, without the mediation of currency and its abstraction of the notion of value from concrete human needs and labor potential. Absent such abstraction, the direct, face-to-face "exchange in kind" may function under the restraint imposed by self-evidence: the impossibility of further production of surplus value beyond a certain point becomes an unarguable physical fact. Without romanticizing an earlier period, its peasant socius, or its relations with an extortionate nobility, one may imagine a model of social organization in which the limits of human productive ability, directly visible to the agents and beneficiaries of oppression, imply relatively effective limitations on greed, rapacity, and cruelty.[54]

The imposition of the banal system, combined with the increasing use of cash, discarded the restraints imposed by a "natural" economy or the exchange of agricultural goods for "services." The banal system shifted the object being requisitioned: from the direct product of local agricultural labor to the semiotic regime of monetary signs. Coins were not only the silver they contained and the "medium" of exchange based on an evaluation and valorization of objects of exchange. Their function as a mediating system of signification between the worlds of "natural" production and that of fiscal captation allowed for their functioning as a separate system of signification. The *deniers* after which the nobility thirsted and hungered, for which the peasants, in the new system of social organization, exchanged the agricultural goods produced by their labor in order to be able to satisfy the lords' exactions, provided what may look, to the jaded modern eye, merely like a valuation of the peasants' labor and the goods it produced. Money, however, in its very mediating function, interposed what became a relatively independent and arbitrary system of objects of value and hence desire. The coins' signifying relation, their relation to the labor required to produce them, weakened as their intermediary function for that labor decreased. Coins became objects of desire independent of that signifying relation, which was also, of course, their source and origin: the *deniers* came to the peasant's hand only as the result of that hand's labor in the field and garden.

The shift from exchange in kind to the representational regime of monetary semiosis became an occasion for increasingly violent oppression. Its source and origin in the labor process forgotten, thanks to the magic masking of money, the desire of the *châtelain* and the insistent requisition of his knights could grow immeasurably: what was to limit the reification of desire in *deniers*, once their source and origin in the representation of human labor and its valuation had been erased?

The other shift of the banal system was equally important. In a major sociocultural shift, the basis of exaction was transformed. The coins were originally substitutes for goods surrendered in concrete and "natural" form. Now, under the banal system, they increasingly were shifted from the function of mere representation of value of goods produced to the category of judicial punishment. "Justice," far from the abstract system of equitableness it supposedly represents in modern thinking, became simultaneously the basis for the extortion of surplus value and its form. The lord was both the judge of the court and the owner of the coffers containing the treasury which accompanied him during his peregrinations throughout his domain, replenished by the fines levied by his judicial judgment or that of his representative. But something profound changed in this switch. The basis of "taxation," as crude and self-serving as it was initially, had at least an ideological basis in an exchange of services: the peasant's labor for the knight's and the lord's protection. But as the basis of extraction shifted from the representation of those concrete goods, given over in exchange for protection, to judicial fines, so did the basis of the exactions. It was no longer an ideologically justified exchange of goods for services, but the surrender of accumulated value caused by culpability under the guise of a juridical system. The victim's judicially established guilt was the new basis on which surplus value was extracted. The extraction was itself colored as a moral and judicial punishment. The extraction of surplus value was transformed into a self-legimating punishment: because it was labeled "fine," the individual being requisitioned was *ipso facto* guilty, and the exaction was a justified and appropriate punishment.[55] The "natural" limitations of the earlier system disappeared, and only the self-restraint of the judge who profited from the imposed fines worked as limitation.

The judicial legitimation of the extraction of surplus value rejoined the larger dimension of theological ideology, as the supposedly universal culpability inherited by all men and women in their descendance from Eve rejoined the more particular culpabilities established by self-interested justice. At this ideological point, the efforts of clerical ideology to justify the submission of the *laboratores* to the exactions of the other two classes of the tripartite system of "orders" obtains its full effect: they are punished for a guilt that is always already pre-ordained. Their very birth into the order of laborers is the sign of their culpability,[56] hence the legitimation of their punishment and the extortion it masks.

Simultaneously with the loosening of the object of value of noble desire from the concrete, physical activities which produced it came a new mode of ideological justification for its extortion, and a new socio-juridical basis for that extortion. At the same time, the accession of the knights to noble status spurred them on to greater and greater feats of extortion, as they themselves emulated an increasingly costly life-style of symbolic consumption from the social betters who were also their overlords. The knights were both the essential element in the mechanisms of manorial exploitation and, thanks to their newly acquired noble identity, increasingly direct beneficiaries of the system of exploitation. Economic self-interest, the "duty" of performing service for their overlords, and the thirst to participate in the display of signs within the symbolic order established by their superiors all combined to increase the fiscal pressures on the peasantry exercised by knightly violence.

But the *Chanson de Roland*, if it displays an ennobled knightly violence exemplarily, does not show its economic functioning. The *Roland*'s performances of noble violence remain entirely within the noble class exercising that violence, and the poem transfers the performance of that violence upon substitute objects marked by religious and cultural alterity. Any reference to an economic origin or functionalization is erased and masked by its sublation into an acceptable ideological systematization of violence as the quest for the social integer of "honor" in the textual diegetic world proposed as an analogue to the world of lived experience. "Honor" becomes the cultural equivalent of money as the abstract representation of value. As the knight rides off on the hungry quest for *deniers* in the performance of his knightly obligation and in pursuit of his joy, nothing in the domain of textual representation is more important than the violent captation and defense of the social value of "honor," acquired, in the text in question, by faithful pursuit and murder of the infidel, ideologically legitimated as a narrative analogue of the contemporary crusade. Nor does any damage seem more grievous, or any attack more irritating to the readiness to resort to violence, than an injured "honor." The distinction between "honor" in the modern sense and the economic realm, of course, is undermined by the medieval ambiguity of *honor*, as both the socio-moral quality of the individual and his lineage, and the actual fief which is the source of wealth required for military force and political power. Language deconstructs the narrative split between textual representation and corporeal political activity. It is a crucial axis in the refractive effects of textuality, separating, recombining, silencing, and exploding threads of signification as they emerge from the complexities of the socius—political, economic, and cultural.

The ultimate question addressed by the *Roland* to the contemporary readers who constitute its most recent Historical Interpretant—to adapt a Peircean notion, perhaps abusively—is whether the indubitable historical components of its violence are a sufficient account of that violence. Contemporary theory has produced crucial insights into hidden forms of violence, in contrast to the open, overt performances of the Middle Ages. Representation itself comports an ineluctable violence, as sign is substituted for the object desired. The system of verbal signification may allow for the symbolic compromises of ideological conflicts. Semiosis can also exacerbate these conflicts in freeing representation from the reality of the represented. The field of representation allows for the (symbolic) resolution of violent conflicts, but the violence of representation, in verbal constructs as well as in coinage, may also rejoin an anterior violence, a self-perpetuating war-machine that continues to function long after the apparent integration of the "nomads" into the social formation. This conjunction of violences appears most clearly in the cycle of the rebellious barons; in the *Chanson de Roland*, it contributes to the profoundly ambiguous relation of the text to the violence it bears and portrays.

But if man is a sign himself,[57] then he and she are created as individuals and subjects by constitutive violences. As a practitioner of the linguistic form of semiosis, as a speaker, as the subject of the linguistic and cultural codes that identify him or her as belonging to a particular human group, and as the political subject of a State, individuals bear the scars of violences that make them what they are. Do we perform cycles of violence that are determined by these beginnings? Do these cycles rejoin a more fundamental violence, one which, Freud argued with good reason, seems as fundamental a human propensity as sexual desire? Lacan dramatizes the issue:

> . . . each time that Freud stops, as if horrified, before the effect of the commandment to love one's neighbor, what surges forth is the presence of that fundamental nastiness (*méchanceté*) which lives in that neighbor. But then, it lives in me as well. And what is closer to me, more my neighbor, than this heart in myself which is that of my pleasure, which I dare not approach? For as soon as I approach it—that's the meaning of *Civilization and Its Discontents*—there surges forth that unfathomable aggressivity before which I withdraw, which I turn around against myself, and which arrives, in the very place of that Law that disappeared, to give its weight to what prevents me from stepping over a certain margin at the limit of the Thing.[58]

This is the ultimate question to which a reading of the *Chanson de Roland* leads, without providing an answer: the aggressivity, the violence which recurs in literature, history, and anthropology, before which Freud recoils in horror, a human essence, whether genetic or derived from the structures of human development? Is not the effort to essentialize human nature itself an oppressive violence, effectuated against the very possibility of freedom and emancipation? Short of the ultimate questions, unanswerable in the absence of a metaphysics of human nature, we are left with the historical, a more limited problematic which also falls short, nonetheless, of providing metaphysically satisfactory answers. It may be that this very limitation of historical discourse is an advantage: the historical forms of social formations are variable, and they allow, the historical record both medieval and modern suggests, at least a modulation of social violence. Insofar as the domain of culture participates in the historicity of the social formation it inhabits, it too is part of that process of modulation.

Given the sliding temporality within which the question of "dating" an oral text like the *Chanson de Roland* must be framed, conjoined with the very great regional variabilities in which social processes occur in the different regions of France and Anglo-Norman England, it is impossible to specify the historical moment to which the text is to be related, in this or that region of France or England. It cannot be identified with a specific date or a specific location. It can, however, be cognitively related to the moments of a phased historical process of evolution, the general social, political, and economic processes which affect the problematics of the social classes it addresses and represents. Above all, it must be read in conjunction with the fundamental processes of historical evolution themselves, in order to produce the full range of meanings and significances whose potentials it bears.

Within that framework, its signifying and ideological productivities are identical. It is not to impose a reign of peace upon a land torn by the endless cycle of violences perpetrated by the newly ennobled instrument of seigneurial oppression, but to capture that violence, assumed as a permanent production of organized society, assumed also as necessary to the continuation of that society, perhaps nomadic in origin or type, by a form of the unitary, monarchical state not yet in existence. So rudimentarily imagined is its proleptic representation that the capture consists entirely in the submission of a feudal class, simultaneously self-destructed and regenerated by the need and word of the monarch, to that monarch, who institutes that subordination by a violence at least as cruel and as graphic as any feudal violence previously displayed. At this point, the state is identified with the function of its leader: king and country, in the thought of the text, are equally inseparable and undefined.

This leaves multiple questions unanswered. Will the ensuing state manage to dominate the force of nomadic violence, or will the state in fact be subverted so as to become the instrument of violence rather than its control? How will the new state create its subjects and their subjectivities in such a manner as to retain and subordinate the violence it continues to require? What will be the categories, simultaneously epistemic and social, which will organize the new political entity called the state? These are questions not addressed by the transformations of the *Chanson de Roland*: other texts, other moments of textualization, will have to address these questions. Indeed, these are the questions to which ensuing European civilization will be constituted as the evolving Historical Interpretant.[59]

For the moment, the text gives voice to the self-destructive dynamic of the social structures that bear its violences, to the necessity of controlling them, to the dimly imagined social instance that will have to either replace or subordinate those of the enunciatory present. It enunciates with remarkable clarity the fundamental juridical principle of this new social order, the subordination and submission of feudal to monarchical right. The poem's formulations are specifically historical symbolizations. Its enunciations are not simply "symbolic formations," however. They are performative speech acts. In the sliding temporality of the text, extending from the turn of the century until a moment between 1150 and 1170, the text remains on the distant side of even the initial stages of State formations that occur during the reign of Philip Augustus (1180–1223), and for which the date of the battle of Bouvines can be taken as a sign: 1214. Well before the actualization of its endpoint on the stage of history, the *Chanson* arises on a wave of textual transformations, not only signaling some of the most urgently felt sociopolitical needs of its time, but cursorily outlining the form of their eventual resolution. As such, it is one of the very first annunciatory signs of the changes it inscribes. As a profoundly ideological construct, it is also one of the crucial cultural and ideological elements bringing about those changes. It may be the first such sign. Is the *Chanson de Roland* prior to the reassemblement of military forces from all over the larger "France" outside of Metz in 1124?[60]

Assuredly it is, in one of its stages, even if not in exactly the form in which we read the text. As such, it is the earliest sign, the earliest ideological act toward the accomplishment of the reign of Philip Augustus: the establishment of the first lineaments of a French nation-state.

Such an accomplishment, such an importance, are ambiguous for a modern reader. Most painfully for the reader constituted in admiration for the object of reading: to what degree must he or she think the texts of the twelfth century, the culture they bear and create, as essentially, as inherently, themselves constitutive of a representational violence imbricated with the social and historical violence it is their task to negotiate? To what degree do the texts bear the violence of their *socius*, either as part of that *socius* or in the form of a necessary displacement, so that our admirative pleasure at their glories can only be a guilty pleasure? To what extent is the violence which the texts transform without discarding to be identified with the later violences that cripple modern civilization and haunt our consciousness?

Such questions are unanswerable. Their responses must remain as speculative as the nature of man, woman, and society. It is, however, in the context of such questioning that the *Chanson de Roland*, the questions of its structures and its production of significations, must be "entertained." The *Chanson de Roland*, characterized by an extraordinary degree of alterity in the values presented, in the modes of their structuration and representation, and their incorporation into larger cultural and social contexts, an alterity defined by its relation to the ideological, cultural, and aesthetic values of the modern reader, is not, for all that, entirely foreign to the problematics of the contemporary reader. Its alterities are negotiable, by means of the patient, assiduous, subtle, and imaginative address to the text "itself," alongside the social text reconstituted by historians, in a process of "reading," of semiotic intepretation, not all that different from the literary reader's challenges. This address of the requisite texts, with the intellectual technologies and problematics developed by contemporary theory, allows for the elaboration of a representation of the text and its co-texts which provides a mirroring effect, not of the text's own, constitutive referents—the realities of the late eleventh and early twelfth centuries—but a distorting mirroring effect that works upon the late twentieth and early twenty-first century reader. A mirroring effect which is not so much a constative: this is the way things are, but an interrogative: is this the way things are, in spite of all the changes that have occurred between the two time-frames? To what degree has the socio-textual problematics changed, between the period of textualization, and that of decoding?

For the negotiation of the textual and cultural alterities of the text brings us to a moment of "beginning" in our own genealogy. It is the Moment where the necessity of subjection of exactly that class which is proudest of the violence of its independence is most brilliantly demonstrated and asserted. It is the Moment when the form of that subject reveals itself as the lineaments of the nascent State: not yet the Nation-State we inhabit with increasing dissatisfaction, and yet, a putative State, unitary, cruelly violent, requiring the creation of new Subjects, and a new form of Subjectivity.

Ours.

Notes

Introduction

1. To borrow Edward Said's distinction. *Beginnings: Intention and Method*, New York: Basic, 1975.

2. Walter Benjamin, "Critique of Violence," in *Reflections*, ed. Peter Demetz, New York: Harcourt Brace (Harvest), 1978, pp. 277–300.

3. Marc Bloch, *La société féodale*, Paris: Albin Michel, 1939/68, pp. 567f.; my translation.

4. Robert Fossier, *Enfance de l'Europe*, 2 vols., Paris: PUF, 1982, vol. 1, p. 117; my translation.

5. Jean-Pierre Poly and Eric Bournazel, *La mutation féodale: Xe–XIIe siècles*, Paris: PUF, 1980, pp. 452f.

6. Fossier, *Enfance de l'Europe*, p. 124; my translation.

7. Pierre Jonin, "Deux langages de heros épiques au cours d'une bataille suicidaire," *Olifant* 9 (1962), 90; my translation.

8. Ibid., p. 91.

9. See Haidu, "The 'Medieval Thing': The Subject of Violence," forthcoming.

10. Ralph de Gorog, *Lexique Français Moderne-Ancien Français*, Athens: Georgia, 1973, under *violence*.

11. Combining the first three definitions of violence in *The American College Dictionary*, New York: Random House, 1964. As one scholar has put it, "[d]efinitions of 'violence' tend to be relatively unhelpful." The term itself has "strong evaluative force" as well as "a pronounced emotive meaning": Robert Holmes, "Emotiveness and Elusiveness in Definitions of Violence," in *Justice, Law, and Violence*, ed. James B. Brady and Newton Garver, Philadelphia: Temple, 1991, pp. 48–52; p. 48.

12. Caesarius of Heisterbach, *Dialogues Miraculorum*, ed. J. Strange, 2 vols., 1851, pp. 345–46. The biblical allusion is to 2 Timothy 2:19. Does the doubt of *fertur dixisse* reflect a question regarding the authenticity of the report, or a distance from the citation's morality?

13. Arno J. Mayer, *Why Did the Heavens Not Darken? The "Final Solution" in History*, New York: Pantheon, 1988, p. 28.

14. Yehuda Bauer, *The Holocaust in Historical Perspective*, Seattle: University of Washington Press, 1978, p. 74.

15. Mayer, pp. 24–35, 216–33, 237.

16. I owe this reference to Larry Crist's kindness. On the generalized assumption that medieval French epics are imbued with the spirit of the Crusades, see D. A. Trotter, *Medieval French Literature and the Crusades (1100–1300)*, Geneva: Droz, 1988.

17. This is true of American thought in general, but it must be tempered in relation to European thought. A contemporary French historian can assert that the Middle Ages are fashionable, medieval history enjoys a good reputation, and that books on the Middle Ages sell well: Jacques Le Goff, in his preface to Agnes Gerhards, *La société médiévale*, Paris: MA Edi-

tions, 1986, p. 13. Compare this to Paul Zumthor's comment, a few years ago, on the marginality of medieval studies (*Parler du moyen âge*, Paris: Minuit, 1980, pp. 101f.). Clearly, intellectual culture differs on the two sides of the Atlantic!

18. "Comment ne pas parler?—Dénégations." *Psyché*, Paris: Galilée, 1987, pp. 535–95.

19. In fact, Foucault did reflect on the medieval case occasionally, with very interesting results: see for instance *La volonté de savoir*, Paris: Gallimard, 1976, pp. 114ff. Foucauldian thought is also represented by one of the most thoughtful discussions of medieval culture, in Timothy J. Reiss's "Questions of Medieval Discursive Practice," *The Discourse of Modernism*, Ithaca, N.Y.: Cornell, 1982, pp. 55–107. The Derridean strain is found in Jesse M. Gellrich, *The Idea of the Book in the Middle Ages: Language Theory, Mythology, and Fiction*, Ithaca, N.Y.: Cornell, 1985; and Robert S. Sturges, *Medieval Interpretation: Models of Reading in Literary Narrative, 1100–1500*, Carbondale & Edwardsville, IL.: Southern Illinois University Press, 1991.

20. Thus, Roland Barthes's useful summary, as applicable to the Middle Ages as to classical antiquity, in "L'ancienne rhétorique," *Communications* 16 (1970), 172–226, and Tzvetan Todorov's brilliant Derridean reading of the *Queste del saint graal* in "La quête du récit," *Critique* 262 (1969), 195–214, with which contemporary medievalists are only beginning to catch up.

21. See Umberto Eco's early work *Opera aperta*, Milan: Bompiani, 1962, early translated into French as *L'Oeuvre ouverte*, Paris: Seuil, 1966; and Julia Kristeva, "Le texte clos," in *Semiotiké*, Paris: Seuil, 1969, pp. 113–42; and *Le texte du roman*, Paris-La Haye: Mouton, 1970. Kristeva's version of the binarism is more subtle than Eco's early work: she sees "openness" and "closedness" coexisting as early as the twelfth century. Unfortunately, she does not extend this simultaneity to modernity to find the "closedness" of the texts of modernism. Eco revises his early and simpleminded opposition in the introductory and title essay of *The Role of the Reader*, Bloomington: Indiana University Press, 1979, pp. 3–43, which should be read in conjunction with another essay in the same volume, "Peirce and the Semiotic Foundations of Openness: Signs as Texts and Texts as Signs," pp. 175–99.

22. The most cogent and overt argumentation of this position is, of course, D. W. Robertson, Jr.'s *Preface to Chaucer* (Princeton: Princeton University Press, 1962), on which see the recent discussion in Lee Patterson's *Negotiating the Past: The Historical Understanding of Medieval Literature*, Madison: University of Wisconsin Press, 1987, pp. 26–39. The theoretical error of the Father is visited upon his progeny, as the tendency continues even in discussions that present themselves as "avant-gardiste" in French medieval studies: Eugene Vance, *Mervelous Signals*, Lincoln: University of Nebraska Press, 1986, and the more recent collection of articles by Evelyn Birge Vitz, *Medieval Narrative and Modern Narratology*, New York: New York University Press, 1989. The latter exceeds the scope of her understanding in attempting to refute Greimas's narrative semiotics: she knows only the earliest works and does not grasp their content. The most sophisticated discussion of the relationship between Christianity and fiction is Alexandre Leupin's *Fiction et théologie*, which I have been privileged to read in manuscript.

23. See the modest, philologically oriented comments of Bernard Cerquiglini, *Eloge de la variante*, Paris: Seuil, 1989, pp. 34–42, as well as my "Medieval Culture: One, Two, or Many Models?," forthcoming.

24. Gilles Deleuze and Félix Guattari, *Kafka: Toward a Minor Literature*, trans. Dana Polan, Minneapolis: University of Minnesota Press, 1986, pp. 16–27.

25. See Haidu, "Making It [New] in the Middle Ages: Towards a Problematics of Alterity," at the occasion of the publication of Paul Zumthor's *Essai de poétique médiévale*, in *Diacritics* (Summer 1974), 1–14. Hans-Robert Jauss then developed the concept of alterity in the title essay of his *Alterität und Modernität des mittelalterlichen Literatur*, Munich, 1977, translated by Timothy Bahti as "The Alterity and Modernity of the Middle Ages," *New Literary*

History 10 (1979), 181–230. In fact, this use of "alterity" is an attempt to recuperate an obviously necessary concept for a larger philosophical framework which is fundamentally incapable of recognizing it without perversion: see Haidu, "The Semiotics of Alterity: A Comparison with Hermeneutics," *New Literary History* 21 (1989–90), 671–91.

26. Roman Jakobson, "Two Aspects of Language and Two Types of Aphasic Disturbances," in Roman Jakobson and Morris Halle, *Fundamentals of Language*, 'S-Gravenhage: Mouton, 1956, pp. 53–82.

27. It is the entire work of A. J. Greimas which must be indexed here. Its *état présent* was provided by Greimas himself with the help of a co-worker, Joseph Courtés, in *Sémiotique: Dictionnaire raisonné de la théorie du langage*, Paris: Hachette, 1979; its English translation, under the title *Semiotics and Language*, translated by Daniel Patte, Larry Crist, et al., Bloomington: Indiana University Press, 1982, contains a useful bibliography. This work is often referred to as the "Dictionary."

Greimas has stressed the fact that narrative semiotics is a permanently evolving model, responding to the notion of the quest more than to a completely formed and self-sufficient "science." His own work develops in surprising ways—see the resurgence of "aesthetics" in *De l'imperfection*, Périgeux: Pierre Fanlac, 1987—and a second generation of what has come to be known as the "Ecole de Paris" is publishing important new expansions and modifications of the original theory.

28. See Haidu, "Text and History," *Semiotica* 33 (1980), 155–69.

29. See Haidu, "Toward a Socio-Historical Semiotics: Power and Legitimacy in the *Couronnement de Louis*," *Kodikas/Code* 2 (1980), 155–69; "Text and History," *Semiotica* 33 (1980), 155–69; "Semiotics and History," *Semiotica* 40 (1982), 187–222; "Considérations théoriques sur la sémiotique socio-historique," in *Aims and Prospects of Semiotics*, 2 vols., ed. Herman Parret and Hans-Georg Ruprecht, Amsterdam: John Benjamins, 1985, vol. 1, pp. 215–28; "La valeur: sémiotique et marxisme," *Sémiotique en jeu: A partir et autour de l'oeuvre d'A. J. Greimas*, ed. Michel Arrivé and Jean-Claude Coquet, Amsterdam: John Benjamins, 1987, pp. 247–63.

30. See the interesting discussion by Jean-Jacques Lecercle, in *The Violence of Language*, London: Routledge, 1990. The theoretical issue itself goes back to the orthodox structuralist and early semiotic periods.

31. In fact, Derrida gave such license in an early comment, which must be acknowledged to provide a fairly weak legitimation, in asserting that any "scientific" semiotics (a formulation I would reject) would "serve" deconstructive analysis: "Sémiologie et grammatologie," an interview with Julia Kristeva, *Positions*, Paris: Minuit, 1972, p. 49. In fact, if the question is approached with sufficient imagination, rather than dogmatism, each of the disciplines will "serve" the other's purposes, and should do so, unless one wishes to impose the most logocentrically doctrinaire theoretical decision of all, namely that one discipline shall reign as mistress and queen of all methodological virtues.

32. The most telling accounts of this historiography are those by Louis O. Mink and Hayden White. Mink's essays have recently been collected and published under the title *Historical Understanding*, Ithaca, N.Y.: Cornell University Press, 1987. The major works of Hayden White are *Metahistory* (1973), *Tropics of Discourse* (1978), and *The Content of the Form* (1987), all published by Johns Hopkins University Press in Baltimore.

33. Three important books reached me too late to be used in this work: Dominique Barthélemy, *L'ordre seigneurial, XIe–XIIe siècle* (Paris: Seuil, 1990); Jacques Le Goff, ed., *L'homme médiéval* (Paris: Seuil, 1992); and Franco Cardini, *La culture de la guerre*, trans. Angélique Lévy (Paris: Gallimard, 1992).

34. A fact whose omission vitiates much medievalism. For an egregious example, compare the treatments of the historical phenomenon of "literacy" in Brian Stock and Jack Goody.

35. The most readily accessible critique of this narrow tradition is to be found in the works of Raymond Williams, *Keywords: A Vocabulary of Culture and Society*, rev. ed. (Oxford: Oxford University Press, 1976/83), and *Marxism and Literature* (Oxford: Oxford University Press, 1977).

1. The Semiotization of Death

1. The positions indicated are those of Robert Francis Cook, *The Sense of the Song of Roland*, Ithaca: Cornell University Press, 1987, from whom I cite two consecutive chapter headings; Karl D. Uitti, *Story Myth and Celebration in Old French Narrative Poetry (1050–1200)*, Princeton: Princeton University Press, 1973, pp. 69–89; Hans-Erich Keller, "The Song of Roland: A Mid-Twelfth Century Song of Propaganda for the Capetian Kingdom," *Olifant* 3 (1976), 242–58; and Stephen G. Nichols, "Fission and Fusion: Meditations of Power in Medieval History and Literature," *Yale French Studies* 70 (1986), 21–42.

2. This section draws on an article published under the same title in the journal *Style* 20 (1986), 220–51 (special number on medieval semiotics).

3. Death, " . . . in the Christian tradition . . . could transcend time and enter eternity." Stephen G. Nichols, Jr., *Romanesque Signs: Early Medieval Narrative and Iconography*, New Haven: Yale University Press, 1983, p. 193.

4. I continue to use the edition which follows the text of the Oxford manuscript most closely, and which also happens to be readily and cheaply available: *La Chanson de Roland*, ed. Joseph Bédier, Paris: Piazza, n.d.; reprinted U.G.E. 10/18, No. 1506. I have also occasionally consulted the editions of T. Atkinson Jenkins (Boston: Health, 1924) and Gérard Moignet (Paris: Bordas, 1969). In establishing English versions of the quoted passage, I have consulted two translations: that of Patricia Terry (New York: Bobbs-Merrill, 1965: "Library of Liberal Arts") and that of Frederick Goldin (New York: W. W. Norton, 1978). I often follow one or the other closely. An excellent bibliographical resource is Joseph J. Duggan's *Guide to Studies on the Chanson de Roland*, London: Grant & Cutler, 1976, which can be supplemented by the extensive bibliographies in the studies of Brault and Cook, cited below. Duggan also produced a research tool I have found most useful, *A Concordance of the Chanson de Roland*, Columbus: University of Ohio Press, 1969. I would be remiss, however, if I did not acknowledge my feeling of coming at the end, and upon the shoulders, as it were, of a strong countertradition of *Roland* scholarship and criticism. In particular, I am thinking of George Fenwick Jones, Matthias Waltz, Karl-Heinz Bender, John Halvorson, Erich Köhler, Albert Gérard, Peter Van Nuffel, and Wayne Guymon—readers whose commentaries can be characterized by the use of historical contextualization to get at hidden meaning, or (in the case of the last two named) the use of particularly modern methods of analysis to get at hidden historical meaning. The near absence of French scholarship in this brief list is not accidental, though I am tempted to add the name of the late Jean-Charles Payen to the list: most of the current production of the French university—in the domain of medieval literary study—is all too readily recuperated by the traditional French ideological values of nationalism and superficial religiosity.

5. For a discussion of the feudal code itself, see K. J. Hollyman, *Le développement du vocabulaire féodal en France pendant le haut moyen âge (étude sémantique)*, Geneva and Paris: Droz and Minard, 1957. For the use of the feudal code in the love lyric, see Roger Dragonetti, *La technique poétique des trouvères dans la chanson courtoise: contribution à l'étude de la rhétorique médiévale*, Bruges: Rijksuniversiteit Gent, 1960.

6. In his classic *La Chanson de geste: essai sur l'art épique des jongleurs*, Geneva and Lille: Droz and Giard, 1955.

7. A. J. Greimas, "Conditions d'une sémiotique du monde naturel," in *Du Sens* [I], Paris: Seuil, 1970.

8. These techniques are simultaneously an essential element of the jongleur's stock in trade, and thus an integral part of the technology of oral literature, and an equally essential part of the classical and medieval traditions of written rhetoric, described in its technological minutiae in the arts of grammar and rhetoric which were a continuous tradition from Quintilian and the late grammarians of the empire through to the twelfth century, when their role began to be taken over by the *poetriae* whose historical import is moot: secularization of a domain of literariness independent of religious function, or summary treatment of literature for MBA's in a hurry to go through the required course in liberal arts (see Alexandre Leupin, "Absolute Reflexivity: Geoffrey of Vinsauf's Poetria nova," *Barbarolexis: Medieval Writing and Sexuality*, tr. Kate M. Cooper, Cambridge, Mass.: Harvard, 1989, pp. 17–38)? The fact that such techniques are contained both in the oral and in the written traditions suggests their universality: amplification, along with its binary opposite, abbreviation, are essential components of any textual construction, and must be accounted for by any textual theory. Hence the fact that, well after the medieval documents, contemporary semiotics rediscovers that technology. See the terms "expansion" and "condensation" in A. J. Greimas and J. Courtés, *Sémiotique: Dictionnaire raisonné de la théorie du langage*, Paris: Hachette, 1979.

9. A. J. Greimas, "The Cognitive Dimension of Narrative," *New Literary History* 7 (1976), 433–47.

10. See the *Preface to Chaucer*, Princeton: Princeton University Press, 1962/69.

11. Eugene Vance has developed this aspect of the text in an essay of remarkable sensitivity and delicacy: "Roland and the Poetics of Memory," in *Textual Strategies*, ed. Josue Harari, Ithaca, N.Y.: Cornell University Press, 1979/81, pp. 374–403. My reservation regarding this article is that the emphasis on a commemorative aesthetic clouds the ideological value of the turn toward the past, and quite disguises the import of the text as a historical event in the present—and future—of the twelfth century.

12. It may be that the medieval tie of avuncularity was a displacement of the paternal caused at least in part by the necessity of training young men in techniques of mortal combat whose practice and exercise might give too ready an opportunity for expressing Oedipal negativities: what seems to us as a strange displacement may be an adaptation to concrete social necessities which, like the adaptation itself, are social practices. Family structures shift markedly in the eleventh and twelfth centuries. John R. Allen derives from these transformations, which include the shift from emphasis on the avunculate bond to the paternal bond, a two-tiered structure of the *Roland* in terms of the familial isotopy ("Kinship in the Chanson de Roland," *Jean Misrahi Memorial Volume: Studies in Medieval Literature*, ed. Hans R. Runte, Henri Niedzielski, William L. Hendrickson, Columbia, S.C.: French Literature Publications, 1977, pp. 34–45). R. Howard Bloch's chapter "Kinship" in *Etymologies and Genealogies* provides both ample bibliographical reference and the recognition that "The history of the family is, at bottom, the history of its land" (p. 74). I would only stress that such "bottom-land" is inescapably part of a materialistic history of economics and politics, concerned with the acquisition, development, and defense of this land, together with the use of labor for its exploitation.

13. Nelly Andrieux-Reix, *Ancien français: Fiches de vocabulaire*, Paris: PUF, 1989, pp. 76–79.

14. Erich Auerbach, *Mimesis: The Representation of Reality in Western Literature*, trans. Willard Trask, New York: Anchor-Doubleday, 1957.

15. One response to the problem has been to interpret the poem as a Christian allegory demonstrating the need for a Christian heroism that, transcending human reason and teaching the necessity to resist the temptation of compromise, is tantamount to a divine folly: see Larry S. Crist, "A propos de la *démesure* dans la *Chanson de Roland*: quelques propos (démesurés?)," *Olifant* 1 (April 1974), 10–20. Rather than being based on an analysis of the text and its structures, this approach follows the model of D. W. Robertson, Jr., to whom it refers, resting on a prior decision that most medieval literature is constructed as Christian al-

legory. This has the advantage of resolving all interpretive problems handsomely, *inter alia* dismissing the peculiar paradox outlined above. It neither responds to modern interpretive criteria, which are summarily dismissed, nor to the observed characteristics of the text.

16. I agree with Tony Hunt that the poem eschews "facile moral judgments" and "simple commendation or criticism of Roland," and that the poem recounts a story that can be called "tragic": Tony Hunt, "The Tragedy of Roland: An Aristotelian View," *Modern Language Review* 74 (1979), 791–805. With all the admiration I retain for the Philosopher (Aristotle is one of the true antecedents of narrative semiotics), I doubt that the unity of plot promulgated in the *Poetics* is the analytic grid onto which to stretch oral narratives. Hunt himself is forced to acknowledge that the poem does not fit this particular procrustean bed, and that the "tragic emotion" he postulates for the poem has been "fatally damaged" by that part of the poem unaccounted for by the claim that " . . . the *Chanson de Roland* satisfies the Aristotelian condition for the highest form of tragedy" (p. 803). Above all, however, I disagree with the conceptualization of *hamartia* as a simple mistake of judgment, which trivializes tragic action by reducing it to the terror of the intellectual: to be caught in an error, a mistake, whether of fact or of judgment.

17. As did George Fenwick Jones, in *The Ethos of the Song of Roland*, Baltimore: Johns Hopkins University Press, 1963.

2. The Gaze of the Other

1. In referring to the general body of Charles's troops, I use the terms "Frank(s)" (adj. "Frankish") as marking a Moment prior to the creation of the nation-state of France, and hence the population of the (properly) French. For a contrary opinion, conceiving of "France" as created in the moment of the creation of the French language, see Renée Balibar, *L'institution du français: Essai sur le colinguisme des Carolingiens à la République*, Paris: PUF, 1985. This fascinating effort, conjoining a sociological history of the language with theoretical considerations drawn from contemporary theory, incorporates the structuralist notion of the centrality of language in the creation of society. Society should not be confused with the State, however. It takes something more than language to constitute the State. Identifying the creation of the French state with the creation of the French language is something of a French tradition, going back at least to Michelet, who traced both back to the Serments de Strasbourg:

> L'histoire de la France commence avec la langue française. La langue est le signe principal de la nationalité. . . . Le premier monument de la nôtre est le serment dicté par Charles le Chauve à son frère, au traité de 843.

Jules Michelet, *Oeuvres*, vol. 4, p. 331; cited by Pierre Chaunu, *L'obscure mémoire de la France, De la première pierre à l'an mille*, Paris: Perrin, 1988, pp. 379 and 466n.

2. Samir Marzouki, "Islam et Musulmans dans la *Chanson de Roland*," *Revue Tunisienne de sciences sociales* 13 (1976), 105–30; Carole Bervoc-Huard, "L'exclusion du sarrasin dans la *Chanson de Roland*: Vocabulaire et idéologie. 'Ço est une gent ki unches ben ne volt' (v. 3231)," in *Exclus et systèmes d'exclusion dana la littérature et la civilisation médiévales*, Paris: Champion, 1978, pp. 345–61; and the excellent discussion of Norman Daniel, *Heroes and Saracens*, Edinburgh, 1984.

3. Matthew Bennett, "First Crusaders' Images of Muslims: The Influence of Vernacular Poetry?," *Forum for Modern Language Studies* 22 (1986), 101–22.

4. Jean-Charles Payen, "Une poétique du génocide joyeux: devoir de violence et plaisir de tuer dans la *Chanson de Roland*," *Olifant* 6 (1979), 226–36. Note that this article, by a French scholar, touching on French know-nothing chauvinism, was published in the United States. For a historical survey of the relationship between nationalism and French literary schol-

arship on the *Song of Roland*, see Joseph J. Duggan, "Franco-German Conflict and the History of French Scholarship on the *Song of Roland*," in *Hermeneutics and Medieval Culture*, ed. Patrick J. Gallacher and Helen Damico (Albany, NY: SUNY, 1989), pp. 97–106.

5. As Pierre Van Nuffel puts it, the Christian poet totally ignores the vision of the Other: "Problèmes de sémiotique interprétative: L'épopée," *Lettres romanes* 27 (1973), 150–62. If so, then why retain the opposition "defend Christianity" vs. "defend Mahomet" as the deep structure of the model of which the *Roland* is supposed to be the most faithful exemplar?

6. Erich Köhler, in many ways the scholar who comes closest to the kind of reading I am attempting, recognized that the twelve peers of the *Roland* have nothing to do with the historical institution in existence at the end of the twelfth century, which was itself based on the literary tradition. For Köhler, the twelve peers of the *Roland* are nothing but a projection of the *grands officiers du roi* of the second half of the eleventh century, heavily modified and archaicized (*Conseil des barons und jugement des barons Epische Fatalität und Feudalrecht im altfranzösischen Rolandslied*, Heidelberg: Winter, 1968 ["Sitzungsberichte der Heidelberger Akademie der Wissenschaften, Philosophisch-historische Klasse, 1968, VI]). Köhler's error, from my point of view, was to consider a single semiotic integer, not the whole of the signifying system within which it is integrated.

7. Louis Brandin, ed., *La Chanson d'Aspremont*, 2 vols., Paris: Champion, 1919 ("Classiques Français du Moyen Age," vols. 19 and 25); 11. 1766–69.

8. The major modern works of scholarship on Capetian kingship are those of Jean-François Lemarignier, *Le gouvernement royal aux premiers temps capétiens (987–1108)*, Paris: Picard, 1965; and his student Eric Bournazel, *Le gouvernement capétien au XIIe siècle (1108–1180)*, Paris: PUF, 1975 ("Publications de la Faculté de Droit et Sciences Economiques de l'Université de Limoges," no. 2). A useful summary of recent scholarship is provided by Elizabeth M. Hallam, *Capetian France (987–1328)*, London and New York, 1980. I have also found most useful Thomas N. Bisson, "The Problems of the Feudal Monarchy: Aragon, Catalonia, and France," *Speculum* 53 (1978), 460–78.

3. Excursus I

1. Karl Marx, *Pre-Capitalist Economic Formations*, translated by Jack Cohen with an introduction by E. J. Hobsbawm, New York: International, 1965/75; as well as the essential "The So-Called Primitive Accumulation," *Capital*, Moscow: Progress, 1954/77, pp. 667–724. A classic discussion by a medieval historian is that of Charles Parain, with Pierre Vilar, in *Mode de production féodale*, Paris: Centre d'Etudes et de Recherches Marxistes, n.d. Two excellent collections of discussions by various hands are those edited by Maurice Dobb and Paul M. Sweezy, *Sur le féodalisme*, Paris: Editions Sociales, 1974; and *The Transition from Feudalism to Capitalism*, London: New Left Books, 1976, which I read in French translation by Florence Gauthier and Françoise Murray: *Du féodalisme au capitalisme: problèmes de la transition*, 2 vols., Paris: Maspero, 1977. In England, the concept was extensively discussed by Barry Hindess and Paul Hirst in *Pre-Capitalist Modes of Production*, London: Routledge & Kegan Paul, 1975, subjected to self-critical appraisal by the same authors in *Mode of Production and Social Formation*, London: Macmillan, 1977. A brief introduction to the feudal mode of production is to be found in Perry Anderson's *Passages from Antiquity to Feudalism*, London: New Left Books, 1974/77, pp. 147–53. A major reconceptualization of the relations between feudalism and the creation, accumulation, and investment of capital is to be found in Isaac Joshua, *La Face cachée du moyen âge: les premiers pas du capital*, Montreuil: La Brèche, 1988.

2. One of the most stringent limitations on medieval historiography results from the classic perception that "history belongs to the victors": the overwhelming preponderance of historical documentation was produced by the ruling class, first the clergy, and then the upper

crust of the nobility. As a result, modern written history is inevitably skewed by the absence of documentation representing the values and perspectives of the overwhelming majority of the population, the peasantry. In spite of this epistemological obstacle, modern historical research has achieved extraordinary successes. Major achievements are those of Georges Duby, *L'économie rurale et la vie des campagnes dans l'Occident médiéval*, 2 vols., Paris: Aubier, 1962; Rodney Hilton, *Bond Men Made Free*, New York: Viking, 1973; and the works of Robert Fossier, especially the two volumes of *Enfance de l'Europe*, Paris: PUF, 1982.

    3. Dobbs, "Du féodalisme au capitalisme," in *Du féodalisme au capitalisme*, vol. 2, p. 16. See also Duby's comment that, except for the fringes of Europe, where no social and economic differentiation may have existed, "everywhere else—and this is the most profound source of growth—a class of lords exploited the peasants, forcing them, by its very presence, to limit the extended periods of leisure which are characteristic of primitive economies, to struggle more obstinately against nature, to produce, in their profound poverty, some surplus destined for the house of the masters." (*Guerriers et paysans*, p. 40; cf. pp. 53, 47, and *passim*.) Robert Fossier's account of the peasantry in Picardy gives more room to the independence and opposition of the peasants, considering them the motor of socioeconomic change: Robert Fossier, *La Terre et les hommes en Picardie jusqu'à la fin du XIIIe siècle*, Paris and Louvain: B. Nauwelaerts, 1968.

    My interpretation of medieval social and political structures is based on the work of a number of contemporary historians of extraordinarily high quality, who are not to be held responsible for the use I have made of their work. Central to my historiographical adventure have been the works of Georges Duby, whose general works combine exemplarily the social, the economic, and the political domains: *L'économie rurals et la vie des campagnes dans l'Occident médiéval*, 2 vols., Paris: Aubier, 1962; *Guerriers et paysans*, Paris: Gallimard, 1973; and *Les trois ordres, ou l'imaginaire du féodalisme*, Paris: Gallimard, 1978, whose chapter "La révolution féodale" (pp. 183–205) summarizes much recent research. Duby set the model for extensive research in a specific geographical area, on the basis of dense and highly specified documentation, in *La Société aux XIe et XIIe siècles dans la région mâconnaise*, Paris: SEVPEN, 1952. This model has been followed by an impressive series of comparable monographical studies, of which three have been particularly important to me: in addition to Fossier's work on Picardy just cited, see also André Chédeville, *Chartres et ses campagnes (XIe–XIIIe siècle)*, Paris: Klincksieck, 1973; and Pierre Bonnassie, *La Catalogne du milieu du Xe à la fin du XIe siècle. Croissance et mutations d'une société*, Toulouse: Association des Publications de l'Université de Toulouse-Le Mirail, 1975. Two additional works of synthesis by Robert Fossier have been crucial to me: *Le Moyen Âge*, 3 vols., Paris: Colin, 1982; and especially *Enfance de l'Europe*, 2 vols., Paris: PUF, 1982. The estimate of the nobility as representing a little more than 1 percent of the total population is Chédeville's (p. 329). Philippe Contamine, focusing on a later period (1300–1340), estimates the nobility as numbering between 1 percent and 2 percent, or between 40,000 and 50,000 families for the entire kingdom ("Introduction," in Contamine, ed., *La noblesse au moyen âge, XIe–XVe siècles: Essais à la memoire de Robert Boutruche*, Paris: PUF, 1976, p. 23).

    4. The classic definition of the *ban* is that of Charles Perrin, *La seigneurie rurale en France et en Allemagne*, Paris: CDU, 1953, p. 343; cited by René Fédou, *l'Etat au moyen âge*, Paris: PUF, 1971, p. 24. For Chédeville, "le ban, c'est essentiellement le pouvoir militaire et le pouvoir judiciaire" (p. 296); for Fourquin, it is "un pouvoir général de commander, contraindre et punir," though this definition is limited to "les hommes libres" (*Seigneurie et féodalité au moyen âge*, Paris: PUF, 1970/77, p. 32). Fossier considers the establishment of banal lordship as "le fait social majeur du XIe siècle" (*Les hommes en Picardie*, p. 560). All of these historians specify the forms of banal lordship; Bonnassie's description has been most useful to me, vol. 2, pp. 582–610. As against the idealized image of medieval nobility that is

current in the texts of the period we call "literary" and that has far too great currency among modern literary scholars, lordship was itself considered "une richesse qui, dans l'esprit de son possesseur, est avant tout l'occasion de perceptions lucratives" (Duby, *La société*, p. 173). In *L'économie rurale*, Duby gives the first half of the eleventh century as the period in which the system is established; the last quarter of the century as a particularly noteworthy period of new exactions (which would make this moment immediately precede the *Song of Roland* in its traditional dating by Bédier); and the twelfth century as the period of the system's completion, with increased attention to village markets around 1150, and the development of the *taille* starting around 1180—the period of Chrétien de Troyes (pp. 452–54).

5. Duby, *Guerriers et paysans*, p. 199.

6. The chronology of this development varies markedly from one region to another. The chronology adopted here is a dominant one, which happens to "make sense" in correlation with the field of textuality. Nevertheless, since the dating of texts is itself highly variable, both chronological models and their correlation must be viewed cautiously, as largely speculative.

7. Chédeville, pp. 294f.

8. Bonnassie, p. 495.

9. Ibid., p. 609.

10. Referring to Bonnassie, Duby writes: "Il a montré le rôle véritable des 'chevauchées': périodiquement, l'escadron chevaleresque conduit par le gardien du château patrouillait la petite principauté, le 'district'—encore un mot qui parle de contrainte—de la forteresse, terrifiante exhibition de force dont le but était . . . d'inciter les manants à s'acquitter sans trop renacler des taxes. Dans la chevalerie, l'oppression s'incarnait" (*Les trois ordres*, p. 191).

11. Duby, *Les trois ordres*, p. 231.

12. Bonnassie, p. 598; Duby, *Les trois ordres*, pp. 183–93. Justifying the expression "*lutte des classes*" in a relatively informal discussion, Duby argues: "Why should I not use it?—since it's true. During the feudal period, there was intense combat by the lords (*seigneurs*) to extend their power to extort and, in the face of their demands, peasant resistances and rebellions" (Georges Duby, Guy Lardreau, *Dialogues*, Paris: Flammarion, 1980, p. 125; my translation). Rodney Hilton stresses the same point in his review of Duby's *Guerriers et paysans* in *New Left Review* 83 (Jan.-Feb. 1974), 83–94: he reformulates Duby's identification of exploitation of the peasants by the lords as the motor of economic development, to state that there is no "hermetic seal" between the ideas of Marxists and non-Marxists, and that it is their interaction that can be mutually beneficial (p. 84). This seems to me exactly right.

13. Bonnassie, pp. 598ff.; Duby, *Les trois ordres*, p. 191.

14. Jean Flori, "La notion de chevalerie dans les chansons de geste du XIIe siècle. Etude historique de vocabulaire," *Moyen Âge* 819 (1975), 211–44 and 407–45. In this context, the prohibition against peasants bearing arms not only reserved the sign of nobility to the knights, it also increased their force relative to the peasants who were its subjects. And of course, the prohibition was enforced by the knights, thereby protecting their own welfare.

15. See Duby, *Les trois ordres*.

16. Georges Duby, *Guerriers et paysans: viie–xiie siècles, premier essor de l'économie européenne*, Paris: Gallimard, 1973: "Les attitudes mentales," pp. 6–86.

17. Compare Judith Kellogg, *Medieval Artistry and Exchange: Economic Institutions, Society, and Literary Form in Old French Narrative*, New York: Peter Lang, 1989 ("American University Studies, Series II: Romance Languages and Literature," vol. 123). Kellogg sees in the presence of economic concerns in the text the early degradation of a "pure" state of knighthood by a commercial ethos (pp. 17–72). Did that state of "pure" knighthood and nobility, untainted by concern with the material realities of life, including the financial and the commercial, ever exist?

18. The issue of the medieval nobility and aristocracy—distinct from that of feudalism—

is exceedingly complicated. Two synthetic overviews are those of Duby, "Les origines de la chevalerie," in *Settimane . . . sull'alto medievo*, vol. 15, no. 2 (1968), 738–61, repr. in *Hommes et structures du moyen âge*, Paris and The Hague: Mouton, 1973, pp. 215–42, which should be read in conjunction with "Histoire et sociologie de l'Occident médiéval: Résultats et recherches," and "Lignage, noblesse et chevalerie au XIIe siècle dans la région mâconnaise," in the same volume, pp. 353–60 and 395–422; and L. L. Génicot, "Naissance, fonction et richesse dans l'ordonnance de la société médiévale. Le cas du Nord-Ouest du continent," in *Problèmes de stratification sociale*, ed. Roland Mousnier, Paris: PUF, 1968, pp. 83–100. Two recent collections of articles on the subject are those of Timothy Reuter, *The Medieval Nobility*, Amsterdam and New York: North Holland, 1979 (which includes a later article by Génicot: "Recent Research on the Medieval Nobility," pp. 17–35); and *La Noblesse au moyen âge: XIe–XVe siècles; Essais à la mémoire de Robert Boutruche*, Paris: PUF, 1976, ed. Philippe Contamine (with an excellent synthetic introduction by the editor, pp. 19–35). A major enterprise, based on semantic analysis but encompassing a general historical synthesis, is to be found in the series by Jean Flori, *l'Idéologie du glaive: Pré-histoire de la chevalerie* and *L'essor de la chevalerie: XIe–XIIe siècles*, Geneva: Droz, 1983 and 1986 respectively; a third volume, *De Roland à Lancelot du Lac: la chevalerie dans la littérature française du XIIe siècle*, has been announced by the same publisher.

19. Poly and Bournazel, pp. 163ff. On the genealogical texts of the nobility, see Duby, "Remarques sur la littérature généalogique en France aux XIe et XIIe siècles," *Hommes et structures*, pp. 287–98; and R. Howard Bloch, *Etymologies and Genealogies, passim*.

20. On the separation of social strata implied by this functional differentiation, see Joseph Strayer's classic article, "The Two Levels of Feudalism," in *Medieval Statecraft and the Perspectives of History*, Princeton: Princeton University Press, 1971, pp. 63–76. Separating the fundamental roles of the dominant class, it identifies the *domini, potentes, magnates, divites*—in the vernacular, the *barons, riches homes*, as well as *ducs* and *comtes*—who ultimately profited from the manorial and banal systems of exploitation, and their agents on the other, who were allowed a limited part of the profits in exchange for their service in assuring the continuation of an adequate surplus productivity on the part of the subject peasant population. The resultant social distinctions were only rarely formulated during the Middle Ages: one exception is that of the Customs of Barcelona, which distinguish four strata within the nobility. See Bonnassie, pp. 782–802; Fossier, pp. 658ff.; Chèdeville, pp. 281ff.; Boutruche, vol. 2, pp. 40–6; and Duby, *La Société*, pp. 317–60.

21. See, for example, Theodore Evergates, *Feudal Society in the Bailliage of Troyes under the Counts of Champagne, 1152–1284*, Baltimore: Johns Hopkins University Press, 1975, pp. 110–13.

22. Bonnassie, p. 798.

23. Duby, *La société*, p. 327.

24. Bonnassie, p. 808.

25. The high nobles who exploit the powers of the ban are "*très rares*": in England, Normandy, northern France, and Germany, the kings, dukes, and counts controlled a monopoly of the *ban* over large territories (Duby, *L'économie rurale*, p. 452).

26. The classic reference on feudalism is F. L. Ganshof, *Qu'est-ce que la féodalité?*, 3d ed., Brussels: Office de Publicité, 1957. Ganshof uses the term "feudalism" to refer to a legally binding system of reciprocal obligations. In his epoch-making *La société féodale*, Marc Bloch used the term to designate an entire society, including its economic and cultural practices. This use does not contradict even the severe strictures of Robert Fossier (*Enfance de l'Europe*, vol. 2, pp. 951–79: "Féodalité et noblesse," in the third part of the entire work, titled "Quelques problèmes"). Marxist historiography, of course, has traditionally used the concept of the "feudal mode of production" as part of its social typology (Karl Marx, *Pre-Capitalist Economic*

Formations, ed. Eric J. Hobsbawm, New York: International Publishers, 1965). Some recent historians have argued against the utility of the feudal model as an analytic instrument, considering it a modern invention, subject to extreme variability, and unnecessary for the explanation of documented historical practices: Elizabeth A. R. Brown, "The Tyranny of a Construct: Feudalism and Historians of Medieval Europe," *American Historical Review* 79 (1974), 1063–88, as well as her review article "Georges Duby and the Three Orders," *Viator* 17 (1986), 51–64; Alain Gerreau, *Le féodalisme: un horizon théorique*, Paris: Le Sycomore, 1980. M. M. Postan's last article, "Feudalism and Its Decline: A Semantic Exercise," might readily fit into this revisionary category, did it not assume a historical referent properly labeled "feudalism" in spite of the inadequacies of all available definitions (in T. H. Aston, P. R. Cross, Charles Dyer, and J. Thirsk, eds., *Social Relations and Ideas: Essays in Honor of R. H. Hilton*, Cambridge: Cambridge University Press, 1983, pp. 73–83). In a 1978 interview in *Le Monde*, Duby characterized "la féodalité" as follows: "l'usage du contrat vassalique et du fief ne fut jamais qu'une couverture superficielle . . . plaquée sur les structures vivantes de la sociabilité. . . . " ("Féodalités méditéranéennes," *Le Monde*, 27 Octobre 1978; quoted by Poly and Bournazel, *La mutation féodale*, p. 483). Robert Fossier, who found the concept of little use in his analysis of Picardy, considers "la féodalité" no more than "une pellicule infime et discontinue" on the surface of medieval society which no more incarnates the period than do the "PDG des 20 premières entreprises nationales" in contemporary France (*Enfance de l'Europe*, vol. 2, p. 952). He finds the attention paid this "moins de 1% de la population" excessive (p. 956) and argues that though "among lords, or within the same manor, the masters might have woven among themselves bonds of interdependence, called feudal, this is an insignificant epiphenomenon (*un épiphénomène négligeable*) which modifies in no way the structure of production" (pp. 1065f.; my translation). Fossier considers it merely "an extremely thin and discontinuous film" on the surface of medieval society ("une pellicule infime et discontinue": *Enfance de l'Europe*, vol. 2, p. 952), and expresses considerable irritation at the disproportionate amount of attention this minuscule level of society receives from historians. Fossier recognizes the epistemological problem: " . . . ce groupuscule oblitère notre vue, encombre l'avant-scène documentaire; c'est pour lui, par lui que la littérature s'exprime, que les chartiers enflent. . . . Que faire alors?" Fossier's answer—"*Compter*, comme toujours . . . "—has undoubted utility for the historian tracking the traces of structures and practices in order to construct a representation of general social functioning. His injunction is less trenchantly decisive for the textual student, whose main focus is on the structures and practices of the texts themselves, and for whom the concrete text is the ultimate "reality" to be represented. Fossier does acknowledge, however, that these bonds existed among kings, princes, counts, castle-masters (*châtelains*), "et quelques gros clients . . . je ne pourrais nier cette évidence" (p. 953). He occasionally has recourse to the concept of feudalism in discussing other social phenomena (e.g., pp. 1068, 1071). And Elizabeth Brown has been forced to recognize that as eminent and admired a historian as Duby continues to use the concept: see the *Viator* article cited above. Indeed, the very title of a recent work of synthesis by two well-established historians suggests that "feudalism" remains an inescapable, if arguable, tool of research: Jean-Pierre Poly and Eric Bournazel, *La mutation féodale, Xe–XIIe siècles*, Paris: PUF, 1980. Oddly enough, the paradox is perhaps more manageable from the perspective of the textual scholar. That the ruling class of the Middle Ages was particularly small in proportion to the population as a whole does not affect the possibility of an internal political organization of some degree of complexity, nor the assumption that the class remains in control of the media of communication, and that its cultural hegemony imposes limitations upon what can directly be stated in those media. Indeed, it is the existence of that hegemony that necessitates semiotic readings such as those of this book. Since that hegemony operates at the level of overt content, the ideological formulations that remain at the level of overtly recognized values are appropriate to the identification of textual ideology at that relatively superficial level. It is a fact that Ganshof's book contains a wealth of formulations and information that complement the text as their implications and presuppositions. While it cannot define the textual deep structure values, or the profound social contradictions that inhered in the historical dynamic of the society, it is of great utility in helping fill in the surface unsaids of the text.

Finally, the *Roland* recognizes feudalism through its centerpiece, the fief, which is mentioned textually, e.g., at l. 2680.

27. Ganshof, pp. 193–99; Duby, *La société*, pp. 149–65.

28. For a study of knighting as ritual from a perspective of historical anthropology, see Jacques Le Goff, "Le rituel symbolique de la vassalité," in *Pour un autre Moyen Âge*, Paris: Gallimard, 1978, pp. 349–420.

29. Two of the best discussions of this complex phenomenon are those of Chédeville, *Chartres*, "Noblesse et chevalerie," pp. 307–24, and Bonnassie, pp. 802–808. In different ways, the symbolic and ideological fusion of the two levels of the dominant class served the purposes of each. The higher level obtained therefrom the functional rationale of its wealth and power: it could be seen to participate in the work of defending the society as a whole. Obviously, the identification of the lower order of professional warriors with the upper class and its interests was highly desirable to the upper crust which depended on the services of the lower order. From the perspective of the knights, one immediate and quite tangible advantage of their "massive accession" to noble status (Bonnassie, p. 802) was the resultant freedom from taxes and impositions that weighed only on the non-noble. In addition, they were probably as susceptible to the flattery of identification with the ruling class as any modern police force.

30. This is obvious from the actantial distribution of Destinator and Subject in the three "cycles" which constitute the traditional subtypes of the epic.

cycle	Destinator	Subject
cycle du roi	(+)	(+)
cycle de Guillaume d'Orange	(−)	(+)
cycle des barons révoltés	(−)	(−)

The bond between the two actantial functions being figured as that of vassality, the issue in this distribution is that of the cause of its misfunction: the lord or the vassal, or both.

4. The Subsystem of the Professional Warrior

1. It was long thought that the description of Ganelon as *anguisables* (l. 280) registered an unworthy fear, characteristic of a traitor. But *anguisables* does not mean "fearful" (or *pénétré d'angoisse*, as Bédier so elegantly put it): it means "caught in a narrow place," an *angustia*. Ganelon is caught between his loyalty to Charles and his hatred of Roland: his condition of being *anguisables* is tantamount to being caught between a rock and a hard place. Cf. Silvio Pelligrini, "L'ira di Gano," *Cultura neolatina* 3 (1943), 161–62, cited by Martin de Riquer, *Les chansons de geste françaises*, 2nd ed., trans. I. Cluzel, Paris: Nizet, 1968, p. 98.

2. Compare this evaluation of Ganelon to Jean Alter's, who considers him an expression of "l'esprit bourgeois" and, since he is limned as a traitor, of the text's anti-bourgeois position: "L'esprit anti-bourgeois exorcisé dans la *Chanson de Roland*," *Romanic Review* 78 (1987), 254–70. Much the same opinion appears in the recent book—admirable in many ways—of Judith Kellogg, *Medieval Artistry and Exchange: Economic Institutions, Society, and Literary Form in Old French Narrative*, New York: Peter Lang, 1989, (American University Studies: Series II: Romance Languages and Literatures, vol. 123) pp. 22–38.

3. As Wayne Guymon has put it, in the context of the internal struggle of the Christian

camp, "their conjunctive qualities predominate"; "The Structural Unity of *La Chanson de Roland*," *Lingua e stile* 12 (1977), 513–36.

4. But see the classic article of André Burger, "Le rire de Roland," *Cahiers de civilisation médiévale* 3 (1960), 2–11.

5. For a study of the *Roland*'s incorporation and deployment of the values of a shame culture, see George Fenwick Jones, *The Ethos of the Song of Roland*, Baltimore: Johns Hopkins University Press, 1963; while few scholars today will be interested by the argument that the text is a Germanic as opposed to a French one, the semantic and valorial study is still useful.

6. Louis Althusser, "Marxism and Humanism," in *For Marx*, London: New Left Books, 1977, pp. 231–36; "Ideology and Ideological State Apparatuses," in *Lenin and Philosophy*, New York: Monthly Review Press, 1971, pp. 127–86.

7. On parataxis, see Erich Auerbach, "Roland against Ganelon," in *Mimesis: The Representation of Reality in Western Literature*, trans. Willard Trask, New York: Doubleday Anchor, 1957, pp. 83–107. Corrections to Auerbach's view can be found in Leopold Peeters, "Syntaxe et style dans la *Chanson de Roland*," and Helge Nordhal, "Parataxe rhétorique dans la *Chanson de Roland*," both in the *Revue des langues romanes* 80 (1972–73), 45–59 and 345–54.

8. Gaston Paris—one of the sharpest nineteenth-century readers of medieval French texts—hypothesized a redactor unable to decide between alternative versions of the same passage, who therefore transcribed one after the other without choosing (*Histoire poétique de Charlemagne* 2nd ed., Paris, 1905, p. 22); T. A. Jenkins considered the second speech the work of an interpolator, possibly the copyist of the O manuscript, and gave several reasons for this opinion (T. A. Jenkins, ed., *La Chanson de Roland*, rev. ed., Boston: Heath, 1924, p. 63, n. to ll. 761ff.).

9. Robert Fossier, *Le Moyen Âge*, vol. 2, p. 476. The importance of counting to interpreting this scene had already been noted by Robert Guiette, "Les deux scènes du cor dans la *Chanson de Roland* et dans les *Conquestes de Charlemagne*," *Le Moyen Âge* 69 (1963), 845–55.

10. Two extensive, religiously inspired commentaries on the *Roland* have been published in recent years: Gerard Brault, *The Song of Roland: An Analytical Edition*, 2 vols., University Park, PA: Pennsylvania State University Press, 1978; and Robert F. Cook, *The Sense of the Song of Roland*, Ithaca, N.Y.: Cornell University Press, 1987. Although both give ample representation to what Brault calls Turpin's "warlike behavior," his "remarkable energy on the battlefield," and his "ardor for combat" (Brault, p. 242), and although Brault does refer to the historical analogues of militancy among contemporary clergymen (pp. 104, 380, 568n.), neither Brault nor Cook deals with the interpretative problem produced for a religious interpretation of the poem by a representation that contravenes the theology of the priesthood so fundamentally. Members of the clergy were forbidden by canon law to bear arms (John Benton, "The *Song of Roland* and the Enculturation of the Warrior Class," *Olifant* 6 [1979], 237–58). The fact is, of course, that "warrior bishops were not lacking in the XIth and XIIth centuries" (Reto R. Bezzola, *Les Origines et la formation de la littérature courtoise en Occident (500–1200)*, 3 vols., Paris: Champion, 1944–63, vol. 2, p. 456), and that their existence was recognized by Church authorities as a *"fâcheuse exception"* to the rule forbidding churchmen to mount horses and bear arms: Jean-Pierre Poly and Eric Bournazel, *La mutation féodale, Xe–XIIe siècles*, Paris: PUF, 1980, p. 229. The issue is not whether such clerics existed or not, but how readily their existence enters into an easy and untroubled religious interpretation of a text whose enacted values are radically elsewhere.

11. Hermann Graf, *Der Parralelismus im Rolandslied*, Inaugural Dissertation, Wertheim-am-Main: Bechstein, 1931; Pierre Le Gentil, *La Chanson de Roland*, Paris: Hatier, 1955/67, pp. 103f.

5. The Destinator's Multiple Roles

1. " . . . for the very reason that personal dependence forms the ground-work of society, there is no necessity for labour and its products to assume a fantastic form different from their reality," as in capitalism: Karl Marx, *Capital*, 4 vols., Moscow: Progress, 1954/77, vol. 1, p. 81.

2. Ganshof, pp. 109–29. An obvious intertextual transformation specifies the relation between fief and protection. In the *Charroi de Nimes*, William of Orange asks King Louis for the grant of Spain as a fief. Louis, quite intelligently, answers that he cannot grant Spain as a fief, since it isn't his, but is controlled by Saracens. William insists, and Louis eventually accedes to his request, but only with the following proviso, whose terms are quite precise:

> "Tenez Espaigne, prenez la *par cest gant*;
> Ge la vos doing *par itel convenant*,
> Se vos en croist ne paine ne ahan,
> Ci ne aillors ne t'en serai garant."
> Et dit Guillelmes: "Et ge mielz ne demant,
> Fors seulement un secors en set anz."
> *Le Charroi de Nimes*, ed. J. L. Perrier,
> Paris: Champion, 1967 ("Classiques français du
> Moyen Âge," v. 66), vv. 585–90.

As suggested by Ganshof, the terms of the contract of vassalism are negotiated quite precisely. Louis's caution in this negotiation assumes that protection of the vassal normally accompanies the grant of a fief. Given the circumstances of the fief when granted, Louis expects William to encounter difficulties in claiming "his" fief and does not want to be held responsible as its guarantor. Further discussions of the historical responsibility of the lord for the protection of his vassal may be found in Ganshof, pp. 125–29; Boutruche, vol. 2, pp. 204–207; Fourquin, p. 124; and Le Goff, "Le rituel symbolique de la vassalité," in *Pour un autre moyen âge*, Paris: Gallimard, 1977, p. 367.

3. Ganshof, pp. 94–105.

4. All readers of the *Roland* have noticed the occasional striking assertions of vassalic duty and responsibility. A handful has commented on the reciprocal obligation of the lord to provide protection to his vassals. André Burger recognized the general duty of the lord to protect his vassal and remarked: "C'est donc à juste titre qu'Olivier se préoccupe de l'honneur de son suzerain." "Les deux scènes du cor dans la *Chanson de Roland*," *La technique littéraire des chansons de geste (Actes de Colloque de Liège (Septembre 1957)*, Paris: Belles Lettres, 1959 ("Publications de la Faculté de Philosophie et Lettres de l'Université de Liège," vol. 150), p. 112. Adelbert Dessau commented that in the majority of cases, the party guilty of treason in the *chanson de geste* is the lord rather than the vassal (" 'L'idée de la trahison au moyen âge et son rôle dans la motivation de quelques chansons de geste," *Cahiers de civilisation médiévale* 3 [1960], 23–6). F. Whitehead acknowledged Roland's duty as *garant* of the rear guard, admitting he had not performed that duty ("L'ambiguité de Roland," *Studi in honore di Italo Siciliano*, 2 vols., Florence: Olschki, 1966 [Biblioteca dell'Archivum Romanicum, serie I, vol. 86], pp. 1203–12); most recently, Wolfgang van Emden made this principle the major point of his article " 'E cil de France le cleiment a guarant': Roland, Vivien et le thème du *guarant*," *Société Rencevals. VIe Congrès International (Aix-en-Provence, 29 août–4 septembre 1973)*. *Actes*, Aix-en-Provence: Université de Provence, 1974, pp. 31–61, applying the principle to Roland, not to Charlemagne.

5. Technically, the vassal is bound only to his immediate suzerain, not to whatever lords might claim that lord's vassalic fealty in turn. But the king's relation is direct to each of his

subjects, and—as we will see below—kingship was normally confused with the feudal relation, so that the relations between king and subjects were represented in feudal cloth.

6. Hollyman, p. 40.

7. The translation of *culvert*, most often used as a general term of injury, by the socio-political term "serf" may surprise. Etymologically, O.F. *culvert* derives from V.L. *cullibertus*, a freed serf, hence one who was formerly a serf. Nevertheless, *serf* is still the first meaning listed in Greimas's *Dictionnaire de l'ancien français*, at *culvert*.

8. It is not only the text of the *Roland* that hesitates at the notion of inculpating lords: modern intertexts do as well. Bédier's translation of a passage that alludes to the notion of *blasme* excises the idea of blame, responsibility, or culpability entirely:

Roland
E Oliver de ferir ne se target,
Li XII per n'en deivent aveir blasme,
E li Franceis i fierent e si caplent. (ll. 1345–47)

Bédier
"Et Olivier n'est pas en reste, ni les douze pairs, ni les
Français, qui frappent et redoublent." (p. 115)

Regarding the problem the term "culpability" raises in view of the alternatives between the anthropologies of "guilt" vs. "shame" in this text, see the comments in the conclusion, *infra*, p. 192.

6. Excursus II

1. Ernst Kantorowicz, *The King's Two Bodies*, Princeton: Princeton University Press, 1959. Other major studies relevant to the ideology of kingship in the Middle Ages are those of Robert Folz, *Le souvenir et la légende de Charlemagne dans l'Empire germanique médiéval*, Paris: Belles Lettres, 1950; and Percy Ernst Schramm, *Der König von Frankreich: Das Wesen der Monarchie vom 9. zum 16. Jahrhundert*, 2 vols., Darmstadt: Wissenschaftliche Buchgesellschaft, 1960 (I owe this reference to Robert Benson). A useful introduction to the general problem is that of René Fédou, *L'Etat au moyen âge*, Paris: PUF, 1971.

2. Robert Fossier, *Le Moyen Âge*, Paris: Armand Colin, 1982, pp. 139f.

3. Perry Anderson, *Lineages of the Absolutist State*, London: Verso, 1974/79, p. 43.

4. Sidney Painter, *French Chivalry*, Baltimore: Johns Hopkins University Press, 1940, p. 7.

5. The classic reference for this opposition is Louis Halphen, "La place de la royauté dans le système féodal," originally printed in the *Anuario de historia de derecho espanol* 9 (1932), 313–21; then in *Revue historique* 172 (1933), 249–56; and reprinted in the collection of Halphen's essays, *A travers l'histoire du moyen âge*, Paris: PUF, 1950, pp. 266–74. Erich Köhler, long ago, made this opposition the historical basis of the *chanson de geste*: "Quelques observations d'ordre historico-sociologique sur les rapports entre la chanson de geste et le roman courtois," *Chanson de geste und höfischer Roman*, Heidelberg: Winter, 1963 ("Studia Romanica," vol. 4), pp. 21–30.

6. M. Pacaut, *Louis VII et son royaume*, Paris: SEVPEN, 1967, pp. 11f.

7. See the first map in Pacaut, at p. 218.

8. Ferdinand Lot and Robert Fawtier, *Histoire des institutions françaises au moyen âge*, 3 vols., Paris: PUF, 1958, vol. 2, *Institutions royales*, pp. 100f.; see also Charles T. Wood, "*Regnum Franciae*: A Problem in Capetian Administrative Usage," *Traditio* 23 (1967), 117–47; Joseph Strayer, "Defense of the Realm and Royal Power in France," in *Medieval Statecraft and the Perspectives of History*, Princeton: Princeton University Press, 1971, pp. 291–9; and

Elizabeth M. Hallam, *Capetian France, 987–1328*, London and New York: Longman, 1980, pp. 78–86. Robert Fawtier, *The Capetian Kings of France, 987–1328*, trans. L. Butler and R. J. Adam, New York: St. Martin's Press, 1960, remains useful as well.

9. Hallam, pp. 86–88; Pacaut, second map at p. 218.

10. Thomas N. Bisson, "The Problem of Feudal Monarchy: Aragon, Catalonia, and France," *Speculum* 53 (1978), 460–78.

11. Jean-François Lemarignier, *Le gouvernement royal aux premiers temps capétiens, (987–1108)*, Paris: Picard, 1965, p. 83.

12. Karl-Heinz Bender, *König und Vassal, Untersuchungen zu Chanson de geste des XII. Jahrhunderts*, Heidelberg: Winter, 1967 ("Studia romanica," 13. Heft), p. 28.

13. Fawtier, *The Capetian Kings*, p. 76.

14. Lemarignier, *op. cit.*

15. Hallam, pp. 75–78; the standard account of Philip's reign is still A. Fliche, *Le règne de Phillippe Ier, roi de France*, Paris: Société Française d'Imprimerie et de Librairie, 1912.

16. Hallam, p. 114.

17. Ibid., pp. 174–79.

18. Hallam, p. 120; Pacaut, pp. 221–23.

19. See Pacaut's detailed discussion, "Gestion et administration," *Louis VII*, pp. 139–60, and the further discussion of John Benton, "The Revenue of Louis VII," *Speculum* 42 (1967), 84–91.

20. Hallam, p. 123.

21. Although Joseph Strayer's classic discussions of the medieval foundations of the French state does not address directly the issue of "ideology," that concept is not far removed from his work in *On the Medieval Origins of the Modern State*, Princeton: Princeton University Press, 1970, and the articles collected in *Medieval Statecraft*.

22. M. Legge, "Gallia und Francia im Mittelalter," *Bonner Historischer Forschungen* (1960), p. 167; cited by Pacaut, p. 222.

23. Hallam, p. 132; Georges Duby, *Le dimanche de Bouvines*, Paris: Gallimard, 1973.

24. Robert-Henri Bautier, "Le règne de Philippe-Auguste dans l'histoire de France," in *La France de Philippe-Auguste: Le temps des mutations*, ed. Robert-Henri Bautier, Paris: Editions du CNRS, 1982, p. 27; my translation. Documentation on Philip-Augustus is greater than for his forefathers, because of the permanent bureaucracy and archives created during his reign. This documentation has produced a large scholarly bibliography. In addition to the more than 1,000 pages of studies in the volume edited by Bautier, see also the brief comments of Heinrich Mitteis, *The State in the Middle Ages: A Comparative Constitutional History of Feudal Europe*, trans. H. F. Orton, Amsterdam: North-Holland, 1975, pp. 267–79; as well as the very full study of John W. Baldwin, *The Government of Philip Augustus: Foundations of French Royal Power in the Middle Ages*, Berkeley: University of California Press, 1986.

25. Fawtier, pp. 156–62.

26. Lot and Fawtier, vol. 2, p. 583.

27. Baldwin, pp. 359–62.

28. Hallam, p. 173.

29. Dominique Boutet, "Les chansons de geste et l'affermissement du pouvoir royal (1100–1250)," *Annales, E.S.C.* 37 (1) (1982), 3–14.

30. Robert Folz, *L'idée de l'empire en occident du V au XIV siècle*, Paris: Aubier, 1953, p. 11.

31. Jacques Le Goff, *La civilisation de l'Occident médiéval*, Paris: Arthaud, 1977, p. 329.

32. Ibid., p. 331.

33. Ibid., p. 130.

34. Ibid., p. 333.

35. Hallam, pp. 176f.

36. Strayer, "France: The Holy Land, the Chosen People, and the Most Christian King," *Medieval Statecraft*, p. 212; A. Bossuat, "La formule: le roi est empereur en son royaume," *Revue historique de droit français et étranger*, ser. 4, vol. 39 (1961), 371–81, cited by René Fédou, *L'état au moyen âge*, Paris: PUF, 1971, p. 100.

37. Hallam, pp. 177–79.

38. Charlton T. Lewis and Charles Short, *A Shorter Latin Dictionary*, Oxford: Oxford University Press, 1958; Robert Fossier, *Le Moyen Âge*, Paris: Armand Colin, 1982, vol. 2, p. 135.

39. See also ll. 333f., 3678f., 3823f., 3999f.

40. Jacques Le Goff, "Le Christianisme médiéval en Occident du Concile de Nice (325) à la Réforme (début du XVIe siècle)," in *Histoire des religions*, 3 vols., Paris: Gallimard, 1972, vol. 2, ed. Henri-Charles Puech: *La Formation des religions universelles et les religions du salut* ("Histoire de la Pléiade"), pp. 749–868; pp. 811–15.

41. Karl-Heinz Bender, "Des chansons de geste à la première épopée de croisade. La présence de l'histoire contemporaine dans la littérature française du XIIe siècle," in *Société Rencesvals. VIe Congrès International* (Aix-en-Provence, 19 août—Septembre 1973), Aix-en-Provence: Université de Provence, 1974, pp. 488–500.

42. John B. Morrall, *Political Thought in Medieval Times*, New York: Harper, 1958/62, p. 27.

43. Louis Halphen, *Charlemagne et l'empire carolingien*, Paris: Albin Michel, 1947/68, pp. 414–17.

44. Fossier, *Le Moyen Âge*, vol. 2, p. 135.

7. Funerary Rituals

1. Parts of this section were printed under the title "Funerary Rituals in the *Song of Roland*" in *Continuations: Essays on Medieval French Literature and Language in Honor of John L. Grigsby*, ed. Norris J. Lacy and Gloria Torrini-Roblin, Birmingham, AL: Summa, 1989, pp. 187–202.

2. See the sensitive reaction to the figure of Charles as survivor in Eugene Vance's "Roland et la poétique de la mémoire," *Cahiers d'Etudes Médiévales* I (1973), 103–15; repr. with changes and in English in *Mervelous Signals, Poetics and Sign Theory in the Middle Ages*, Lincoln, NE: University of Nebraska Press, 1986, pp. 51–85.

3. I am using the English word "Moment" in the sense of the German *Momente*, indicating both temporal sequentiality of successive events and their incorporation of successive phases of a process: the dual isotopies of temporality and social process are combined by this usage.

4. See ll. 2414, 2417, 2419, 2428, 2446, 2456, 2517, 2519, 2524; and later in the narrative: ll. 2873, 2880, 2936, 2946. The study of these verbalizations should prove semantically interesting.

5. It also verbalizes the link between the present action and the prolepsis voiced by Turpin in discussion with Oliver and Roland: see *supra*, pp. 82–83.

6. *Supra*, pp. 111–15.

7. Bédier mistranslates here: "il (= Gabriel) la (= the battle) lui montre par des signes funestes," which means little.

8. See ll. 2859, 2870, 2876.

9. See K. J. Hollyman, *Le développement du vocabulaire féodal en France pendant le*

haut moyen âge (étude sémantique), Geneva: Droz, 1957, p. 40; Georges Matoré, *Le vocabulaire de la societé médiévale*, Paris: PUF, 1985, pp. 144f.; Nelly Andrieux-Reix, *Ancien français: Fiches de vocabulaire*, Paris: PUF, 1989, pp. 76–79.

10. See 11. 2859, 2870, 2876, 2885, 2894, 2920.

11. On marriage in the Middle Ages, see Georges Duby, *Medieval Marriage*, Baltimore: Johns Hopkins University Press, 1978; and *The Knight, the Lady, and the Priest*, trans. B. Bray, New York: Pantheon, 1983; as well as R. Howard Bloch's second chapter, "Kinship," in *Etymologies and Genealogies, A Literary Anthropology of the French Middle Ages*, Chicago: University of Chicago Press, 1983.

12. The exception that marks this ideology is, of course, the American devotion to insurance. This is probably best seen as the effort of American ideology to deny death and transcend history. Even when some social element or principle of governmental responsibility can be alleged in the issue of mortality, it is extremely difficult to assert the principle of the State's obligation to its members and to obtain compensation for a particular death.

13. See R. Howard Bloch, *Medieval French Literature and Law*, Berkeley: University of California Press, 1977, pp. 28–42.

8. Textual Coherence and the Dialectics of Ideology

1. The works that have been particularly important to my own thinking are the following: Albert Lord, *The Singer of Tales*, New York: Atheneum, 1968; Eric Havelock, *Preface to Plato*, Cambridge, MA: Harvard University Press, 1963; Jean Rychner, *La Chanson de Geste, Essai sur l'art épique des jongleurs*, Geneva: Droz, 1955; Franz Baüml, "Varieties and Consequences of Medieval Literacy and Illiteracy," *Speculum* 55 (1980), 237–65; Ruth Finnegan, *Oral Poetry*, Cambridge: Cambridge University Press, 1977; as well as the work of two sociologists, Jack Goody, *The Domestication of the Savage Mind*, Cambridge: Cambridge University Press, 1977, and Brian Stock, *The Implications of Literacy: Written Language and Models of Interpretation in the Eleventh and Twelfth Centuries*, Princeton: Princeton University Press, 1983; a major study of the *Roland* from the perspective of orality is that of Joseph J. Duggan, *The Song of Roland: Formulaic Style and Poetic Craft*, Berkeley: University of California Press, 1973. Duggan is also the "author" of a research tool that has been of capital importance to me, the *Concordance to the Chanson de Roland*, as well as the editor of the collection of essays *Oral Literature: Seven Essays*, Edinburgh: Scottish Academic Press, 1975.

2. Duggan, *The Song of Roland*, the chapter "The Episode of Baligant," pp. 63–104, esp. pages 75 and 103f. The assumption that the accretive process must be long, slow, and multi-secular strikes me as both pre-Foucaldian and unnecessary. A major narrative sequence like the Baligant could well have been pondered and elaborated in a matter of weeks and produced in a form very similar to what we have—or even identical to it—in a single performance. In addition, the process of "accretion" must be understood to include "subtraction," "multiplication," "fusion," and "transformation" as well. One of the rare scholars to avoid the "attempt to use aesthetic considerations as a basis for making factual judgments" as to the (in)authenticity of the Baligant episode is John Robin Allen, of whom see "Du nouveau sur l'authenticité de l'épisode de Baligant," in *Société Rencesvals, VIe Congrès International*, ed. Jean Subrenat, Aix-en-Provence: Université de Provence, 1974, pp. 147–56; repr. in English, with changes, as "On the Authenticity of the Baligant Episode in the *Chanson de Roland*," in *Computer in the Humanities*, ed. J. L. Mitchell, Minneapolis: University of Minnesota Press, 1974, pp. 65–72; and Allen's "Stylistic Variants in the *Roland*," *Olifant* 6 (1979), 351–63.

3. Oral and literate cultures coexist in the same socio-geographical space. Even the *Roland*—the ultimate "oral" text in Old French—cites a written *geste francor* as its legitimating source. While the study of particular texts may attempt to establish a distribution of oral and

literate traits in an evenhanded manner, one of the two categories is likely to seem dominant, or perhaps fundamental, by comparison to the other.

The dating of the *Roland* is both a perplexing problem and a false issue. In attempting to come up with a usable date, two events must be distinguished: the performance of the text to be dated and its manuscript inscription. The (romantic) fascination with origins, and the valorization thereof, resulted in efforts to date "literary texts" as early as possible; by contrast, the paleographic evidence of actually existing manuscripts tended to be seen as "late." Thus, Bédier's dating of the poem placed it at the very end of the eleventh, or the very beginning of the twelfth century: he proposed 1098–1102, and—in good conscience—immediately admitted there was something disquieting about such a precise dating. At the same time, Bédier thought the Oxford manuscript in the Bodleian Library might date from around 1170 (*La Chanson de Roland: [Commentaires]*, 2nd ed., Paris: Piazza, 1927, pp. 58f. and 66; the UCLA copy is inscribed "A mon cher collègue, Wm. A. Nitze, Souvenir fidèle, Joseph Bédier"). Nevertheless, Pierre Le Gentil asserted that "tout le monde est d'accord sur ce point," i.e., a dating of the manuscript in the second quarter of the twelfth century (*La Chanson de Roland*, Paris: Hatier, 1955, p. 23). A recent survey of the literature on this point finds a fair degree of agreement with Bédier on the dating of Digby 23, as around 1170 or the third quarter of the twelfth century, with some notable exceptions: Gerard Brault's review of André Burger, *Turold, poète de la fidélité*, in *Olifant* 5 (1977), 120–24. The conditions of performance in an oral cultural context make the entire issue most likely a false one. Although a single performance of an oral text is theoretically possible, it is unlikely to find its way into the written records of its culture. The text we read in Digby 23 is most likely to represent simply that stage of development attained by the tradition at the time it was recorded. As a result, the text will undoubtedly contain a palimpsestic structure, incorporating traits from various performances at various historical moments. As a result, it seems appropriate to consider the "date" of the *Roland* to consist, not of a punctual moment indicated by a three or four digit number (as a recent and seemingly authoritative publication would have it: the *Harvard History of French Literature*), but by a continuum which stretches minimally from the opening years of the twelfth century over at least three generations toward the end of the same century. Over this period, I would further guess that the content of the Roland-sequence and Ganelon's trial remained fairly stable, but that the Baligant episode was added somewhere along the way, probably fairly late within this time frame. Given the existence of historical references of markedly earlier dates, I would further assume that at least some elements of the Roland-sequence antedate the beginning of the twelfth century. Such a reconceptualization of the problem of dating the text would recognize the pertinence both of early datings (such as Karl-Heinz Bender's: the last two decades of the eleventh century [*König und Vassal*, p. 38]) and relatively late datings (such as Hans-Erich Keller's: "The *Song of Roland* and Its Audience," *Olifant* 6 [1979], 259–74). The theoretical crux then becomes: for a method of reading that specifies the socio-historical co-text as at least partly determinative of the text's meaning and significance, how does such a chronologically "sliding signifier" operate?

If the date of the text is open to question, so is the place of its composition: the facts that the earliest manuscript of the text was found at Oxford, and that a form of medieval French was spoken by the conquerors of medieval England, are pertinent to the possibility of a Norman or even Anglo-Norman composition. For a thoughtful discussion of this possibility, see David Douglas, "The *Song of Roland* and the Norman Conquest of England," *French Studies* 14 (1960), 99–116.

4. Ferdinand de Saussure, *Cours de linguistique générale*, ed. Tullio de Mauro, Paris: Payot, 1972, pp. 155–58. This would seem to be the end result of the co-presence of variants proposed by Bernard Cerquiglini in the last chapter of his book *Eloge de la variante*, which appropriately ridicules philological efforts to reconstitute lost "originals" likely to have never

existed, only to recommend a reconstitution—equally ahistorical—of all variants in the co-presence allowed by a computer screen: the important ahistoricity is not the use of electronic instruments of research (this is being typed on a Macintosh SE), but the simultaneous presence of all variants, a condition which never existed for vernacular works of fiction.

5. For a sophisticated semiotic analysis that remains resolutely synchronic, see Larry S. Crist, "Roland: Héros du vouloir: Contribution à l'analyse structurale de la *Chanson de Roland*," *Marche Romane* 7 (1978), 77–101; (*Mélanges Jeanne Wathelet-Willem*), which deals persuasively with the structural relation between the Roland and Charles sequences.

6. Several critics have drawn attention to the possible effect of epic performance on medieval audiences in somewhat different terms: Hans-Erich Keller, "*The Song of Roland*: A Mid-Twelfth Century Song of Propaganda for the Capetian Kingdom," *Olifant* 3 (1976), 242–58, and "*The Song of Roland* and Its Audience," *Olifant* 6 (1979), 259–74; John F. Benton, "'Nostre Franceis n'unt talent de fuïr': *The Song of Roland* and the Enculturation of a Warrior Class," *Olifant* 6 (1978/9), 237–58; and Joseph J. Duggan, "Social Functions of the Medieval Epic in the Romance Literatures," *Oral Tradition* 1 (1986), 728–66.

7. See the impressive efforts by Paul Zumthor to resurrect—by imagination, by the deepest resonances of a sympathetic subjectivity—all that has been lost: *La lettre et la voix: De la "littérature" médiévale*, Paris: Seuil, 1987.

8. Maurice Delbouille, *Sur la genèse de la Chanson de Roland*, Brussels: Palais des Académies, 1954, p. 36; cited by Duggan, *The Song of Roland*, pp. 74f.

9. Duggan, *The Song of Roland*, p. 74.

10. Gérard Genette, "Vraisemblance et motivation," *Figures II*, Paris: Seuil, 1969, pp. 71–100.

11. See the reference to Bisson, *supra*, note 10, chap. 6.

12. See Albert Gérard's important article, "L'axe Roland-Ganelon: valeurs en conflit dans la *Chanson de Roland*", *Moyen Age* 75 (1969) 445–65.

13. *Supra*, pp. 76ff.

14. Robert Francis Cook, *The Sense of the Song of Roland*, Ithaca: Cornell University Press, 1987, p. 107.

15. In Benedict Anderson's phrase; see *Imagined Communities: Reflections on the Origin and Spread of Nationalism*, London: Verso, 1983/89, p. 15.

16. Ernest Renan, "What Is a Nation?," trans. Martin Thom, in Homi K. Bhabha, ed., *Nation and Narration*, London: Routledge, 1990, pp. 8–22; see as well Thom's own contribution to this volume, which follows Renan's essay directly: "Tribes within Nations: The Ancient Germans and the History of Modern France," pp. 23–43.

9. Ganelon's Trial, or the Monarch's Revolution

1. The overriding debt of this section to John Halverson's article "Ganelon's Trial," *Speculum* 42 (1967), 661–69, will be obvious to all who know it. An early study, still useful, is M. Pfeffer, "Die Formalitäten des gottesgerichtlichen Zweikampfs in der altfranzösischen Epik," *Zeitschrift für romanische Philologie* 9 (1884), 1–74: it is worth noting that of the eleven steps Pfeffer identifies as legally sanctioned and generally followed, the *Roland* omits those that are specifically religious (the night's vigil in a church, mass, confession, and the swearing of an oath). See also Ruggero M. Ruggieri, *Il proceso di Gano nella 'Chanson de Roland'*, Florence: Jansoni, 1936.

2. Petit de Juleville, cited by Gérard Moignet, ed., *La Chanson de Roland*, Paris, Bordas, 1969, p. 263n.

3. See Erich Köhler, "*Conseil des barons*" und "*jugement des barons*": *Epische Fatalität und Feudalrecht im altfranzösischen Rolandslied*, (Sitzungsberichte der Heidelberger Akademie

der Wissenschaften, Philosophisch-historische Klasse, 1968, IV) Heidelberg: Winter, 1968. I see no basis for Köhler's argument that two different types of court were required, at the period of the *Roland*, to pass on political matters and on judicial issues. On the contrary, these distinctions, which seem so fundamental to a twentieth-century consciousness, appear to have been irrelevant to the practice of the eleventh and twelfth centuries. Cf. Maria Luisa Meneghetti, "*Conseil des barons*: L'Oratoria deliberativa dall'epopea al romanzo," *Retorica e Politica. Atti del II Convegno Italo-Tedesco*, Bressanone, 1974.

4. Moignet is quite right, I think, in considering this line a response to the specific accusation that he betrayed *por aveir*; his comment that "l'un est aussi peu vrai que l'autre," in his note to line 3758, suggests the possibility that Charles as well as Ganelon is lying.

5. In addition to the references above to the work of Halverson, Köhler, Meneghetti, Pfeffer, and Ruggieri, see R. Howard Bloch, *Medieval French Literature and Law*, Berkeley: University of California Press, 1977.

6. Wood, p. 114.

7. Marc Bloch, p. 496.

8. M. Bloch, pp. 456 and 497; Boutruche, pp. 134f.

9. Pierre Maranda, *French Kinship*, Paris and The Hague: Mouton, 1974, pp. 22f.

10. Duby, *La société*, pp. 169ff.

11. Ibid., p. 330.

12. M. Bloch, p. 188.

13. Philippe de Beaumanoir, *Coutumes de Beauvaisis*, ed. A. Salmon, Paris: Picard, 1899; quoted by R. Howard Bloch, *Medieval French Literature and Law*, p. 66.

14. Compare Cook, p. 114, to R. Howard Bloch, *Medieval French Literature and Law*, pp. 40f.

15. "La noblesse féodale considérait la guerre privée comme une voie de recours parfaitement légitime . . . une procédure parfaitement admise . . . un droit incontestable . . . *qui ne mettait pas en cause le principe de la royauté*." Lot and Fawtier, *Histoire des institutions françaises*, vol. 2, p. 37; my emphasis.

16. On the *judicium dei* and the growing preference for various forms of mediation, arbitration, and compromise, see Lot and Fawtier, *Histoire des institutions françaises*, vol. 2, pp. 306–308; R. Howard Bloch, *Medieval French Literature and the Law*, pp. 13–62; Yves Bongert, *Recherches sur les cours laiques du Xe au XIIIe siècle*, Paris: Picard, n.d. (1949?), pp. 103–11, 228–39 and the conclusion; and Duby, *La société*, pp. 165–72 and 427–32.

17. Bédier, whose edition is used in this study as one that stays relatively close to the manuscript, emends Digby 23. He gives "Tierri" at l. 2883. As Moignet notes, however, the manuscript has "Henri" here, and it is in order to bring the text in line with the trial scene, according to nineteenth-century notions of aesthetic economy, that Bédier "corrects" the manuscript.

18. Duby, *La société*, pp. 169f.

19. Both this public quality and the function of torture distinguish Ganelon's case from those studied by Elaine Scarry, in her brilliant book of remarkable equanimity, *The Body in Pain*, Oxford: Oxford University Press, 1985. In Scarry and the modern world, torture is the unmaking of a world; in the cases drawn from the *ancien régime*, it is the constitution of a political world. In the latter, it is a public act, which could not obtain its effects in private; in the former, it is illegal, immoral, shameful, and hence hidden in the privacy of closed doors and drawn curtains. In the latter case, the torture is viewed as the political act of the sovereign; in Scarry's book, the torture is viewed from the victim's perspective, assuming—to the author's credit—the sanctity or claim to respect of the individual body. *The Body in Pain* defends the claims propounded by the modernist ideology of individualism—as admirable as it is *hors de jeu* in an earlier world of values.

20. Michel Foucault, "Torture," in *Discipline and Punish: The Birth of the Prison*, trans. Alan Sheridan, New York: Random House (Vintage), 1977/79, pp. 3–67. Matilda Bruckner kindly reminds me of the other modern text that bears comparison in this context, Kafka's "Harrowing," or "In the Penal Colony."

21. Compare Edward Peters, *Torture*, Oxford: Blackwell, 1985, pp. 44–54, and R. I. Moore, *The Formation of a Persecuting Society*, Oxford: Blackwell, 1987.

10. Conclusion

1. Should this be considered a token of Fredric Jameson's "political unconscious" (*The Political Unconscious: Narrative as a Socially Symbolic Act*, Ithaca: Cornell University Press, 1981)? There is no reason not to do so, but I find no imperative reason to assume that the significations displayed in this text were not available to its original audience. It is one of the effects of medieval alterity to render the boundary between the consciousness and the unconscious of medieval subjects very uncertain. As the intentional consciousness of the medieval speaking subject cannot be affirmed, the same is true of his or her unconsciousness.

2. Alexander Murray, *Reason and Society in the Middle Ages*, Oxford: Oxford University Press, 1978, pp. 97f.

3. Anthony Giddens, *A Contemporary Critique of Historical Materialism: Volume II: The Nation-State and Violence*, Berkeley: University of California Press, 1987, p. 13. Giddens's definition—"circumscribed arenas for the generation of administrative power"—must be expanded, in this case, to include the military power which, as Giddens explains later, is associated with the origin of administration: " . . . it was to a large extent in the military sphere . . . that administrative power in its modern guise was pioneered" (p. 113).

4. Duby, *Les trois ordres*, p. 190.

5. Duby, *Les trois ordres*, pp. 191f.; my translation.

6. Duby, *Les trois ordres*, pp. 187f.

7. To consider feudalism as ideology might go some way toward reconciling the views of two groups of historians: those who, like Elizabeth Brown and Alain Gerreau, persuasively find the concept of feudalism worthless, confused, or unnecessary, and those who, like Duby, Bonnassie, and Chédeville, find it impossible to operate without it; see *supra*, pp. 220–22n.26. The self-flattering idealization of the "classical" form of feudalism is itself an indicator of its ideological function. The fact that this ideology was developed in the domain of secular textuality before being codified by Beaumanoir in the thirteenth century defines the crucial importance of that cultural field in developing ideology and power relations, factors that in turn determined economic functioning. This restricted view of feudalism acknowledges the aptness of Fossier's irritation at the modern fascination with the ideology of less than 1 percent of the population at the expense of any effort at understanding and imagining the lives of the huge majority of the population: this fascination is a signal of the fundamental political prejudice or escapism of modern historians and their readership (Fossier, "Féodalité et noblesse," in *Enfance de l'Europe*, 2 vols., vol. 2, "Structures et problèmes," Paris: PUF, 1982, pp. 951–79).

8. Michel Foucault, *Histoire de la sexualité*, vols. 2–4: *vol. 2: L'usage des plaisirs; vol. 3: Le souci de soi; vol. 4: Les aveux de la chair* (Paris: Gallimard, 1984). The first volume, in a different and smaller format, more tentative and scattered, is closer to the concerns of the present book: *Histoire de la sexualité, vol. 1: La volonté de savoir* (Paris: Gallimard, 1976).

9. Foucault, *L'usage des plaisirs*, p. 11; my translation.

10. Ibid., p. 12; my translation.

11. See Etienne Balibar, "Citoyen sujet," *Cahiers confrontations* 20 (Winter 1989) 23–47, the special issue titled "Après le sujet QUI VIENT."

12. See Jean-Luc Nancy's interview with Derrida, " 'Il faut bien manger,' le calcul du sujet," ibid., pp. 91–114.

13. Michel Foucault, *Résumé des cours, 1970–1982* (Paris: Julliard 1989); R. I. Moore, *The Formation of a Persecuting Society* (Oxford: Blackwell, 1987/90).

14. See Haidu, "The Constitution of the Subject," forthcoming.

15. "History is the western myth": Vincent Descombes, *Modern French Philosophy*, trans. L. Scott-Fox and J. M. Harding, Cambridge: Cambridge University Press, 1980/82, p. 110.

16. Sigmund Freud, "Reflections on War and Death" (1915); *Beyond the Pleasure Principle* (1919–20); "Why War?" (1932); and *Civilization and Its Discontents*. The essays are available in *Freud, Character and Culture*, ed. Philip Reiff, New York: Collier, 1963. I cite *Beyond the Pleasure Principle* in the James Strachey translation (New York: Bantam, 1959/67); and the last title in Joan Rivière's translation, in an undated reprint by the University of Chicago of the edition by Leonard and Virginia Woolf at the Hogarth Press and the Institute for Psychoanalysis. Jacques Lacan, *Le séminaire: v. VII: L'éthique de la psychanalyse*, Paris: Seuil, 1986. René Girard, *La violence et le sacré*, Paris: Grasset, 1972. Jesse Byock, *Medieval Iceland: Society, Sagas, and Power*, Berkeley: University of California Press, 1988/90. Pierre Clastres, *La Société contre l'état*, Paris: Minuit, 1974. Georges Sorel, *Reflexions sur la violence*, Paris: Marcel Riviere, 1912/46. Walter Benjamin, "Critique of Violence," *Reflections*, ed. Peter Demetz, trans. Edmund Jephcott, New York: Harcourt Brace Jovanovich, 1978. Derrida's recent detailed discussion of the Benjamin essay (UCLA, April 26, 1990) omits the issue of the general strike as a political method of particular moment at a particular Moment in history. A cursory approach to some of the issues implicit in this reading list can be found in Haidu, "The Medieval Thing," forthcoming.

17. One might consider the concept of the "world war" a contemporary devolution of the medieval crusade, as much as the concept of the "holy war": indeed, there is substantial overlap between the two models.

18. See the comments of Michael Herzfeld, who argues convincingly that "a critical semiotics of nationalism" must address the absolutization of ethnic differences that accompanies nationalism: "Of Definitions and Boundaries: The Status of Culture in the Culture of the State," in *Discourse and the Social Life of Meaning*, ed. Phyllis Pease Chock and June R. Wyman (Washington, D.C.: Smithsonian Institute, 1986), pp. 75–93.

19. R. I. Moore, *The Formation of a Persecuting Society: Power and Deviance in Western Europe, 950–1250*, Oxford: Blackwell, 1987.

20. See the comments of Mireille Corbier, "Pélèvements, redistributions et circulation monétaire dans l'empire romain (Ier–IIe siècles)," pp. 15–27, and Michel Le Mené, "Conclusion du point de vue du médiéviste," pp. 239–41, both in *Genèse de l'état moderne: Prélèvement et redistribution*, ed. J.-Ph. Genêt and Le Mené, Paris: CNRS, 1987, pp. 16 and 239.

21. "Tout de même, ne pas oublier les invasions barbares," in *L'identité de la France: Les hommes et les choses*, Paris: Arthaud-Flammarion, 1986, p. 84. One regrets finding the word "*barbares*," redolent with such traditional prejudices, from the pen of the great historian. On the invasions themselves, see the classic work of Louis Halphen, *Les Barbares, des grandes invasions aux conquêtes turques du XIe siècle*, Paris: Alcan, 1936; Lucien Musset, *Les invasions: Les vagues germaniques*, Paris: PUF, 1965, and Emilienne Demougeot, *La formation de l'Europe et les invasions barbares*, 3 vols., Paris: Aubier, 1969–79. A useful introduction in English is J. M. Wallace-Hadrill, *The Barbarian West, 400–1000*, rev. ed., Oxford: Blackwell, 1967/85.

22. C. W. Prévité-Orton, "The Crumbling of the Empire in the West, 395–476," in *The*

Shorter Cambridge Medieval History, 2 vols., vol. 1: *The Later Roman Empire to the Twelfth Century*, Cambridge: Cambridge University Press, 1952, pp. 77–102.

23. Braudel, p. 85; my translations.

24. Patrick J. Geary, *Before France and Germany: The Creation and Transformation of the Merovingian World*, Oxford: Oxford University Press, 1988. See also Prévité-Orton, ch. 7: "The Barbarian Kingdoms of the West," pp. 128–84.

25. Braudel, p. 101.

26. Jacques Le Goff, *La civilisation de l'occident médiéval*, Paris: Arthaud, 1964, pp. 27–71.

27. We must beware of the "orientalism" that may hover behind a notion such as "nomadism," simultaneously hypostasizing "violence" (for which no neutral term exists in English: the term is marked by negativity) and attributing it exclusively to originary "outsiders." On Orientalism, see Edward Said, *Orientalism*, New York: Random House/Vintage, 1978/79.

28. Gilles Deleuze and Félix Guattari, *Mille plateaux*, Paris: Minuit, 1980, p. 435.

29. Deleuze and Guattari, *Mille plateaux*, pp. 453f.

30. The term, in modern usage, itself comports a dysphoric seme characteristic of our civilization, and quite foreign to a civilization that gloried in its performances.

31. Deleuze and Guattari, *Mille plateaux*, pp. 434–446.

32. In M. Bloch, p. 66.

33. Ibid., same page; both translations mine. More recently, see also Robert Fossier, *Enfance de l'Europe*, 2 vols., Paris: PUF, 1982, vol. 2, p. 803f.

34. Prévité-Orton, pp. 128f.

35. Georges Duby, "Les 'jeunes' dans la société aristocratique dans la France du Nord-Ouest au XIIe siècle," *Hommes et structures du moyen âge*, pp. 213–25.

36. Braudel makes the important point that, as early as the third century, the social crisis is such that it engenders the "jacquerie" of the Bagaudes among the peasant masses, "*une jacquerie impossible à éteindre*"—an inextinguishable guerilla movement. Among historians of the Middle Ages, those that have focused on the active role of the peasantry as a major determinant are Pierre Dockès, Robert Fossier, Rodney Hilton, and Georges Duby.

37. A readily available example is John Benton's translation of Guibert de Nogent's "autobiography," under the title *Self and Society in Medieval France: The Memoirs of Abbot Guibert de Nogent*, New York: Harper & Row, 1970; see especially Book III.

38. If we have not read Lacan on the constitution of split subjectivity! Jean-Jacques Lecercle's *The Violence of Language*, London: Routledge, 1990, reached me too late to be used for this study.

39. Fossier, *Le Moyen Âge*, vol. 1, pp. 117f.

40. Ibid., p. 124; Patrick J. Geary, "Vivre en conflit dans une France sans Etat: typologie des mécanismes de règlement des conflits (1050–1200)," *Annales ESC* 41 (1986), 1107–33.

41. Max Weber, *The Theory of Social and Economic Organization*, trans. A. M. Henderson and Talcott Parsons, ed. Talcott Parsons, New York: Free Press, 1947/64, p. 156.

42. Anthony Giddens, *A Contemporary Critique of Historical Materialism, Volume II: The Nation-State and Violence*, Berkeley: University of California Press, 1987, p. 18.

43. Ibid., p. 172.

44. Fredric L. Cheyette, "The Invention of the State," in *Essays on Medieval Civilization*, ed. Bede Karl Lackner and Kenneth Roy Philp, Austin: Texas, 1978, p. 163.

45. The renegade moments of the Federal Bureau of Investigation, of the Central Intelligence Agency, and the operations of the "enterprise" that surfaced in Watergate are so many moments of resurgent "nomadism" in contemporary history. So are My Lai, the police assassination of sleeping Black Panther leaders in Chicago in December 1970, and the self-regener-

ating death squads of various South American dictatorships. The brutal violence exercised by an armed gang of police repeatedly beating up Rodney King, exploding on TV newscasts in American living rooms, followed by the violence to law and common sense of an all-white jury's verdict, ricocheted in the urban insurrection in the streets of Los Angeles in the spring of 1992, with its highly specific targets: local stores that habitually profited from the neighborhood population. The narrative of events implicated the police, communications, judicial, and commercial system of the American polity. The joy of killing, beating, and torture has not been suppressed by omnipresent bureaucratized State. On the contrary, their perfect marriage was achieved in the bureaucratization of extermination in the *Rausch* of the Holocaust.

46. Georges Duby, *Le dimanche de Bouvines*, Paris: Gallimard, 1973, p. 100.

47. This hegemony was imperfect, a fact of crucial importance in cultural history.

48. Georges Duby, *Les trois ordres, ou l'imaginaire du féodalisme*, Paris: Gallimard, 1978.

49. Duby, *Guerriers et paysans*, Paris: Gallimard, 1973.

50. René Girard, *La violence et le sacré*, Paris: Grasset, 1972, pp. 301f.; my translation. To Girard goes the credit of having been the first among the theoreticians of (post-)structuralism to have insisted on the problem of violence. The limitation upon his thought is evidenced by its precise aptness to medieval historical experience: it has not advanced beyond the epistemological categories of the twelfth century, in spite of its attempt to grapple with Freud. Ultimately, the question to be addressed to Girard is: why would one expect such sublimated externalization under the aegis of religion as he recommends to work today, when it didn't in the past, and particularly when contemporary civilization has run out of "exteriors" to which to export its own violences?

51. See the texts collected by Edward Peters in *The First Crusade: The Chronicle of Fulcher of Chartres and Other Source Materials*, Philadelphia: University of Pennsylvania Press, 1971, especially the version of Robert the Monk, pp. 2–5.

52. Duby, *Guerriers et paysans*, pp. 60–87.

53. *Supra*, p. 51.

54. Such limitations are entirely relative, of course: the suffering of the victims in the extermination camps of World War II was perfectly visible to their guards. Indeed, their suffering and their victimization was the point of a pondered program to humiliate and desubjectify the victims: see Haidu, "The Dialectics of Unspeakability: Language, Silence, and the Narrative of Desubjectification," in *Probing the Limits of Representation: Nazism and the "Final Solution,"* ed. Saul Friedländer, Cambridge, MA: Harvard University Press, 1992, pp. 277–99.

55. The analogy to the self-punishments inflicted by the super-ego on the guilty psyche in an ever-intensifying cycle of severity is striking.

56. See the classic pages of Georges Duby, "La révolution féodale," in *Les trois ordres, ou l'imaginaire du féodalisme*, Paris: Gallimard, 1978, pp. 183–205.

57. Charles Sanders Peirce, *Collected Papers*, Cambridge, MA: Harvard University Press, 1934–63, vol. 5, p. 185.

58. " . . . à chaque fois que Freud s'arrête, comme horrifié, devant la conséquence du commandement de l'amour du prochain, ce qui surgit, c'est la présence de cette méchanceté foncière qui habite en ce prochain. Mais dès lors elle habite aussi en moi-même. Et qu'est-ce qui m'est plus prochain que ce coeur en moi-même qui est celui de ma jouissance, dont je n'ose approcher? Car dès que j'en approche—c'est là le sens du *Malaise dans la civilisation*—surgit cette insondable aggressivité devant quoi je recule, que je retourne contre moi, et qui vient, à la place même de la Loi évanouie, donner son poids à ce qui m'empêche de franchir une certaine frontière à la limite de la Chose." Jacques Lacan, *Le Séminaire, livre VII, L'Ethique de la psychanalyse*, ed. Jacques-Alain Miller, Paris: Seuil, 1986, p. 219; my translation.

59. In strictly Peircean terms, historical evenementiality itself cannot figure as an Interpretant: civilization, like culture a signifying construct, can theoretically do so, however, but its signification will, inevitably, remain a developing and a complexly open "text."

60. See Haidu, "Fragments in Search of Totalization: Roland and the Historical Text," in Brigitte Cazelles and Charles Méla, eds., *Modernité au moyen âge: le défi du passé*, Geneva: Droz, 1990, pp. 73–99.

Bibliography

Adorno, Theodor W. "Cultural Criticism and Society," in *Prisms*, tr. Samuel and Sherry Weber. Cambridge, MA: MIT Press, 1981/84, pp. 17–34.

Allen, John Robin. "Du nouveau sur l'authenticité de l'épisode de Baligant." In *Société Rencesvals, VIe Congrès International*, ed. Jean Subrenat. Aix-en-Provence: Université de Provence, 1974, pp. 147–56.

———. "Kinship in the Chanson de Roland." In *Jean Misrahi Memorial Volume: Studies in Medieval Literature*, ed. Hans R. Runte, Henri Niedzielski, William L. Hendrickson. Columbia, S. C.: French Literature Publications, 1977, pp. 34–45.

———. "On the Authenticity of the Baligant Episode in the *Chanson de Roland*." In *Computer in the Humanities*, ed. J. L. Mitchell. Minneapolis: University of Minnesota, 1974, pp. 65–72.

———. "Stylistic Variants in the *Roland*." *Olifant* 6 (1979), 351–63.

Alter, Jean. "L'esprit anti-bourgeois exorcisé dans la *Chanson de Roland*." *Romanic Review* 78 (1987), 254–70.

Althusser, Louis. "Ideology and Ideological State Apparatuses." In *Lenin and Philosophy*. New York: Monthly Review Press, 1971, pp. 127–86.

———. *For Marx* trans. Ben Brewster. London: New Left Books ("Verso"), 1977/79.

———. "Marxism and Humanism." In *For Marx*, pp. 231–36.

———. "The 'Piccolo Teatro': Bertolazzi and Brecht." In *For Marx*, pp. 129–51.

Anderson, Benedict. *Imagined Communities: Reflections on the Origin and Spread of Nationalism*. London: Verso, 1983/89.

Anderson, Perry. *Lineages of the Absolutist State*. London: Verso, 1974/79.

———. *Passages from Antiquity to Feudalism*. London: New Left Books, 1974/77.

Andrieux-Reix, Nelly. *Ancien français: Fiches de vocabulaire*. Paris: PUF, 1989.

Auerbach, Erich. "Roland against Ganelon." In *Mimesis: The Representation of Reality in Western Literature*, trans. Willard Trask. New York: Doubleday Anchor, 1957, pp. 83–107.

Badiou, Alain. *Théorie du sujet*. Paris: Seuil, 1982.

Baldwin, John W. *The Government of Philip Augustus: Foundations of French Royal Power in the Middle Ages*. Berkeley: University of California Press, 1986.

Balibar, Etienne. "Citoyen sujet." *Cahiers Confrontations* 20 (Winter 1989), 23–47.

Balibar, Renée. *L'institution du français: Essai sur le colinguisme des Carolingiens à la République*. Paris: PUF, 1985.

Barthélemy, Dominique. *L'ordre seigneurial, XIe-XIIe siècle*. Paris: Seuil, 1990.

Barthes, Roland. "L'ancienne rhétorique." *Communications* 16 (1970), 172–226.

Bauer, Yehuda. *The Holocaust in Historical Perspective*. Seattle: University of Washington Press, 1978.

Baüml, Franz. "Varieties and Consequences of Medieval Literacy and Illiteracy." *Speculum* 55 (1980), 237–65.

Bautier, Robert-Henri. "Le règne de Philippe-Auguste dans l'histoire de France." In *La France de Philippe-Auguste: Le temps des mutations*, ed. Robert-Henri Bautier. Paris: Editions du CNRS, 1982.

Bédier, Joseph, ed. *La Chanson de Roland*, "édition définitive." Paris: Piazza, 1921/66; reprinted U. G. E. 10/18, No. 1506.

———. *La Chanson de Roland (Commentaires)*. 2d ed., Paris: Piazza, 1927.

Bender, Karl-Heinz. "Des chansons de geste à la première épopée de croisade. La présence de l'histoire contemporaine dans la littérature française du XIIe siècle." In *Société Rencesvals. VIe Congrès International, Aix-en-Provence, 19 août-Septembre 1973*. Aix-en-Provence: Université de Provence, 1974, pp. 488–500.

———. *König und Vassal, Untersuchungen zu Chanson de geste des XII. Jahrhunderts*. Heidelberg: Winter, 1967 ("Studia romanica," 13. Heft).

Benjamin, Walter. "Critique of Violence." In *Reflections*, ed. Peter Demetz, trans. Edmund Jephcott. New York: Harcourt Brace Jovanovich, 1978, pp. 277–300.

Bennett, Michael. "First Crusaders' Images of Muslims: The Influence of Vernacular Poetry?" *Forum for Modern Language Studies* 22 (1986), 101–22.

Benton, John. "The Revenue of Louis VII." *Speculum* 42 (1967), 84–91.

———. "The *Song of Roland* and the Enculturation of the Warrior Class." *Olifant* 6 (1979), 237–58.

———, trans. *Self and Society in Medieval France: The Memoirs of Abbot Guibert de Nogent*. New York: Harper & Row, 1970.

Bervoc-Huard, Carole. "L'exclusion du sarrasin dans la *Chanson de Roland*: Vocabulaire et idéologie. 'Ço est une gent ki unches ben ne volt' (v. 3231)." In *Exclus et systèmes d'exclusion dans la littérature et la civilisation médiévales*. Paris: Champion, 1978, pp. 345–61.

Bezzola, Reto R. *Les Origines et la formation de la littérature courtoise en Occident (500–1200)*. 3 vols. Paris: Champion, 1944–63.

Bhabha, Homi, ed. *Nation and Narration*. London: Routledge, 1990.

Bisson, Thomas N. "The Problem of Feudal Monarchy: Aragon, Catalonia, and France." *Speculum* 53 (1978), 460–78.

Bloch, Marc. *La société féodale*. Paris: Albin Michel, 1939/68.

Bloch, R. Howard. *Etymologies and Genealogies: A Literary Anthropology of the French Middle Ages*. Chicago: University of Chicago Press, 1983.

———. *Medieval French Literature and Law*. Berkeley: University of California Press, 1977.

Bongert, Yves. *Recherches sur les cours laïques du Xe au XIIIe siècle*. Paris: Picard, n.d. (1949?)

Bonnassie, Pierre. *La Catalogne du milieu du Xe à la fin du XIe siècle. Croissance et mutations d'une société*. Toulouse: Association des Publications de l'Université de Toulouse-Le Mirail, 1975.

Bossuat, A. "La formule: le roi est empereur en son royaume." *Revue historique de droit français et étranger*, ser. 4, vol. 39 (1961), 371–81.

Bournazel, Eric. *Le gouvernement capétien au XIIe siècle (1108–1180)*. Publications de la Faculté de Droit et Sciences Economiques de l'Université de Limoges, No. 2. Paris: PUF, 1975.

Boutet, Dominique, "Les chansons de geste et l'affermissement du pouvoir royal (1100–1250)." *Annales, E.S.C.* 37 (1) (1982), 3–14.

Boutruche, Robert. *Seigneurie et féodalité.* 2 vols. Paris: Aubier, 1968.

Brandin, Louis, ed. *La Chanson d'Aspremont.* Classiques Français du Moyen Âge, vols. 19 and 25. Paris: Champion, 1919.

Braudel, Fernand. *L'identité de la France: Les hommes et les choses.* Paris: Arthaud-Flammarion, 1986.

Brault, Gerard. Review of *Turold, poète de la fidélité* by André Burger. *Olifant* 5 (1977), 120–24.

———. *The Song of Roland: An Analytical Edition.* 2 vols. University Park, PA: Pennsylvania State University Press, 1978.

Brown, Elizabeth A. R. "Georges Duby and the Three Orders." *Viator* 17 (1986), 51–64.

———. "The Tyranny of a Construct: Feudalism and Historians of Medieval Europe." *American Historical Review* 79 (1974), 1063–88.

Burger, André. "Les deux scènes du cor dans la *Chanson de Roland.*" In *La technique littéraire des chansons de geste, Actes de Colloque de Liège, (Septembre 1957).* Publications de la Faculté de Philosophie et Lettres de l'Université de Liège, vol. 150. Paris: Belles Lettres, 1959.

———. "Le rire de Roland." *Cahiers de civilisation médiévale* 3 (1960), 2–11.

Byock, Jesse. *Medieval Iceland: Society, Sagas, and Power.* Berkeley: University of California Press, 1988/90.

Caesarius of Heisterbach. *Dialogus Miraculorum*, ed. Josephus Strange. 2 vols. Coloniae: J. M. Hebrerle (H. Lemperts), 1851.

Cardini, Franco. *La culture de la guerre*, tr. Angélique Lévy. Paris: Gallimard, 1992.

Cerquiglini, Bernard. *Eloge de la variante.* Paris: Seuil, 1989.

Chaunu, Pierre. *L'obscure mémoire de la France. De la première pierre à l'an mille.* Paris: Perrin, 1988.

Chédeville, Andre. *Chartres et ses campagnes (XIe–XIIIe siècle).* Paris: Klincksieck, 1973.

Cheyette, Fredric L. "The Invention of the State," in *Essays on Medieval Civilization*, ed. Bede Karl Lackner and Kenneth Roy Philp. Austin: Texas, 1978, pp. 143–78.

Clastres, Pierre. *La Société contre l'état.* Paris: Minuit, 1974.

Contamine, Philippe, ed. *La Noblesse au moyen âge: XIe–XVe siècles; Essais à la mémoire de Robert Boutruche.* Paris: PUF, 1976.

Cook, Robert Francis. *The Sense of the Song of Roland.* Ithaca, N.Y.: Cornell University Press, 1987.

Coquet, Jean-Claude. *Le discours et son sujet*, 2 vols. Paris: Klincksieck, 1984.

Corbier, Mireille. "Prélèvement, redistributions et circulation monétaire dans l'empire romain (Ie–IIIe siècles)": see J.-Ph. Genêt and M. le Mené, eds., *Genèse de l'état moderne: Prélèvement et redistribution*, pp. 15–27.

Crist, Larry S. "A propos de la démesure dans la *Chanson de Roland*: Quelques propos (démesurés?)." *Olifant* 1 (1974), 10–20.

———. "Roland: héros du vouloir: Contribution à l'analyse structurale de la *Chanson de Roland.*" *Marche Romane* 7 (1978), 77–101 ("Mélanges Jeanne Wathelet-Willem").

Daniel, Norman. *Heroes and Saracens: An Interpretation of the Chansons de Geste.* Edinburgh, 1984.

Delbouille, Maurice. *Sur la genèse de la Chanson de Roland*. Brussels: Palais des Académies, 1954.

Deleuze, Gilles, and Félix Guattari. *Mille plateaux*. Paris: Minuit, 1980.

———. *Kafka: Toward a Minor Literature*. Trans. Dana Polan. Minneapolis: University of Minnesota Press, 1986.

Demougeot, Emilienne. *La formation de l'Europe et les invasions barbares*. 3 vols. Paris: Aubier, 1969–79.

Derrida, Jacques. "Comment ne pas parler?—Dénégations." In *Psyché*. Paris: Galilée, 1987, pp. 535–95.

———. *De la grammatologie*. Paris: Minuit, 1967.

———. " 'Il faut bien manger,' le calcul du sujet." *Cahiers Confrontations* 20 (Winter 1989), 91–114 (interview with Jean-Luc Nancy).

Descombes, Vincent. *Modern French Philosophy*. Translated by L. Scott- Fox and J. M. Harding. Cambridge: Cambridge University Press, 1980/82.

Dessau, Adelbert. "L'idée de la trahison au moyen âge et son rôle dans la motivation de quelques chansons de geste." *Cahiers de civilisation médiévale* 3 (1960), 23–26.

Dobbs, Maurice, and Paul M. Sweezy. *Sur le féodalisme*. Paris: Editions Sociales, 1974.

———. *The Transition from Feudalism to Capitalism*. London: New Left Books, 1976. French translation: *Du féodalisme au capitalisme: problèmes de la transition*, trans. Florence Gauthier and Françoise Murray. 2 vols. Paris: Maspero, 1977.

Dragonetti, Roger. *La technique poétique des trouvères dans la chanson courtoise: contribution à l'étude de la rhétorique médiévale*. Bruges: Rijksuniversiteit Gent, 1960.

Duby, Georges. "La diffusion du titre chevaleresque sur le versant méditerranéen de la Chrétienté latine." See Contamine, ed., *La Noblesse au moyen âge*, pp. 39–70.

———. *Le dimanche de Bouvines*. Paris: Gallimard, 1973.

———. *L'économie rurale et la vie des campagnes dans l'Occident médiéval*. 2 vols. Paris: Aubier, 1962.

———. "Féodalites méditerannéennes." Interview in *Le Monde*, 27 Octobre 1978.

———. *Guerriers et paysans*. Paris: Gallimard, 1973.

———. *Hommes et structures du moyen âge*. Paris and The Hague: Mouton, 1973.

———. *The Knight, the Lady, and the Priest*. Translated by B. Bray. New York: Pantheon, 1983.

———. *Medieval Marriage*. Baltimore: Johns Hopkins University Press, 1978.

———. "Les origines de la chevalerie." In *Settimane . . . sull'alto medievo*, vol. 15, no. 2 (1968), 738– 61; repr. in *Hommes et structures du moyen âge*, pp. 215–42.

———. *La Société aux XIe et XIIe siècles dans la région mâconnaise*. Paris: SEVPEN, 1952.

———. *Les trois ordres, ou l'imaginaire du féodalisme*. Paris: Gallimard, 1978.

Duggan, Joseph J. *A Concordance of the Chanson de Roland*, Columbus: University of Ohio Press, 1969.

———. *Guide to Studies on the Chanson de Roland*. London: Grant & Cutler, 1976.

———. *Oral Literature: Seven Essays*. Edinburgh: Scottish Academic Press, 1975.

———. "Social Functions of the Medieval Epic in the Romance Literatures." *Oral Tradition* 1 (1986), 728–66.

———. *The Song of Roland: Formulaic Style and Poetic Craft*. Berkeley: University of California Press, 1973.

Eco, Umberto. *L'Oeuvre ouverte*. Paris: Seuil, 1966; translation of *Opera aperta*. Milan: Bompiani, 1962.

———. *The Role of the Reader*. Bloomington: Indiana University Press, 1979.
Evergates, Theodore. *Feudal Society in the Bailliage of Troyes under the Counts of Champagne, 1152–1284*. Baltimore: Johns Hopkins University Press, 1975.
Fawtier, Robert. *The Capetian Kings of France, 987–1328*. Translated by L. Butler and R. J. Adam. New York: St. Martin's Press, 1960.
Fédou, René. *L'Etat au moyen âge*. Paris: PUF, 1971.
Finnegan, Ruth. *Oral Poetry*. Cambridge: Cambridge University Press, 1977.
Fliche, A. *Le règne de Phillippe Ier, roi de France*. Paris: Société Francaise d'Imprimerie et de Librairie, 1912.
Flori, Jean. "La notion de chevalerie dans les chansons de geste du XIIe siècle. Etude historique de vocabulaire." *Moyen Âge* 819 (1975), 211–44 and 407–45.
———. *De Roland à Lancelot du Lac: la chevalerie dans la littérature française du XIIe siècle*. Geneva: Droz, forthcoming.
———. *L'essor de la chevalerie XIe–XIIe siècles*. Geneva: Droz, 1986.
———. *l'Idéologie du glaive: Pré-histoire de la chevalerie*. Geneva: Droz, 1983.
Folz, Robert. *L'idée de l'empire en occident du V au XIV siècle*. Paris: Aubier, 1953.
———. *Le souvenir et la légende de Charlemagne dans l'Empire germanique médiéval*. Paris: Belles Lettres, 1950.
Fossier, Robert. *Enfance de l'Europe*. 2 vols. Paris: PUF, 1982.
———. *Le Moyen Âge*. 3 vols. Paris: Colin, 1982.
———. *La Terre et les hommes en Picardie jusqu'à la fin du XIIIe siècle*. Paris and Louvain: B. Nauwelaerts, 1968.
Foucault, Michel. *La volonté de savoir*. Paris: Gallimard, 1976.
———. *Discipline and Punish: The Birth of the Prison*. Translated by Alan Sheridan. New York: Random House (Vintage), 1977/79, pp. 3–67.
———. *Histoire de la sexualité*. 4 vols. Paris: Gallimard, 1976.
———. *Résumé des cours, 1970–1982*. Paris: Julliard, 1989.
Fourquin, Guy. *Seigneurie et féodalité au moyen âge*. Paris: PUF, 1970/77.
Freud, Sigmund. *Beyond the Pleasure Principle* (1919–20). Translated by James Strachey. New York: Bantam, 1959–67.
———. *Civilization and Its Discontents*. Undated reprint by the University of Chicago of the edition by Leonard and Virginia Woolf at the Hogarth Press and the Institute for Psychoanalysis.
———. "Reflections upon War and Death" (1915). In *Freud, Character and Culture*, ed. Philip Reiff. New York: Collier, 1963, pp. 107–33.
———. "Why War?" (1932). In *Freud, Character and Culture*, pp. 134–47.
Ganshof, F. L. *Qu'est-ce que la féodalité?*. 3d ed. Brussels: Office de Publicité, 1957.
Geary, Patrick J. *Before France and Germany: The Creation and Transformation of the Merovingian World*. Oxford: Oxford University Press, 1988.
———. "Vivre en conflit dans une France sans Etat: typologie des mécanismes de règlement des conflits (1050–1200)." *Annales, ESC* 41 (1986), pp. 1107–33.
Gellrich, Jesse M. *The Idea of the Book in the Middle Ages: Language Theory, Mythology, and Fiction*. Ithaca: Cornell, 1985.
Genêt, J.-Ph., and Michel le Mené, eds. *Genèse de l'état moderne: Prélèvement et redistribution* ("Actes du Colloque de Fontrevault, 1984"). Paris: CNRS, 1987.
Genette, Gérard. "Vraisemblance et motivation." *Figures II*. Paris: Seuil, 1969, pp. 71–100.
Génicot, L. L. "Naissance, fonction et richesse dans l'ordonnance de la société médiévale.

Le cas du Nord- Ouest du continent." In *Problèmes de stratification sociale*, ed. Roland Mousnier. Paris: PUF, 1968, pp. 83–100.

———. "Recent Research on the Medieval Nobility." In *The Medieval Nobility*, ed. Timothy Reuter. Amsterdam and New York: North Holland, 1979; pp. 17–35.

Gerard, Albert. "L'axe Roland-Ganelon: valeurs en conflit dans la *Chanson de Roland*." Moyen Âge 75 (1969), 445–65.

Gerhards, Agnès. *La société médiévale*. Paris: MA Editions, 1986.

Gerreau, Alain. *Le féodalisme un horizon théorique*. Paris: Le Sycomore, 1980.

Giddens, Anthony. *A Contemporary Critique of Historical Materialism, volume II: The Nation State and Violence*. Berkeley: University of California Press, 1987.

Girard, René. *La violence et le sacré*. Paris: Grasset, 1972.

Goldin, Frederick, trans. *The Song of Roland*. New York: W. W. Norton, 1978.

Goody, Jack. *The Domestication of the Savage Mind*. Cambridge: Cambridge University Press, 1977.

Graf, Hermann. *Der Parralelismus im Rolandslied*. Inaugural Dissertation. Wertheim-am-Main: Bechstein, 1931.

Gramsci, Antonio. *Selections from Cultural Writings*. Edited by David Forgacs and Geoffrey Nowell-Smith; trans. William Boelhower. Cambridge, MA: Harvard University Press, 1991.

Greimas, A. J. "Conditions d'une sémiotique du monde naturel." In *Du Sens* [I]: *Essais Semiotiques*. Paris: Seuil, 1970.

———. " The Cognitive Dimension of Narrative." *New Literary History* 7 (1976), 433–47.

———. *De l'imperfection*. Périgueux: Pierre Fanlac, 1987.

———. *Dictionnaire de l'ancien français*. 2e éd. revue et corrigée. Paris: Larousse, 1968.

Greimas, A. J., and Joseph Courtès. *Sémiotique: Dictionnaire raisonné de la théorie du langage*. Paris: Hachette, 1979; English translation: *Semiotics and Language*, trans. Daniel Patte, Larry Crist, et al. Bloomington: Indiana University Press, 1982.

Guiette, Robert. "Les deux scènes du cor dans la *Chanson de Roland* et dans les *Conquestes de Charlemagne*." Le Moyen Âge 69 (1963), 845–55.

Guymon, Wayne. "The Structural Unity of *La Chanson de Roland*." *Lingua e stile* 12 (1977), 513–36.

Haidu, Peter. "Considerations théoriques sur la sémiotique socio-historique." In *Aims and Prospects of Semiotics*, 2 vols., ed. Herman Parret and Hans-Georg Ruprecht. Amsterdam: John Benjamins, 1985; vol. 1, pp. 215–28.

———. "Fragments in Search of Totalization: *Roland* and the Historical Text." In *Modernité au moyen âge: le défi du passé*. Edited by Brigitte Cazelles and Charles Méla, 73–99. Geneva: Droz, 1990.

———. "Funerary rituals in the *Song of Roland*" in *Continuations: Essays on Medieval French Literature and Language in Honor of John L. Grigsby*, ed. Norris J. Lacy & Gloria Torrini-Roblin, Birmingham, AL: Summa, 1989, pp. 187–202.

———. "La valeur: sémiotique et marxisme." *Sémiotique en jeu: A partir et autour de l'oeuvre d'A. J. Greimas*. Edited by Michel Arrivé and Jean-Claude Coquet, Amsterdam: John Benjamins, 1987; pp. 247–63.

———. "Making It [New] in the Middle Ages: Towards a Problematics of Alterity." Review of Paul Zumthor's *Essai de poétique médiévale*, *Diacritics* (Summer 1974) 1–14.

————. "Semiotics and History." *Semiotica* 40 (1982) 187–222.

————. "Text and History." *Semiotica* 33 (1980) 155–69.

————. "The Semiotics of Alterity: A Comparison with Hermeneutics." *New Literary History* 21 (1989–90), 671–91.

————. "The Semiotization of Death: Open Text or Closed?" *Style* 20 (1986), 220–51.

————. "Toward a Socio-Historical Semiotics: Power and Legitimacy in the *Couronnement de Louis*." *Kodikas/Code* 2 (1980), 155–69.

Hallam, Elizabeth M. *Capetian France (987–1328)*. London and New York: Longman, 1980.

Halphen, Louis. "La place de la royauté dans le système féodal." *Anuario de historia de derecho espanol* 9 (1932), 313–21. Reprinted in *Revue historique* 172 (1933), 249–56. Reprinted in Louis Halphen, *A travers l'histoire du moyen âge*. Paris: PUF, 1950, pp. 266–74.

————. *Les Barbares, des grandes invasions aux conquêtes turques du XIe siècle*. Paris: Alcan, 1936.

————. *Charlemagne et l'empire carolingien*. Paris: Albin Michel, 1947/68.

Halverson, John. "Ganelon's Trial." *Speculum* 42 (1967), 661–69.

Havelock, Eric. *Preface to Plato*. Cambridge, MA: Harvard University Press, 1963.

Herzfeld, Michael. "Of Definitions and Boundaries: The Status of Culture in the Culture of the State," in *Discourse and the Social Life of Meaning*, ed. Phyllis Pease Chock and June R. Wyman. Washington, D.C.: Smithsonian Institute, 1986, pp. 75–93.

Hilton, Rodney. *Bond Men Made Free*. New York: Viking, 1973.

————. Review of *Guerriers et paysans* by Georges Duby. In *New Left Review* 83 (Jan.-Feb. 1974), 83–94.

Hindess, Barry, and Paul Hirst. *Mode of Production and Social Formation*. London: Macmillan, 1977.

————. *Pre-Capitalist Modes of Production*. London: Routledge & Kegan Paul, 1975.

Hollyman, K. J. *Le développement du vocabulaire féodal en France pendant le haut moyen âge (étude sémantique)*. Geneva and Paris: Droz and Minard, 1957.

Holmes, Robert. "Emotiveness and Elusiveness in Definitions of Violence," in *Justice, Law, and Violence*, ed. James B. Brady and Newton Garver. Philadelphia: Temple, 1991, pp. 48–52.

Hunt, Tony. "The Tragedy of Roland: An Aristotelian View." *Modern Language Review* 74 (1979), 791–802.

Jakobson, Roman. "Two Aspects of Language and Two Types of Aphasic Disturbances." In Roman Jakobson and Morris Halle, *Fundamentals of Language*. 'S-Granvenhage: Mouton, 1956, pp. 53–82.

Jameson, Fredric. *The Political Unconscious: Narrative as a Socially Symbolic Act*. Ithaca: Cornell University Press, 1981.

Jauss, Hans-Robert. *Alterität und Modernität des mittelalterlichen Literatur*. Munich, 1977.

————. "The Alterity and Modernity of the Middle Ages." Translated by Timothy Bahti. *New Literary History* 10 (1979), 181–230.

Jenkins, T. Atkinson, ed. *La Chanson de Roland*. Rev. ed. Boston: Heath, 1924.

Jones, George Fenwick. *The Ethos of the Song of Roland*. Baltimore: Johns Hopkins University Press, 1963.

Jonin, Pierre. "Deux langages de heros épiques au cours d'une bataille suicidaire." *Olifant* 9 (1962), 83–98.

Joshua, Isaac. *La Face cachée du moyen âge: les premiers pas du capital*. Montreuil: La Brèche, 1988.

de Juleville, Petit, trans. *La Chanson de Roland*. Paris: Lemerre, 1878.

Kantorowicz, Ernst. *The King's Two Bodies*. Princeton: Princeton University Press, 1959.

Keller, Hans-Erich. "The *Song of Roland* and Its Audience." *Olifant* 6 (1979), 259–74.

———. *The Song of Roland*: A Mid-Twelfth Century Song of Propaganda for the Capetian Kingdom." *Olifant* 3 (1976), 242–58.

Kellogg, Judith. *Medieval Artistry and Exchange: Economic Institutions, Society, and Literary Form in Old French Narrative*. New York: Peter Lang, 1989 ("American University Studies," Series II: Romance Languages and Literature, vol. 123).

Köhler, Erich. "*Conseil des barons" und "jugement des barons": Epische Fatalität und Feudalrecht im altfranzösischen Rolandslied*. Sitzungsberichte der Heidelberger Akademie der Wissenschaften, Philosophisch-historische Klasse, 1968. Heidelberg: Winter, 1968.

———. "Quelques observations d'ordre historico-sociologique sur les rapports entre la chanson de geste et le roman courtois." In *Chanson de geste und höfischer Roman*. Heidelberg: Winter, 1963 ("Studia Romanica," vol. 4) pp. 21–30.

Kristeva, Julia. "Le texte clos." In *Semiotiké*. Paris: Seuil, 1969, pp. 113–42.

———. *Le texte du roman*. Paris and the Hague: Mouton, 1970.

Lacan, Jacques. *Le séminaire: v. VII: L'éthique de la psychanalyse*. Paris: Seuil, 1986.

Lecercle, Jean-Jacques. *The Violence of Language*. London: Routledge, 1990.

Le Gentil, Pierre. *La Chanson de Roland*. Paris: Hatier, 1955/67.

Le Goff, Jacques. "Le Christianisme médiéval en Occident du Concile de Nice (325) à la Réforme (début du XVIe siècle)." In *Histoire des religions*. 3 vols., v. II: ed. Henri-Charles Puech: *La formation des religions universelles et les religions du salut*. Paris: Gallimard, 1972 ("Histoire de la Pléiade"), pp. 749– 868.

———. *La civilisation de l'Occident médiéval*. Paris: Arthaud, 1964/77.

———. "Le rituel symbolique de la vassalité." In *Pour un autre Moyen Âge*. Paris: Gallimard, 1978, pp.349–420.

Le Goff, Jacques, ed. *L'homme médiéval*. Paris: Seuil, 1992.

Lemarignier, Jean-François. *Le gouvernement royal aux premiers temps capétiens (987– 1108)*. Paris: Picard, 1965.

Leupin, Alexandre. *Fiction et théologie*. forthcoming.

———. *Barbarolexis: Medieval Writing and Sexuality*, tr. Kate M. Cooper. Cambridge, Mass.: Harvard, 1989.

Lewis, Charlton T., and Charles Short. *A Shorter Latin Dictionary*. Oxford: Oxford University Press, 1958.

Lord, Albert. *The Singer of Tales*. New York: Atheneum, 1968.

Lot, Ferdinand, and Robert Fawtier. *Histoire des institutions francaises au moyen âge*. 3 vols. Paris: PUF, 1958.

Lugge, Margret. "*Gallia" und "Francia" im Mittelalter*. Bonner historische Forschungen, No. 15. Bonn: L. Roterscheid, 1960.

Maalouf, Amin. *The Crusades through Arab Eyes*. Translated by Jon Rothschild. New York: Schocken, 1984.

Maranda, Pierre. *French Kinship*. Paris and The Hague: Mouton, 1974.

Marx, Karl. *Capital*. 4 vols. Moscow: Progress, 1954/77.

———. *Pre-Capitalist Economic Formations*. Edited by Eric J. Hobsbawm, translated by Jack Cohen. New York: International Publishers, 1965.

Marzouki, Samir. "Islam et Musulmans dans la *Chanson de Roland.*" *Revue Tunisienne de sciences sociales* 13 (1976), 105–30.

Matoré, Georges. *Le vocabulaire de la société médiévale.* Paris: PUF, 1985.

Mayer, Arno J. *Why Did the Heavens Not Darken? The "Final Solution" in History.* New York: Pantheon, 1988.

le Mené, Michel. "Conclusions: Point de vue du médiéviste." See J.-Ph. Genêt and M. le Mené, eds., *Genèse de l'état moderne: Prélèvement et redistribution*, pp. 239–41.

Meneghetti, Maria Luisa. "*Conseil des barons*: L'Oratoria deliberativa dall'epopea al romanzo." *Retorica e Politica. Atti del II Convegno Italo-Tedesco.* Bressanone, 1974.

Mink, Louis O. *Historical Understanding.* Ithaca, N.Y.: Cornell University Press, 1987.

Mitteis, Hienrich. *The State in the Middle Ages: A Comparative Constitutional History of Feudal Europe.* Translated by H. F. Orton. Amsterdam and New York: North-Holland and American Elsevier, 1975.

Moignet, Gérard, ed. *La Chanson de Roland.* Paris: Bordas, 1969.

Moore, R. I. *The Formation of a Persecuting Society.* Oxford: Blackwell, 1987.

Morrall, John B. *Political Thought in Medieval Times.* New York: Harper, 1958/62.

Murray, Alexander. *Reason and Society in the Middle Ages.* Oxford: Oxford University Press, 1978.

Musset, Lucien. "L'aristocratie normande au XIe siècle." See Contamine, ed., *La Noblesse au moyen âge*, pp. 71–96.

———. *Les invasions: Les vagues germaniques.* Paris: PUF, 1965.

Nichols, Stephen G., Jr. "Fission and Fusion: Meditations of Power in Medieval History and Literature." *Yale French Studies* 70 (1986), 21–42.

———. *Romanesque Signs: Early Medieval Narrative and Iconography.* New Haven: Yale University Press, 1983.

Nordhal, Helge. "Parataxe rhétorique dans la *Chanson de Roland.*" *Revue des langues romanes* 80 (1972–73), 345–54.

Odo of Cluny. *Collationes.* In Migne, *Patrologia latina*, 133.517–638.

Pacaut, M. *Louis VII et son royaume.* Paris: SEVPEN, 1964/67.

Painter, Sidney. *French Chivalry.* Baltimore: Johns Hopkins University Press, 1940.

Parain, Charles, and Pierre Vilar. *Mode de production féodale.* Paris: Centre d'Etudes et de Recherches Marxistes, n.d.

Paris, Gaston. *Histoire poétique de Charlemagne.* 2nd ed. Paris, 1905.

Patterson, Lee. *Negotiating the Past: The Historical Understanding of Medieval Literature.* Madison: University of Wisconsin Press, 1987.

Payen, Jean-Charles. "Une poétique du génocide joyeux: devoir de violence et plaisir de tuer dans la *Chanson de Roland.*" *Olifant* 6 (1979), 226–36.

Peeters, Leopold. "Syntaxe et style dans la *Chanson de Roland.*" *Revue des langues romanes* 80 (1972–73), 45–59.

Peirce, Charles Sanders. *Collected Papers.* Cambridge, MA: Harvard University Press, 1934–63.

Pelligrini, Silvio. "L'ira di Gano." *Culture neolatina* 3 (1943), 161–62.

Perrier, J. L., ed. *Le Charroi de Nimes.* Classiques français Moyen Âge, vol. 66. Paris: Champion, 1967.

Perrin, Charles. *La seigneurie rurale en France et en Allemagne.* Paris: CDU, 1953.

Peters, Edward, ed. *The First Crusade: The Chronicle of Fulcher of Chartres and Other Source Materials.* Philadelphia: University of Pennsylvania Press, 1971.

————. *Torture*. Oxford: Blackwell, 1985.

Pfeffer, M. "Die Formalitäten des göttesgerichtlichen Zweikampfs in der altfranzösischen Epik." *Zeitschrift für romanische Philologie* 9 (1884), 1–74.

Poly, Jean-Pierre, and Eric Bournazel. *La mutation féodale, Xe-XIIe siècles*. Paris: PUF, 1980.

Postan, M. M. "Feudalism and Its Decline: A Semantic Exercise." In *Social Relations and Ideas: Essays in Honor of R. H. Hilton*, ed. T. H. Aston, P. R. Cross, Charles Dyer, and J. Thirsk. Cambridge: Cambridge University Press, 1983, pp.73–83

Prévité-Orton, C. W. *The Shorter Cambridge Medieval History*. 2 vols. Cambridge: Cambridge University Press, 1952.

Reiss, Timothy J. *The Discourse of Modernism*. Ithaca: Cornell, 1982.

Renan, Ernest. "What Is a Nation?" Translated by Martin Thom. In Homi Bhabha, ed., *Nation and Narration*. London: Routledge, 1990, pp. 8–22.

Reuter, Timothy, ed. *The Medieval Nobility*. Amsterdam and New York: North Holland, 1979.

de Riquer, Martin. *Les chansons de geste françaises*. 2nd ed. Translated by I. Cluzel. Paris: Nizet, 1968.

Robertson, D. W., Jr. *Preface to Chaucer*. Princeton: Princeton University Press, 1962/69.

Ruggieri, Ruggero M. *Il proceso di Gano nella 'Chanson de Roland'*. Florence: Jansoni, 1936.

Rychner, Jean. *La Chanson de geste: essai sur l'art épique des jongleurs*. Geneva and Lille: Droz and Giard, 1955.

Said, Edward. *Beginnings: Intention and Method*. New York: Basic, 1975.

————. *Orientalism*. New York: Random House/Vintage, 1978/79.

de Saussure, Ferdinand. *Cours de linguistique générale*. Edited by Tullio de Mauro. Paris: Payot, 1972.

Scarry, Elaine. *The Body in Pain*. Oxford: Oxford University Press, 1985.

Schramm, Percy Ernst. *Der König von Frankreich: Das Wesen der Monarchie vom 9. zum 16. Jahrhundert*. 2 vols. Darmstadt: Wissenschaftliche Buchgesellschaft, 1960.

Silverman, Kaja. *The Subject of Semiotics*. Oxford: Oxford University Press, 1983.

Sorel, Georges. *Reflexions sur la violence*. Paris: Marcel Rivière, 1912/46.

Stock, Brian. *The Implications of Literacy: Written Language and Models of Interpretation in the Eleventh and Twelfth Centuries*. Princeton: Princeton University Press, 1983.

Strayer, Joseph. *Medieval Statecraft and the Perspectives of History*. Princeton: Princeton University Press, 1971.

————. "On the Medieval Origins of the Modern State. Princeton: Princeton University Press, 1970

Sturges, Robert S. *Medieval Interpretation: Models of Reading in Literary Narrative, 1100–1500*. Carbondale and Edwardsville: Southern Illinois University Press, 1991.

Terry, Patricia, trans. *The Song of Roland*. "Library of Liberal Arts." New York: Bobbs-Merrill, 1965.

The New Harvard Dictionary of French Literature. Cambridge, MA: Harvard University Press, 1989.

Todorov, Tzvetan. "La quête du récit." *Critique* 262 (1969), 195–214.

Trotter, D. A. *Medieval French Literature and the Crusades (1100–1300)*. Geneva: Droz, 1988.

Uitti, Karl D. *Story Myth and Celebration in Old French Narrative Poetry (1050–1200)*. Princeton: Princeton University Press, 1973.

van Emden, Wolfgang. " 'E cil de France le cleiment a guarant': Roland, Vivien et le thème du *guarant*." *Société Rencesvals. VIe Congrès International (Aix-en-Provence, 29 août–4 septembre 1973). Actes*. Aix-en-Provence: Université de Provence, 1974, pp. 31–61.

Van Nuffel, Pierre. "Problèmes de sémiotique interpretative: L'épopée." *Lettres romanes* 27 (1973), 150–62.

Vance, Eugene. "Roland et la poétique de la mémoire." *Cahiers d'Etudes Médiévales* I (1973), 103–15; English version: "Roland and the Poetics of Memory." In *Textual Strategies*, edited by Josué Harari. Ithaca, N.Y.: Cornell University Press, 1979/81, pp.374–4030. Reprinted with changes and in English in *Mervelous Signals: Poetics and Sign Theory in the Middle Ages*. Lincoln, NE: University of Nebraska Press, 1986, pp. 51–85.

Vitz, Evelyn Birge. *Medieval Narrative and Modern Narratology*. New York: New York University Press, 1989.

Wallace-Hadrill, J. M. *The Barbarian West, 400–1000*. Rev. ed. Oxford: Blackwell, 1967/85.

Weber, Max. *The Theory of Social and Economic Organization*. Translated by A. M. Henderson and Talcott Parsons. Edited by Talcott Parsons. New York: Free Press, 1947/64.

White, Hayden. *The Content of the Form*. Baltimore: Johns Hopkins University Press, 1987.

———. *Metahistory*. Baltimore: Johns Hopkins University Press, 1973.

———. *Tropics of Discourse*. Baltimore: Johns Hopkins University Press, 1978.

Whitehead, F. "L'ambiguité de Roland." In *Studi in honore di Italo Siciliano*. 2 vols. Biblioteca dell'Archivum Romanicum, ser. I, vol. 86. Florence: Olschki, 1966, pp. 1203–12.

Williams, Raymond. *Keywords: A Vocabulary of Culture and Society*, rev. ed. Oxford: Oxford University Press, 1976/83.

———. *Marxism and Society*. Oxford: Oxford University Press, 1977.

Wood, Charles T. "*Regnum Franciae*: A Problem in Capetian Administrative Usage." *Traditio* 23 (1967), 117–47.

Zumthor, Paul. *La lettre et la voix*. Paris: Seuil, 1987.

———. *Parler du moyen âge*. Paris: Minuit, 1980.

General Index
(Terms of art and common nouns)

Index of Proper Nouns
(Excludes actors and place-names in the *Chanson de Roland*)

Index of Foreign Terms and Phrases
(Excludes common terms such as *chanson de geste, jongleur*, and *laisse*)

réalisation: 62
recreant, recreantise: 73, 86, 169
regnum, regnum Franciae: 104, 110, 114,
    225
reguli: 114
res publica: 189
rex, reis: 101–19
rex Franciae, rex francorum: 109
rex and sacerdos: 112

saives, sage: 80
soldeier, soudoyer: 56

taille: 50
tenir: 101
Träger: 61, 100
traïsun: 157, 224

ubi sunt: 121, 125

valor: 54
vavasseur: 60
vraisemblance: 141, 147
violer: 3

wergeld: 131

PETER HAIDU is Professor of French at UCLA. His earlier publications include *Aesthetic Distance in Chrétien de Troyes: Irony and Comedy in Cligès and Perceval, Lion-queue-coupée: L'écart symbolique chez Chrétien de Troyes,* and a large number of articles in medieval literature and contemporary theory.

DATE DUE

~~DEC 01 2008~~		
~~NOV 27 2009~~		
~~NOV 2 1 20~~		
NOV 0 7 2009		

GAYLORD · PRINTED IN U.S.A.